# MAN THROUGH THE AGES

JOHN BOWLE

# MAN THROUGH THE AGES

ATHENEUM

NEW YORK

1977

*Library of Congress Cataloging in Publication Data*

*Bowle, John.*
   *Man through the ages.*

   *Includes bibliographical references and index.*
   *1. World history.   I. Title.*
*D21.B77   1977     909     76–30532*
*ISBN 0–689–10797–8*

# CONTENTS

# PREFACE

'It is fitting,' wrote Diodorus Siculus, that early and unreliable exponent of world history, who began at the Creation and ended his voluminous works at 59 BC, 'that all men should ever accord great gratitude to those writers who have composed universal histories since they have aspired to help by their individual labour human society as a whole.' But although through the centuries the demand for such history has been perennial, today professional historians are seldom forward to bestow encomia on those who attempt to write it.

Indeed with vastly more knowledge but increased specialization, most professionals are as little concerned with the Ming or the Gupta, the Ashanti or the Incas, as they are with biochemistry. Every aspect of Merovingian Gaul has been researched, while vast tracts of Asian and African history remain unheeded, and where patches of the home ground are exhaustively cultivated they are unrelated to the outer world.

Yet in a civilization of jet aircraft and television by satellite, the time is obviously ripe for a view of the landmarks in world history; nor is it impossible to achieve it. Anyone with the will to do so can today discern the main events in the development of the chief civilizations of mankind. And their sequence can today become as intelligible and familiar as, for an Englishman, that Tudors, Stuarts and Hanoverians succeeded one another; or, for an American, that the oligarchy of Washington and Jefferson was succeeded by Jacksonian democracy, or the original preponderance of the eastern states by the impact of the middle west. Yet, while communications increasingly annihilate distance and television presents a panorama of the world, few people are familiar with even the outlines of the history of the Far East, or of the Hindu and Muslim civilizations, let alone with the background of Africa or of pre-Columbian America. Yet all are highly relevant to the modern world. The debt of our own civilization to Greece, Israel and Rome is widely appreciated, but few Europeans who are not experts understand the debt of Cambodia, Thailand, Burma and Indonesia to southern India, or of the Japanese to China. Yet even those knowledge-able about their own continents are beginning to appear provincial unless they apprehend at least the rudiments of the past, the environment and the mentality of the rest of mankind, a grasp which may become commonplace to future generations.

Scholars may concentrate on their own fields, but specialists must take broad views if they desire to encourage their pupils to make the most of life and broaden their minds. Moreover, as we are forced into some form of world order, and supra-national institutions develop, a sense of world citizenship is no longer a vague aspiration but realism.

In these circumstances it is no mere hobby to master the essentials of world history, and this survey is designed to give a contemporary and compendious introduction to the essentials of world history as they appear to a Western European. No one is 'qualified' to write such a book; but the writer, as editor of the *Concise Encyclopedia of World History*, to whose contributors he pays full acknowledgment, is perhaps less unqualified than most historians to survey the whole scene. That editorial task, undertaken fifteen years ago, not only greatly widened his own horizons, but has perhaps made for a certain objectivity.

A composite volume, however expert, cannot have the impact of the work of one mind, but a single author must admit his predilections. I am concerned mainly with the physical setting and human interest of the past, not with world-historical theories or economic 'explanations' of history, and, in face of much professional opinion, I hold that history, at least vicariously, should be enjoyed. The narrative is thus an outline, with many inevitable omissions, but it is pointed with contemporary detail which indicates that its characters were once alive. It is also closely related to geography and climate, and is designed to help travellers and television viewers to get more out of what they see, as well as to suggest unfamiliar fields of historical interest.

I am grateful for much help. In particular Dr A. L. Rowse, Professor Glyn Daniel, Dr Raghavan Iyer, the late Mr Wyndham Ketton-Cremer, Professor Hugh Lloyd-Jones and Mr Quentin Davies have read and advised; Mr Charles Saumarez Smith has greatly assisted in a thorough revision of the book for this present edition, and Mr Andrew Wheatcroft has suggested the scope of the Epilogue. I would also like to thank Mrs Barbara Phillips for her typing of an exacting script.

JOHN BOWLE
Oxford, February 1976

# One

# ARCHAIC ORIGINS

## 1

The vistas of prehistoric time are desolate and enormous. Man has a gruelling evolution behind him and the subconscious bears the mark of the beast; indeed, it is still an open question whether the exotic process called civilization achieved in the brief time span of recorded history is not too exacting. Yet out of the prodigality of instinct there emerged mind.

How this evolution occurred is outside the scope of the present version of this survey, designed essentially as a history of civilizations. But here Archbishop Ussher, in the seventeenth century, who conjectured that the world was created in 4004 BC, deserves some credit. His interesting hypothesis has long been scouted, but for dating the rise of the earliest civilizations, as distinct from the Creation, he was not so wide of the mark. By 4000 BC the Near East had become more arid; oases and river valleys and the Nile flood were therefore even more attractive. By then, also, village agricultural settlement was already old, the decisive inventions had been made, and a tenuous web of commerce was beginning to bring metals and precious stones from the mountains and the uplands to settlements in the Delta, Upper Egypt and the fertile crescent. The Indians and Chinese had a rather similar, if independent, background, though there were contacts by sea between Sumer and Mohenjo Daro, and the use of bronze penetrated to China across the steppe.

Large cities were first founded in Mesopotamia and Egypt, but there had been a surprising prelude in an odd place. At Jericho, in the Jordan valley, twelve hundred feet below the level of the sea in the deepest abyss in the world, the most ancient of all strongholds has been discovered. The three-thousand-odd inhabitants, akin to the Natufians of Carmel, did not even use pottery, but they built towered stone walls and cut ditches out of the living rock. They had a curious habit of decapitating their dead and embalming the heads; they were rather handsome and have left the earliest authentic record of the human face. By radio-carbon dating, this settlement seems to have begun sometime round 7500 BC, but like the Palaeolithic Magdalenians, these talented people did not last. They were succeeded by a squalid peasant encampment.

The massive archaic civilizations took root in areas exceptionally well suited for them: between the Tigris and Euphrates, along the Nile and the Indus – all great rivers, with fertile soil and a strong sun. In northern China winters were sharper, the soil friable, there was a rougher sea; but here, too, the Yellow River encouraged settlement.

By 4000 BC lower Mesopotamia was being colonized, probably from Iran, by a people now called Ubaidians from a site near Ur. They were no longer Neolithic; they had copper, but not bronze, and they tackled the untamed swamps that bordered the Persian Gulf. Immense works of drainage and irrigation had to be undertaken – the waters separated from the land. They built with clumped reeds and mud brick, and cultivated date palms, which flourish only in the southern part of the estuary. They built temples on which much more elaborate structures were to be superimposed; they were the forerunners of the classical Sumerian temple states from which the Babylonian, Hittite and Assyrian cultures largely derived. They founded Eridu, then on the coast, and Ur; Erech and the sacred city of Nippur were only forty miles upstream. The ruins of these, and of other cities, are now stranded by the shift of the river, desolate mounds of immense antiquity; all lie in the sun-baked flats between the Tigris and Euphrates, an area (not much bigger than Wessex or Long Island) which retains the most ancient concentration of cities in the world.

By 3000 BC the Sumerians had succeeded these pioneers. They, also, had come from the hills; they were of the Caucasian race, accustomed to woollen garments and felt cloaks, with an agglutinative language, unlike the Semitic tongues, and they built methodically on a great scale. They enlarged the temples; bored perhaps by the alien monotony of the plains and associating their gods with the hills, they constructed great Ziggurats of painted, patterned, brick, with processional staircases, and trees and shrubs on the platforms. They commanded a massive labour force and built and irrigated as no one had ever done before.

Such enterprise implied records, and records, writing. The first pictographs on tablets of clay list flocks, barley, subsistence allowances. There was now a far-flung traffic in metal and precious stones; transactions were witnessed and property registered by seals; standardized weights and measures were devised; the ideograms became phonetic and cuneiform. Sumerian aims were intensely practical: around the black and red Ziggurats rising above flat-roofed cities, stretched broad acres of wheat and barley, polders and palm groves. The Sumerian farmer, plodding into market and temple, set a pattern which was to last. And his theocratic rulers, storing their grain and wool, counting their wealth and using it, were the first capitalists and the first organizers. They had achieved high civilization and they commanded their people through religion.

How great was that faith is apparent from the royal burials at Ur which contain the wealth of a culture that is already long established. King A-bar-qi and Queen Shub-ad took their whole households with them into eternity. All the resources of Sumerian art were lavished on superb vessels of fluted gold, a sledge chariot decorated with mosaic, lapis lazuli and silver, a gaming board exquisitely inlaid; splendid vessels of alabaster and marble; chalices and lions' heads; elaborate harps and lamps. But this Aladdin's cave was a charnel-house. Ninety men and women, three oxen and two asses died with their rulers. The household were laid out very decently, and it is thought that they processed into the vault in full finery, then lay down and died of a drug. Doubtless the human victims thought their fate a privilege.

After this splendid but ambivalent prelude to the history of civilization, one turns to the humbler relics which depict Ur-Nina of Lagash (*c.* 2800 BC). This solid archaic benefactor balances a basket on his shaven head; he wears a flounced kilt and his sons stand round him in hieratic, serviceable, order.

By now there was not only civilization, but also war. At Ur a mosaic standard depicts feasting and tribute and its background, rudimentary chariot fighting. The business-like Sumerians have left monuments of highly organized carnage, disciplined spearmen advancing in wedge formation behind square shields. They were a tough, Iranian people, accustomed to the life of the uplands and, when they found wealth in Mesopotamia, knew how to defend it. There was also endemic war between the temple states: water rights have always been a classic bone of contention. Already they had civic emblems, heraldic birds, the baleful double-headed eagle of later empires. They had a weird mythology, full of composite animals, man-faced bulls, winged gryphons and chimeras; on the seals heroes hurl lions to the ground. Their legends determined the themes for art for peoples long after them: as Rome was to medieval Europe, so was Sumer to the Near East.

Hereafter, Mesopotamian civilization became Semitic. Sargon I, originally a gardener, ruled from the 'Lower' to the 'Upper' Sea; from the Persian Gulf to the Levant. The Akkadian epic of Gilgamesh – the oldest epic in the world – reveals the dynamic but fatalist spirit of these peoples in its tale of heroic effort and doom.

# II

By the fourth millennium the archaic civilization of Egypt had also emerged from its Neolithic background. The country was richer than the city states of Sumer and Akkad; it was early united, and the Pharaoh owned the entire land; he was no mere deputy, rather a god in his own right. The monuments of Egyptian grandeur are world-famous and they survive, not from the Delta, but from Upper Egypt, where the long valley of the Nile winds between isolating deserts. Though influenced by

Mesopotamia, Egypt was a law unto itself. By *c.* 3200 BC the first authentic Pharaoh is recorded. Narmer-Menes, a chieftain of the Falcon clan, ruled the whole country and founded the first 'dynastic' phase of Egyptian history. The 'palette' of Narmer commemorates him, on one side grasping an enemy by the forelock and brandishing a mace; on the reverse, advancing briskly behind the falcon standards above the entwined necks of two symbolic cheetahs. Already the *fellaheen* of Egypt had entered their millennial servitude.

The most massive effort of the Old Kingdom went into building gigantic limestone and granite pyramids. By the time of the fourth dynasty, the great pyramid of Cheops at Gizeh rose to 481 feet – higher than St Peter's at Rome, or Salisbury or Ulm. Each of the four sides of this colossal monument was 755 feet long. This monstrous, and futile, achievement marks the culmination of the Old Kingdom, and is roughly con-temporaneous with Ur-Nina of Lagash. From the fourth dynasty also dates the vivid head of Queen Nefert, who stares with such monumental and impassive arrogance at posterity.

The archaic Egyptians were already obsessed with a materialist view of an afterlife and they harnessed their rich resources to secure the immortality of their mummified Pharaohs and magnates. Fortunately, artists were thus induced to depict scenes of everyday life with great precision, for it was thought – as in Ur – that the dead would need all the amenities and service of a great household and, in Egypt, that these could be provided by painting them. So they plastered tombs with pictures of all the vivid life of the Nile, illuminated by ideographic inscriptions – a humane alternative to human sacrifice. Passports to immortality were later available for less important Egyptians, and they stuffed and embalmed totem animals and worshipped them.

The river also occasioned a calendar from which our own directly derives. The wealth of the country depended on the Nile flood, and it was observed that the interval between the annual inundations was roughly 365 days; but this measurement was not strictly accurate, so that the tidy-minded authorities checked it by a more exact phenomenon. Probably in the fifth millennium, pre-dynastic priests, watching in the dawn, had observed that Sothis (Sirius), the morning star, made its latest visible appearance before sunrise just when the river began to flood. A 'Sothic' calendar was adopted: it proved to be more useful than the Sumerian, which was lunar and adjusted periodically to the solar year, with the months, as in pagan Anglo-Saxon practice, called after the activities of the seasons – brick making, sheep shearing, irrigation, harvest. So the Egyptians devised the first sidereal year as a more accurate measurement of time.

Archaic dynastic Egypt thus moved heavily forward into recorded history, the first totalitarian state. It was African; ruled by a god-king, administered by corporations of priests and hereditary landowners, with large tracts of land dedicated to the building and upkeep of gigantic monuments to the dead. The wealth of the Pharaoh's court provided a living for artisans, jewellers and smiths, and encouraged a conservative, expert craftsmanship. Most of the people were cultivators, their poverty mitigated by a favourable climate. But archaic Egypt took long to make bronze; the wheel was unknown, and the government controlled commerce. In spite of the wealth of the land, the immense effort of building pyramids and adorning tombs, carried on for generations, gradually sterilized much of the capital of this massive society. By 2260 BC it had lumbered into political and economic decline.

Towards the end of the Old Kingdom, a sun cult became more popular. The high priest of Ré, originally 'the Great Chief of Artificers', became a secular lord; Userkaf of On even seized the throne, calling himself Sa-Ré – Son of the Sun. The cult of the Pharaoh took on a new splendour and the conventionalized figures of Egyptian painting now proceed with posed hands and fixed expressions; their serenity expressed a culture able to survive the vicissitudes which intervened between the archaic Egypt and the richer and more far-flung society of the New Kingdom of the full Bronze Age.

# III

The civilization of northern India has a very different flavour. It was younger than both Sumer and Egypt, for the cities of the Indus plain cannot be dated before 2500 BC. Although archaic, they were contemporary with the Middle Kingdom in Egypt and with Babylon, not with Sumer, but they lasted for about a thousand years. Their culture was already very Indian. The people worshipped gods recognizably ancestral to the Hindu deities; a proto-Siva with his 'linga', a pipal tree with a horned god, a sacred dewlapped bull. These gods are bedizened with bracelets and bangles, and tiger, rhinoceros, elephant and buffalo do them honour. Figures survive in postures common among Indian holy men, often with familiar head-dresses, earrings, necklaces and robes.

It was a civilization broad-based on a wide plain, and extended for nearly a thousand miles from the great city of Harappa in the Punjab, to Mohenjo Daro, two hundred and fifty miles from the coast. Both cities are brick-built, with large fortified citadels and straight streets: their drainage was more efficient than anything achieved until Minoan and Roman times, and their bathrooms would have astonished sixteenth-century Europeans. The houses of the rich were spacious, built round an open court, and if the dwellings of the poor were cramped, they were solid. These people, dominated by priests, practised ritual ablutions: at Mohenjo Daro a large cloistered temple is built round a well-made tank. Their records have perished and the script on their elaborate seals has never been deciphered.

But they were skilled sculptors. An accomplished torso in red sandstone already displays the full curves of Indian art; a dancing girl, slender and provocative, hints at orgiastic ritual; festoons of shining beads and jewellery adorned the richer women, and the children had ingenious toy monkeys on sticks; the seal engravers of Harappa have left a whole gallery of miniature jungle animals. It must have been an easy-going civilization, not without its gaieties, and it had considerable contacts outside its borders.

Round the cities the peasants cultivated cereal crops and were the first people to grow cotton. They had humped cattle and bullocks and the ubiquitous eastern water-buffalo; they traded with the Iranian plateau and with central Asia through the Khyber, and exported their cotton to Mesopotamia. Their fortifications were elaborate, but their weapons not very efficient. They seem to have been a priest-ridden mercantile oligarchy, profoundly conservative. About 1500 BC they were overrun by Aryan conquerors, yet they had laid the foundations of the original Indian society on which the Aryan castes were to be superimposed.

# IV

At the western end of the Eurasian landmass the Neolithic revolution had quickly percolated across the seaways of the Levant and, more slowly, into central and western Europe. Neolithic colonizers spread up the Danube into Bohemia and along the main rivers of the Continent, the Vistula, Rhine and Meuse. They were hunters who practised hoe cultivation and mixed farming. At a stockaded settlement near Cologne they built barns not dissimilar to those still common on the northern European plain, but, in general, they soon moved on, leaving exhausted ground to revert to wilderness. This shifting agriculture was still practised by the German barbarians who fought Julius Caesar.

The other main stream of European settlement came through the Iberian Peninsula. Pastoral peoples moved across France into Normandy and Belgium and up into Scandinavia. On the Wessex downs they left encampments and long barrows; the eastern part of Maiden Castle in Dorset is Neolithic. Some of them settled down in pile dwellings by lakes, as near Konstanz or in Switzerland, and near Glastonbury in Somerset. By 3000 BC both the Danubians and the western pastoralists were well-established, but two millennia after the urban revolution in Mesopotamia and Egypt, and five hundred years after the rise of Harappa, they were still in the late Stone Age – barbarian villagers and tribesmen.

Yet they were often technically proficient. Their maces, axes and pottery, their amber necklaces and polished beads, imply a long and laborious tradition. The most striking monuments of the western peoples are the even older Megalithic tombs and stone circles which are found from the Iberian Peninsula to the Baltic, and in the western Mediterranean and Malta. This entirely Neolithic culture reached its astonishing climax in the Megalithic temples of Tarxien, Hajar-Kîm and Mnaidra in Malta and Jigantea on Gozo. Nowhere, save in the Yucatan, where the Maya peoples much later built the most elaborate Neolithic monuments in the world, has Stone Age carving left such impressive remains. The magnificent temple of Tarxien, with its circular chambers opening from one to the other, its friezes of sacrificial animals and spiralled screens, its massive entrances and well wrought walls, is the most complex Megalithic monument in Europe.

In Brittany the mighty avenues of Carnac, in England, Avebury (*c.* 2800 BC) and the older circles at Stonehenge attest how far flung was this apparently spontaneous cult, while in Denmark, on the Island of Åls, lie the long barrows of Blommeskobbel, nearly two hundred feet long, intercepted by two chamber entrances and surrounded by an oval of large stones. In beech woods which today fringe the Baltic, are the largest Megalithic barrows in the north; from Denmark, too, comes the finest northern example of late Stone Age pottery, the Skarpsalling bowl, with its silvery patina and precise decoration.

This Neolithic culture, in the cool north, originated before the rise of full civilization in Egypt and was not, as once believed, 'diffused' from it. In the Levant, on the other hand, in Crete, mainland Greece, the Cyclades and the Ionian coast, in Sicily and southern Italy, Neolithic barbarism was influenced by the Near East. As early as 3400 BC the first Minoan phase had begun in Crete and an Helladic culture was taking root in southern Greece and the Islands. In Cyprus – the island from which copper takes its name – the population multiplied, and Crete was the natural focus and intermediary for both Egyptian and Mesopotamian influence. Egyptian vases from the time of Narmer have been found near Knossos and early Minoan jars in Egypt. The foundations of Minoan wealth and commerce were already being laid, and Troy began as a small fortified trading post commanding the entrance to the Dardanelles and the trade to the Black Sea.

The structure of the Greek peninsulas and islands, where the mountains run down steeply to the sea, made for independent strongholds in the relatively few accessible and fertile areas, while in the south the sunny climate favoured olives and vines. Helladic and Minoan fishermen killed octopus, tuna and mullet and netted the swarming Levantine fish, still a standby of Greek cuisine.

Thus Near Eastern culture spread across what the Egyptians termed the 'Great Green Sea': for the first time civilization had become maritime. The sea-girt citadels of early Minoan Crete and Helladic Greece foreshadow the great Hellenic culture of antiquity. Farms on terraced hillsides, embowered with vine, olive and fig; goats browsing on aromatic herbage; fishermen handling their nets from sharp-prowed boats that ride a glittering sea, mark the transmission of civilization from the Near East to Europe.

# Two

# BRONZE AGE
# EMPIRES OF ASIA

## I

The archaic and solid civilizations in Mesopotamia and Egypt now suffered confusion and attack, even if they survived as the basis of richer, more dynamic societies. In Iran, Syria and Anatolia, successive military empires dominated the Near East and the Levant, while, beneath changing politics, the old massive cultures carried on directly into the great Persian Empire, whose influence in the East was to be culturally comparable to that of Graeco-Roman civilization for Europe, and which long continued, in Sassanian and Muslim forms, as the dominant political and cultural fact for the Near East and northern India.

Although in Egypt the Old Kingdom had subsided into feudal conflict, by 2000 BC the 'Middle Kingdom' was in being; by the seventeenth century, the Semitic Hyksos, charioteers, originally out of the desert, had succeeded it. By 1500 BC at the height of the Bronze Age, a native 'New Kingdom' overran much of Palestine and Syria, and held its own with the empires of the East. Increasing wealth in slaves, trade and plunder was reflected in colossal sculpture and architecture.

In India, about that time, as already observed, the native culture of Harappa and Mohenjo Daro was overrun by Indo-Europeans, akin to the Hittites and Iranians, and speaking a language related to Greek, Latin and the Germanic tongues. These invaders were new to India, coming out of the Iranian uplands and the southern Russian steppe; they transformed the native culture and imposed a caste system which has made Indian civilization different from any other. They developed an Old Sanskrit oral literature, the Vedic hymns and sutras (invocations) which depict an heroic society akin to that described by Homer, and the later prose *Upanishads*, the foundation of Hindu literature and divinity for over three thousand years. In China, by 1500 BC the Bronze Age dynasty of Shang was established, with its capital at Yin Hsu, near the modern Anyang in Honan. Although its wooden architecture has perished, it has left inscribed oracle bones and fine bronzes, jades and ivories which prove that this hitherto legendary dynasty lasted for many centuries.

In terms of European history these far-flung events coincided with the

9

last phase of Minoan maritime dominion which ended with the fall of Knossos and, in Britain and Denmark with the climax of the Bronze Age. All these great long-established Babylonian, Egyptian, Indian and Chinese societies had created permanent traditions, while Europe, north of the Mediterranean, was still barbaric.

## II

The Sumerians had entered Mesopotamia from Iran; the native Semites, better adapted to the climate and backed by desert manpower, gradually closed in on them. The dominion of Sargon I had been followed by invasions from Gutium, but the Ammorite Hammurabi (fl. *c.* 1750 BC) founded the first Semitic dynasty of Babylon. His famous laws, found inscribed on a block of black diorite at Susa, are preceded by a magisterial account of his exploits of conquest and consolidation.

Already Babylon on the Euphrates was a large city, with a network of canals and a rich hinterland of corn and barley fields, orchards and palm groves. It was the forerunner of the much later walled, turretted neo-Babylonian capital of Nebuchadnezzar in the sixth century BC, which was to be dominated by the eight-storied Tower of Babel, the 'Gate of God'. Hammurabi, in his own words, cut down his enemies 'like dolls of clay'; he 'put order in the land': 'I dug,' he boasts, 'the canal *Hammurabi-Nukush-Nishi* which brings copious water to the lands of Sumer and Akkad. The top of the wall of Sippar I raised with earth like a great mountain.'

This business-like and formidable ruler commanded a complex society with over two millennia of civilized life behind it. The laws of Hammurabi depict a well-ordered and highly organized economy, slave-owning but not caste-ridden, in which priests were giving way to military and commercial interests and to an efficient secular administration. There was no coinage, but standardized silver bars and shekels; contracts were witnessed and ratified, deeds of partnership drawn up, property registered, elaborate wills devised. The peasant farmers borrowed at stiff rates from city money-lenders, whose loans were secured on the harvest, and the temples owned large properties. Produce was ample, with much wheat for the pancake-like bread, still baked by the Arabs, and barley for beer. The date harvest meant not only a staple food, but date treacle and arrack wine. Citrus fruits, aubergines, apricots and melons were heaped in the teeming *suks*, where merchants from Anatolia and Iran brought metals and precious stones, and fishermen from the gulf their catch. Flocks and herds produced wool and leather; cedarwood from Lebanon and the Taurus commanded a great price.

Outside the cities, the peasants still lived in the rush-built houses already described, and in low black tents similar to those of the Bedouin today. All depended on irrigation. As in modern Holland, canals ran often above the land and it was a routine task to keep them from silting up. If solid-wheeled, creaking farm carts were still primitive, the design of the crescent-prowed boats, still used in the marshes, was efficient. The civilization of Hammurabi's Babylon was based on the rivers and canals.

Hammurabi's laws are not general principles, but remedies for specific occasions, with the stamp of public authority upon them.

There were now scribes, auditors and doctors, liable to punishment if they made their patients worse. The wages of skilled artisans and bricklayers were fixed; architects might be executed if their mud-brick houses collapsed. Violence was severely dealt with, and penalties were heaviest among the upper class. These laws were enforced by police and administered by judges, who heard cases by set procedures. It was a society not only rich and solid, but also ordered, if, beneath its wealth, we sense the already ancient dust, disease and squalor of the teeming East.

Hammurabi's dynasty did not last long. Hittite and Kassite barbarians destroyed it after two centuries; but though the political power of Babylon went into long eclipse until its revival under Nebuchadnezzar, the social cohesion and economic life of Mesopotamia was not destroyed. On balance, indeed, the civilization of the Middle East was invigorated by the incursions of new peoples.

But the focus of power now shifted north-west: the Hittites at the height of their power (*c.* 1400–1100 BC), whose domination was based on the plateau of Asia Minor, were mainly Indo-Europeans, possibly akin to the Etruscans who contributed so much to the civilization of Rome. They controlled the vital junction between Europe and Asia, and long ousted Semitic land power from the Levant. Their most important city was Boghaz Keui, deep in the interior of modern Turkey, nearer the Black Sea than the Mediterranean, where their archives have been discovered and read. They worshipped a sun god and a god of war, and practised divination through the liver; their laws were milder than those of Hammurabi, morally less severe. They had horses ('the ass from the East') and swift chariots; they were pioneers in the mining and use of iron. These Anatolian people from beyond the snow-capped Taurus, came out of surroundings very different from the hot Mesopotamian plain; their art is at once massive and naive, influenced by the civilizations they conquered, but with a strong accent on hunting, chariot-racing, archery and war. They built on a great scale, and avenues of stone lions and winged gryphons led to palaces decorated with animal reliefs which reflect the motifs of central Asia. From their tough profiles, they must have been a forceful people.

The Assyrians succeeded them, extending their rule to the lowlands from Nineveh on the Tigris. Originally Semitic nomads, they have an oriental splendour, a wolfish people also capable of large-scale administration and commerce, of discipline and sustained effort. Their art is magnificent but uninspired – heavy winged bulls and muscle-bound lions – but already they used the yellow and blue glazed tiles, which long after, reached a delicate climax in the mosques of Iran. Their border patterns reflect or anticipate the designs of oriental rugs, and they excelled in depicting hunting and battle scenes in bas-relief. They were mighty hunters, bending great bows from light chariots; their artists depicted the rush of the chase, the leap of their great hounds, the defiance of their speared and roaring prey. The serried ranks of their spearmen and archers have an impressive, rigid monotony. Assyrian magnates wore close-cut coats extending to the ankle, patterned with bold stripes and squares, their dark faces set off by square-cut black beards and curled locks. They were connoisseurs in the art of siege and sack.

# III

In Egypt the lives of the *fellaheen* had long been overlaid by feudal anarchy and by Hyksos invasion. But in the sixteenth century a great native ruler came to power. The Pharaoh Amose drove out the Hyksos, put down the feudal magnates, subdued Nubia and created a strong army. The dreaded Egyptian archers, like the English bowmen of the later Middle Ages, became the nucleus of the striking power of the most wealthy and far-flung of all the Bronze Age empires in the Near East. The New Kingdom reached its climax under Thutmose III, 'Binder of the Barbarians' and victor of Megiddo on the northern slopes of Mount Carmel (1479 BC), and under Ramses II, who flourished in the first half of the thirteenth century BC. Egypt was not simply a land power: her war fleets dominated the eastern Mediterranean and the capture of Phoenicia gave the armies a base for combined operations against the Hittites and the rulers of Canaan.

Thutmose III – the survivor of a partnership with Queen Hatshepsut, one of the greatest builders in history – exploited an inherited bureaucracy. He ruled from the southern Sudan to Syria. Unlike their archaic predecessors, the rulers of the New Kingdom were not interested in pyramids: instead they put up gigantic colonnaded temples and obelisks ninety feet high. The famous Valley of the Kings, the pillars and statues of Karnak and Luxor, commemorate them. The tribute of predatory empire was lavished on these monuments and Egypt, like Rome, was inundated with outlandish slaves. But Thutmose III was no mere militarist: he was an able administrator. He came up the Nile to Thebes with captive kings hung head downwards from the royal barge, but his chroniclers wrote: 'Lo, His Majesty was one who knew what happened.' Egyptian commerce now ranged from Anatolia and the islands to Dafur and eastern Abyssinia.

With greater sophistication and foreign ideas, even the orthodoxy of Egyptian religion was disturbed. When Amenhotep IV succeeded to the throne in 1370 BC, he proved to be a cultivated religious visionary, with a passion for pantheistic monotheism. He worshipped Aton, the sun, in a land where golden-plated barges and glittering ornaments were the insignia of royalty and where, not content with gold and silver, the rulers plastered their chariots and obelisks with electrum. These unorthodox opinions infuriated the powerful priests of Amon and Osiris; Amenhotep, who had changed his name to Inknaton, 'he whom Aton approves', did not long survive. Imperialist and orthodox ways were resumed, but not before the artists patronized by the amiable and eccentric Pharaoh had achieved naturalistic paintings whose free and delicate style is akin to the art of Crete.

The extent and wealth of this totalitarian empire won Egypt immense prestige, and her civilization had a more obvious effect on Minoan and Mycenaean art and architecture, and subsequently on the Greeks, than that of the Asiatic powers, though theirs too was decisive. Anyone who visits the Parthenon can detect Egyptian influence behind it, for if Egypt's political power waned, her gigantic monuments were intact. Nowhere else had such feats of architecture and sculpture ever been attempted.

Her reputation for wisdom was less deserved. The Egyptians were obsessed with a materialistic religion, with magic, and with a dismal cult of the hereafter. Medicine was a rule-of-thumb science, mixed up with spells and incantations, and mathematics limited by clumsy symbols and calculations. The Egyptians could not multiply except by two: for abstract theory they had no capacity at all. On the other hand, like many near-eastern peoples, they were good organizers, docile workers and shrewd men of business. There was nothing they did not know about the arts of bureaucratic intrigue or fleecing the taxpayer. After the death of Ramses III in 1167 BC the empire gradually collapsed. But, in spite of poverty and toil, the *fellaheen*, then as now, were a cheerful people. The country life of great Egyptian households could be gay; and an easy-going peasantry, with their roots in the Old and Middle Kingdoms, survived the hectic period of the new imperialism, in a way of life that was to continue for thousands of years.

Such, by the close of the second millennium, were the fortunes of the heirs to the two most archaic civilizations in the world which had grown up in Mesopotamia and Egypt. Important events had meanwhile been going on in India and the Far East.

# IV

As already recorded, by about 1500 BC the Bronze Age Aryan invaders of India, related to the Iranian conquerors of Persia, were descending on the subcontinent out of north-western Asia through the Kabul valley. They overwhelmed the literate civilization of Mohenjo Daro and Harappa, and probably wrecked its irrigation, but they did not destroy the basis of the archaic culture. Their power centred first in the Punjab, the 'Land of the

Five Rivers' tributary to the Indus; then in what they termed the 'Middle Lands' round the upper waters of Ganges and Jumna. They later penetrated into western Bengal. Today Umballa, Delhi and Benares mark the stages of their gradual expansion; it was to form the background of the Persian invasions of north-western India in the sixth century BC, to the teaching of the Buddha in the sixth and fifth, to the raid of Alexander in 326–325 BC, and to the establishment of the first Indian empire by the Mauryas in 322 BC.

Aryan power took much longer to penetrate south of the plains and of the Ganges hinterland; south of the Vindya mountains, its influence was comparatively superficial and the people continued to speak their own bewildering variety of Dravidian tongues.

The illiterate pastoral invaders were led by chieftains (rajas) and priests with a cult of ritual sacrifice. Like the early Romans and Celts, they reckoned wealth in cattle, and their novel light chariots, like those of the Hittites – horses 'spurning the dust and champing at the bit' – terrified the sedentary plainsmen. The Aryans had an elaborate pantheon of *Devas* (shining ones) – Indra the Thunder God, Agni the God of Fire, Rudra the Archer, and Varuna the Spirit of Order. Warriors and gamblers, they despised and distrusted the dark alien peoples whom they came to rule. Aryan literature was elaborate and its unbroken tradition is the oldest in the world; the hymns of the *Rig Veda* (1500–1000 BC) still form the core of the Hindu sacred books. They were transmitted orally for centuries before they were written down in classical Sanskrit. This language is ancestral to Pali, from which Hindi and Punjabi descend, and closely connected with Iranian and Old Persian; it is also akin to the European branches of the Indo-European speech,* in particular to Lithuanian, and even to Romany, the gipsy tongue, which began as a dialect of northern India.

The origin of the Indo-European peoples, who divided into European and Asian branches in the general folk-wanderings of the second millennium BC, remains an historical enigma. They probably came from the Baltic–Black Sea corridor and from southern Russia, rather than from central Asia: all had a pastoral and nomadic background that derived from Mesolithic times. The Aryan invaders slowly adapted themselves to the village and urban society of India. Their fluid tribal organization contrasted with the static urban bureaucracies of Mesopotamia and Egypt; their shifting dominations were at first mere casual tribute and plunder. But as they penetrated south-east, they went native. The great Indian epics, the huge *Mahabarata*, and the later *Ramayana*, depict settled warring kingdoms with luxurious courts, perhaps contemporary with the Trojan war, already based on the teeming population of the rice lands now subjugated. Where

---

* 'Brother', for example, is *broeder* in Dutch, *Bruder* in German, *phrator* in Greek, *frater* in Latin, *bhrator* in Sanskrit.

the original Aryans had lived off wheat crops and cattle and dressed in goat hair and wool, their descendants ate rice and curry and wore muslin cotton and silk.

These 'heroic' Bronze Age invaders in their sub-tropical environment, ruling over strange peoples of 'hostile' speech, early imposed a colour bar. Their whole society became set in a strange system of orders and castes (from *casta*, Portuguese for 'lineage'), an aspect of '*dharma*' (duty). The four major *varnas*, or 'orders', persisted for over three thousand years and subdivided into a great many functional varieties of caste (*jati*). Like Hindu literature, the Hindu caste system has unbroken continuity, much older than any social pattern in the West. There were four orders: the revered Brahman priests, the Khsatriya warriors, the Vaisya farmers and the Sudra serfs. Successive conquerors of India ruled over this intensely conservative society. Thus the native *Dasas* (in Sanskrit, 'slave') were to be held in permanent subjection. But there were more Dasas than Aryans; racially, *apartheid* failed. The pastoral, patriarchal invaders had become, by the early first millennium, dark glittering princes, adept at diplomacy and intrigue, sitting cross-legged in their divans:

> All decked in fragrant garlands
> With bright gems in their ears.

Vedic poetry is full of pastoral similes, as when

> . . . the grasshopper replies
> To the distant lowing of cattle,

or when the approach of the goddess of the forest can be heard

> Like the distant sound of moving wagons,

but in the later epic, the *Ramayana*, Rama is helped in his wars by the jungle king of the monkeys.

If the archaic native civilization absorbed the invaders, they gave it a new impetus. Already silks, brocades and carpets were meticulously designed, for the rajas encouraged the detailed and traditional skill of a swarm of craftsmen. Slow caravans moved over the passes to and from central Asia and Iran, and with minute specialization oriental artificers wrought fine weapons, jewels and ivory. A novel variety of vegetables, of fruit and flowers, was already available to the potentates of India in the late Bronze Age, and their lavish entertainment of jugglers, acrobats and musicians surpassed in scale the luxury even of the Mycenaean princes, who were contemporary with the full Aryan settlement. Nothing survives of Aryan architecture, which was mainly in wood and bamboo: the urban and court culture had a background of mud and thatched villages spread out over the great plains, then far better timbered than they are today.

Yet the hopeless poverty of the swarming populace appalled the Buddha. He was not the first genius to try to escape from the 'wheel of things'; hermits, ascetics and holy men had long existed in the ancient Indus civilization: the Aryans, after many centuries, gave their meditations definition. The pantheistic idea of a universal soul, 'he who encircles all things, radiant and bodiless', is formulated in the *Upanishads*; the ascetic tries to merge his soul in the universe, and to escape into a higher reality from the evils of incarnation. The aim of this kind of Indian religion was not, like the prevalent aboriginal phallic cults, to increase fertility, or, like that of Egypt, to preserve the personality, but to transcend it; not to ensure plenty and plunder by sacrificing oxen to a patriarchal god, or to promote civilization by a Confucian cult of right conduct and moderation, but to fade out of the dust, heat and cruelty into *moksha* (liberation). These ascetics developed methods of expanding consciousness, an important aspect of Indian religion.

So, by the middle of the first millennium, the Aryan invaders who had entered India a thousand years before and transformed the archaic native culture, had themselves been changed. The migrating warriors had become a sophisticated ruling class and, in their attempt to retain their identity, had elaborated the Indian caste system. This society was to suffer the impact of Persian expansion, as the Levant was to feel it at the time of Marathon, as well as the famous incursion of Alexander: more lasting were the influence of Buddhism and of the establishment of the Maurya Empire.

## V

The fourth great area of Bronze Age civilization was the broad valley of the Yellow River in north-eastern China. Tenuous contacts between this culture and the West have already come to light; as in India, the flavour of an original civilization is already recognizable. China faced eastwards towards the Pacific: what slender western contacts it had were with the steppe peoples of central Asia, not with the Mediterranean or the Middle East, and temperamentally the Chinese were very different from the Indians. Where Indian religion was imaginative, sometimes fantastic and other-worldly, the Chinese was more pragmatic, concerned with ritual and right conduct. But if, like the Indian, Chinese civilization was less ancient than that of Mesopotamia and Egypt, its social continuity was to be unbroken from the Bronze Age into modern times: of all cultures the Chinese has been the most directly related to its Neolithic village origins, religion and the way of life.

Out of the Neolithic background of Chinese history at Yangshao and Lung-shan, a Bronze Age culture had emerged. But, until the excavations at Anyang in Honan, north of the Yellow River, the Bronze Age Shang dynasty (which flourished about 1384–1100 BC and so coincided with late

Minoan Crete and Mycenae, the Egyptian and Hittite empires and the Aryan invasions of India) was thought to be legendary, like the still indeterminate Hsia, which may have existed on a small scale in southern Shansi about 2000 BC, and which perhaps reflected influences from the Turki steppe peoples in the north. The Shang was a well-established and literate culture, whose bronzes, jades and ivories foreshadow the style of the best Chinese art – the famous cicada pattern, the characteristic solidity and fine proportions of the bronzes, the patina of the jades. There was a rudimentary form of writing from which later Chinese script in part derives. Human sacrifice was common, to promote the fertility of the land – a tradition which long persisted.★

But the Shang supremacy collapsed, about a century after the Trojan war, before the Chou (1028–257 BC), a steppe people, whose paramountcy gave place to the feudal conflicts of the Ch'un-ch'iu age, and of the period of the Warring States (481–221 BC). The later Chou formed the setting of the teaching of K'ung Fu-Tzu, known to the West as Confucius (552–479 BC).

The Shang culture had been based on the lowlands round the Yellow River in north-eastern China, an area exposed to a severe and fluctuating climate, with winter winds and dust from the north. In compact physique, its Mongoloid, narrow-eyed people contrasted with the lightly built Dravidians of India or with the taller Caucasian Aryans and Iranians. But there is a similar rhythm of conquest: the hunters and nomads of the hill country of the interior moved down, through the centuries, to plunder and rule the peasants of the valley and plain. Population multiplied: the Chinese were to colonize north-eastward into Manchuria; more heavily, south into the warm rice lands, first of the Yangtze River and later down into southern China. Peasant agriculture made the most of every acre, of every patch of fertile ground: the Chinese cultivated wheat, millet, barley and rice; cucumbers, melons, pears and mulberries. The Shang already used silk, and the industry further developed under the Chou – the secret was not smuggled into Europe until the sixth century AD. They had also devised a spirited and elaborate music of gongs, tambourines and bells. They had rudimentary money – cowries, bone tokens and stamped leather – but it was later, under the centralized Han Empire, that metal currency was widely employed. Taxes and duties were generally paid in kind and, under the Chou, there was already an elaborate and corrupt hierarchy of tax-collectors and customs officers. There was now a considerable commerce, in particular in metals; market towns had begun to expand into centres of

★ When in historic times these sacrifices were prohibited, the Chinese would hold water festivals, with processions of boats. 'A great boat festival was held in the spring, to which many crews came crowded in . . . narrow boats. At least one of the boats had to capsize; the people who were thus drowned were a sacrifice to the deities of fertility.' Wolfram Eberhard, *A History of China* (London 1960), p. 23.

greater wealth and more complex administration, while royal scribes, treasurers, judges and local governors ruled a hierarchy of districts and departments. In theory, both justice and military power derived entirely from the king (*wang*), the paramount 'Son of Heaven'; in practice, the big feudatories and governors were independent. But the social cohesion of this conservative society was never entirely disrupted by political strife. The rulers performed rain sacrifices and fertility rites. They were particularly concerned with oracles: great quantities of oracle bones have survived, scratched with ideograms ancestral to the Chinese script. Inquirers would write on tortoise-shell and read their answers from the cracks in the heated carapace. The finest Shang and Chou works of art are ritual vessels for libations.

The Bronze Age Chinese made a cult of the spirits of rain and harvest, forest and river, and personified the powers of nature in benevolent and hostile dragons. The Chinese pheasant was also already a sacred symbol. They had a strong sense of order, which their rituals symbolized, reinforced by a cult of the ancestral spirits of the clan which was to give certain Chinese families the longest pedigrees in the world. If the male line died out, they thought that their ancestors would become famished and turn dangerous; indeed the greatest catastrophe to family or State was if 'the sacrifices were interrupted'. But this cult of pedigree was confined to the upper classes, the *Shih*, who practised elaborate marriage customs: the peasantry, the *nong*, on the other hand, held communal spring festivals, which derived from Neolithic times, when village youths and girls followed their own inclinations, sometimes afterwards ratified. Chinese religion thus derived from the weather, the soil and the family: all the immense, precise elaboration of later Chinese cults, of which the post-feudal 'emperors' (Huang-ti) were to be the supreme exponents, aimed to ensure survival, propitiate the forces of the universe, and win the favour of the unseen.

There was no separate priesthood as in India. Kings and nobles performed their religious and oracular functions themselves, and the magicians and sorcerers who advised the peasants never formed a celibate order. The equivalents of the Indian Brahmans were to be the very different 'scholar gentry' who, after the establishment of the centralized Han Empire, administered China from the second century BC to AD 1905.

Meanwhile, under the Bronze Age Shang and Chou and in the Ch'un-ch'iu period, a feudal aristocracy flourished. On sturdy ponies from the steppes, Chinese warriors charged with swords and axes and shot from the saddle with a short bow. By the late second millennium, cavalry was superseding chariots, and considerable armies were organized. The feudatories challenged, but never permanently destroyed, the sacrosanct power of the kings, whose authority over the feudal confederacies was moral and religious; indeed sacred kingship was to culminate in the emperor, who was to inherit the Chou title 'Son of Heaven'. He alone was to focus the unity and power of an immense culture, in which the rulers enjoyed great wealth, and in which the peasant masses, though subject to flood and famine and incessant toil, shared their conviction that China was the centre of the civilized world.

# VI

By 500 BC there were thus four great cultures solidly established: in the Near East, in Egypt, in India and in China. All were based upon riparian agriculture of great antiquity, and all had hot climates, though the northern Chinese had a harder winter. The Near Eastern peoples and Egyptians cultivated cereal crops; the Indians of Bengal and the Chinese of the Yangtze and the south lived off rice. All these cultures had long been literate and the Near Eastern peoples were already using iron. In a great arc, girdling half the world from the Nile to the Yellow River, four massive civilizations were already old.

Western chronology traditionally assumes that a sudden break in world history occurred under Augustus. The turning point is rather about 1500 BC. These centuries saw the rise of the Near Eastern and Egyptian empires, the entry of the Aryans into northern India and the establishment of the Shang in China. If the palace dominations of the Near East lived for plunder and war and dispersed much of their subjects' wealth, successive great kings imposed public law, after their lights, over large areas; they were served by bureaucracies coming down from Sumer and Akkad, and their literature derived from Sumer. The Pharaoh, meanwhile, much richer than his Near Eastern rivals, at the height of his power ruled from the southern Sudan to Syria and over the 'Great Sea'. An Indian empire was not yet established over the whole sub-continent, but there were flourishing kingdoms with wealthy courts and large, if ill-organized, armies; the Aryans had been acclimatized and ancient India had been changed. In China the wide political over-lordships of Shang and Chou were past, and political confusion was setting in; more important was the establishment of a generally accepted Chinese way of life and the expansion into the interior and to the south. And all this was to be consolidated, after the time of the Warring States, in the Han Empire, from which the Chinese to this day are known as the people of Han.

# Three

# BRONZE AGE EUROPE

## 1

Across the Aegean Sea, between Greece and Egypt, lies the mountainous island of Crete. The most fertile and sheltered of the Greek islands, it was long immune from attack, and here, at the western extremity of the half-circle of civilizations extending from the China Sea, the first maritime empire grew up. It derived in part from the Neolithic cultures of mainland Greece, but it was also linked with Asia Minor and with Egypt; like the culture of the Indus, it was buried in total oblivion until the twentieth century.

The Minoans were literate, at least for business, and civilized. Their earliest native script remains obscure, but the archaic Greek of their rulers in the fifteenth century has been deciphered, and a brilliant art and complex architecture speak for themselves. Through the Dark Age that set in after the collapse of the Minoan-Mycenaean Bronze Age, the Dorian and Ionian Greeks retained the memory of Crete, and the civilization of Knossos is ancestral to that of Europe. This wealthy Levantine culture went down before the Dorian tribes who came out of northern Greece – never subdued by Mycenae – at about the time that the Hittite Empire collapsed in Anatolia. It was not until the eighth century that the Greeks fought their way out of an Heroic Age and that classical Hellenic civilization began.

These events took place against the background of Asiatic and Egyptian empires already recorded: other changes were also going on in central Europe and on the outer fringes of Bronze Age culture round the Baltic and out in the West. First, by 1700 BC, 'Battle Axe' and 'Beaker' warrior peoples, skilled in the use of metals and chariots, moved in on the Neolithic peasantry; then, contemporary with the Dorian Greeks, Celtic aristoc-racies imposed a widespread domination, extending during the La Tène period over much of the West and, contemporary with fifth-century Athens, into Ireland. Finally the Germans moved heavily out of ancient Baltic homelands, through the forests of Wurtemberg, Thuringia and the Ardennes, and spread into the Rhineland and the Low Countries and north-eastern Gaul. These Celts and Germans were the ancestors of the war-like barbarians whom Julius Caesar encountered in the first century BC and whom he and Tacitus described.

## II

The Neolithic culture of Crete is immensely old. Crete was in touch with the Old Kingdom of Egypt, and as far back as 3000 BC there was commerce with the Delta and the Anatolian coast: by 2000 BC there were palaces at Knossos, Phaestos, and Hagia Triada. They formed a nucleus of sea power and commerce which brought wealth and luxury and, what was rarer, peace.

Their priest-kings lived in a maze of buildings where elaborate inventories were kept, and in whose cellars six-foot jars of olive oil were stored. Vivid frescoes adorned Minoan walls and the pillars of loggia and staircase tapered oddly at the base. Evans's restorations, which have made this culture so familiar, may have been over bold, but they recapture the spirit of this vivacious maritime people who first combined the influences of Asia and Egypt with something European. Their affinities were more eastern than Egyptian; with an oriental cult of the pillar and the double axe, the snake goddess, the gryphon and the bull. But their women were not shut away, and games and bull-baiting foreshadowed the athletic contests of Hellas. Minoan art was brilliant, it was imported by Mycenae, and it influenced Greece. One of the earliest frescoes (*c.* 2000 BC) depicts a boy gathering saffron in a field of crocuses; the Candia cat stalks a pheasant with realistic concentration;* flying fish swoop over blue water, the octopus of Gournia writhes in life-like convolutions, and the dining room in the guest house at Knossos was decorated with a frieze of partridges.

Earthquakes, not invasion, were the main enemy, but broken palaces were rebuilt. Minos may have employed Sudanese mercenaries, but artists do not record scenes of battle. The long-haired 'chieftain' of the Knossos painting, slender in loin-cloth, necklace, bracelets and peacock-plumed hat, moves with a grace unknown to the pompous and terrible potentates of the East. Knossos, on the northern coast, had many inhabitants; Phaestos, Mallia and Gournia were all considerable cities, and the main routes across the island were well constructed. The principal streets were paved; Minoan plumbing was unsurpassed until the twentieth century. There were bathrooms near the low-built palace doorways which led to living quarters, separate from the storerooms and magazines. Externally, the huddle of flat-roofed houses cannot have been impressive, and the legend of the labyrinth, 'the House of the Axe', recalls the bewilderment of strangers in the crooked stairways and chambers of this Levantine hive.

The Minoan culture centred on great households more than on cities, and their social order was at once feudal and dependent on the palaces, for elaborate records of stores and citizens and slaves were kept. We can read

---

*The *Cambridge Ancient History* is more cautious and describes a 'feline animal creeping stealthily through the undergrowth to spring upon an unsuspicious fowl', II, p. 34.

the late Minoan Linear B script which is in primitive Greek, but not Linear A in the earlier language.

The Cretans were enterprising traders, mainly to Egypt, mainland Greece, southern Italy and Sicily; and must have long held control of the sea.

But Knossos was wrecked by earthquake and sacked by invaders from the mainland about 1400 BC. The catastrophe was sudden and total, and the palace never recovered. The disaster was a culmination of a long shift of power. Since 1600 BC the barbaric princes of Mycenae and Tiryns, Orchomenos and Athens had enjoyed a wealth and consequence which could challenge the Minoans. These Indo-Europeans were the prototypes of Homer's 'well-greaved Achians', the most spectacular of the Bronze Age aristocracies of Europe. The inheritors and exploiters of Levantine culture, they were racially quite different from the Minoan stock. They were the first people to use chariots in Greece and they have affinities with southern Russian and Hittite aristocracies. According to their funerary masks, they were bearded, unlike the Minoans. They spoke primitive Greek, though they retained, and passed on, words from the non-Indo-European Cretan tongue – hyacinth, narcissus, cypress, hymn, abyss and *thalassa*, the sea, a word for which a steppe people had no equivalent. The place-names Corinth, Halicarnassos, Parnassos and Larissa all come down from the old civilization. Trained in Minoan techniques, artists wrought daggers and bronzes for Mycenaean lords which surpassed those of Crete; the Cyclopean architecture of the Lion Gate at Mycenae and the royal tomb of the 'treasury of Atreus' are solid masterpieces which find no parallel in the old civilization. Mycenae was a Peloponnesian land power subject to attack from the untamed northern hinterland: cities were heavily fortified; their organization was massive, and their interests cosmopolitan, akin to the Near Eastern land powers with their elaborate palaces, courts and bureaucracy. The relatively simple economies of the later city states of Hellas emerged from a much more primitive society.

The Mycenaean *wanax*, or over-king, like the potentates of the East, ruled through sub-kings (*basileis*) whose title would outlast his own; beneath them a feudal aristocracy paid tribute in kind. Inventories were kept in the 'Linear B' script as in Crete; chariots, helmets and armour, sheaves of arrows, piles of shields and oars are meticulously recorded: all the working population were registered and their functions defined. The rulers stored up elaborate furniture and heaped treasure in their massive strongholds. This wealth implies far-flung trade. Like the kings of the East, the Mycenaean princes were mighty hunters of lions and wild boars, which they faced with spears, bows and huge oblong or eight-shaped shields. A dagger blade from the shaft grave at Mycenae depicts a lion at bay before five hunters, while two other great beasts bolt. Suntanned slaves lead hunting dogs, and brindled mastiffs hurl themselves on a huge boar: the legends of Hercules and the Nemean Lion and the Erymanthine boar recall these times. The centre of this dominion was in the plain of Argos in the north-east Peloponnese, commanding the sea routes out of the Saronic Sea, and the Isthmus of Corinth across the mountains. Nowhere in Europe is there a more dramatic site than that of Cyclopean Mycenae, crouched in its strategic position.

By 1150 BC these Bronze Age lords were being overwhelmed by new invaders from the north with iron weapons and greater manpower. Most of the massive Mycenaean strongholds perished by fire and sack. The Dorian Greeks and those akin to them were illiterate, incapable of the organization which sustained Minoan-Mycenaean culture; for centuries Greece reverted to a primitive way of life. The heroes of the *Iliad*, who behaved like Dorian Greeks, though their legend is Mycenaean, are warriors akin to the heroes of sagas everywhere. The famous war against Troy, which commanded the Hellespont, probably records a genuine expedition, undertaken at the end of the thirteenth century BC, perhaps to promote colonization on the Black Sea, not by Mycenaeans, but by Dorian Greeks.★ These heroes are northerners; they feast on fat oxen and recognize only a shadowy pre-eminence of their war-lords. They are aristocrats, touchy on points of honour, apt to sulk in black tents, avid for women and plunder; they are alien to the retainers of a highly organized Mycenaean palace, or to the courtiers and bureaucrats of a great king; they lead passionate lives and suffer their ordained fates. But the populace whom they exploited and despised continued to cultivate the olive terraces, orchards and vineyards, and herd their goats and gather their harvests; craftsmen still worked the mines and made the pottery. The basic skills of Minoan-Mycenaean antiquity were never lost.

## III

North of the Mediterranean, beyond the Balkans and the Alps, the Neolithic Danubian peasants of central Europe had long been colonizing the valleys of the Meuse, the Rhine and the Elbe, and spreading into the surrounding lands. They had intermarried with the descendants of Mesolithic peoples, and by 2500 BC they were fairly thick on the ground. In the West the Megalithic cattle breeders had settled in and multiplied. Then a superior Bronze Age culture had also spread westward from central Europe into France, the Iberian Peninsula and the Baltic countries. These 'Battle Axe' warriors had horses and chariots, and the kindred 'Beaker' folk

★ The excavation of Troy VIa has yielded actual evidence of sack and probably of siege. 'Every house or hut in Troy VIa which could still be examined told the same story – a story of the utmost violence and destruction, legible in debris of burnt brick, charred wood and brittle stones.' There was a great accumulation of storage jars to stand a siege. *Antiquity*, XI: 129 (March 1959), p. 29.

brewed beer, a drink new to the Neolithic peoples, who had apparently made shift with repellent decoctions of berries and honey. These conquerors, who brought trade with them, invaded Britain and in 2200 BC developed the original Neolithic circle at Stonehenge into the elaborate temple famous today. They buried their dead in round barrows – the Neolithic people had often made long ones – and their arrival may have coincided with a warmer climate.

The full Danish Bronze Age (*c.* 1500–800 BC) is particularly interesting. The amber trade brought wealth, and elaborate grave goods have survived. Even garments have been preserved, the oldest textiles in the north. Cut to resemble skins and precariously secured, brown woollen tunics were fastened behind by bronze buttons under bare shoulders, while long cloaks were surmounted by brimless caps. At Skrydstrup the most dramatic of these relics has come to light: wrapped in a cowskin in a great oaken coffin, lay a woman in an elaborate coiffure, swept low across her forehead, and in her ears gleamed spiral rings of gold; tall and enigmatic, she lies today under a glass case at Copenhagen.

The Danes also, conveniently, buried votive offerings in bogs. The sun car of Trundholm (*c.* 1000 BC) attests a cult borne out by rock carvings and solar symbols, but the most spectacular finds are the strange *lurs*, trumpets, peculiar to Scandinavia. These large slender instruments, modelled, like the drinking cups, on animal horns, curve into sounding-discs from which a mournful bellow can still be coaxed, recalling weird ceremonies in a Bronze Age dawn.

The Danish relics are only the most celebrated. There were considerable cultures in Britain, northern France and Spain, for Europe was getting richer. Shifting slash-and-burn agriculture and hoe cultivation had often given place to the plough; in favoured areas, Neolithic wattle huts to log houses. Central and much of northern Europe and the West was a going concern when Mycenae was flourishing; free from Neolithic mists, it already looked south to the glow of a Mediterranean civilization.

But the Bronze Age peoples beyond the Alps were not merely passive before southern influence. Astride the amber routes over the Brenner to Bohemia and the Elbe, the Aunjetitz and Lausitz peoples were now exploiting the metals as well as the agriculture of central Europe, while the ancestors of the primitive Germans were already established from Brandenburg to the Elbe, and forebears of the Scandinavians infiltrating beyond the Baltic into the far north. The great reservoir of Germanic manpower, from which invaders were to come from the time of Ariovistus to the Vikings, was already building up; Franks, Vandals, Goths, Burgundians and the Swedish founders of Kievan Russia were to come out of it.

Before Celts and Teutons had become formidable, a Bronze Age social pattern is thus apparent. Neolithic peasants, intermarried with original Mesolithic stocks, had colonized large areas of Europe; they were dominated by warriors from the Baltic–Black Sea corridor, who combined Mesolithic and Palaeolithic hunting instincts with the martial enterprise and flair for trade of the richer Mycenaean princes – the most successful of their kind. The history of these prehistoric peoples, and of the Celts and Teutons who succeeded them, is inevitably obscure, but there was a growing weight of manpower in the barbarian world. In time it was to prove decisive even for the Roman Empire.

# IV

Bronze Age Europe, like Mycenae, now had to face the infiltration of new invaders. The Celts, like the Dorian Greeks, emerged from the Dark Age which followed the collapse of Hittite, Egyptian and Mycenaean power. By 750 BC, about the time of Homer, they had settled along the Upper Danube and the Upper Rhine, in southern Bohemia, Bavaria, the Salzkammergut and in Switzerland between the Jura and the Alps. They were a central European people, probably out of Caucasia or southern Russia.: it was only later that some of them moved west into Burgundy and northern France; finally into Ireland and southern Britain. They also penetrated the Balkans and established themselves in Asia Minor, as well as in northern Italy, whence they attacked Etruria. In 390 BC they sacked Rome; as late as 105 BC Celtic and German hordes combined to inflict a savage defeat on the Romans at Orange in Provence.

The Celts were the first people north of the Alps to use iron. There are three main phases of their culture: the Hallstatt dates from the eighth century; the La Tène from the fifth, and when they got into Ireland, their pagan way of life long flourished in picturesque confusion, so that Christian missionaries, as late as the seventh century AD, found an elaborate native literature in the Indo-European tradition of *Mahabarata* and *Iliad*. It was inferior to both, but, once written down, it became the third oldest literature in Europe.

Hallstatt, not far from Salzburg, is high up by a mountain lake – a contrast to the Atlantic coasts of later Celtic history. It is near lucrative salt mines and well-placed for raids or commerce into the Adriatic coast or northern Italy. The peaked Celtic helmets, with their ornaments of enamel, coral and gold, the sword hilts chased with zig-zag patterns, smack already of Central Europe: Strabo remarks that all the Celts were 'war-mad'.

They wore trousers, and may, indeed, have first introduced these garments to the West. According to their coins, they wore long moustaches and stiffened their fair or rufous hair with a horrid dressing of lime. They would fight naked, save for helmet, torque and belt, believing in the magical protection of their gods. They were head-hunters who thought that the ghosts of decapitated enemies would serve them in the afterlife, and they were organized in tribes, whose chieftains were surrounded by retainers who lorded it over the subject peasantry they had overrun.

The early Hallstatt phase was eclipsed by the La Tène culture named from a site at the northern end of Lake Neuchâtel. After 500 BC, these Celts spread out into Burgundy, Gaul and Spain, and their descendants were found by Caesar in stone-built *oppida* in Gaul. They acquired a veneer of Greek and Etruscan luxury and they imported much wine. But even the Celts of the Côte d'Or and the Rhineland never cultivated vineyards – beer was the common Celtic drink. Spirited, loquacious and quarrelsome, they were a farming warrior aristocracy who never built towns on any scale; they were doubtless, like their descendants, politically unstable. Their artistic flair, individualism and dash contributed to the history of France, the country in which their influence was most important.

The literature of the Celtic Gauls has perished, but in Ireland, unpruned by Roman discipline, the Celtic epic exuberantly survived. The saga of Cuchulain is a catalogue of fantasy. The protagonists of Celtic epic leap over mountains and hurl trees at one another: sometimes, they forgot what they set out to do; as one critic puts it, 'they display the quality of non-arrival'. Yet their fantasies are lit by a strange beauty and by legends of Atlantic isles.

# V

While these settlings and shifts of population in central and outer Europe were decisive for a distant future, the principal economic impulse of the nascent civilization of the continent remained Levantine, connected with Egypt and the mainland cultures of the Near East. On the fringe of Asia, in Palestine, two Bronze Age peoples, in particular, linked Asia and the Aegean. The Philistines are familiar through the alarm they provoked among the Jewish hill tribes upon whom their superior culture and armaments left an indelible impression:* the Phoenicians, Semitic traders who took to the sea and whose colonists founded Carthage in Tunisia and, indirectly, the Carthaginian settlement in Spain, made a lasting contribution to history since they invented a simplified alphabet. It was taken over by the Greeks and attained world-wide importance.

The Philistines, or Pulesati (hence Palestine), were a people of Minoan affinities. In collaboration with the Shardarna from Sardinia, and the Carians from Asia Minor, they had raided Egypt in the thirteenth century; beaten off, they settled at the expense of the Canaanites in the fertile plain of

*The term 'Philistine', as popularized by Matthew Arnold when he attacked the Victorian middle classes, is derived from German students' slang applied originally to those who had not attended a university. It did good service for Arnold, but misrepresents a people more civilized than the Jews.

Sharon, and their principal cities were Gaza on the southern extremity of the coast, Ashdod (Ashkelon), which has the best climate in Palestine and Ludd, today the site of the air port of Israel. Here, by the time of the Trojan War, along the dune-fringed coast and in the fields and olive groves which skirt the Judaean hills, they maintained a society strategically comparable, both in its strength and weakness, to the crusading states of Outremer. They commanded the roads up to Judea and Samaria and the defiles into the plain of Esdraelon. Like the Minoans, they had a cult of sacred pillars and bulls – calf-worship, the Jews called it – and they made their captives perform in gladiatorial games, as when the blinded Samson made sport for them. They had bronze armour, for Goliath had the equipment of an Homeric warrior, save that his spearhead was tipped with iron, and are depicted by Egyptian artists wearing feather circlets in battle.

In their miniature area, Jews and Philistines conducted long intermittent wars, the Jews harrying the plain, the Philistines counterattacking into the hills. This struggle forced the Jewish tribes into some political unity in the days of Saul and David, who once took refuge with the enemy and later employed a Philistine bodyguard. As in the time of the crusades, in the long run the Semites triumphed, and the Philistines were assimilated into the native population.

North of Mount Carmel and Acre, the sandy coast gives place to hills and wooded country which run down steeply to the sea from the snow-capped mountains of the Lebanon. Here a Semitic people were well placed to exploit the trade routes between Syria and the interior and the eastern Mediterranean. The decline of the Hittite and Egyptian empires in the thirteenth century BC gave the Phoenician cities a short-lived inde-pendence, and afterwards they were far too useful for the Assyrians and Persians to destroy. Their cities stretched from Ougarit (Ras-Shamra), opposite the eastern cape of Cyprus, down to Byblos, Tyre and Sidon. Here rich mercantile oligarchies controlled hereditary kings. The Phoe-nicians cultivated the Lebanese vineyards and olive groves, and were rich in sheep and cattle, but their main interests were commercial. After the fall of Crete they exploited the monopoly of the murex dye and developed a textile trade. They specialized in luxury goods and supplied the Mycenaean magnates with jewellery and glass; they monopolized the tin trade from the Iberian Peninsula. With good timber from the Lebanon, rare in the East, they built strong ships: they turned their backs on Asian conquests and became the best sailors of their time. They explored the coasts of Africa for the Pharaohs; pushed out on their own account into the far western Mediterranean; sailed beyond Gibraltar and founded Cadiz, though there is no evidence that they traded directly with Iberian Cornwall. Sometimes they kidnapped the natives and sold them as slaves; more often they conciliated them. They fought rival Greek explorers and for long kept their knowledge of the West to themselves. By the time of Homer they had founded Carthage (*Kart Hadasht*, the New City), brought the entire North African coast into their sphere of influence, as well as Sardinia, the Balearics and the coasts of Spain and Sicily. This network of commerce grew up even through the period of confusion between the decline of Mycenae and the rise of the cities of Ionian Greece. This was the first great Semitic commercial enterprise on the sea.

The Phoenicians worshipped eastern gods: Baal, God of Thunder and Storm; Dagon, Lord of Harvest; Ashtaroth, the Mother Goddess. They also had local gods, Mel Karth of Tyre; Adonai (the Lord), a fertility god who was sacrificed and rose again, whose cult, as that of Adonis, spread over the Levant; and Moloch into whose brazen maw the Carthaginians, in times of panic, thrust their infants in sacrifice. Like many other Semites, the Phoenicians were exploiters more than originators, but, as observed, they invented an important alphabet. By 1500 BC the merchants of Ougarit had devised one of thirty consonants; two centuries later, they were reduced to twenty-two. The Phoenicians had discarded the hieroglyphics of Egypt and the clumsy cuneiform of Mesopotamia. These economical signs, written backwards from right to left, at first sight seldom seem recognizably like our own, but already they were not ideograms but syllables – neutral, flexible sounds. Amplified by Greek vowels, these Semitic characters became the basis of Graeco-Roman and western script.

So the Phoenicians took over and developed the commerce of Crete, but, save at Carthage, they preferred riches to empire. As Levantine middlemen, they retained their wealth and influence until the rise of Rome, when the Romans, after a gruelling struggle with Carthage, broke their power in the West. In the Levant the keen traders of Beirut and Lebanon carried on into Byzantine, Arab and Turkish times; even today they have not lost their flair.

# VI

The centuries from 1700 to 700 BC witnessed the climax and the collapse of Cretan civilization, the rise and destruction of Mycenae, and, after a period of barbarism, the settlement of the Hellenes in mainland Greece and Ionia, while the Phoenicians inherited and greatly extended the commerce which had been the basis of Minoan wealth. Out of this background, by the seventh century, the brilliant civilization of Hellas was to emerge. It was to prove the most creative in the world, but only when the Hellenic culture had become Graeco-Roman could it compare in scale to the great societies already established in Iran, India and China.

# Four

# IRAN: INDIA: CHINA

While the Hellenes were beginning their famous civilization and the warrior aristocracies of outer Europe were working their own development and coming into the light of Mediterranean culture, far more populous societies were already established in the Middle East, India and China, and giving rise to the earliest world religions. In Iran, Cyrus the Great and Darius I made the first great centralized empire, for until the Han Empire, the Chinese paramountcies were shadowy. After Alexander, the idea of empire became acclimatized in the Levant, to be taken over by Rome, Byzantium, and medieval Europe. Moreover, in the seventh century BC, the Iranian Zoroaster founded a cult which was to have wide influence.

In India Gautama the Buddha, a Sakya prince, taught a religion which was to dominate much of India until the early Middle Ages, to inspire the first important Indian architecture and sculpture, then to spread into Indonesia, China and Japan and into Tibet, where a form of it is still the prevalent belief. Then, about two and a half centuries later, Chandragupta built up the first Indian Maurya Empire based on Pataliputra (Patna). His grandson, the famous Aşoka (269–232 BC), ruled in Bengal from northern India nearly to Madras: he turned Buddhist, in disgust at war, and was the first ruler to try to impose a universal peace on religious principles.

The Mauryas did not long keep their authority: by the early second century BC, when Rome was becoming the first power in Italy, their empire was breaking up, and it was not until AD 350, when the western Roman empire was in decline, that a second great empire arose under the Guptas in northern India. It was to flourish when western Europe was reverting to barbarism.

In China the paramountcy of Chou collapsed into a period of feudal conflict, but not before K'ung-Fu-Tzu had formulated the *Ju Chia*, or Scholars Doctrine, a code of conduct to be adopted about four centuries later by the government as the official cult of the Han Empire, the first great centralized Chinese State.

While the early Greek lyrics and philosophy were being written in Ionia, the Buddha attained revelation under the pipal tree at Gaya, and his contemporary, K'ung-Fu-Tzu, like Plato after him, was seeking an enlightened prince in vain. The Buddha died three years before the Greeks routed the Persian fleet at Salamis, and K'ung-Fu-Tzu a year after. Across the old world from Hellas to China decisive political, artistic and religious developments had set the pattern of later history, but in the Americas, Australasia and most of Africa mankind remained in Palaeolithic savagery, at best, in Neolithic barbarism.

## II

The Iranian plateau, comparable on its grander scale to the uplands of Castile, is very different from the maritime and miniature environment of Greece, and from the hot alluvial flats of Egypt, Mesopotamia or the Gangetic plain. Like Anatolia, it is accessible from the Eurasian steppe, and it commands the north-western passes into India. Here the Assyrians and Neo-Babylonians were now outclassed. Since 1500 BC Aryan horsemen, akin, as already remarked, to the conquerors of northern India, had been encroaching upon this wide and then, probably, more fertile land. By the eighth century, when the Dorians were settling in Greece and beginning to colonize the shores of the Mediterranean, Medish and Persian clans dominated the area from Lake Urmia, near the modern Tabriz and eastern Armenia, down to Ecbatana (Hamadan) behind the Zagros mountains which flank Mesopotamia. By 612 BC the Medes had sacked Nineveh and broken the Assyrians. The Persians, farther down at Susa, in the foothills south-east of modern Baghdad, now subdued the Medes: Susa remained their winter headquarters, but they built an official capital at Persepolis near Shiraz in the warm latitude of Kuwait.

The first Persian monarch, Cyrus the Great (559–530 BC), who had supplanted his Medish grandfather, Astyages, claimed descent from a legendary tribal king, Achaemenus. He extended his power westward over Lydia and the Ionian coast, then north, beyond the Caucasus and modern Bukhara, as far as Uzbekstan, and east to the Afghan and Baluchi mountains which dominate the plains of West Pakistan. He mopped up Babylon; magnanimously restored the captive Jews to Jerusalem where they rebuilt their temple; and planned to annexe Egypt. But he was forestalled by the Scythians, who defeated him, and are said to have thrown his head into a skinful of human blood: at last, they said, the conqueror could drink his fill. His tomb still stands in the plain of Pasargadae. His son, Cambyses, overran Egypt, but cut himself on his own sword as he leapt into the saddle, and so perished young. The Greeks thought him a drunken tyrant, though the Iranian monarchs themselves regarded it as their sacred mission to extend a salutary *Pax Iranica*, an aspect of history generally ignored.

The empire was refounded by the youthful Darius I, the Charlemagne of

Iranian history. Master of the most ancient kingdoms in the world, this descendant of nomadic Indo-European tribesmen became *Shahanshah* of Iran and its dependencies, an oriental King of Kings, hedged about with elaborate ceremonial. The Chosen of his subjects' gods, he was the heir of Hammurabi and the divine Pharaohs, if, among his own nobles, still first among equals. His successors became palace despots surrounded by catamites, eunuchs and women. So Alexander found and conquered them.

Darius soon descended into India, extended his empire as far as the Indus, and then tried to outflank the Greeks through Macedonia and Thrace. He failed to master the mountainous peninsula itself, and in 490 BC his troops came to disaster at Marathon. But he retained the coasts of Ionia, and his successor, Xerxes, ten years later, tried again, to suffer final defeat at Salamis and Plataea.

A survey of the bounds of Darius' empire brings home the power which the Greeks faced, defeated, and, through the genius of Alexander and his generals, counterattacked and conquered. It extended from Salonika and the mouths of the Danube over all Anatolia, the Caucasus, Cyprus, Palestine and Egypt, with spheres of influence in Libya and Arabia: it stretched from the Caspian and Turkestan to the Persian Gulf and the Indian Ocean; over Afghanistan and Baluchistan to the Indus. Even after Alexander's conquests, Parthian and Sassanian Iran remained the only power in the accessible world to treat on equal terms with Rome and Byzantium, on whose armies it inflicted memorable defeats. To this day the area presents appalling difficulties: anyone who has seen the mountains of southern Iran from the air, let alone travelled in the desert, can appreciate the administrative problems of the 'Great King'.

He succeeded, if his successors failed. Darius divided the empire into twenty provinces ruled by satraps keeping semi-regal state, with royal viziers at their elbows and travelling officials to keep an eye on them. The satraps, when loyal, raised armies and tribute: gigantic sums flowed into the royal treasury; enormous, if motley, levies were at the royal command. Over roads which were a wonder of antiquity, post-horses carried the Great King's decrees. All centred on the court, with its household troops, the robed Immortals, depicted on the reliefs at the Spring Palace at Persepolis. Here, over a foundation-stone of pure gold, pillars seventy feet high still rise in majestic desolation, and Darius himself is depicted with curled hair and beard beneath a parasol of State. The Great King moved about his empire from his winter capital at Susa to Persepolis; in the summer up to Ecbatana, and he would hunt in parks from which the word 'paradise' derives.

The heavy taxation, from which Medes and Persians were exempt, was suited to the various satrapies: Cilicia provided horses, Babylon droves of young eunuchs and much silver. But although the king was immensely rich and introduced a gold coinage, most of the wealth was sterilized: Persian nobles did not possess or desire the Greek and Phoenician flair for trade. The official language of the empire was Aramaic, a Semitic tongue with an easy script, taken over from the Assyrians. Darius practised a version of the Zoroastrian cult of Ahurah Mazdāh, the High God of Order and Light, which gave the ancient and practical tradition of Hammurabi an abstract sanction. Such was the great empire which Cyrus and Darius made.

Iran set not only new standards of empire but also of religion. Zarathushtra or Zoroaster (*c.* 628–551 BC) was a prophet of a monotheist religion, afterwards travestied in official cults by the priests he denounced. He was born in Media, but found his first followers in Khorasan, western Afghanistan and what is today the Turkmen Republic. He proclaimed the conflict between *Asha* and *Druj* – Truth and the Lie, which probably reflects the 'universalization of a concrete political and social situation in which a peaceful pastoral and cattle breeding population was constantly threatened by the inroads of fierce nomadic tribes'.* Like Jesus, he was tempted in the wilderness, and afterwards proclaimed a revelation. He denounced the ordinary Aryan sacrificial cults of the Magi (from whom 'magic' derives). He called them *Karapans* or 'mumblers', with their cult of intoxication with *Soma* ('when will thou strike down the filthy drunkenness with which the Karapans delude the people?'); and he proclaimed a cosmic conflict between *Spenta Mainyu*, the Bounteous Spirit, or Good Mind, and *Angra Mainyu*, the Spirit of Evil and Confusion. This conflict was crystallized in the struggle between Ahurah Mazdāh, afterwards identified with the Good Mind, and his twin brother, Ahriman, prototype of the Devil. The one created light, order and life; the other darkness, confusion and death. Ahurah Mazdāh wills good, but he is thwarted by his medium, Matter and Time. The Bounteous Spirit created man free to increase light or diminish it, and all are held to strict account: the good will attain heaven and the wicked hell, the House of the Good Mind and the House of the Lie; for doubtful cases, there is a neutral zone. In later elaborations of this conflict for the soul of man a Miltonic hierarchy of archangels and devils takes part; Zarathushtra had cast the *Devas* of the old Aryan Pantheon for the evil role.

The original doctrines are expressed in the *Zend Avesta*, still the sacred book of the Parsees. Metrical *Gāthās* preserve some of the original teaching; *Yashts*, hymns akin to those in the *Rig Veda*, the poetry. Both come down from remote antiquity, for though the original scriptures in

*R.C.Zaehner, *The Dawn and Twilight of Zoroastrianism* (London 1961), p. 34 for the best account. The pastoral background of the original teaching is vividly recalled in the dialogue between the soul of the Ox and Ahurah Mazdāh. 'For whom did ye, Mazdāh, create me?' the Soul of the Ox demands, 'Who was it that fashioned me? Violence, fury, cruelty, frightfulness and might have me in their grip. No other husbandman have I but you, so assign me good grazing lands.' (p. 35). An early formulation of the problem of evil (p. 34).

old Persian have perished, the Sassanians revived the cult and wrote down the books on sacred cow-hides in Pahlavi. The *Zend Avesta* also contains rules of worship and conduct, later elaborated by the Magi whom the founder denounced, but who assimilated and distorted his teaching into an official cult. Worshippers now drank *soma*, took sacraments and worshipped fire; like the Parsees, they neither buried nor burnt their dead, but exposed them.

The dualist conflict between spirit and matter, with its later elaborate mythology, so alien to the pagan cult of life, had wide influence. It could inspire self-discipline, even kindness; the religion of Mithras, the sun-god, with its mysteries and sacraments, descends from it. But there were those who, on the evidence, thought that Ahriman, the Devil, was bound to win, and so worshipped him instead. With its cosmic conflict between God and Satan, its judgement, heaven and hell, angels and devils, this Iranian religion, like that of the Manichees, was deeply to influence Christianity.

# III

While, from the Iranian uplands, the Medes and Persians had created the greatest empire hitherto known, and Zarathushtra and his interpreters had devised their elaborate creed, momentous religions and political events had been going on in Magadha, in the heat haze of the Lower Ganges.

In the late sixth and early fifth centuries BC, when Athenian civilization was coming to its climax and Darius was at the height of his power, the Buddha founded one of the great world religions; then, two and a half centuries after his death, Chandragupta Maurya (322–298 BC) created the first Indian empire, which was based upon Magadha, with its capital Pataliputra. His grandson, Aşoka, extended his rule over Kalinga (Orissa) on the Bay of Bengal, and came to rule all India save the southern part of the peninsula below what is today Madras. Aşoka, who emerged from a fierce warrior background and who was himself a great conqueror, became converted to Buddhism, and proved to be a pacific despot, who ruled a vast and rich empire according to the precepts of his religion and encouraged the development of fine sculpture and art. The lions and the wheel of the celebrated column at Sarnath have become the emblem of modern India. Already the command of the Maurya monarchs over luxuries of all kinds and skilled craftsmanship in all the manual arts was not inferior to that enjoyed by the Mughal Emperors eighteen centuries later.

The innumerable religions of India derive in part from the Aryan *Vedas* already described, and in part from many native cults, the beliefs of the Dravidians in the south. As early as the seventh century BC, only a hundred years after Homer, the notion of reincarnation according to the *Karma* or deserts of the soul was widespread. This painful belief, though sometimes regarded as a 'doctrine of hope', naturally led to a desire for *mukti* (escape) and to a great proliferation of ascetic practices. The lofty teaching of the Buddha, with its ultimately worldwide influence, came from a Brahman background, as did the even more ascetic cult of the Jainas, whose founder, Vardhamana Mahavira, fasted to death. Both the austere religion of the Brahmans, deriving from the *Vedas* in remote antiquity, and the lush ramification of popular Hindu cults were thus already long established before Buddhism; and by the second century AD, Khanishka, a contemporary of Hadrian from central Asia, who ruled the great Kushan empire from Peshawar, had sponsored the Mahayanan version of Buddhism, which was much closer to Hinduism. By the thirteenth century Buddhism had been largely swamped out of India by Hindu cults, which have lasted, in both highly intellectual and primitive forms, until today. Nowhere else has such a variety of anthropomorphic and zoomorphic beliefs been devised. But it was not until the second century BC that Patanjali developed in the Yoga Sutras the most original aspect of Indian religion – the psycho-physical methods whereby consciousness can be altered and enlarged. *Rajayoga* means intense meditation in the 'lotus' posture, elaborate breathing exercises, the emptying of the mind of all preoccupations and desires: it can give its exponents extraordinary powers. The contortions of *Hathayoga*, less reputable, can also produce curious effects. The Yogis were ascetics of the kind common in India since remote antiquity and Buddhism owes much to them.

Siddhartha Gautama (563–483 BC) was the son of a raja from the hills of the eastern Himalayas. A prince surrounded by luxury, he became appalled at poverty, old age, illness and death, and determined to renounce the world. So he escaped from his palace, and took to desperate austerities, until, at Gaya, beneath the Bodhi tree – a pipal or fig tree – he attained enlightenment. Forty-nine days he meditated, unmoved by the temptations of power and passion, by earthquake and disaster. Then, in the Deer Park at Benares, he began to teach *Dharma* and founded the first saffron-robed Buddhist monastic order. He died, at Kusinagora, aged eighty, a mystic of indefatigable serenity, having founded the *Sangha*, one of the great religious orders of the world. One disciple, Upali, set out the rules of the Buddhist order; another, Ananda, the doctrine. A great monastic movement spread far over India: the Buddhists built monasteries and erected huge *stupas* which commemorate the founder's attainment of *Nirvana*. Buddhism was at first an impersonal discipline, a way of life, but, by the end of the first millennium, the image of the Buddha was being worshipped as a god. The events and scenes of his life became sacred: Buddhist monuments became magnificent, the monks wealthy. Then, in the second century AD, the religion became divided into its two great sects, *Mahayana* and *Hinayana* Buddhism; the religion of the 'greater vehicle' which transformed the Buddha from a teacher into a saviour and which was to attain vast influence in northern India and the Far East, and that of the 'lesser vehicle', contained in the Pali scriptures, which flourished in Ceylon, Burma and Indonesia.

Buddhism is a religion both of escape and compassion. 'I go for refuge,' say its followers, 'to the Buddha, to the Doctrine, to the Order.' Individuality, the thirst for pleasure, the lust for power, inevitably bring sorrow: *Nirvana* ends it. The world, personality itself, are transient illusions, and the goal is not immortality but transcendence and annihilation of self. The followers of this almost agnostic religion must work out their own salvation. But many Buddhists came to believe in Bodhisatvas, who, in successive incarnations, help all creatures on their way. A whole realm of these beings grew up.

The process was paralleled by the elaboration of Hindu beliefs. By the sixth century BC their two main cults are already apparent: first, that of Vishnu, who created the world, and of his successive incarnations in the protean hero Krishna; the second, of Shiva, Lord of Beasts, in part a pre-Aryan fertility god, worshipped as a *linga*, and in part Rudra, the Aryan archer. Unlike Vishnu, the merciful, Shiva could be incalculable and malevolent. Hinduism, in contrast to the original Buddhism, developed in a baroque exuberance which surpassed even the cults of Mediterranean image-worship. Already there were Ganapati, the Wise Elephant; Hanumant, the Monkey King; Kama the Love God, whose sugar-cane bow was strung with bees, and whose erotic skill is collected in the *Kama Sutra*, the oldest extant treatise on manners and the art of love. Demonic *asuras*, lascivious *apsaras*, snake spirits, spirits of springs and hills, made up the Hindu pantheon. The great rivers were already sacred: the Ganges flowed from Vishnu's foot, and in the Himalayas dwelt the great Gods themselves. The Hindus accepted and elaborated the Aryan cult of the cow and extended it to other animals. Many higher castes became vegetarians; the extreme advocates of non-violence refused to kill even flies or fleas. Long before Christianity or Islam, Buddhists and Hindus between them had made Indian civilization the greatest world centre of religion.

The Buddha had lived in the world of competing kingdoms carved out by the Aryan conquerors, but his teaching attained wide influence under the Maurya Empire, founded after Alexander's incursion into India, when Chandragupta Maurya defeated Seleucus, one of Alexander's successors, turned East and conquered the country in which the Buddha had spent most of his life.

Soon Chandragupta ruled from the Indus to the Bay of Bengal. Megasthenes, an envoy of Seleucus, whose fragmentary report is lost but quoted by other writers, described his elaborate court, with huge wooden fortified strongholds, similar to those built in Burma in more recent times, well-organized armies and a guard of ferocious women. To his Brahman vizier, Chanakya, or Kautilya, who was a power behind the throne, is attributed the first Indian treatise on politics, the famous *Arthaśastra*, a document which vividly depicts Indian society and sometimes makes Machiavelli look humane. The prince, writes Kautilya, should be affable and enthusiastic, strong and brave, with 'flashing intelligence'; not procrastinating or fickle. But he must spy on everybody and keep his councils so secret that birds cannot hear them, 'for it is said that the secrecy of councils is divulged by parrots'. He must have secret passages in his palace, test all food for poison, and shut up his sons in forts or at least encourage them to dissipation, since 'princes, like crabs, eat their begetters'. The ruler should never bathe where there are crocodiles or ramble in forests where there are snakes, and he must combat corruption, though he will never suppress it, for 'just as a fish moving under water cannot possibly be found out either as drinking or not drinking water, so government servants employed in government work cannot be found out when taking money'.[1]

'The victory of kings in battle,' says Kautilya, 'depends mainly upon elephants,' always best in wet country. Forests, roads, bridges and reservoirs must be kept up; sugar-cane, rice and fruit cultivated; tigers and serpents destroyed, while forts should be well-stocked 'with bamboo sticks with pointed edges made of iron'. Armies can be deployed in 'diamond', 'cartlike' and 'crocodile' formations; camps must be well-planned; there should be a medical corps and, always, adequate reserves. There are hints, too, for courtiers; princes are particularly dangerous when they breathe hard and smile to themselves for no apparent cause. 'Self preservation,' indeed, 'should be the constant thought of a wise man, for the life of a man under the service of a king is aptly compared to a life in fire.'[2] The treatise, familiar in India, but little known in the West, deserves more attention.

Much Indian political thought, however, like medieval thought in Europe, stresses the moral basis of society. Where the *Arthaśastra* is a treatise on how to obtain wealth and power, most Indian philosophers were concerned, like Plato, with *Dharmaśastra*, the art of the moral law. This concept of *Dharma* is fundamental. 'The essential gift of Indian civilization,' writes Dr Mukerjee, 'is the sense of *Dharma* for each individual, ethnic group, caste and vocation; each must pursue, accomplish, and, finally, transcend, a certain code of duties according to life's demands. Dharma . . . is what contains both the social and the cosmic order, which in Indian thought is continuous . . . Dharma defines and regulates both the functions of social life and the goals of the individual and is interpreted across the centuries as the unbounded extension of social relations, as the liberation derived from interdependence and solidarity. The individual's aim of perfection is the same as the group's aim of culture, complete, balanced and practical.'[3] The parallel to European Divine law, in particular as interpreted by Dante, is clear. The distinction between society and government, basic to European constitutionalism, is predominant in Indian thought, so that 'the state, politics, and conquest are far less significant in India than metaphysics, religion, myth and art as factors in social integration. There are hardly any people in the world who have been ruled so little by political occurrences.'[4]

This outlook was expressed in policy by Aşoka. His rock-cut edicts and columns attest his power and enlightenment. 'The Beloved of the Gods,' he wrote, 'desires safety, self-control, justice and happiness to all beings.' This ruler actually promoted *ahimsa*, 'non-violence', while his officials toured his empire to promote peace.

From his reign dates Mauryan sculpture, with its simplicity and solid forms, an expression, perhaps, of the ancient Harappa traditions touched by Greek influence. It reached a more characteristically Indian complexity, after his reign, at the Buddhist monastery at Sanchi in Bhopal, with its crowded friezes of elephants and *yaksi* or spirits. The earliest paintings in the Ajanta caves in the Deccan were now made; masterpieces which depict with superb artistry the lives of the Buddha and of the Bodhisatvas, and which were still being executed under the Guptas centuries later. For subtlety of colour, feeling and design, these paintings are one of the greatest achievements of Indian art, and they combine intense religion with a panoramic realism.

Aşoka began the cult of the domed brick stupas over the ashes of the Buddha, which came to be distributed all over India. They were glorified barrows, crowned with a ceremonial umbrella in wood or stone, and the most gigantic are in Ceylon. They were to determine the form of much Buddhist architecture not only in India but in Burma, Indonesia and Thailand. The Buddhists of the first century AD also cut huge cave temples out of the rock, of which the Ajanta caves are only the most famous, and which were to reach their climax at Ellora in the early Middle Ages. Although it was not until the Gupta period, in the fourth and fifth centuries, that Indian temple building began to develop, and although, after Aşoka's death, the Mauryan dominion broke up, the first of the great Indian empires had set its seal on the varied cultures of a subcontinent, and already, from the Kalinga coast, the tide of colonization and cultural influence was setting towards South-East Asia.

# IV

In China, as already remarked, K'ung-Fu-Tzu was teaching his doctrines in the late sixth century, when the paramountcy of the Chou had broken down into the feudal conflicts of Ch'un-ch'iu. He taught, not a religion, but a way of life, and it was extremely worldly. Virtue, family piety and urbane conduct, he insisted, along with the strict observance of traditional ceremonial, could greatly ameliorate society. Suitably adapted, this ancient doctrine of the Scholars or *Chun-Tzu* (literally 'true gentlemen'), was to be officially recognized six centuries later in the great empire of the Han, and to influence the administrators of China into modern times.

Plato advocated calm and the rule of law among the sharp, mercurial, Athenians, and K'ung-Fu-Tzu (the Grand Master K'ung) taught circumspection and formality among the hard-working and enterprising Chinese. He was born in 552 BC in the dukedom of Lu in modern Shantung, the son of the district commander. He was appointed a keeper of parks and lakes, married at nineteen, and at twenty-two started what might be called a seminar for intelligent boys. In 517 he left Lu for the neighbouring state of T'si, but, in middle age, returned and proved an able administrator. Four years later, ostensibly put out because the duke spent his time with dancing girls supplied by the rival ruler of T'si, in fact because he was denied power ('he was not used'), the philosopher took to wandering over China in an ox wagon, accompanied by disciples, to find an enlightened prince. In old age he came back to Lu and, seven years later, in 479 BC, having remarked 'since no intelligent ruler arises to take me as his master, my time has come to die', decorously expired. To this day his magnificent tomb remains, together with a cypress avenue, a statue and a ceremonial gate. His doctrines were reinterpreted by Meng Tzu (Mencius, 372–289 BC).

K'ung-Fu-Tzu did not found a religion, he formulated a code of conduct. 'While you do not know life,' he remarked sensibly, 'what can you know about death?' But he inspired great devotion. Many of his pupils attained high rank, so that Confucius himself was once denied office since his protégés ran the government already, and it seemed too much to have the sage as well. He taught that the superior man should do as he would be done by, and that criminal power politics could be shown up sarcastically, by 'the rectification of terms'. In the *Annals of Spring and Autumn*, he writes very ironically: in a strictly formal way, he will give a character, not the title he claimed or even possessed, but only that conferred on his ancestors by the legitimate emperor, whose representative was now a puppet. The result, for Chinese readers, was devastating. Confucius taught that everyone should fulfil their role in society, which was not so much a state as a great family. But all depended on right conduct, a flimsy barrier to arbitrary power.

The parallel teaching of an even more venerable sage, Lao-Tzu (the Old Master), whose *Tao* or Way meant cynical detachment and a cult of nature, was perhaps more akin to the Chinese temperament.* He thought that the people should be kept well-fed but ignorant, as they were obviously beyond improvement, and he pointed out that 'striving or crying were ridiculous'. He preached a doctrine of 'passive achievement', *wu-wei*; 'the

---

*Some modern opinion places him in the mid-fourth century, perhaps a contemporary of Aristotle.

more craft and cunning men have, the more useless and pernicious contraptions will they invent.' 'If I work through Non-action,' says the sage, 'the people will transform themselves.'[5] The *Tao* appealed to the scepticism, aesthetic sense, and endurance of his countrymen, and inspired many Chinese aristocrats with an escapist detachment, as well as being distorted into popular cults.

The breakdown of the Chou feudal supremacy indeed produced extremely cynical political theories. Hsun-Tzu, a later Confucian, whose doctrines were repudiated during the Confucian revival under the Han, closely anticipates the ideas of Hobbes. 'Man's nature,' he writes, 'is evil. Anciently the sage kings knew that man's nature was evil, partial, bent on evil, corrupt, rebellious and without good government. Hence they established the authority of the Prince to govern men.' When the Age of Confusion was ended by the ruthless Ch'in, disillusioned sages reflected that 'a country which loves talking is dismembered', and attacked culture as enervating. 'The way of the sage,' it was said, 'is to eliminate knowledge and cleverness: if knowledge and cleverness are not eliminated, it will be difficult to establish stability.'

Plato and even Kautilya, are hopeful compared to the Chinese. They had, indeed, already achieved a stifling social sophistication, conditioned by the entire dependence of the individual on social approval, by an acceptance of arbitrary power, and by a romantic escapist cultivation of the pleasures of life and of acute sensibility to nature. There is a merciless judgement of men, a flair for the essentials of sad or futile situations. The men of action were wont to punctuate their careers with poignant verse, and officials were often poets. Already the Chinese élite 'had acquired a new means of expressing their inmost feelings; they wrote poetry, and, above all, painted'.[6]

In spite of the philosophers, the period of the Warring States – there were a great many of them, slowly reduced to fourteen – went on. In 221 BC it was ended by a ferocious tyrant, the ruler of the tough and relatively primitive western State of Ch'in, in the present Shensi and western Kansu, which had become wealthy through trade with Turkestan and practised conscription of the peasantry. Shih Huang Ti, 'The First Emperor' (221–210 BC), destroyed all the feudal kingdoms. He was a real revolutionary; he transported the high eastern aristocrats from their estates to Shensi and broke their territorial influence, concentrating them in the capital of Ch'in which became a great centre of luxury.* He disarmed the entire population of the fourteen feudal states, save for his own armies;

---

*He was descended from the last feudal Prince of Ch'in whose son, by a concubine, married the daughter of a horse dealer Lu Pu-wei, who had made his fortune trading with rival feudatories. Shih Huang Ti, the offspring of this marriage, was thus of combined aristocratic and mercantile descent – an unprecedented background for a ruler at that time.

established uniform weights and measures and a common script, and constructed roads over much of the immense empire. At appalling cost in human lives, he built most of the Great Wall of China, which runs fifteen hundred miles, from the mountainous interior to the sea, to protect the empire from the Hun nomads of the steppe. This gigantic, but not very effective, work was maintained until the seventeenth century AD.

Shih Huang Ti also ordered a notorious 'burning of the books'. His minister, Li Ssu, pointed out that the scholars were irreconcilable to the new order: the emperor therefore decreed that they must, every one of them, save a few 'scholars of great learning', bring in all books, except those on medicine, agriculture and divination, to be burnt by the magistrates. If any scholar after thirty days disobeyed this command, he was to be branded and sent to forced labour on the Wall. Hundreds of the *Chun-Tzu* were buried alive, recalcitrant to the last gasp. But their power was broken, and Chinese literature immeasurably impoverished.

These totalitarian methods unified China, but they did not preserve the dynasty. The tyrant, in theory, ruled indirectly through his ministers; as the Son of Heaven he became primarily a religious symbol whose journeys were determined by the astrologers; he lived immured in his palaces surrounded by eunuchs and slaves; after his demise, all his political intentions were frustrated. By a forged decree Li Ssu induced the heir to commit suicide, but was soon himself tortured to death by the chief eunuch, Chao-Kao, who then accounted for the emperor's incompetent second son. The empire now rose in revolt, and by 206 BC a peasant soldier from eastern China, Liu Pang, or Liu-Chi, had seized power. After writing a pathetic poem, the aristocratic warrior Hsiang Yü killed himself, and autocracy was reimposed. So was founded the first great Chinese empire of the Han dynasty.

The parvenu Han emperors were more subtle than Shih Huang Ti. They accepted a façade of aristocracy, deprived the old families of the remnant of their power by bringing them to court and, instead of persecuting the scholars, they exploited them. In 191 BC the remnants of the ancient books were reinstated, and an elaborate rewriting of history began. The old Confucian ideal served a centralized despotism and a 'scholar gentry', of real ability and mainly derived from landowning families, some of whom kept power for more than a millennium, manned the bureaucracy. This system, peculiar to China, was developed under the T'ang and, in the seventh century AD, the public examinations were elaborated.

The Han Empire was a society of great wealth and splendour: iron weapons belatedly superseded bronze; literature and the arts flourished. The throne was handicapped by the murderous palace intrigues which chequered its power, and abject submission alternated with revolt, but the administration overcame great economic difficulties and established a culture which was never destroyed. The records of this great empire, which pushed out between the Altai and the Kunlun mountains to the Tarim basin and the Hindu Kush, and south-west to Tongking, are relatively ample. Ssu-ma Ch'ien, the first important Chinese historian, compiled the earliest source book of Chinese history; he even chose the dishonour of castration rather than the grander alternative of Suicide Under the Imperial Displeasure, simply to complete his work.*

But it is Han art which most directly recalls this culture. The Chinese now imported fine horses from central Asia, and their artists modelled them in marble and bronze; they also began their unique mastery of ceramics, and, by the first century BC, were making lacquer. Chinese silks, exported at a great price to the Roman Empire or to bribe the chieftains of the Huns, were already superb. In a deserted tower near Lou Lan in Turkestan, Sir Aurel Stein discovered a store of these silks preserved by the dry climate. At Hsiao-T'ang Shan in Shantung, just such elaborate robes are depicted in the famous bas-reliefs in the tombs of the Wu, designed, facing inward, to provide entertainment for the occupants. Above is a battle scene in which three nobles, having wounded their adversary in his chariot, line up to offer him polite congratulations, since his charioteer has saved his life; below is shown the dramatic escape of the tyrant, Shih Huang Ti, from assassination. In this spirited scene, the monarch bounds to safety behind a pillar, leaving half his severed sleeve falling to the ground, while his would-be murderer, in a huddle of flying draperies and wearing a huge pointed hat, flings out both arms in a turkey-cock gesture of despair. These figures already wear the kind of ceremonial garments, inconvenient for action, but pleasing to the eye, worn by Chinese officials for nearly two thousand years, for the Han Empire stands to Chinese civilization as Graeco-Roman antiquity to Europe.

*This remarkable man, who 'galloped up and down the centuries', the Herodotus of the Far East, wrote the *Shih Chi* or *Records of the Historian*. He had incurred his disgrace – 'the Palace Punishment' – by defending the reputation of a defeated general, thus reflecting on the Chinese establishment, for his relatives were too poor to buy him off. 'Worthless old creature that I am,' he wrote, 'I have yet heard something of the teachings of the great men of old.' His outlook shows profound pessimism and insight, with a cyclic recurrence of tyranny and catastrophe taken for granted. 'It is only those who are masterful and sure who are remembered,' he wrote. He addressed himself to posterity. 'There is an old saying,' he observed, 'who will you do it for, and who will you get to listen to you? . . . If [my history] may be handed down to men who will appreciate it, and penetrate to the villages, and great cities, then, though I should suffer a thousand mutilations, what regret should I have?' For himself, he could only go with the tide, 'follow with the vulgar, floating and sinking and bobbing up and down with the times, sharing their delusions and madness' (p. 67). For, as he explained ironically, he had 'no glories of generals slain or enemy pennants. . . . I have not, by piling up the days and sticking to my labours, achieved any high position or large salary.' His insight is devastating: 'When the fierce tiger dwells in the deep hills, all the other beasts tremble with fear. But when he is in the trap or the cage, he wags his tail and begs for food.' And he can describe 'the barbarian Lords in their robes of felt'. In the end his reputation won through. As a later scholar wrote, 'he discourses without sounding wordy, he is simple without being rustic, his writing is direct and the facts sound. He does not falsify what is beautiful nor does he conceal what is evil.' As his books achieved fame, his senior descendant was sought out and made Viscount Master of History. See Burton Watson, *Ssu-ma Chi'en, Grand Historian of China* (New York 1958), pp. 58, 67–8.

# Five

# HELLAS AND ALEXANDER

## I

The Hellene tribesmen of the Iron Age, who moved down through Thessaly and Boeotia, took Corinth, burnt Mycenae and overran the Peloponnese, found difficult country, often comparable to the west coast of Scotland in a Mediterranean setting. It is hard going from Larissa to Athens; worse from Corinth to Sparta: Greece was not even rich, though the gaunt mountains were then better forested. There was sunshine, but in winter a bitter Macedonian wind.

The invaders took over the old cities or made new ones, each with its small hinterland, and were early forced to take to the sea. By the eighth century, they were founding new cities along the Ionian coast of Asia, on the Black Sea, along the fine bay of Taranto and in Sicily. Many colonists now grew rich, trading oil, corn and wine with Egypt, Asia and the western Mediterranean; artisans found new markets and this prosperity spread to the parent cities. New men now challenged the landed interest, and tribal dooms came to be superseded by written laws and open law courts. A social revolution separates the autonomous city state with a constitution, whether oligarchic or democratic, from its tribal original. The basic blend of Hellene and Levantine was still there, but the Achaeans plundered an ancient civilization and the Dorians rose from the penury described by Hesiod in the eighth century to create the most brilliant culture in world history.

## II

This claim is made advisedly. The originality of Hellas is incomparable; and, after Alexander, Hellenization was to spread eastward as far as northern India, as well as along both shores of the Mediterranean, round the Black Sea and north-west, in Roman form, to Gaul and Britain and along the Rhine. The Greeks created the vocabulary of European philosophy, politics, science and the arts. Since nineteenth-century sentiment has cleared and archaeology has unearthed new evidence, this extraordinary people can be better understood. They faced life directly, without illusions, and still this high pagan past is relevant.

The Greeks first devised constitutional self-government by the citizens of a slave-owning society, and Plato and Aristotle analysed politics more deeply than Confucius, whose ethics only mitigate arbitrary power, or than Kautilya, with his crooked recipes for benevolent but unscrupulous kingship. Indo-Europeans, accustomed to tribal moots and assemblies, had long appealed to custom rather than to the fiat of personal rule, but the Greeks organized elaborate assemblies, councils and voting, gave them theoretical sanction and defined the rule of law. They hated lawless power: 'Aristotle of Athens,' as Hobbes put it, 'seldom spoke of kings but as wolves.'[1] Man, the social animal, Aristotle believed, 'should not merely live but live well'. When, in the fourth century BC, the great Hellenistic kingdoms swamped the city states, and dynastic kingship came in, this ideal of moral purpose, formulated in old Greece, inspired a concept of universal order, a commonwealth of all civilized mankind.

But the rule of law was first evoked as a practical measure against the land-owning oligarchs of the tribal city. By the seventh century BC, heavy-armed citizen infantry dominated the battlefield and coinage had stimulated production and trade: at first the change was embodied in protecting tyrants – an Anatolian term *Turannos*, not yet derogatory. Some of them granted laws and constitutions; most had to be put down. The most important constitution was made in Athens, a comparatively wealthy city which had not entirely lost its continuity with Mycenaean times. As early as 594 BC, Solon gave laws to the citizens, and at once went abroad for ten years so that no one could ask him to amend them. In Sparta an elaborate arrangement put the ancient dual kingship in balance with an oligarchy. Other cities made their experiments: in their miniature states the Hellenes were creating original methods of government.

By the sixth century they were already fairly prosperous; they had forceful sculpture and fine buildings; their geometric patterned vases had given place to more naturalistic and spirited designs. But Greece was now threatened by the enormous Iranian empire already described, demanding tribute and slaves. Led by Sparta, the Hellenes defeated this threat; first at Marathon, when in 490 BC the Great King, Darius I, landed troops against Attica; and ten years later, after Xerxes had crossed the Hellespont with a gigantic armament, overwhelmed the Spartans at Thermopylae (where he decapitated and crucified the body of Leonidas, one of the Spartan kings) and burnt most of Athens. But the Athenians took refuge on Salamis and lured the Persian fleet into the narrows off the island; then, by a brilliant manoeuvre devised by Themistocles, they destroyed it. As Aeschylus, who fought at Salamis, put it, the Persian dead were flayed by the fishes, 'silent children of the undefiled'. Then, in 479 BC, the Persian army was defeated at Plataea, the Greeks seized the strategically vital Hellespont and liberated most of Ionia.

Unlike the Spartans, who were a small aristocracy concerned mainly with war and supported by the labour of the Helots, the Athenians saw their chance and took it. The Delian league gave them a short-lived maritime empire, and the 'city of cities', with its crown of violet hills, became the glittering centre of a power which extended, in the words of Euripides, from Ionia 'to the outward Ocean of the West'. Even today, when paint and ivory and gold are gone, the superb prospect from the Propylaea on the Acropolis, out over Salamis and Phaleron, symbolizes and recalls this greatness. All collapsed in ruin when, in 413 BC, the fleet sent to capture Sicily and bring the resources of the West into the war was destroyed off Syracuse. 'Fleet and army,' wrote Thucydides, 'perished from the face of the earth, nothing was saved', and Athenian citizens were flung into the sinister quarries still to be seen behind the town. A second fleet was destroyed at Aegospotami in 405 BC and the long walls of Athens razed to the ground. Sparta did not benefit much from her victory and its sequel of 'death, devastation and cold-eyed hate': Thebes attacked her; Athens revived; in the end Nemesis came down in the shape of Philip II of Macedon from the country behind Salonika. The Macedonians had perfected a new battle-order from Thebes: their *phalanx* broke the hoplite armies at Chaeronea in Thessaly (338 BC), and put the city state politically out of business. But the Greeks were at last united, at a price, and Philip's son, Alexander, went out to conquer the East.

# III

The literature of Hellas was the inspiration of antiquity and so, preponderantly, of Europe. The poetry has a wonderful range, from the racing hexameters of Homer, through poignant lyric and lapidary epigram and the choruses of Pindar, to the austere drama of Aeschylus and Sophocles, and Euripides' telling insight. As in pagan Teutonic literature, there is a power to look at life as it is, an acceptance of fate. 'Women of Trachis,' writes Sophocles, after the appalling tragedy of Herakles' death:

> You have seen strange things,
> Unheard of sufferings,
> And all that you have seen is Zeus.

For Euripides 'even wisdom is only happening to guess right': the gods symbolized passions uncontrollable by the conscious mind, but life could be justified by beauty, compassion and hard achievement. All this literature is pervaded by the Greek landscape, bright light and hard shadow, ilex and olive, poplar and resinous pine, the rhythm of the cicada and 'the salt swell of the sounding sea'. And Aristophanes, in gross comedy and roaring satire, recalls the life of Levantine streets.

Prose writers, too, reflect all aspects of life. The famous old tales of

Herodotus are full of psychological insight; he is a pioneer anthropologist and sociologist.[2] Thucydides is the first objective, analytic, historian of contemporary events. 'In politics,' he writes, 'the powerful exact what they can, and the weak grant what they must'; democracies, he rightly points out, are 'only amenable to discipline while the fright lasts', and many political and social crimes arise, not through avarice, but through disinterested hatred – 'the envy which equals feel for one another'. The searching argument and poetic vision of Plato, and Aristotle's sharp observation and classifying power, show a flair for essentials which no other peoples had then attained, nor have there since been many competitors. The Greeks possessed a superb language: 'With its strength and majesty,' wrote Sir Maurice Bowra, 'it remains supple and sinuous and easy to manage. From its rich store of words and innate resourcefulness, it is able to go straight to the point, to say with clarity and assurance just what has to be said.'[3] The Hellenes had a trenchant power of mind, cleverness, swift contrivance. The Chinese élite admired Superior Persons who observed sedately the traditional rites, whose family piety was impeccable, and who could generally outface a crisis by an imperturbable demeanour, while for the Buddhists, then spreading their way of life in India, detachment was the price of serenity; but the Greeks seized upon all facets of experience, and investigated the entire moral and physical order of the world:

> The unaging order
> Of deathless nature, of what it is made
> And whence and how.

The conviction that cosmic laws exist, 'sure' as Sophocles writes, 'as the perennial rotation of the Great Bear in the High Firmament', came early on the philosophers of Ionian Greece. Here prosperous cities, founded by emigrants from the mainland, were in touch both with Asia and Egypt. By the early sixth century, Thales of Miletus speculated on the structure of matter, studied eclipses, tried to predict the weather for the olive harvest: water, he concluded, was the 'element from which everything was made'. Pythagoras of Samos proved that the square on the hypotenuse of a right-angled triangle equals the sum of the squares on the other sides – the beginning of theoretical geometry. Democritus, in the late fifth century, even guessed at an atomic theory of matter, of a vast universe proceeding automatically by ascertainable laws, while Hippocrates of Kos (fl. 430 BC) is said to have founded the theory of medicine. Diseases, he apparently declared, against all the weight of priestly and popular superstition, are not sent by God or the Devil, but result from ascertainable causes. 'In my opinion,' he is reputed to have written, 'every doctor must have a knowledge of nature, and, if he is to do his duty, make every effort to learn the relation of the human organism to articles of food and drink.' He related disposition to environment, and is said to have composed the famous physician's oath: 'Whatever in my professional practice, or outside, in the life of the world, I see or hear, which ought not to be spoken of abroad, I will not divulge, considering that such things should be kept secret.'

Science thus began in Ionia, but by far the greatest Greek scientist was Aristotle (384–322 BC) whose influence on European civilization has been greater than that of any other philosopher. The weight of his immense learning, from physics and zoology to politics, which he rightly regarded as a branch of biology, make him the outstanding scientific coordinator of classical antiquity; his belief that society should aim at the 'good life' within the bounds of the human condition is the most important principle of political theory, in terms of Humanism and Christianity. Thus the scientific speculations of Ionia spread back to mainland Greece, whose philosophers often surpassed their mentors.

This kind of analysis had also been applied to philosophy and ethics. In Athens Socrates had been put to death in 399 BC; with his indefatigable dialectic he had for years compelled and cajoled the youth of Athens to examine the basis of their conduct and beliefs. In Plato's *Symposium* Alkibiades declares: 'I have been bitten by philosophical discourse, which implies pain sharper than the adder's sting in the young and sensitive intelligence it attacks.' Doubtless the pain was pleasurable for the scintillating wits of the Agora. Plato (427–347 BC), who was influenced by Indian ideas, sought to find 'reality' in the shift of change: his doctrine of permanent 'forms', which phenomena reflect, may have misled philosophy, and his advocating an authoritarian closed society is a counsel of despair, but the beauty of his exposition and the balanced candour of his judgements are incontestable. This trenchant Greek science and philosophy anticipate a weight of mind, a power to classify and use knowledge, which, when backed by inventions achieved mainly after the sixteenth century AD, were to be the most original contribution of Europe to world history and, at length, to make a world civilization a possibility.

This proportion and balance is also manifest in Greek architecture, with its convenience and economy of line. Derived from a primitive timber structure, Greek temples also early reflect Egyptian influence, but not Egyptian scale. The Doric Parthenon cunningly combines lightness with dignity, and the Ionic Erechtheum is well suited to Mediterranean elegance. The architecture of southern Europe, and of its northern imitators, are modelled on Greek originals, which set the style of the entire Graeco-Roman world from Britain and Spain to northern India.

Greek sculpture had an equally far-flung influence. It ranges from the forceful archaic work of the seventh century to the naturalistic figures of the Periclean Age, unequalled until the Italian Renaissance. If the set smile of a priestess recalls Minoan cults, and if the hard gaze of an early Apollo is enigmatic, the Hermes of Praxiteles is compassionate; and if the Parthenon frieze depicts sturdy cobs, ridden bare-back by strong boys, their grace reflects a confident humanism.

Greek vases pass through a comparable development, from the geometrical designs of the eighth and ninth centuries, with their rows of black conventional figures, through pictures of combat in the sixth, to the more genial designs of ships, dolphins and olive trees, of which Exekias' vase of the shipborne Dionysus is a splendid example. Artists now presented both the old legends, in cunning design and finished detail, and scenes from daily life – a girl crowning a youth, an elegant dinner party. By the time of Plato, technique had become so skilful that episode and character are sketched in a few deft lines.

So, in intellect and art, the Greeks achieved the depth, style and lucidity which mark greatness. But the civilization of old Greece was tiny and, by modern standards of life, primitive: at Marathon only 9000 men were mustered, and at Salamis 180 triremes made up the entire fleet. The citizens of Plato's Athens probably did not exceed twelve thousand, and of these perhaps only three thousand were well-to-do, and a thousand rich. The Greeks had slaves, but never, like the Roman magnates or Virginian planters, owned droves of them. Citizenship went by tribal descent, and many citizens were small farmers and fishermen. Socrates was a stone-mason. Small households would contain few slaves, and save when citizens were sold after a war, Greek slavery was seldom iniquitous; if in some plays servants appear shifty, in others they are reliable confidantes. Naturally the Greeks, a Mediterranean people, conducted vendettas and intrigues with passion, and their politics were often murderous: death or exile were the penalties of miscalculation. Their religion, too, was haunted by bloody primeval cults, often pre-Hellenic, and by the cruelty of their own shining warrior gods. Many characters in their tragedies are hard and fatalistic; sexual passion is accepted, not as the Jews taught, as shameful, but as a frenzy none can resist, which can raise mortals to a brief moment of divine, if sometimes fatal, power. Further, although as one authority suggests, the opinion of philosophers that women should be silent and secluded 'need not be taken too literally, since they plainly contain an element of wishful thinking and it is hard to imagine any Greek woman being silent for long',[4] women were kept in the background, and the 'love songs of Ibycus and Anacreon express feelings which might in different circumstances be given to girls'.[5] The cult persisted in antiquity, an integral part of Hellenism. This lack of inhibitions and acceptance of all kinds of passionate feeling makes much Greek poetry and art more akin to that of China and Japan than to that of medieval or Protestant Europe.

Yet, Hellas contrasted profoundly with Far Eastern civilization through its far-darting curiosity and impulse to understand and exploit. Though the Chinese compiled much knowledge, this spirit of dynamic and ordered inquiry was wholly original.

# IV

Of Alexander's conquests in Asia, Kavafy has written:

> And out of that wonderful
> Pan-Hellenic Expedition,
> The victorious, the illustrious,
> The renowned, the glorified,
> As none has been glorified else,
> The incomparable expedition,
> We have come out,
> A new Greek world and Great.[6]

Athens and Thebes and Corinth had been states in miniature, and relatively poor: the Hellenistic world was to be large, cosmopolitan, and extremely wealthy.* Old Greece largely created the intellectual capital of European civilization, but the Hellenistic world diffused, elaborated, enriched and vulgarized it.

· For Alexander the Great (355–323 BC) now changed the course of world history. A Balkan background early proved his metal. When his father, Philip II of Macedon, left him in charge of a kingdom at fifteen, he had at once put down a revolt, and he had succeeded to the throne four years later, when Philip was murdered by one of his own guards. Through his mother, Olympias, Alexander was an Epirote from the harsh Illyrian mountains; she probably connived at her husband's murder, and was killed six years after her son's death, having massacred most of the leading families of Macedonia. Philip, who was assassinated at forty-seven, had organized the armies that Alexander led, and had himself planned the invasion of Asia. The Macedonian *phalanx* was a deep wedge of pikemen, whose weapons in the rear ranks were twenty feet long, and whose right arms were overlapped by the next man's shield. They were employed with heavy cavalry to protect their flanks and to envelop the enemy when the *phalanx* had smashed into him. These tactics were deadly against large and ill-organized oriental armies, which often still used chariots.

Alexander's meteoric career lasted only twelve years and eight months. He conquered the entire Persian Empire, and deliberately Hellenized it. He founded many cities, of which Alexandria at a mouth of the Nile was the most important, strategically chosen as the economic capital of a

*The term 'Hellenistic' originally applies to non-Greeks who admired and imitated Greek civilization.

civilization extending from the Adriatic to the Indus. Alexander had been taught by Aristotle, whom he revered and subsidized, and although he put Callisthenes, a tiresome philosopher who had accompanied him to Asia, in chains, speared his kinsmen Cleitus in a tipsy argument, and set fire to the Achaemenid palace at Persepolis probably as a gesture of pan-Hellenic revenge, he may have believed in the pan-Hellenic ideas of Isocrates, who had written: 'The term Hellene no longer signifies a race but an intelligence.' Alexander naturally used Persians to administer his gigantic conquests, and his assumption of divine honours was a political necessity in the East.

His first objective was to secure his Macedonian base. So he made a punitive expedition against the barbarians on the Danube and also taught the dangerous Illyrian tribesmen a lesson: he then moved south and razed all Thebes to the ground – save for the house of the poet Pindar – and sold the citizens into slavery. Having cowed the city states, he then invaded Asia with 35,000 men across the Dardanelles. To secure his communications, he now marched down the Ionian coast to seize the harbours and ships. Here he was intercepted by the Persians on the river Granicus, and utterly defeated them; he took Miletus and other cities, then moved inland behind the Taurus and descended through the Cilician gate on the coast of what is now the Gulf of Iskanderun (Alexandretta). Here the incompetent, if dignified, Darius III tried to cut him off on the Issus plain: Alexander turned, destroyed his army and captured his harem; then, while Darius fled eastward, took Sidon and laid siege to the Phoenician stronghold of Tyre, where his Greeks, with a new expertise in siege-craft and aided by ships, built a causeway and took the island city after seven months. The Phoenician fleet was now at Alexander's disposal: the second objective had been achieved.

Alexander now advanced on Egypt, which he secured, and in 331 BC returned to base at Tyre. He then launched his main attack into the interior. The army marched through Syria, straight for the heart of the Iranian Empire, and at Gaugamela, near the modern Mosul, won a hard-fought victory over an enormous Persian host. Darius escaped into Parthia, south of the Caspian, where he was murdered by his own people. The third and final objective had been won – the conquest of the Near East.

Alexander swiftly turned south and occupied Babylon, then took all the Persian capitals – Susa, Persepolis and Ecbatana, and advanced north-east into Bactria, where he married Roxana, a local princess. With a Graeco-Persian army he even crossed the Hindu Kush, and invaded the Punjab, where he defeated the Indian monarch, Paurava (Porus), at the battle of the river Jhelum, for the Indian cavalry was outclassed and the elephants bolted from the Greek archers. Paurava, whose bravery and bearing impressed the Greeks, now became an ally, and Alexander pressed on east towards the

Ganges valley and Magadha, where, a century and a half before, the Buddha had taught his disciples. But the rains set in, and the generals feared mutiny: Alexander returned through southern Baluchistan and the Makran to Susa and so to Babylon, where, in 323, he died of fever, aged thirty-two.

His generals now fought it out for the inheritance, and his posthumous son, Alexander, was murdered before he was twelve. But this brilliant and hectic career of conquest had not been ephemeral, for the scale of Greek civilization had been enlarged. The kingdoms of the successors were far richer and better organized than old Greece, and their rulers promoted Hellenism, while the idea of a universal civilization became widely accepted. And, as the Han Empire in China was to create the Chinese State which thought itself the centre of the civilized world, so Rome was to weld the Hellenistic kingdoms and the cities of the West into her empire. Thus the decisive continuity between Europe and her most ancient Near Eastern centres of civilization came about. Even today, when the Pope, enthroned between ostrich feather fans and wearing the triple crown, gives his benediction *urbi et orbi*, or the Monarch of the British Commonwealth is anointed and crowned, the origins of both ceremonials go back over thousands of years, through the Byzantine and Roman empires to the Hellenistic monarchies and priesthoods of the East, and through them to the oldest of all civilizations in Mesopotamia, to Hammurabi and the Sumerian kings.

Yet this cult of empire was un-Greek, since the city state, oligarchy or democracy, attempted self-government; un-Indo-European, since the original tribes had recognized only war leaders or tribal and local kingship. The contrast between the originally oriental concept of far-flung absolute power and bureaucratic administration with small-scale self-government has run through Western history. It is the last that is more original.

# V

When the empire of Alexander broke up, it divided into several kingdoms, ruled by Macedonian military dynasts with all the trappings of Eastern monarchy. The largest share fell to Seleucus: based on the great city of Antioch in Syria, and extending to Seleucia, near modern Baghdad, over part of Anatolia and most of Iran. But the Seleucids could not long hold territories beyond the Euphrates; by 250 BC the Asian Parthians counter-attacked and became a first-class power on the Tigris at Ctesiphon, the inheritors of the Achaemenid Empire and the forerunners of the mighty Sassanian power. But the Seleucids still flourished in Syria, where Hellenistic civilization remained dominant until the Arab invasions of the seventh century AD.

The other great successor State was Egypt, where the Ptolemies ruled with all the absolute bureaucratic power of the Pharaohs. They were the richest of all these dynasts, and they made Alexandria the intellectual capital of the Hellenistic world: after the death of their descendant, Cleopatra, in 30 BC, the Romans annexed the country. In Anatolia the kingdom of Pergamum was established by the Attalids, who drove a horde of invading Celts into Galatia in the interior, and reigned until 133 BC, when the last ruler bequeathed the entire State to Rome. The original Macedonian kingdom was the shortest lived; the last of the Antigonids, having defied the Romans, was deposed by them in 165 BC.

The founders of these dynasties were all soldiers, and their diademed descendants, who in Egypt and Seleucia were generally expected to marry their sisters to keep the stock pure, had to combine a show of dash and glamour with business acumen and patronage of the arts. In the Mesopotamian tradition, they called themselves *Euergetes*, the Benefactor, or *Soter*, the Saviour, but they were apt to perish in fratricidal palace revolutions, so that one Ptolemy, who had finished off two of his brothers, was surnamed, ironically, Philadelphus (Brotherloving).

All these kingdoms had fought themselves to exhaustion before Rome mopped them up, but they remained immensely wealthy. Greek traders and settlers had been moving into Asia long before the fourth century BC; after Alexander's conquests, they swarmed far into what had been the Persian Empire. They found rich territories and docile peoples, whose skills derived from the archaic civilizations in which the urban revolution had begun, and they exploited their opportunities. The huge capital of gold stored up by the Achaemenids was minted and put into circulation; enlightened Hellenistic despots competed to found cities, to build and extend ports, to encourage commerce and exploration. Alexander had taken geographers with him and sent his fleet to explore the Arabian Sea. The Pharos of Alexandria, the biggest lighthouse in antiquity, 480 feet high, was begun under Ptolemy Soter in 284 BC, and Sostratus, the architect, played the monarch a neat trick, cutting his own name in marble beneath the king's in plaster, so that in due time the building stood dedicated 'to the saviour Gods for the Benefit of Sailors', not by Ptolemy, but by its designer. New roads and bridges were constructed; sparsely populated areas brought to life, the towns complete with colonnades, agora, temples, fountains and public baths. Sculpture attained an unsurpassed virtuosity, if not the sublimity of Praxiteles; the superb 'Winged Victory' of Samothrace dates from the middle of the third century BC, and the luscious 'Venus of Milo', so popular in the nineteenth century, from the second. The new cities, Pergamum, Seleucia, Priene, were well planned, and new methods of cultivation and better strains of livestock were introduced. Iron agricultural implements became common, while citrus fruits and melons spread from the East into Greece and then into Italy, where poultry were now, for the first time, introduced into the West. In the first century BC, water mills, driving rotary grinding stones, became common. Vineyards and olive groves were extended into fresh areas of Africa and Asia; state factories produced textiles and luxury goods; Asian manpower was set to new methods of production. The Near East saw Greek civilization expand to the Iranian plateau and to northern India, while, westward, in North Africa and southern Europe, the Greek colonies flourished as new markets were opened up. Pytheas of Massilia was already sailing out into the Atlantic and round Scotland to the Kattegat for amber when Alexander was marching east.

# VI

All this wealth meant leisure for the rich, who assimilated and vulgarized the old Hellenic culture. Athens retained immense prestige as a university city, and new universities multiplied. On the beautiful island of Rhodes flourished the most fashionable school of rhetoric, but the biggest library and university were at Alexandria, where new standards of philosophical and critical scholarship were set. Egypt produced papyrus, and Pergamum, parchment, so that books became more common. New 'universal' philosophies now became fashionable – Epicurean, Cynic, Stoic – all aiming at 'self sufficiency' after the close community of the city state had been superseded. Epicurus (341–270 BC) taught self sufficiency in a universe indifferent to the fate of man, and a sceptical toleration of the varying customs, religions and morals which a variety of environments has elicited from the human race. Far from being the hedonists of popular legend, the Epicureans were extremely wary of life and advised moderation and withdrawal; 'live unobtrusively' they said; they regarded fanaticism as stupid. They have much in common with the more aristocratic Taoists, who advocated a similar withdrawal and contemplation, and they were influenced by Indian philosophies, with their negative but benevolent attitude to life.

Stoicism, founded by Zeno (342–270 BC), who taught in the porch or loggia of Pisianax in Athens, was a more positive philosophy, widely accepted by men of affairs, which stressed the obligations of public duty, more akin to Confucian than to Taoist doctrine. The just and tenacious man, he taught, ought to preserve his dignity, though the world crash about him . . . *'si fractus inlabitur orbis'*, as Horace was to write, *'inpavidum ferient ruinae'*. Since all men possessed reason, they participated, if in varying degrees, in the universal and eternal soul of the world, which was sustained and ordered by Natural Law, a concept which, in various forms, was to have great influence on political theory, supporting the moralization of power. Though the process of life is often indifferent to human desires, the philosopher ought to accept it without complaint and play his part with dignity on the stage of existence. This self-sufficient and fine acceptance of the limitations of fate, was then, as now, obviously needed – especially in the Roman Empire. The prestige of these philosophers is comparable, after their grim fashion, with that of St Francis and St Dominic. Oriental religions – the cult of Sarapis and Isis; of Mithras, with its Zoroastrian background; of Orpheus and Adonis – ramified through the cities. The last of these eastern salvation cults was Christianity, a branch of Judaism which spread to the Gentiles, while the main Jewish tradition remained aloof.

The medium of culture was the *Koiné*, derived from Attic Greek, the language of a large secular literature, most of which is lost. It is the tongue of the Septuagint and the New Testament, the common language of the Hellenized East, of the Greek fathers of the Christian Church and of Byzantium. The *Koiné*, which doubtless seemed odd in accent and limited in vocabulary at Athens, retained the old Attic flexibility and clearness.

Hellenistic literature and its Latin imitators owed much to the East. In the early third century BC a new pastoral poetry was written by Theocritus, who lived in the delectable islands of Sicily and Kos, as well as in Alexandria, and evoked, in the dialogue of sunburnt and conveniently literate goat-herds, the Mediterranean landscape of harvest, fig tree and vine. Callimachus wrote epigrams; the best known to English readers is on a friend, Heraclitus, with the refrain:

> Still are thy pleasant voices, thy nightingales awake,
> For death he taketh all away, but them he cannot take.

This romantic regret often goes along with a fierce disillusionment, as in the epitaph:

> I've entered port: Fortune and hope adieu,
> Make game of others, I have done with you.

A whole range of 'modern' sensibility is expressed in Hellenistic poetry, at once hedonist and stoical.

It was the philosopher, Theophrastus (372–287 BC), a pupil of Aristotle, who preserved the works of his master, and was the best botanist before the eighteenth century Swede, Linnaeus. Eratosthenes of Alexandria was a pioneer cosmographer, and the astronomer Hipparchus collaborated with Babylonian colleagues; Euclid, born in the year that Alexander died, extended the study of geometry, and Archimedes (287–212) was a famous pioneer of mechanics, while Heron invented a small steam engine, but no one put it to use.

The theoretical discoveries of Hellenistic science were, indeed, remarkable, but they were seldom applied, since the bias of education was rhetorical and literary, and any mechanical occupation was thought to be banausic. Though technological progress was greater than has traditionally been admitted (in the making of bread, for example, great skill was achieved), while there was a huge slave population augmented by wars and piracy, there seemed no need to economize in manpower. 'Natural philosophers', as scientists were termed, were further handicapped since they had no adequate instruments of precision, no telescopes, microscopes and accurate chronometers. The ruling classes of antiquity, save for their interest in ballistic instruments of war and siege engines, felt no more enthusiasm for such things than did the élites in India or China. Save in Europe after the fifteenth century AD, a technologically conservative and indolent outlook has generally gone along with privilege. Moreover, there was a fundamental weakness in this culture of cities. A native peasantry – the Roman Christians were to call them the *pagani*, the country folk – were biding their time. Hellenistic civilization in the East flourished for many centuries, but the Semitic peasants outlasted it: today great Hellenistic ruins rise above the mud huts of eastern villages, while in Britain, at the other extremity of the Graeco-Roman world, the towns and villas of civilized landowners were deserted after more than three centuries, and sub-Roman survivors lurked among the ruins, or Germanic barbarians sent them up in flame and smoke, while, at best, an Anglo-Saxon poet, more sensitive than the others, is found muttering, 'Wondrous is this wall stone . . . the work of giants is crumbling.'

Outside the broad Mediterranean-influenced areas of its origin, the civilization of antiquity never went deep; it was baffled by economic problems, it upset the trade balance with the East, and never created the great internal markets which expansion and prosperity demand. Nonetheless, after the inclusion of the Sicilian Greek and Carthaginian spheres of influence in the central and western Mediterranean and the extension of Roman power into Spain, the Rhineland, the Low Countries, Britain and Gaul, it was a society on very great scale, comparable to the Indian dominions of Aşoka or to the Han Empire that was now being consolidated in China. Old Greece had largely created the intellectual capital of this civilization, but it had been enlarged and enriched by the wealth, manpower and technical skills of the Near East, by the resources which Alexander's conquests and Roman expansion opened up. And the framework of the universal empire envisaged by Alexander was now to be created by the Romans, the political architects of Europe.

# Six

# ROME

## I

Anyone who looks down from Tusculum across the Roman Campagna, will observe, to the west of the dome of St Peter's, the gleam of the sea, and, to the east, an amphitheatre of famous hills. Here, behind Tivoli, lies the Sabine country and, beyond the peaks of Soracte and Lucretilis, the mountains of the Abruzzi, while below, to the left, the ancient Via Appia runs direct between ruins and cypresses to Gaeta and the south. From this great prospect the strategic and commercial advantages of the city, the natural capital of the Mediterranean, will be obvious. Situated on the swift Tiber, at the nearest bridgeable point to the coast, and with access to the shore at Ostia Antica, whose shell remains the best example of a Roman port, the mosaic tokens of the shipping lines still clear on the pavements, Rome was well set to command the trade of the western flank of central Italy in the curve of the Apennines as they strike towards the Adriatic.

Here, from tenacious peasant beginnings, there grew up a dominion which extended round the entire Mediterranean world and, finally, from Scotland to the Euphrates, from the Sahara to the Rhine. It came to cover all Europe, save for Bohemia, the northern German and eastern plains and Scandinavia; it included the Balkans, much of Hungary and all Romania, besides vast territories in North Africa, Egypt and the Near East. The transmitter of Hellenistic culture and of Alexander's idea of an hegemony coterminus with civilization itself, the progenitor of the papacy and the Holy Roman empire, and, directly, of Byzantium, Rome became the cardinal political fact of European history. This empire can be compared in scale and duration only to the Han and T'ang dynasties in China, with their influence radiating throughout the Far East through Korea to Japan, for the city outlasted the empire of Aşoka, which was at its brief climax when Rome fought Carthage for the domination of the Tyrrhenian Sea. And Rome had two incarnations, pagan and Christian: the autocrat of Byzantium carried on unbroken the tradition of Constantine and Theodosius, with all that it meant to Russia and the Balkans through the Orthodox Church, while, as Roman pontiff, Gregory the Great took the leadership of Italy and the West.

The history of the city falls naturally into three parts; first of the Republic and its rise to Mediterranean world power, then of the Augustan Principate, which was Italian, and shaded into the empire of Vespasian and Hadrian, Diocletian and Constantine, which was increasingly cosmopolitan and despotic. As the empire expanded, its rulers might, and did, come from anywhere, while the armies, in particular the palace guards so decisive in politics, were increasingly drawn from the Balkans and Germany. This barbarian infiltration had been going on long before the outer warbands got into the ruined western territories. So great is the just prestige of the Romans that the brutal and treacherous way in which their supremacy was built up, the ferocity of their class conflicts and civil wars, the epidemic rate of suicide and political murder, and the damage done as military plutocrats fought one another across the known world, is often disregarded. The novel discipline of camp and road construction, of organized supply and defence – the well-found *limes* stretching along the frontier against the barbarians – went along with incapacity to control the armies, a problem much better solved by the Byzantines, and with a technological and fiscal conservatism which prevented this great slave-ridden society from creating the markets which its rudimentary capitalism came to demand, so that the whole vast structure was eroded by a gradual and, at that time, inexplicable decline. And the Romans, after all, had only barbarians to conquer in the west and north; tribes without discipline or considerable towns; in Germany without civilization at all. Yet, when the armies got off their own ground, as did Varus in the Teutonic forests, or Crassus against the Parthians, and Valerian against the Sassanians in the deserts of the East, they could come to spectacular defeat.

The culture of the Roman Empire was mainly derived from Hellas, though the Romans could give it a new turn, as in prose or satire. But the old native *virtus* and *gravitas* of the Republic, the majestic vision of Augustan and Antonine Rome, the sense of a peculiar responsibility to the divine power which inspired Constantine and Justinian, his Byzantine successor, were politically dynamic, making Byzantium still the focus of European civilization into the twelfth century. If Hellas was the intellectual inspiration of Europe, Rome was decisive for its scholarship, its architecture, for its very language in the Romance-speaking countries and their colonies overseas; above all, for its main tradition of administration and law.

## II

In the opening decades of the first millennium BC, when Dorian invaders were penetrating Greece, Iron Age peoples were also settling in Italy. The best known of them, the Villanovans, settled near Bologna and used pottery with geometric designs similar to those of early Hellas. On these autochthonous inhabitants two much more highly civilized cultures were superimposed. The expansion of Greek cities in Sicily, southern Italy and along the Riviera coast at Antibes, Nice and Marseilles is generally familiar, but the Etruscans, who much more intimately influenced Rome, are a strange people.

They certainly began as Aegean pirates and almost certainly they came from the East, from Lydia, as Herodotus declares. They settled in Tuscany, dominated central Italy from the Arno to the Tiber, and extended their power north to the Po valley and the foothills of the Alps, and south as far as Salerno. They formed a league of hill cities – Perugia, Siena, Orvieto and Arezzo have survived – and they exploited Tuscan copper and zinc deposits and the iron mines of Elba. They were bold sailors, with Tuscan timber for their ships; as previously observed, they traded pottery, wine and ornaments with the Celts beyond the Alps. They thus became a wealthy, high-living aristocracy which flourished during the sixth century, before the full brilliance of Greece in the fifth, and Etruscan *Lucumones* (overlords) long dominated the farmers of Latium and ruled as 'kings' in Rome. It was not until 510 BC, only twenty years before Marathon, that the Romans followed the Greek cities in getting rid of their '*tyrants*' and expelled the Tarquins. But these rulers had left their mark: some of the most famous Roman institutions, the lictors, the fasces, the augurs, the gladiatorial contests – originally funeral games when blood flowed to nourish the dead – the 'Roman' arch, even the toga (*tebennos*), are Etruscan. Thus, apparently, Asia set its mark on Europe; for an eastern origin is attested by the mythological animals and demons of Etruscan art, by their costume, with its turned-up eastern shoes, by their religion, with its cult of divination through the liver, the seat of life, by their still largely unintelligible and un-Indo-European language, and by the evidence of place names in Asia Minor.

The Etruscans were also partly Hellenized. Their divinities accord with the Graeco-Roman Pantheon, save that they have garbled names – Persephone becomes Phersiphae; Neptunus, Nethumus; and Bacchus, genially, Fufluns. Like the Romans, the Etruscans feared or acclaimed thunder, according to the quarter of its origin in the sky, and took omens from the flight and position of birds. They constructed elaborate rock-cut tombs, subterranean replicas of houses, in which the apparatus of their lives and the scenes of their revels are reproduced. Since the tombs, of which the most famous are at Cerveteri and Tarquinia-Corneto, between Pisa and Rome, were sealed for more than two thousand years, these frescoes were found marvellously preserved, while most other classical painting has perished. Compared to Greek art, Etruscan sculpture and bas-relief is rustic, if forceful, but their painting was heavily influenced by Ionian and Attic styles, and may well have been done mainly by Greeks. It is splendid, comparable, though less subtle, to that of the Indian Ajanta caves, showing how much has been lost in the paintings of Greece itself. At Tarquinia-Corneto, in the *tomba della Caccia e della Pesca*, there is a brisk painting of a hunt after birds at sea, and a boy dives smartly from a rock. But the most gorgeous, in its splendour of blue and red, green and yellow ochre, is the famous tomb of the Hunting Leopards, where the laurel-crowned dancers whirl in abandon to lyre and flute, flinging out hands and draperies to the rhythm, while Etruscan magnates and their women, who held an honoured place, feast with invincible satisfaction. If haunted by Asian superstitions, they were well at home in the sunny countryside of Umbria and Tuscany, so that their predominantly Hellenic art even shows odd anticipations of the Florentine Renaissance, some of whose artists may, indeed, have had Etruscan ancestry.

By the sixth century Italy was thus divided into wealthy Greek and Etruscan spheres of influence, while the Phoenicians, who dominated Sardinia, picked up what they could. But the unimportant Roman farmers of Latium were now to profit by a Graeco-Etruscan conflict. After the expulsion of the kings, the Republic began to develop its own formidable institutions, similar in principle to those of other city states, but with a peculiar solidarity. The Roman oligarchy, the patricians who formed the Senate and elected the two consuls, came to terms with the plebs, and the State was *Senatus Populusque Romanus*. This prosaic agricultural people – 'they had at least seven words for "pig"'[1] – early showed an iron determination and a shrewd eye for business. Even their religion was practical: 'they were ritualistic in their way of performing even the simplest customary act, and they consecrated the best way of doing it. . . . Their real gods were, in short, efficiency and good luck.'*

The earliest tale of Romulus and Remus is legendary, but the Gallic invasion of 390 BC, when the geese are said to have saved the Capitol, certainly occurred, and while Athens was crippled in the aftermath of the Peloponnesian war, Rome was already the greatest power in central Italy. Half a century later, when Alexander's successors were carving up the East, Rome also survived the backwash of these wars. The Epirote King Pyrrhus, who used elephants, which the Romans called 'Lucanian cows', and who had been brought in by the Greek cities, was worn down by the discipline and manpower of Rome and her allies; by the resolution of what he termed the 'Hydra-headed' Senate.

But the Romans had now to face another enemy: Carthage, the North African Phoenician focus of Semitic power. The colony of Tyre, looking

---

* Even the patrician surnames, Goad points out, were chiefly country nicknames, 'especially those derived from domestic animals, vegetables, colours, or bodily defects'. 'Flavius' means 'blond', Rufus 'red-headed', Naso 'nosey', Balbus 'stammer', Scipio 'stick', Galba 'Paunch', Porcius 'pig' and Mucius 'mouldy'.

across what is now Tunis Bay, with its fertile hinterland, to the dramatic silhouette of mountains falling to Cape Bon, commanded the strategic and commercial sea routes of the central and western Mediterranean. The Carthaginian oligarchy had a civic constitution admired by Aristotle, for it was not only Indo-Europeans who could make a city state, with two annually elected '*Sofetim*' (magistrates) and a secret Council of Ten. In sharp practice they surpassed the Romans and they are said originally to have bought even the famous Byrsa, the hill behind the city, by a trick. They maintained large mercenary armies, complete with war elephants in the eastern fashion, ocean-going keeled 'round' merchant ships (*Kirkarahs*) with high bulwarks, and long war galleys with banked oars and figureheads of their horrid gods. Moreover, they had abandoned the old fashion of navigation, practised by Noah, of sending out long-sighted birds – generally crows – and steered to Ophir and to Senegal by the stars.

The climax of the inevitable and atrocious struggle occurred after 218 BC in the second phase of the Punic War. Hannibal was forced into his famous and desperate invasion of Italy over the Alps, since the Romans were strangling Carthage at sea. 'The elephants,' writes Livy, 'caused considerable delay owing to the difficulty of getting them over the narrow and precipitous places; on the other hand, they rendered that part of the column safe from attack where they were'.[2] The Celtic mountaineers were beaten off; rocks broken up with fire and vinegar; tracks constructed, and, after heavy losses, Hannibal, like Napoleon, was loose in the plains of Lombardy. The Romans suffered appalling disaster at Trasimene and Cannae, but the very ground Hannibal occupied changed hands in the Roman market at a normal price, '*nihil ob id deminuto pretio*'.[3] Then the Senate, in apparent extremity, took the correct strategic decision, comparable to the British dispatch of tanks to Egypt before Alamein, of attacking Hannibal's base in Spain, while, in Italy, Q Fabius Maximus '*cunctando restituit rem*', 'restored the position by delay'.

There could be only one end: Hannibal could not reduce fortified cities, and in 202 BC the Romans carried the war to Africa and finished the campaign at Zama. Thus blooded as a great power, with no one her equal in all the Mediterranean, but impoverished and disrupted by gruelling wars, Rome turned east, where the main stages of her expansion have already been recorded, and by 146 BC she was strong enough to extirpate Carthage entirely.

The Republic, with its cautious peasant mentality and narrowness, and its stern ancient virtues, was now confronted with a situation beyond its control. The Senate was pushed into incongruous responsibilities and new businessmen (*equites*) got an increasing hold on policy. In spite of the misguided, if idealistic, attempt of the Gracchi to democratize the oligarchy, the old institutions broke down. The yeoman farmers, the backbone of the State, were ruined by war and inflation, following the influx of loot and slaves and the swarming of an idle proletariat into Rome; the balance of trade was upset by excessive imports, and Senatorial plutocrats plundered the provinces. Roman arrogance, myopia and cruelty, all the worst sides of their character, had full scope; for the civil wars of Marius and Sulla now marked the emergence of dictatorship on the Hellenistic model, and of the irresponsible power of the armies. Then the Senatorial magnates, Julius Caesar and Pompey, fought it out, with Caesar subjugating and plundering the West to redress the balance of oriental power. The former emerged as the winning tyrant, and laid the foundations of a new, far-flung administration; but he was assassinated by replublican plutocrats. This terrible phase of the breakdown of the Republic was ended when Caesar's great-nephew, Octavian, the Imperator Caesar Augustus (63 BC–AD 14), defeated Antony at the sea battle of Actium under the Illyrian mountains, and Cleopatra's galleys turned and fled for Egypt. Octavian gave the Roman world a new deal – conservatively termed *Respublica Restituta*.

<h1 style="text-align:center">III</h1>

The Principate of Augustus was thought by Virgil to begin a new age: '*Magnus ab integro saeclorum nascitur ordo.*' The *Princeps* was in theory the First Citizen, who had revived and personified the *auctoritas* of Senate and People; in fact, his power largely derived from his private wealth and from his being *Imperator*, Commander-in-chief. The cold intelligence of this immensely able man, whose sharp features and level eyes show the habit of cunning and command, made him the architect of a new system: in spite of recurrent crises, it maintained peace over a greater area of space and time than had then ever been known in Europe. The Principate assimilated the Hellenistic cult of the divine ruler, the saviour and benefactor, standing between humanity and the gods, and it was buttressed by an official cult, in theory universal, quite beyond the range of local household rites and ancestor worship. Where the Republic had failed, the new regime worked.

But too much depended on the *Princeps*. Already in AD 69–70, little more than fifty years after Augustus' death, the madness of Caligula, who is said to have conferred the Consulate on his horse; the oddity of Claudius, and the sheer criminality of Nero,[4] contributed to a crisis. 'These things,' thought Tacitus, who described them, 'came of the wrath of the Gods against Rome.'[5]

The Julio-Claudians were replaced by Vespasian, a leathery old Sabine soldier, the son of a tax farmer and founder of the Flavian house, who had in person commanded the assault on Maiden Castle, the Iron Age Celtic hill fort in Dorset in Britain at one end of the empire, and by his son Titus, whose triumphal arch at the eastern entrance to the Forum commemorates the capture of Jerusalem at the other. The Flavian Principate was even more far-flung, based on the armies outside Italy; and the Roman world reached its most impressive prosperity and peace under Trajan, a great administrator; under the brilliant, cosmopolitan, Hadrian; under his able and humane successor, Antoninus Pius, and under the philosopher, Marcus Aurelius Antoninus. The problem of succession was often solved by adoption; but with Commodus, the son of Marcus Aurelius, who succeeded him in AD 180, the Principate, which had always had to sustain severe wars along the frontiers without an adequate strategic reserve, collapsed.

Its bane, the unbridled power of the armies, now had to be its desperate remedy. Septimius Severus, an African emperor who died in York, abandoned the old constitutional forms and established a military dictatorship, but Caracalla and the Syrian boy-emperor, Heliogabalus, vied with Nero in running the gamut of illustrious crime. The situation was only retrieved by Diocletian (284–305), who imposed a bureaucratic despotism, based on a semi-barbarized army, and so set the stage for the massive autocracy of Constantine and Theodosius and the Christian Byzantine sequel, coincident with the Guptas and the T'ang.

Such, in bare essentials, was the main course of political events from the establishment of the Principate after the failure of the Republic, through the rise of the highly civilized cosmopolitan empire of Hadrian, to the lapse into political confusion, retrieved by the coarsened and orientalized but formidable autocracy which long sustained the foundering Graeco-Roman world, and carried on, in a Christianized form, into Byzantium.

The Roman Empire, in spite of the frequent atrocity of its politics, thus created the political framework of European civilization. It embodied a Mediterranean way of life whose inspiration was Greek, and whose administration, derived from the Republic and the household of the *Princeps*, was also modelled on Hellenistic bureaucracy. In spite of the modern revolution in industry, scientific knowledge and overseas settlement, which have since dwarfed the Mediterranean world, the Roman tradition is still relevant.

In this universal society all citizens were subject, save for endemic political murder, to a common rule of law, and looked to a semi-divine ruler in whom the original consular *imperium* had been transmuted into a world power. This *imperium* was reinforced by the Hellenistic cult of kingship, as old as Babylon and Sumeria; Julius Caesar received divine honours as *Divus Iulius, Pater Patriae*; Augustus, ostensibly First Citizen, was hailed in the East as 'Son of God'; the *lares* and *penates* of the *gens Iulia* were worshipped at public altars – *Ara Romae et Augusti* – and the dying Vespasian made a wry joke of his divinity when he remarked, succinctly, *'ut puto, deus fio'* ('I think I'm becoming a God'). The *Princeps* became the living symbol of civilization necessary in so vast and varied a society. The cult later became orientalized and theocratic in terms of sun-worship and Christianity.

In this empire, coterminous, like China, in the eyes of its inhabitants, with civilization itself, there grew up a common, universal law. It emerged from the *ius gentium*, applicable to those outside the old *ius civilis* of the citizens, and it was primarily commercial. With the extension of citizenship through military service and the foundation of the *Colonia* whereby Rome clamped her power upon the provinces; with the expansion of trade and administration, and the growth of Stoic ideas of the natural equality of free men, who were '*cives totius mundi*', 'citizens of the whole world', this law, long administered in the courts, was codified and reinforced by imperial edicts. By 91 BC, citizenship had been widely extended in Italy. Under the restless Spanish-born Hadrian, who constantly toured the empire and was as much at home in Greece or Bithynia as in Rome, the privileges of Italians were greatly diminished; citizenship was extended wholesale to Britains, Gauls, Spaniards and Africans, as the legions came to be recruited in their own territories. By AD 212 the *Constitutio Antonina* granted citizenship to all free-born men who thus became more liable to taxation. Thus a civilization, not of nations, but of cities, was united in a common web of rights and procedures, and law was defined, no longer as that of Athens or Sparta, still less as that of different barbarian tribes – a personal attribute – but as the expression of Right Reason, in which all civilized free men participated. In practice this law was absolute, a firm focus of order: but its impartiality was never entirely forgotten, so that though the Goths and Visigoths, Lombards and Franks, had overrun the empire, the old Roman Law was never stamped out; it remained entrenched in Byzantium, and was to be revived in Italy by the twelfth century.

The civilization of antiquity, though urban, was not much industrialized. A rustic flavour pervades Latin literature: the farms of Lombardy and Umbria, with their vines and olive groves, their white oxen plodding through the scented dusk, their lively children and bronzed peasantry, formed the preponderant background to the life of street and forum. But in Italy war and class conflict had brought gradual ruin to many citizen farmers of the Republic. The kind of farming admired by Cato, supervised by the proprietor and his family and worked by household dependents, was often swamped out by the estates of grossly rich magnates, which were cultivated by slaves. If, in Lombardy, where the Gallic population had been absorbed, a flourishing agriculture went on, which Provence was to become, as its Roman buildings still testify, the most prosperous western part of the empire, in central, and, in particular, southern Italy, the *latifundia*, the great estates, became a social and economic liability. Already the millennial poverty of the south was setting in.

By the time of Diocletian (AD 284–305) it had become only one aspect of a general economic decline, a major cause of the decadence of the empire. Inflation resisted the government's attempts to fix prices; an adverse trade balance mounted up since the empire was steadily exporting its gold to buy eastern luxuries, instead of paying for them by its own exports, for there was a large trade with India and the Far East. Grinding taxation – which, under Augustus, had been light – offset the benefits of a European trading area. Taxes began to be paid, not in currency, but in kind, and the *curiales* of the *municipia*, the administrative and fiscal backbone of the empire, had to meet their obligations out of their own resources. They began to evade office, so that the government tried to make it hereditary, and the crude expedient was applied to farmers, traders and artisans. When the Germanic war bands came in, many Romans preferred their casual domination to that of the imperial bureaucracy.

Another major cause of this great civilization's decline was probably psychological. The élite of antiquity were inspired by an austere Stoic philosophy, whereby a man played out his part on the stage of life. The magnanimous Marcus Aurelius is its most famous exponent. 'Let it be thy hourly care,' he wrote, 'to do stoutly what thy hand findeth to do, as becomes a man and a Roman.' He held that intellect was the manifestation of God in which men could participate; that human enmities should not be taken too hard, 'since in a little while both thou and he will be no more'; as for death, it was 'nothing save what is consonant with the nature of rational life', and not 'repugnant to the laws of our being'.[6]

The less tough-minded took to emotional mystery cults from the East which guaranteed 'salvation'. The close little *religio* of the gods of family and farm, of the Earth Mother and the spirits of grove and stream, were satisfactory – as they still are, in a different idiom – to peasants, hunters, shepherds and fishermen. In the cosmopolitan cities more elaborate eastern cults soon became fashionable, while to the court of the Caesars flocked every kind of sophist, mystic and charlatan, who provided a Nero or an Heliogabalus, their catamites and their women, with a new sensation. Among the legions Mithraism, with its sun worship and initiation rites, descending from the Zoroastrian religion already described, was the most popular cult, as attested by many shrines, one of them lately discovered in the heart of the City of London.* But it was Christianity that proved the predominant, and finally the sole, official religion. Extended by St Paul beyond its original Jewish setting, it overcame its own Gnostic heresies, and in AD 312, with the conversion of Constantine, and the edict of Milan a year

---

*Mithraism originated among Iranians settled in Asia Minor. The capture and sacrifice of the bull promoted the harvest, and was combined with the cult of the sun. It was a virile religion, without priests; popular in the army, with grades of initiation like Freemasonry. It set standards of duty and honour but, since it did not include women, it was handicapped in competing with other religions.

later, it was an established religion of the empire. The Emperor Julian (361–3) tried to restore the finer of the old Hellenic and Roman traditions, but he perished on a campaign against the Sassanians of Iran. His last words, '*Vicisti Galilea*' – 'Thou hast conquered,' as Swinburne put it, 'O pale Galilean' – marked the end of official paganism.* Popular paganism, of course, carried on.

With Theodosius (378–95), established Christianity, centred on Byzantium, dominated the empire. When, in 421, after the sack of Rome by Alaric and with the Vandals besieging his Tunisian see, St Augustine finished his *City of God*, the empire had been permeated by Christian influence and organization for over a hundred years. Graeco-Roman society had entered its Christian phase long before the final collapse in the West, with the appropriately named Romulus 'Augustulus' gone to ground in Ravenna in 476. This transformation, as it appears to a Catholic, has been brilliantly described:

> Constantine had made terms with a new ally of unknown strength; he had shelved a problem. So it might seem to the strategists of the East who counted the order of battle, legion by legion, granary by granary; so, perhaps, it seemed to Constantine. But as the news spread everywhere in Christendom, from every altar a great wind of prayer gathered and mounted, lifted the whole squat smoky dome of the Ancient World, swept it off and up like the thatch of a stable, and threw open the calm and brilliant prospect of measureless space.[7]

# IV

So a Mediterranean and officially Christian civilization determined Europe's political and religious future; in literature, architecture and the arts this influence was equally overwhelming, directly, and through the Renaissance – a term unfashionable but just. For Roman writers gave Hellenic and Hellenistic literature a new turn, and it was mainly through Latin that civilization filtered through to the western barbarians, if the Byzantine legacy to Russia was Greek, and, during the twelfth century, the West regained contact with Hellenistic literature and science through the Arabs. It is, indeed, impossible to imagine modern western civilization without this background, for the northern literature of epic and saga, though sometimes magnificent, is in general murky and barbaric. The order and clarity of Latin was decisive in the transmission of the rudiments of culture, in the organization and discipline of the Church, in law and administration, so that when a Norman king said *Moneo et praecipio* at the beginning of a writ, the words still echo the commands of Rome.

The earliest Latin literature, Annals, Fasti and religious ritual – *sacra solemnia obeunto*, 'observe the sacred rites' – are limited, if revealing; but by

*See Ammianus Marcellinus, who accompanied him on his campaign.

the early second century, Ennius was adapting the Greek hexameter, while the Umbrian Plautus' boisterous comedies and the more pointed wit of the emancipated African slave, Terence, had brought a version of the Greek theatre to Rome. By the late Republic the full force of a native literature is deployed, when the Greek models have been fully assimilated. Now came the great figures who were to be models of learned Europe for nineteen centuries, names that are still familiar. Cicero (106–43 BC), so long admired by barristers and politicians, the most influential of all Roman orators and prose writers for posterity, could change his mood through piled up denunciation and ironic narrative to the lucid demonstration that black was white. Julius Caesar's studied simplicity became the model of generals turning their campaigns to account in political warfare. Livy (59 BC–AD 17) from Padua, who wrote a history *Ab Urbe Condita* to the Macedonian wars, preserved the legends of ancient Rome, setting himself, in what he thought an age of decadence, to recall 'by what sort of men and what sort of conduct in peace and war the Empire has been acquired and extended'. But Tacitus is the greatest Roman historian, in the tradition of Thucydides, compact, economical, with a piercing eye.

In lighter vein, Petronius' fragmentary *Satyricon* gives a cross-section of the shady Roman underworld, with a classic caricature of the newly rich Trimalchio and a picaresque narrative of the adventures of that resourceful trio, Encolpius, Ascyltos and Gito.[8] In frigid contrast to this engaging story, are ranged the portentous ranks of Roman moralists, of whom Seneca was the most popular. Among the great Latin poets, Virgil, courtier of Augustus, has pre-eminence.

> Wielder of the stateliest measure
> Ever moulded by the lips of man.*

His epic glorification of Rome expressed the majesty of the empire, while his shorter poems, in the manner of Theocritus, evoke the Italian summer when, after a hot day, shadows lengthen with the setting sun, *et sol crescentis decedens duplicat umbras.*[9] Lucretius, before him, had transposed Epicureanism into Latin, attempting to deliver men from superstition by a materialist explanation of the universe, but the direct personal appeal of Catullus and Horace has always been much more popular. Catullus' love poetry dissects various lyrical and agonizing situations: how, for example, he asks, can I love and hate at the same time?

> Odi et amo. Quare id faciam, fortasse requiras?
> Nescio, sed fieri sentio et excrucior.[10]

More happily, he describes his girl's laughter, saying that it makes him feel

*Tennyson: *To Virgil*. Written at the request of the Mantuans for the nineteenth centenary of Virgil's death.

luckier than the Gods, though struck dumb by delight.[11] The Apulian Horace, urbane and perspicacious, who wrought Latin into such complex Greek metres, has always been admired by the worldly; he shows a shrewd grasp of affairs, and an abiding love of the country, if his voice can be rather husky from good living. But Ovid was the most popular Latin poet in the Middle Ages, with his brisk memorable legends and *risqué* touch, while Martial's pungent epigrams range from a romantic sensuality – *pocula da labris facta minora tuis* ('give me the cup 'minished beneath thy lips')[12] – to stabbing Iberian hatred, as when he describes his enemy's face as 'like that of a man swimming under water'.[13]

These writers are only the most celebrated. The fierce and sensual Mediterranean emotions they expressed were to be the background of northern as well as of southern European literature; oddly enough, of Protestant English public schools, where the paradox created has never been quite resolved. More congenial to austerer climes was the dogged moralizing (translated by King Alfred) of the unfortunate Boethius, in prison, awaiting agonizing execution by the Visigoths in the full decadence of the empire.

The classical Latin of literature was different from the vulgar speech, from which the Romance languages of Europe descend. Hellenistic civilization had used the lucid *Koiné*, but the slaves, provincials and Romanized barbarians of the empire used dialect and jargon. Out of Africa the colourful prose of St Augustine embodied a new patristic style, influential in the Middle Ages, but, with the depression of élites, this gap widened and contributed to cultural decline.

The poets, very few of whom were native Romans, give a Latin interpretation of Hellenistic culture; similarly, in the arts and architecture, as in religion, Graeco-Roman society brought eastern as well as Italian influence to bear on Europe. Roman painting followed Greek models, and although, like the legendary masterpieces of Apelles, court painter to Alexander, all the large paintings have perished, and provincial Pompeii, overwhelmed in AD 79, remained buried until the eighteenth century, the baroque interior decoration of Nero's Golden House influenced Renaissance artists: many motifs there anticipate patterns familiar on Venetian glass, and the very word 'grotesque' derives from the 'grottos' of this mile-square warren which fifteenth century antiquaries explored.

But Roman sculpture was much more important. The equestrian statues, the portrait busts now in the museum of the Capitol, the finished, pagan and lively animal sculptures in the Vatican, are unsurpassed of their naturalistic kind: one can sense through them the spirit of this civilization, domestic as well as public and grand. There are also clumsy sarcophagi and inept portraits from the fourth and fifth centuries, not to mention vulgar representations of circus animals and brutish gladiators. One art flourished as the western Empire foundered: the earlier mosaic floors and wall decorations, and even their distant provincial imitations, as at Chedworth in the Cotswolds, with its personified seasons – a man coming in with a hare, a girl holding a bird, a boy with a garland – are pleasing. But in the late empire in Rome, and in particular in Ravenna, superb masterpieces, cunningly contrived, shimmered from designs of blue and green and gold, the domed basilicas swimming in light; or soft and mysterious, as in the famous fifth-century tomb of Galla Placidia. The fullest flowering of the art is Byzantine, but it springs directly from Rome. Further, all sorts of marble, malachite, porphyry, serpentine, onyx, were used by Roman architects for cool interiors in the southern heat, and they laid out fine villas, looking inwards on fountains and gardens. Hadrian's villa – in fact a great palace – with its vast grounds and sheets of ornamental water, its colonnades and statues, must have surpassed Versailles and symbolized a wider dominion. The figures walking there, too, would already have been more colourful than the togaed bundles of the Republic, who must have appeared not dissimilar to a crowd in modern Tangiers; and by the time of Constantine the dress of imperial guards and courtiers was already as gorgeous as those depicted in the mosaic of Justinian.

Technically, Roman architects were innovators. They inherited much from the Etruscans and the East, but they characteristically invented concrete, which they faced with brick, the material of the buildings of the Republic. The Augustan Vitruvius lived before the greatest monuments of the empire had been built, but his extremely practical *De Architectura* was to inspire, sometimes to constrict, the enterprise of Renaissance and Baroque builders, so that a seventeenth-century writer, still in the tradition, could observe "twas *vox Europae* that named Inigo Jones Vitruvius Britannicus'. By the time of Vespasian and Titus, great theatrical triumphal arches, forerunners of similar monuments over all Europe, were going up. Trajan's column accurately depicts the details of savage campaigns, marred only by the difficulty of examining them as they spiral upwards, an embodied triumph; while the almost indestructible Colosseum, gross and efficient (AD 80), scene of how many bestial public spectacles, was always considered particularly impressive by the barbarians.

But the most original Roman architectural exploit was the dome. Hadrian's Pantheon has a huge one: under Diocletian, vaults were set in novel fashion on a square base, a style which reached its much more elaborate climax in the domes of Haghia Sophia. The great public baths – those of Caracalla still stand in majestic ruin – had barrel vaults lit by high windows above vast marble floors; they were models for the Christian basilicas and so of Romanesque cathedrals. The brick exteriors of these churches can appear mean, though they point the splendour within, and Roman windows had heavy grills and opaque glass; but massive architecture remains the most obvious material aspect of the legacy of the empire. Roman roads, too, striking direct across country, remain the basis of much of the present system; they enabled the armies to be switched from one area to another, and barbarian war bands to move fast. Ordinary civilians did not, of course, command the facilities of the imperial couriers who depended on the relays of post-horses which the young Constantine hamstrung when he fled from Galerius.

# V

So the peasant farmers of Latium, overshadowed by Etruscan power, uncouth beside the rich cites of Sicily and the Tarentine Gulf and outclassed by the alien sea-going Carthaginians, came first to the mastery of Italy; then of the central and western Mediterranean and Spain; then to the domination of Greece. They grasped Greece, Anatolia, Syria and most of Mesopotamia; took Egypt, and pushed north-west beyond the mountains through Switzerland into the Côte d'Or and the Celtic interior of Gaul; then on to the Low Countries and along the Rhine, while they thrust beyond the Danube into Dacia. From homely religion and plain language, the Romans, under Hellenistic influence, created elaborate literature and art, and brought the architecture of humanism into Europe. From provincial beginnings they formulated a universal theory of law and administered the entire Mediterranean world and its periphery. Cicero, in the decadence of the Republic, had defined the statesman's aim as 'to make human life nobler and richer by our thought and effort'.[14] In spite of atrocious defects, massive slavery, callousness and sadism, the empire sometimes achieved that aim.

In the West economic and technological incompetence, perhaps a failure of political nerve, and certainly the failure to subordinate the armies to civil authority and to maintain a strategic reserve, together with the pressure of aliens within and unconquered Germanic barbarians without, slowly but inevitably brought this great society down. But in the lands of its cultural inspiration, to which the capital had been shifted by Constantine, it went on vigorously, for the court of the Christian Byzantine Basileus, to the East always the ruler of the *Romaioi*, remained, until the barons of the Fourth Crusade crippled it in 1204, the seat of a culture, an administration and an economy which dwarfed the rural and barbaric feudal realms of the West, and long fought on until conquered by the Ottoman Turks.

# Seven

# ISRAEL: THE RISE OF CHRISTIANITY

## I

The traveller going up to Jerusalem through the tortuous, rocky defiles from the coastal plain, first sees the city on the brow of a stony hill. At nearly three thousand feet, it has brisk air and vast prospects, eastward the ground falling to the rift valley of the Jordan and the chasm of the Dead Sea, with the mountains of Moab beyond. This barren setting contrasts with the variety of sea and mountains which frames the Acropolis and with the comparatively rich hinterland of Rome. This impression of austerity is enhanced by the supposed tomb of King David on Mount Zion. Nothing homely, not an image; only the silver-cased Rolls of the Law on a catafalque draped with a purple carpet, with texts, embroidered on velvet, on the walls. A few worshippers sway slightly as they intone a psalm. And this austerity is significant; Moses, Jesus and Muhammad, all inspired great Monotheist religions; all of them derived from the Word of God, of Abraham – *Ibrahim Khalil*, the Friend of God.

The Semites who overwhelmed and assimilated the culture of Sumer, who made the empire of Hammurabi, and who had descended on Egypt as the Hyksos Kings, had so far influenced the West mainly through Phoenician commerce and by war; by the fourth century AD, an originally Semitic religion had come to dominate the Roman Empire. Such diffusion of ideas is not unusual; Buddhism won its most lasting influence outside India; an Hellenic Pantheon had been accepted by cosmopolitan classical civilization, dominating its literature and art; while Zeno, the founder of Stoic philosophy, was Phoenician. Mohammedanism was to spread far beyond Arabia, and the Teutonic doctrines of Karl Marx were not to be confined to the West.

The history of the Jews is often treated by Christians as a mere prelude to the expansion of their own religion, but the original Hebrew scriptures remained, through millennia of persecution, the inspiration and discipline of world Jewry, and formed an important aspect of the background of Islam. Whether manifest in Moses descending from Sinai with the Tables of the Law, in Jesus on the mount above the Sea of Galilee or upon the Cross, or in the Prophet of Allah, bringing out of the blazing desert revelation and the sword, Jewish influence was to be decisive.

## II

Certain Israelites – the Egyptians called them the Habiru – probably came down into Egypt by 1400 BC, about the time of the climax and fall of Minoan Crete: by the thirteenth century, when the Egyptian and Hittite empires were in decline and confusion came to the Levant, they escaped from the Pharaohs into the desert. Their leader was Moses, a Jew versed in Egyptian learning; and folk-memory of this exodus and of Moses' reception of the Law, still celebrated all over Jewry, is very ancient; older even than the beliefs of the Zoroastrian Parsees or of the Buddhists and Confucians, and much older than those recorded by Christianity or Islam. After wandering as Bedouin in the Siniai peninsula, these Israelites settled into Palestine, where there were probably other Jews, and where the Canaanites, in part, perhaps, distantly descended from the Natufians of Carmel and the inhabitants of Stone Age Jericho, practised fertility cults revolting to the austerer Hebrews, and were harried by the Philistines, with their maritime Levantine background.

Then, as afterwards, the Hebrews were not absorbed; rather the tribal cult of Yahweh intensified and the kingship was created in the Philistine wars. David, their first royal hero, reigned about 1000–980 BC, roughly two centuries after the Trojan War. He seized the natural stronghold of Jerusalem and made it the religious capital of the tribes; there, in the early tenth century, Solomon built the Temple with the aid of Phoenician artificers. The memory of his rich but ephemeral kingdom, with its relatively far-flung contacts and commerce, the climax of Jewish temporal power, was ineradicably imprinted on Israelite tradition.

After Solomon, the kingdom was divided. In the north Israel tended to come to terms with Phoenician and local cults; in Judah, in the hills, Monotheism was consolidated. But both kingdoms were now overwhelmed by the new Iron Age empires of the Near East. First, in the eighth century, Israel was overrun by the Assyrians, and the Lost Ten Tribes faded out of history – the best course under Assyrian attack, and one which has since given rise to some odd legends. In about 700 BC Jerusalem was also besieged; but the Assyrians drew off after imposing a swingeing tribute. Then, after the Persians had smashed Assyria, the Neo-Babylonian power of Nebuchadnezzar moved against the Jews: by 589 BC, Zedekiah, the last king of the House of David, had been deported, with the élite of Judah, to Babylon.

After the rise of the Persian Empire under Cyrus in 549 BC, the second phase of Jewish history began. Though the kingdom was not restored, the tolerant Persians allowed the Jews to return. A religious community was now established in Jerusalem under Persian protection, and in the fifth century BC the already ancient Temple was rebuilt. But the old cult of Yahweh had been altered: in Babylon the exiles had not only elaborated the Law; they had taken over many Zoroastrian beliefs in a cosmic conflict between good and evil, in angels and devils and in a judgement. To the original covenant of the chosen people with God, this Iranian sense of a drama working out through time had been added.

While the priests had preserved the Law and rallied the exiles, the main inspiration of Hebrew religion had always been the prophets. They had been generally of peasant origin, and since Elijah, in the ninth century and the first Isaiah in the eighth, they had denounced all other cults and proclaimed a religion which sometimes went beyond tribal exclusiveness. Jeremiah lamented the Neo-Babylonian destruction of Jerusalem, and Ezekiel was the prophet of the Exile. These two strains had always run parallel in Israel – the discipline of the Law and the visions of ascetics.

To the rest of the Levantine and Near Eastern world the Jews had long appeared peculiar, even repellent; they were not even politically important, though their communities had already spread far beyond Palestine. For when Alexander overran the Near East and the tide of Hellenism followed him, the Jews of Jerusalem remained quaint and conservative in their hill city, already the religious centre of a Diaspora. Only a well-to-do or politically minded minority compromised with Hellenism and its cult of divine rulers and gymnasia, embarrassing to a people who, unlike the Greeks, thought nakedness shameful and a statue an abomination. But as guardians of the *Pentateuch* – the Five Books of the Law – the priests of the Temple drew great revenues from the Jewish colonies, now rapidly exploiting the newly released wealth of the Achaemenid Empire. With riches, some of the hierarchy became more cosmopolitan: the Diaspora even made proselytes and translated the scriptures into Greek in the Septuagint, so called because seventy scholars were set individually to translate them and all miraculously concurred, a singular evidence of inspiration. These writings ranged from the older books, which had come down from the time of the Old Kingdom and the earliest prophets and from the Exile, to the Psalms, Proverbs, Daniel, the second Isaiah, and the book of Job, the finest of the Old Testament scriptures, all written in Hellenistic times. The hard core of puritanism and exclusiveness remained.

Then, in 167 BC, when the eccentric, stage-struck, Seleucid monarch, Antiochus *Epiphanes* – the Illustrious – made the Jews sacrifice to Zeus in the Temple itself, and the behaviour of Hellenized Jewish youths gave mortal offence to conservatives, a fanatical resistance flared up. It even flared into nationalist rebellion. Judas Maccabeus, the Hammer, proved to be a brilliant soldier: after fierce vicissitudes, his brother Jonathan routed the Seleucid armies and established the Hasmonaean House (142 BC) as rulers of most of Palestine.

But the Romans now intervened in the Near East. Dynastic and priestly feuds played into their hands; after sanguinary intrigues, the last Hasmonaean priest-king, Hyrcanus II, was deposed: by 63 BC the country was annexed. During these operations, Antipater, a Hellenized Arab from Idumaea, had ingratiated himself at Rome: his son, Herod, a brilliant and ruthless prince, an intimate friend of Augustus, was put to rule Palestine from 37–4 BC as a client king. His son proved untrustworthy, and although his nephew, Herod the Tetrarch, ruled in Galilee, most of the country was subjected to a Roman procurator with headquarters on the coast at Caesarea, north of modern Tel Aviv. This collapse of the Maccabean kingdom, and the foreign occupation, had deeply embittered the nationalist Jews, many of whom believed in passionate and vengeful fantasies of a Messiah – the original title of King David, meaning the Lord's Anointed, applicable to kings and priest-kings as well. He would lead Israel, they were convinced, to the conquest of the world. At that time, too, the Sadducees and Pharisees first appeared, the one ready to compromise, the other meticulously standing by the Law. These Pharisee 'Rabbis' – the term came in during the first century AD – were to compose the *Talmud*, the Book of Instruction, first codified by the third century AD and destined to play so great a part in Jewish history. Such was the menacing background, feverish with hatred, fantasy, and expectation, to the life of Jesus.

Under Nero, seething discontent again broke into rebellion: it was raging in full fury in AD 67, the year of the death of St Paul. Vespasian then brought the full weight of Roman arms to bear upon this intransigent people: in AD 73 Jerusalem was taken and sacked by Titus. His soldiers are depicted on his great arch carrying off the ark of the covenant and the Menora, the seven-branched candelabra, the most sacred symbols of Judah. Even that catastrophe was not final. In the reign of Hadrian, rebellion broke out again under a leader calling himself Bar Cochba, the Son of the Star, who claimed to be the Messiah. After a gruelling struggle, the Jews were finally mastered: Jerusalem, like Carthage, was extirpated, all resistance stamped out.

Militarily the Jews had given a good account of themselves: ideologically they were to prove even more formidable. The alert vitality of the Jewish stock, the tenacity, the toughness, had long been amply proved and are distilled in their scriptures. 'Hebrew,' it has been said, 'may be called primarily a language of the senses . . . there is a prevalence . . . of the harder, heavier consonants, including a greater variety of gutturals than Western alphabets contain . . . it is urgency more than beauty, emphasis more than melody, which strike the ear as characteristic.'[1] When Isaiah describes the raging of the multitude:

Woe, the booming of peoples multitudinous
Like the booming of seas they boom,

he writes:

> Hoi hᵃmôn 'ammim rabbîm
> Kahᵃmôth yammîn yehᵉmayûn:

While the famous lines of the twenty-third psalm,

> The Lord is my Shepherd, I shall not want,
> He leadeth me beside the waters of comfort,

become in the original:

> Yahweh Ro'i lo'-'ehs-ar
> 'Al-mê mᵉnûhôth yᵉ nahᵃlēni.

This heavy Semitic literature, with its bold, square characters, became the medium for colourful, repetitive poetry; for denunciation, yearning and compassion, as well as for the Code of the Law, the nucleus of a moral tradition.

So inspired, the Jews held aloof; they saw life, not as cyclic recurrence, presided over by negligent, if anthropomorphic, Olympians, but as the working out of a divine purpose; of that conflict between righteousness and evil familiar in Zoroastrian doctrines, and set in terms of the Babylonian myth of Creation and Fall, as well as of the ancient Covenant between the Chosen People and their desert God.

Such a powerful myth could dwarf the quaint polytheism of peasant farmers, or the sceptical hedonism of Hellenized aristocrats; and a searing vision of conflict, suffering and redemption may give more permanent psychological satisfaction than traditional piety, or ritual orgies and their aftermath. Politically, too, the myth increased Jewish nationalism, and provided their traditional *chesed* – their code of right conduct and mutual benevolence – with a new hope. It combined hatred of the foreigner, of 'the lawless ones who laid waste our land',[2] and the desire 'to purge Jerusalem from the nations that trample her down to destruction',[3] with glimpses of a kingdom of universal righteousness. After the Maccabean wars, some Jews also began to accept the idea of an apocalypse and immortality, dim or absent in the old scriptures. It was now felt that the heroes of the rebellion and their enemies, in particular Antiochus *Epiphanes*, must have their rewards. These beliefs could be very dangerous in politics, an empirical art at which the Jews have seldom collectively excelled, and they led to disaster. Jewish ascetics, muffled in complicated garments, were also deeply alien to the civilization of Mediterranean antiquity, which took beauty and pleasure for granted and celebrated them in official religion as well as in esoteric cults. To Anacreon or Theocritus, to Horace or Catullus, the idea that love was 'unclean' and only 'justified' by the command 'be fruitful and multiply', so necessary for a people hemmed in by enemies, whose oldest legends were legends of escape, would have appeared deplorable. It was deeply to influence Christianity.

Jewish religion was, indeed, often akin to the beliefs of Iran and parts of India: its theocratic monotheism also contrasted with the ritual and conduct of circumspect Confucian morality; with the code of honour of Homeric or German barbarians; with the inquiring and anthropocentric outlook of the Greeks, and with the tolerant scepticism and sense of world responsibility of the finer minds of Rome.

Against this background, Jewry was to develop during the seventeen centuries from the destruction of Jerusalem to the foundation of modern Israel, and out of it two world religions, Christianity and Islam, were to expand.

The fall of the Maccabean kingdom had intensified the nationalism of the Jews, and encouraged the compensatory beliefs in an apocalypse which the Sadducee traditionalists opposed; this fanaticism contributed to the revolt which Vespasian and Titus had suppressed. But the enlightened or indifferent Hadrian, while he saw to it that Jerusalem was destroyed as a focus of rebellion and that a Roman *Colonia* was planted on the site, still tolerated the Jewish religion, and officially recognized a Jewish patriarch. The Rabbis rallied their people and kept contact with the Diaspora. The *Torah*, or Doctrine, based upon the Pentateuch, had already been defined: by AD 219 the patriarch, Rabbi Judah I, had compiled the *Mishna*, or Instruction, the first part of the *Talmud*, while by AD 408, the *Gemara* or Commentary had been completed. A famous centre of rabbinic studies grew up in the hill town of Safad in Galilee, and a body of Law and Scripture was elaborated which served as a focus and a discipline for the Jews. They now, with the rise of Christianity, had to face first discrimination which cut them off from official employment, then persecution by the Christian authorities.

Not only Christians were anti-Semitic. Before the revolt of AD 66 there had been anti-Jewish riots in Alexandria and Rome, in Antioch and Ephesus; during the first century, Mnaseas, a Greek writer, popularized the damaging belief that the Jews worshipped a donkey's head, and the soldiers of Titus shouted 'Hep, Hep' (*Hierusalem est perdita*) as they stormed the walls of the Holy City. The cry was to continue down the Christian centuries – an ironical turn of fate.

# III

Jesus of Nazareth grew up in a city high in the hills between the Mediterranean coast and the Lake of Tiberias, scene of the calling of the disciples, the draft of fishes, the embarkation. Immediately below the site of the Sermon on the Mount, in spring covered with young barley with a few tufa rocks scattered among the crop, lie flourishing olive groves;

southward along the low western shore are broad meadows bounded by trees reflected in the lake. Beyond, the hills fall in a smooth curve from the Horns of Hattin, where the crusaders met disaster in the twelfth century; at Tiberias fishing boats still put out, gulls wheeling about them, while at Kfar Nahum, the Capernaeum of the Bible, lie the grey ruins of a synagogue built in the second century AD, the star of David cut among the Hellenistic foliage of its capitals. In such surroundings, the teaching of Jesus began: they contrast with the harsher scene of the crucifixion.

'Blessed,' said Jesus, 'are the merciful.' Here is the most original aspect of Christianity. Although Jesus is plainly in the ancient line of the Jewish prophets, his message is even more intimate. This kindliness, the sublimation of human solidarity, sprang from the conviction of the common fatherhood of God. The Buddha's compassion led to detachment, and his aim was annihilation in *Nirvana*; the original Gospel asserts God's care for individuals and wins converts not by argument, still less compulsion, but through active benevolence. This unusual idea has never been stamped out, and it sometimes achieved extraordinary and swift success, in particular among primitive peoples, whether western barbarians in the fifth and sixth centuries or among savage converts in the nineteenth. Further, by valuing personalities, whether slave or free, and asserting that the deepest springs of action are beyond the reach of the State, Jesus, like the Buddha, and, unlike Confucius, made a fundamental criticism of government. The stern *Pantokrator* of Byzantine Mosaics of the Judgement is not the oldest representation of Christ, but the beardless 'good shepherd' of the catacomb paintings, a youthful and kindly God, with affinities more with Hellenistic saviours than with any judge of the dead. The bells of Christian Churches and the colourful hierarchy of Christian Saints make Judaism and Islam, the other versions of Hebrew religion, seem sombre and fatalistic in comparison.

Along with this strange hope and mercy, went a fierce prophetic fire, which denounced the arrogant Pharisees, scorned social distinctions and wealth, drove the money-changers from the Temple and declared that the kingdom of God was not temporal, but an immediate inner experience. So the perennial conflict between prophet and priest, between genius and mediocrity, blazed into judicial murder. The hierarchy thought to break Jesus, as it had broken rebels before. In AD 33 they induced the worried procurator, Pontius Pilate, who was to end his days at Vienne in Provence, unaware of the millennia of infamy reserved for him, to hand over the apparently false Messiah to his fate.

By doing so they assured the future of Christianity. The crucifixion, and its sequel, manifested the prophet to his followers as the incarnate God. In daily expectation of the return of the *Christ* – the Greek translation of Messiah – and of an *apocalypse*, they organized themselves in intimate coteries which included *presbyters* and a *bishop*, whose leaders met in *Synods* as the movement spread. From that tiny organization, which was pushed out of Jewry rather than left it, the Christian Church directly descends.

But it was St Paul who transformed the beliefs of a Jewish sect into one of the great world religions. A Hellenized Jew from the big city of Tarsus in Anatolia, he had studied with the Pharisees in Jerusalem. After his conversion, he journeyed up and down the Levant, to Greece, to Rome, organizing, exhorting, corresponding. When the conservative Jews attacked him, he appealed, as a Roman citizen, to Caesar. The spread of Christianity outside Palestine was swift and decisive: when St Paul died, less than forty years after the crucifixion, there were Christian communities all round the Mediterranean, in Greece, Italy, Africa and Spain. The intense hatred he provoked in the Diaspora was natural: his ideas were revolutionary, an appalling heresy – no less than to assert that the ancient Israelite covenant with God had been superseded by a new, potentially universal, covenant in Christ, 'grafted on', as he wrote to the Christians in Rome, 'like a shoot of wild olive', to the Jewish stock.

But current Hellenistic ideas also left their mark. The *Agape* or love feast, the sacramental centre of Christianity, derives not from Jewish but from Hellenistic and pagan ritual. The original *Eucharist* (Prayer of Thanksgiving), of which the ritual and phrasing is already by AD 150 closely akin to that familiar today, originated in the laying of bread and wine as an offering on the altar. As the hope of a second coming faded, the ritual came to commemorate Christ's sacrifice, and then to be thought to reenact it. 'Here,' it has been said, 'we have quite plainly before our eyes an idea of primitive religion transferred to a Christian cult. The solemn rehearsal, or dramatic re-enactment of some event in the history of the Gods, releases the same divine forces and produces the same effects as were once displayed at the time of the original occurrence.'[4] The organization of the Church, also, was to be paralleled by the hierarchies of the Gnostics and Manichees, and even, though its vocabulary was Greek, to become predominantly Roman in the West, with a tradition of world empire behind it; and although the new religion derived from an event in time – part of a Jewish cosmic drama, the fulfilment of Biblical prophecy – it was also a typical salvation cult in which all could participate, not merely a grade of 'perfect ones' or advanced initiates. St Paul preached *salvation* by faith:

> As in Adam all die,
> Even so in Christ shall all be made alive.[5]

'Man was no longer the victim of the malice of countless demon powers . . . the victory over the demons had been won once and for all time, and that victory could be appropriated by the humblest Christian through Faith.'[6] Other mystery religions claimed to rescue their initiates from the grip of evil, for the time was one of deepening gloom. Most Hellenistic philosophers were disillusioned with analytic reason; no experimental science anchored their restless minds; astrology had a persuasive and depressing influence.[7] Beyond the *pietas* of family and farm, these urban intellectuals were haunted by eastern 'demons' and 'powers' like those depicted in later Etruscan art, and sought magic to control them. The followers of Mithras were protected from the Zoroastrian devil, and the official and popular Sun cult, which was to be blended with Constantine's Christianity, offered *safety* to its devotees. Even the high classic tradition had been sceptical: '*Nobis*' Catullus had written:

> cum semel occidit brevis lux,
> Nox est perpetua una dormienda

– 'for us, our brief day over, there is perpetual night'. For Christians there might be eternal life.

The new religion, as already emphasized, spread astonishingly fast. By AD 64, in the reign of Nero, there were enough Christians in Rome to be scapegoats for his reputed escapades. Already by AD 150, as well as Baptism and the Eucharist, celebrated on Sunday morning, and derived from the Agape originally held like the Passover at night, Easter and Pentecost had been established. The former derived from the Passover commemorating the exodus from Egypt, but now turned to rejoicing at the resurrection, and was transferred from the night of the full moon in the spring month to the preceding Sunday. And although the first great systematic persecution was not to occur until a century later, under Decius and Valerian, the blood of many martyrs had already become the seed of the Church. The mob believed that the Christians, who could not undertake military service or civic office, like the Jews worshipped a donkey, devoured children and practised evil rites; but Christian enthusiasm had already outfaced the torture chamber and the arena.

Christianity was first established officially in the eastern parts of the empire, where Hellenization was thin and where, by the third century, a militant-frontier religion was needed against the attack of the Sassanians, who had superseded the Parthians and revived the Persian Empire. In Osrhoene in Syria, and in Palmyra, Christian influences predominated by the middle third century; the kingdom of Armenia was Christian by 303, nine years before the opening of Constantine's reign, and over a century before St Augustine finished his *De Civitate Dei*.

The four hundred years between the birth of Christ and that epoch-making book saw the formulation of Christian doctrine from a welter of competing and elaborate Hellenistic ideas. They all assumed a dualistic vision of the universe; matter and 'spirit' inevitably opposed. For many minds the bloom was off Hellenic paganism long before the rise of

Christianity, and civilization rotten with pessimism, particularly among intellectuals. This dualism was Greek as well as eastern: Plato had taught, and by AD 250 the Egyptian Plotinus had reinterpreted him, that reality was unchanging, a pattern of 'ideas' behind phenomena. The Stoic philosophers also thought that reality was rational order, and the *Logos* or *Word* the means whereby order became manifest. Thus by AD 100 St John began the fourth, and Hellenized, Gospel by writing: 'In the beginning was the *Word*' – the mediator between Godhead and the world of sense perception. Add to this Platonic and Stoic theory the eastern idea that matter is intrinsically evil, a distorting medium, so that the world is a gross caricature of God's order and light, and that men can escape from the nightmare through magic and sacrament, and there is a powerful myth. But the religion of profoundest despair was preached in Iran by Mani, who was put down by the Zoroastrian Magi, in the middle of the third century. It taught that man was actually begotten by Satan and, as will later be described, won its widest popularity in the deserts of central Asia, though it also inspired an underground movement in medieval Europe, leading to notable massacres in northern Italy and Provence, and flourishing in Bulgaria.

Against this background, Irenaeus, bishop of Lyons, in his Latin *Five Books against the Heretics*, had defended the Christian scriptures against Gnostic heresies, and the Greek Father, Origen, who died in AD 253, ransacked Greek learning with an Aristotelian vigour to systematize Christian belief. Like other Greek and Latin fathers of the Church, he pulled Christianity out of a world of complex and misty superstition. The elaborate creed of Athanasius is the most familiar example of this theological virtuosity.

But established Christianity, though purged, largely through its clear-cut Jewish background, of the grotesque Gnostic ideas, retained a fundamental dualism.* The Latin father, Tertullian, in the early third century, who coined the memorable phrase '*Credo quia absurdum*' – 'I believe *because* it is crazy to believe', detested *Romanitas*, the code of Graeco-Roman civilization, even to its learning and poetry. Where the classical poets, from Homer onwards, had glorified life, and even its tragedies, Tertullian set no store by it at all. '*Quid est volaticum mundi gaudium?*' he demanded, 'What is the fleeting pleasure of the world?' When

---

*The Gnostic heresy was an attempt to clothe Christianity with the abstract ideas which were then fashionable among intellectuals and their following in good society. Its best exponent was Valentinus (fl. 130–150) and it can most charitably be explained in terms of psychological symbolism. In brief, the Gnostics held that out of Bythos, the Deep (the unconscious) emerged Nous (Mind) and from Nous, Sophia (philosophy), who tried, in vain, to understand Reality. In this attempt, as sceptical philosophers might expect, Sophia failed, but in the process gave birth to a monster with a disordered mind. This monster was the World. But Sophia was rescued by Horos on the Cross, who crucified the philosophy out of her, as Wittgenstein's followers have for Hegel's.

St Augustine, who had been a Manichaean, came to sum up Christian belief, he sharply distinguished between the city of man and the city of God. All men – and particularly women – through the fall of Adam, are born in sin; but the elect, redeemed by Christ, will attain heaven.

## IV

Such, by the early fifth century, was the world picture which established Christianity presented to the barbarians who were now overrunning the empire. The Church was most securely established in the East, where the Byzantine emperor combined the religious and secular powers of Constantine; but in western Europe, where the authority of the empire broke down, a theocratic Christian Church was to grow up, the bishops taking over the authority that fell from the hands of the decadent emperors and seizing the initiative towards the barbarians. So the totalitarian front of imperial government in the West was broken; a new distinction was made between Church and State – following Jesus' swift answer; 'Render to Caesar the things that are Caesar's and unto God the things that are God's.'

Further, by this clear-cut scheme of fall, redemption and salvation, the White Christ became a God intelligible to the heathen, a hero, even, in terms of the old mythology of the north. But the most novel aspect of the new religion remained its original compassion. This benevolence, akin to Buddhism, but more positive, brought an unheard-of good cheer and gentleness both into the jaded, demon-haunted world of late antiquity, and into the cruel and fatalistic cults of the north, with their vague sense of Teutonic tragedy, of weird monsters and fated gods, their dour code of holding fast, at best, to honour and endurance. As western civilization went down, and as Byzantium withdrew into its eastern territories after the short-lived attempt under Justinian and Belisarius to regain North Africa and Italy in the sixth century, the West confronted the future in an intellectual, economic and technical degradation unparalleled by any great contemporary civilization. But it possessed in the Christian religion, which, like Graeco-Roman culture, had come out of the East, a creed full of obstinate Semitic vision and fire, inspired by a novel charity and hope.

It was as well. Western Europe was now under attack; first from Germany and Scandinavia, then out of the Arabian desert, where a sudden wave of Arab expansion was to carry the flags of Islam to Mesopotamia and central Asia, over Syria and Palestine to the defences of Byzantium, and along North Africa into Spain. But before turning to the shattering effect of the third Semitic religion, one must observe what has been going on in the great empires of the Near, Middle and Far East during the climax and the decline of the Roman Empire, and trace the rise of civilization in Japan.

# Eight

# SASSANIANS:GUPTAS: THE FAR EAST

## I

While the Roman Empire flourished, and during its decline when Byzantium alone maintained the direct tradition and the West fell into degradation, the great civilizations of India and China, in spite of political disasters, did not suffer comparable social collapse. The Gupta Empire was culturally more remarkable than the Maurya, and the T'ang dynasty even more creative than the Han, while, during the western Dark Ages, there arose a highly sophisticated court culture in Japan.

But the development of the oldest of all civilizations demands attention first. In Iran the Scythian-Turki Parthians had gradually regained most of the territories taken by the Seleucid successors of Alexander, and in the late third century BC had established their capital at Seleucia-Ctesiphon on the Tigris. Mithridates I had proclaimed himself 'great king' in the second century BC, and his overlordship extended from the Persian Gulf to the Caspian: but the Arsacid dynasty ruled an aristocracy of great landowners, an armoured, fighting baronage with a nomadic background.

They were ousted by the Sassanians, who came, not like the Parthians, from the north-eastern frontier steppe, but from Persis in the heart of the district of Fars and Shiraz. In AD 226 Ardashir, the grandson of Sassan, a high priest of the temple at Istakr near Persepolis, was crowned Shahanshah of Iran, and acknowledged from Mesopotamia and Bahrein to Bactria and the Punjab. His dynasty was to last until AD 640, when predatory hordes of Muslim Arabs, who had captured Mesopotamia, overran the heartland of Persia. Ardashir centralized the feudal Parthian overlordship into a neo-Achaemenid oriental despotism, made Zoroastrianism an official Church and had it defined in the Avesta, already described. In 260 AD his son Shapur I (242-72), captured the Roman Emperor Valerian by a trick near Edessa and, according to disaffected Christian writers, used him as a footstool, flayed and salted him, and hung his skin, tanned and stuffed, in a Mazdian temple. The famous rock reliefs in Fars depict Shapur as a dashing horseman, in contrast to the gross and bewildered Roman; they point the difference between Aryan Iran and the urban civilization of antiquity as it appeared to its enemies.

But the Sassanian Empire was elaborately organized. The magnates combined an Hellenistic and Iranian way of life above the poverty-stricken peasantry, and the mail-clad Sassanian cavalry were long the redoubtable adversaries of Byzantium. In the sixth century Khusru (Chosroes) I captured Antioch, and, in the early seventh, Khusru II raided Jerusalem, carried off the True Cross, and penetrated to Egypt. Even after the Arab conquest, the adaptable and highly sophisticated Sassanian-Persian culture was to stand to the Abbasid caliphate of Baghdad as classical antiquity to medieval Europe.

Shapur I also left a less attractive legacy, for he encouraged the Manichees. Mani (fl. AD 242–c. 275) devised a parody of Christianity and Zoroastrianism and was crucified by Shapur's grandson, Bahram I. The universe, he taught, was divided into 'a god land' of order and light and 'a hell land' of anarchy and darkness. But the darkness 'smelt' . . . something nice and invaded the light: so, to defeat the incursion, the light-god created primal man and the elements. The sun and moon were rescued, but the powers of darkness seized the elements and botched together Adam and the world: creation was thus the supreme evil. When Adam tasted the fruit of the tree of knowledge, he realized his fate: 'Woe, woe,' he cried, 'to the creator of my body', and determined at least to be the last of his kind. But Eve seduced him; they begot Seth, from whom the whole miserable race of men descend.

On this deplorable scene appeared Jesus the Redeemer: he conveyed men's souls to the moon, which, waxing, receives them and waning, empties them, purged, into the Milky Way. Hence the old Manichean hymn:

Thou art God and Full Moon, Jesus Christ.

At the Judgement, of course, the mistaken process would be wound up: all the light would be rescued, and the dust and ashes perish in a cosmic bonfire lasting 1468 years. The world 'smudge' would be erased.

Sorry, not for humanity but for the light, the Manichees organized a vegetarian elect, celibate and destitute, like Indian ascetics. An order of plain Hearers kept the holy men alive; '*Manaster Hirza*,' they would intone, '*cleanse our spots*': the supreme crime was to breed.

This deplorable religion, which developed a highly elaborate literature, influenced St Augustine, spread rapidly, inspired some delicate art, survived longest in Chinese Turkestan, spread secretly among the Muslims, and was to infect medieval Europe. It was the last dualist religion to emanate from Persia. In its homeland it was swamped, like Zoroastrianism, by the cleansing monotheism of Islam.

Sassanian architects, meanwhile, developed vaults and domes ancestral to the great mosques of Muslim Persia, and the gigantic ruin at Ctesiphon still shows the scale of building under Khusru I. Luxury trade in silks through Turkestan out of China, in textiles, ceramics and jewellery, flourished from Mesopotamia to central Asia and India: the manners and etiquette of the court of the Abbasid Harun al-Rashid were predominantly Sassanian-Persian, while Sassanian influence on Byzantine costume and ceremonial was decisive. The most ancient culture in the world, coming down direct through the Achaemenids and Babylon from Sumer, was to remain substantially unimpaired until the Mongol assault in the thirteenth century and even to civilize the descendants of the Mongols themselves.

## II

While these events were enacted in Iran, in India the Maurya Empire of Aşoka had broken down by the beginning of the second century BC: but by the time of Constantine a new, Gupta, empire was established. By AD 320 another Chandra Gupta I reigned in Magadha, and his son, Samudra Gupta, ruled from Pataliputra to the Punjab and the Indian Ocean. The reign of Chandra Gupta II (375–415) saw the greatest age of Hindu civilization, comparable, for pre-Muslim India, to the fifth century for Greece. But by 450, the Gupta Empire was shattered by the White Huns out of central Asia, and a century later, extinct. The revival under the brilliant Harśa-Vardhana (606–658) was vigorous but ephemeral, and for the next three and a half centuries, there was no great empire in northern India. Then, in 1001, and for nearly twenty years after, the Muslim Mahmud of Ghazni brought armies of Turkis and Afghans to loot and harry the Punjab, and the millennial conflict between Muslim and Hindu began. His mounted archers, like their Turki kinsmen who were to fight the crusaders, outmanoeuvred the native elephants and cavalry. A Ghaznavid dynasty lasted until the twelfth century, when, in 1192, Muhammad of Ghor defeated a great Indian army and finally secured Muslim domination of north-western India.

Peninsular India resisted the Muslim attack. Harśa-Vardhana, in the seventh century, had attempted to conquer the south, but had been defeated by Pulakesin II, whose elephants, maddened by drugs, dispersed the invaders. The southern Dravidian populace spoke Tamil and Telegu and other non-Aryan tongues, but their rulers had assimilated Buddhism and Sanskrit literature since the time of Aşoka. The Pallavas of the Eastern Deccan and the Coromandel coast and the Kalingas of Golconda exploited their economic position between the Roman and Arab worlds and the rich islands of Indonesia. They penetrated the Malacca straits and founded the powerful Buddhist kingdom of Srivijaya in Java, while other southern Indian settlers circumnavigated the Malay peninsula and dominated Cambodia, where most of the famous Khmer Hindu Temples of Angkor Wat, with their great artificial lakes, were built, by western reckoning, at the time of the later Angevins and Hohenstaufen. In Indonesia and Cambodia Indian art achieved some of its greatest sculpture and building.

In the north, the Gupta Empire saw the most creative age of Indian literature. The Sanskrit court poet and dramatist, Kalidasa (fl. 375–455), is the Shakespeare of Hindu India. His poems vividly evoke nature. He compares the rocks of the Vindhya hills to the 'pattern of stripes on the flank of an elephant', or apostrophizes a drifting cloud:

> Smell the most fragrant earth of the burnt out woodlands,
> And, as you release your raindrops, the deer will show you the way.

His love poetry is characteristic:

> I see your body in the sinuous creeper, your gaze in the startled eyes of deer,
> Your cheek in the moon, your hair in the plumage of peacocks,
> And in the tiny ripples of the river I see your sidelong glances.

He can also evoke terror:

> . . . the flaming ends of heaven were filled with smoke
> and bore the dull hue of the neck of an ass;

or, again:

> Before the host of the foes of the Gods
> dogs lifted their muzzles to gaze on the sun,
> then, howling together with cries that rent the eardrums,
> they wretchedly slunk away.
>
> – śvānaḥ svareḥ śravahanta-śātinā
> mitho rudantaḥ karuḥena niryayuḥ.

Kalidasa was also a fine dramatist. His most famous play is the *Recognition of Sakuntala*, in which the monarch, Dusyanta, marries the lovely Sakuntala; then, under a spell, forgets and disowns her, until the curse is broken and they are reunited. The play is most artfully devised, worldly as well as romantic.

Many poets followed, sometimes overelaborated, Kalidasa's technique: notably Bhartrhari in the seventh century, who wrote erotic and religious poetry, and his contemporary, Amaru, and Bana, who wrote *The Deeds of Harsa*, and the Kashmiri poet, Bilhana, in the eleventh century. There is a lush medieval Hindu literature of lyric, narrative and dramatic poetry. Dandin's *Tales of the Ten Princes* are absorbing narrative, and Bana also wrote prose romance, while Indian fables are the sources, through Persian, Syrian and classical translations, of many tales in the *Arabian Nights*, of La Fontaine's *Fables* and of the story of *Reynard the Fox*.

Besides this Sanskrit court literature, there were popular writers in Pali and Tamil. The literature is contemporary with the famous Ajanta cave paintings already described, which reflect a whole panorama of Indian life and express intense and highly subtle religious emotion. These exquisite, now fading, paintings were most masterly under the Guptas, when the Anglo-Saxons were barbarians in Jutland and Frisia. In the West only the mosaics of Ravenna were then fit to compare with them.

The Buddhist stupas of Aşoka's time were now elaborated and enlarged: the gigantic *Dagabas* at Anuradhapura in Ceyon date from the second century AD: 'Mighty currents of Graeco-Buddhist and Gupta art . . . flowed in successive waves to Central Asia, China, Nepal, Tibet, Further India and Indonesia by the mountain routes to the north and the east, and the sea-route to the south. It was this art of India that spread Indian myth, metaphysics and dharma.'[1] The cult of Hinayana Buddhism spread into Burma and Indonesia where architecture developed in fantastic elaboration. In the Deccan and Hyderabad enormous temples and even monasteries were cut from living rock, and the Pallava kings had temples carved out of whole hills. From the Gupta Age into medieval times massive and ornate temples, covered with complex writhing sculptures, rose over southern India.

Buddhist sculpture also reached a climax in the superb images of the Buddha at Mathura and Sarnath. They were a prelude to a proliferation of Indian sculpture and metal work, to the Tamil bronzes of the eleventh century and the Orissan sculptures in the twelfth. All derive from the Gupta Age, when Hindu culture was at its zenith.

This colourful civilization was overrun by successive conquerors but never destroyed. It was self-sufficient, a teeming native culture, with its riches and abject poverty, its ascetic and erotic cults. It developed in its own way, for the Himalayas and Tibet cut India off from China, save indirectly through Turkestan and through Cambodia by sea; nor did the trade with Rome and the Arabs much affect India, though Hellenistic influence was strong through Bactria in the north-west. The vitality of this original and ancient society is plain from its expansion into Burma and Indonesia, and the spread of Buddhism into Tibet, China, Thailand and Japan.

# III

During these centuries, the Han dynasty in China, which had created the centralized empire, had been consolidated; then, after a phase of disunion and political decline, reunited under the Sui and T'ang dynasties in the late sixth and early seventh centuries.

The Han emperor, who exercised the 'mandate of heaven', was hedged about by an elaborate bureaucracy; his court secretariat supervised the numerous ministries: justice, transport, supply, state sacrifices, the harem, the interior and foreign affairs. But at its peak, the régime was not overcentralized; the provincial administration could carry on even if the central power was in political eclipse. The Emperor Wen Ti (179–157 BC) ruled a peaceful empire. 'For the first time since the beginning of Chinese history, great areas of continuous territory were under unified rule . . . the creation of so extensive a region of peace produced great economic advance.'[2] The new 'scholar gentry' became a more homogeneous class, and began to revive the ideals of the old landed nobility as defined by Confucius. The new examination system, established by the late second century, became a settled procedure – its object 'not to test job efficiency but command of the ideals of the gentry and knowledge of the literature inculcating them: this was regarded as sufficient qualification for any position in the service of the state'.[3] This long-established and massive society, which in spite of political vicissitudes and internal revolt which led to the refounding of the dynasty by Kuang-wu Ti (AD 25–57), embarked upon wide conquests to the west. A large army advanced through Turkestan to the Caspian, and 'washed their swords in the surf of Parthian seas'. In the second century they sent envoys to the Roman Empire: Marcus Aurelius, whom they called *An Tun* (Antoninus), returned the compliment. The exchange marks the closest official contact between the two civilizations. But this expansion preceded internal disruption and decline. Palace intrigues and vendettas between the eunuchs and the bureaucracy and the personal incompetence of the emperors led, as in the Roman Empire, to military revolt. Among the people the secret society of the 'Yellow Turbans' rebelled, inspired by religious fanaticism and economic distress. The last of the Han emperors in the early third century was at the mercy of his generals: by AD 221, the last Han Son of Heaven had abdicated. The murderous Age of the Three Kingdoms began; later, wrongly, romanticized.

China saw a growing conflict between north and south, and a shift of wealth and population to the rich and climatically favourable area of the lower Yangtze. By 311 the northern provinces were overrun by Hun invaders, who had long threatened the empire but had assimilated much of Chinese civilization, and who captured the ancient capital of Loyang. These events, and their sequel, provoked a large-scale migration to the south to the territories of the former kingdom of Wu, near the modern Nanking. The northern territories were divided between Hun and, in Shensi, Tibetan rulers, but an invasion from the north was defeated in 383 at Fei hui, and it was long before northern armies were able to penetrate a country of hills and paddy fields, unsuited for cavalry. When they did, they were Chinese. Meanwhile, the immigration of northerners to the south greatly stimulated economic development. The wealthy aristocracy, who had already lived in luxury under the Han, brought new standards. 'We hear soon of water-cooled houses for the gentry, artificial ponds for pleasure and fish breeding, artificial water courses, artificial mountains, bamboo groves and parks, with parrots, ducks and large animals.'[4] The main diet of the south was rice, supplemented by vegetables and sea-food, where the northerners had wheat and pork.

By 588, a Chinese Sui dynasty had overcome the Hun, Tibetan and Turki rulers and consolidated a native power in the north, subdued the south and reunited China. They were the precursors of the great T'ang dynasty.

In 618, four years before Muhammad's *Hijra*, Li Shih-min, a young aristocrat who had made an alliance with a Turki army, founded the mighty T'ang Empire, which saw the most creative period of Chinese history. As the T'ang Emperor T'ai-tsung, he restored the northern capital of Ch'ang-an, and proved the greatest of ancient Chinese rulers. He commanded a formidable military power, based on a militia conscribed from the peasantry; the civil administration was more centralized; taxation tightened up. There was an enormous revenue and great luxury, while the great provincial cities also flourished – the basis for a widespread prosperity and cultural achievement. After the demise of the emperor in 650, his son ruled a gigantic and flourishing State, humming with economic enterprise and intellectual activity, with extensive trade with Korea, India and the now-Muslim west.

But again palace intrigues weakened the government. One of the old emperor's concubines, Wu Chao, was taken over by the new emperor: after her new protector's death, she ousted her own son, and ruled as empress dowager until 701, when she was murdered. Then the young emperor Hsüan Tsung (712–756), presided over the most creative epoch of Chinese culture, though he was finally driven to abdicate.

For in the later eighth century, the dynasty had lost grip on the north, and the shift of Chinese power and civilization to the southern provinces was confirmed. There followed exacting wars against Tibet, and much territory was lost in central Asia. But though the later T'ang dynasty petered out, it had seen a flowering of literature and art which influenced vast areas beyond China in the north and in central Asia, and which had largely inspired the civilization of Japan.

After a phase of political confusion, the T'ang dynasty was succeeded by the highly sophisticated Sung (960–1127). It was founded by a shrewd warrior, Chao Kuang-yin, who pensioned off all his generals by lavish endowments and secured prosperity and peace, while he abandoned the north to the Mongol Khitans.

Under both T'ang and Sung, Chinese civilization became more massive and brilliant. The later Han period had seen the spread of Mahayana Buddhism from India; it first became a court fashion; then, gradually, in a Chinese version offering a complicated mythology and an after life in the 'western heaven', it became a popular religion. The empress dowager, Wu

Chao, was a Buddhist; monasteries were heavily endowed, and Buddhism, like Taoism, became an integral part of Chinese life. Both were tolerated by the Confucians who manned the bureaucracy: 'it is related that a celebrated Chinese sage, known as "the noble minded Fu", when asked whether he was a Buddhist, pointed to his Taoist cap; when asked whether he was a Taoist, pointed to his Confucian shoes, and, finally, being asked whether he was a Confucian, pointed to his Buddhist scarf'.[5] This attitude contrasts with the intolerance of Christianity and Islam.

The extraordinary examination system which sustained Chinese society had grown up under the Han. It was elaborated by the T'ang and Sung emperors and the 'scholar gentry'. When most Europeans were illiterate, Chinese candidates were locked up in cells and told to write, in exquisite calligraphy, two essays and a poem. Those who passed won life-long privileges – often snug appointments. The more ambitious could take a stiffer examination, while the ablest attained a final degree, conferred after an ordeal held in the imperial palace itself, and could become mandarins of the highest class, privileged to wear the purple sash and commanding lucrative perquisites and appointments. Nearly all educated Chinese, whether successful bureaucrats or feckless poets, were caught in some part of this elaborate net. Moreover, civil appointments had much more prestige than posts in the army: 'The sword,' wrote one of the poets, 'is a cursed thing, which a wise man uses only if he must.' This attitude did not prevent war lords from winning great reputations among the people.

The culture of the bureaucracy was esoteric, for the Chinese ideographic script took years to learn; as the hierarchy expanded, the administration became more stifling and complacent, to become eventually an arrogant and corrupt anachronism, blind to the realities of the outer world. In its great days it proved the backbone of China.

The T'ang period was the golden age of Chinese literature. Li Po (701–62) is one of the great poets of the world. His contemporary, Tu Fu, wrote, engagingly:

> I rejoice in clear wine of Enlightened Men:
> I fly, moreover, from thick draughts of Virtuous Worthies.

Both sought promotion at the imperial court: but poets were apt 'to become estranged from the Illustrious Ruler', call themselves 'the Six Idlers of the Bamboo Grove', and write poems on 'drinking alone by moonlight'. They were commonly believed to be 'banished immortals', and their oddities condoned. Even in translation, the best of their poetry, with its poignant evocation of place, of the brevity of life, of nature and friendship, is still moving.

> The little waves [writes Li Po] were like dragon scales,
>     and the sedge leaves were pale green.

> When it was our mood we took girls with us and gave
>    ourselves to the moments that passed,
> Forgetting how soon they would be over – gone like
>    willow-down, like snow.

Or, again:

> The wine of Lu is like amber, the fish of Wen River
> Have scales of dark brocade. . . .

Li Po could also depict tragedy. A young conscript is symbolized by the white poplar:

> A foreign wind has stirred the horsemen of Tai,
> To the north they are blocking the pass of Lu Yang.
> Weapons of Wu glint on the Snowy lake . . .
> On the White Poplar the autumn moon shines cold;
> Soon it will fall on the hills of Yu Chang . . .
> This song has a tune, but the tune cannot be played.
> If the soldiers heard it, it would make their hair go grey.

> A Half Moon [he could write] hanging in the blue sky.
> And how many clenched bracken fists
> Growing along the paths where I used to walk?

Such was the poetry written in China when the rustic Merovingians were trying to rule Gaul.

The T'ang civilization is also celebrated for its ceramics and painting. Though figure sculpture had never been important among the Chinese, northern China produced some Buddhas and Bodhisatvas of monumental serenity. But the most famous T'ang figures come from the tombs of the well-to-do, placed there as a substitute for the old Chinese custom of sacrificing a living household. They are finished works of art which give a vivid cross-section of T'ang society.

T'ang and Sung painting is among the finest in the world. Brush calligraphy was invented in the Han period, but the early paintings have perished. In the eighth century, Han Kan's and Wu Tao Tzu's romantic landscapes are delineated with exquisite economy, while, in the twelfth, Chao Pu-chu's 'Entry of the Founder of the Han dynasty into Kuan chung' is a symbolic masterpiece. The last Sung emperor, Hui-tsung, founded an academy of painting and has himself left a wonderful study of a 'Pigeon on a Peach Branch', painted on silk.

But the rulers of China were not mere court aesthetes: Li Shih-min, in particular, was efficient, versatile and magnanimous. They regarded themselves as the summit of the world. When the emperor I-tsung received some Muslim envoys in 872, he remarked, in an Olympian manner: 'As for the Flood, we do not believe it. The Flood did not submerge the whole world. It did not reach China or India.' 'Moses,' he said, 'was not important, and his people were few.' As for Jesus: 'He lived only a short time. His mission lasted only thirty months.' Muhammad he took more seriously, since 'he founded an empire, which he did not see completed, but his successors have'.

The Son of Heaven was, indeed, the ruler of far the most populous empire anywhere. The census of China taken under the T'ang revealed a population of nearly fifty-eight million; under the later Sung, it was nearly doubled. Beneath the ruling classes, who were exempt from taxation, the peasant masses multiplied. Wheeled traffic was uncommon in the south: pack mules and litters and coolies provided transport. But traders pushed into northern Siberia and central Asia, south to Annam, Cambodia and Indonesia; Chinese civilization entirely dominated the Far East. In spite of the bias of the rulers, it was not unpractical. Engineers made good bridges and roads: the northern fortifications were immense. Further, by the tenth century, the Chinese classics were in print, five hundred years before the art spread to Europe. Gunpowder was invented, though not exploited in war. The life of the rich was luxurious, their gardens adorned with peach-trees, wistaria, peonies, all unknown in the West. At that time the rulers of China represented the richest, most stable and most cultivated civilization in the world.

## IV

That civilization had developed in the alluvial plains of the Yellow River; it had spread south to the Yangtze estuary and its hinterland and so into the interior. But the mountainous islands of Japan, to the Chinese 'the country of the Wa (dwarfs) . . . south east of South Korea in the Middle of the Ocean', were very different. Both cultures, like all South-East Asia and most of India, depended on rice, and in both the people were predominantly Mongoloid, but the mercurial and martial Japanese had a southern as well as an aboriginal Ainu strain. They seized on Chinese culture but gave it their own interpretation.

The legendary history of Japan goes back to the divine emperor, Jimmu Tenno, a descendant of the sun goddess, in the seventh century BC. From a rudimentary Neolithic culture they plunged into the sphere of influence of the advanced civilization of Han. In response to this continental stimulus, the clans of the southern islands entered the threshold of authentic history when the Empress Jingo (fl. *c.* AD 360), who ruled Yamato in central Japan, subdued the Ainu and sent her armies to raid Korea. In the early fifth century the rulers of Yamato imported Chinese *literati* and adapted Japanese to Chinese ideograms. The imperial dynasty, now far the oldest in the world, dates from the fourth century, with even a legendary descent from Jimmu Tenno: but the ruler controlled only his own clan, and 'The

Manifest God ruling over the Great Land of many Islands' was apt to get strangled or abdicate. The emperors were polygamous: there was no fixed succession, but the dynasty survived as a sacred institution, while power was vested in successive great court families.

The early history of Japan falls politically into three phases. First, the centuries when there was no fixed capital; next the period, coincident with the later T'ang, when the capital was at Nara (AD 710–782); then the Heian age of Kyoto (Heian-kyo) 794–1185, near Lake Biwa in central Japan. During these centuries Chinese and Buddhist culture were assimilated by the court, though the mass of the people remained primitive. But the fighting clans of the north superseded the rule of the 'cloistered emperors', and imposed from Kamakura a relatively efficient rule. Under their successors, the Hojo Regents, the Japanese, helped by storms, defeated two Mongol invasions ordered by Kublai Khan in the late thirteenth century.

The first known statesman of the pre-Nara age was the Prince Regent, Shotoku Taishi (AD 593–621), who codified the laws, encouraged Buddhism and witnessed a flowering of Japanese art and architecture under Chinese and Indian influence. In 646 Fujiwara Kamatari, the founder of the great Fujiwara family, who had apparently attained power by his politeness to the heir apparent on the football field, devised the reforms of Taikwa (Year of Great Enterprise). They created a bureaucracy on the Chinese model but never broke the military aristocrats, and although Chinese examinations were introduced, they never properly took root. Posts were always reserved for the well-born.

The Nara period, though culturally brilliant, saw murderous court intrigues. The Buddhist priest, Dokyo, the favourite of the deplorable Empress Shotoku, who had already once abdicated as the Empress Kogyuku but had returned to enjoy a second reign, attempted to oust the dynasty itself. He failed, and the Japanese decided to have no more empresses. An able emperor, Kwammu (782–805), a contemporary of Charlemagne, now moved to Kyoto, where, in luxury and splendour, the etiquette and ceremonial of T'ang China were acclimatized under the *de facto* rule of the Fujiwara. But although the first Seii-ti Shogun (Barbarian-subduing Generalissimo) pushed the imperial power to the north, the emperors never dominated the great territorial magnates. In 1156 the fighting Tairas from the north seized power, at a time hopefully termed 'the Age of Peaceful Rule', but they were defeated by the Minomoto on land at Ichi-no-Tani (1184) and at sea in the Shemonoseki straits in the following year. Minamoto Yoritomo (1185–1199) then established a military government at Kamakura in Eastern Japan: behind the cultured façade of the court, the arbiter of Japan remained the sword. The age of feudalism and the Samurai had begun, and it was to last, in various phases, until the seventeenth century.

Nara literature imitated the Chinese, but the first Japanese Chronicle, *The Record of Ancient Matters*, was written in AD 712, and the *Anthology of the Myriad Leaves* was collected in 760, while the Buddhist Scriptures were transcribed by a department of Imperial household. In the Heian period a phonetic script was developed, and while the cult of Chinese learning continued, Japanese court ladies wrote romances and diaries in their native tongue. Between 1008 and 1020, Murasaki Shikibu wrote the classic *Genji Monogatari*, the Tale of Genji, with an insight comparable to Jane Austen's.

'In the stillness of the evening,' she writes, 'under a sky of exquisite beauty, here and there along the borders of his palace some insect croaked its song: the leaves were just beginning to turn'; or again, 'the princely scent of the sleeve which he had raised to brush away his tears filled the low and narrow room.'

The Heian court-aesthetes lived in elegant pavilions with red lacquered balustrades and roofs tiled in red, emerald and blue. Since the expansion of Buddhism in the time of Prince Shotoku, who himself expounded the *Sutras* – one of his compositions in exquisite Chinese script has survived – temple architecture had flourished. By the early seventh century the huge Golden Hall of the Huryugi monastery, the oldest surviving wooden building in the world, with its curved roofs and elegant proportions, had been built. At Nara the six-tiered pagoda of Yakushiji was erected in 718, and the gay Phoenix pavilion of the Byodo in the middle of the eleventh century. Buddhism also inspired fine sculpture – the delicate Kwannon of the Chuguji and the Nara image of the monk Ganjin, solid, aloof, benevolent.

But the native Shinto religion, with its nature worship and ritual purifications, was a fertility cult of life. Sin was not a moral outrage, but unpropitious, a defilement, a social offence. One goddess was called 'Rich Food Princess'; the harvest festival celebrated 'crops in ears long and in ears abundant, things in the great moor plain . . . in the blue sea-plain, the broad of fin and the narrow of fin, seaweed from the offing, seaweed from the shore . . .'[6]

The greatest Divinity was a sun-goddess, 'the Heaven shining Deity who dwells in Ise, whose glance extends as far as where the Wall of Heaven rises; as far as where the bounds of the earth stand up, as far as the blue clouds are diffused, as far as where the white clouds settle down opposite.' This popular Shinto religion was blended with the official cult of the celestial emperor, himself descended from the goddess of the sun. Both were compatible with Confucian ethics and with popularized Buddhism, though Japanese monks were often warlike and are said to have invented Ju-Jitsu.

The ethics of the aristocracy were still symbolized by the sword, the *Katana*. The cult of *Bushido* – honour – reached fantastic elaboration in the feudal age. Japanese warriors were expert bowmen, but the sword was thought more romantic. Already, in the Nara period, their swords must have been the finest in the world, single edged, razor sharp yet heavy, sometimes six foot long; beautifully curved and balanced. The sword-smiths fasted, prayed and donned special garments before making them, and their owners carried a shorter sword as well, either to decapitate their beaten enemies, or to commit ritual suicide, should they themselves suffer disgrace, or even slight.

Such, from the beginnings to the end of the twelfth century, were the salient aspects of the civilization of Japan. It was indebted to the brilliant Chinese culture, at its zenith under the T'ang, which dominated the whole Far East, and to Buddhist influences from India; but it was also insular, peculiar, and unique. The court culture was flimsy, and its chivalry, to western eyes, has a touch of hysteria, but Japanese society was sturdy, based on the large peasant population, living on rice, seaweed and fish, which swarmed in the Islands of the Great Sea.

# V

Across the whole continent of Asia, from Syria and the Tigris through Iran and India, down to Burma, Cambodia and the Indonesian islands; and, from Iran, through Turkestan and the Chinese interior down to the plains of the Yellow River and the Yangtze, and across to Korea and Japan, three great civilizations had thus developed directly from their prehistoric origins. The Iranian Mesopotamian culture was the most ancient; the Indian presented the greatest variety of religions, and the Chinese was the most massive, the best administered and the most creative, radiating its influence to Japan and north to Mongolia and the Siberian hinterland. All were flourishing when western Europe was sunk in barbarism. Had anyone been able to survey the prospects of humanity in the seventh century AD, they would have regarded T'ang China as far the most promising of the cultures of the world, superior in scale to Byzantium, and incomparably more advanced than western Europe – still more than the extraordinary ceremonial cultures of the Maya in Yucatan, which, developing since the first century AD, had reached their first peak of achievement in the fourth, the most peculiar civilization in the New World.

# Nine

# THE EXPANSION OF ISLAM

## I

At the other extremity of Asia, beyond the Persian Gulf and the Rub' al Khali, where, between Hijaz and Yemen, the caravans from Syria converged upon Yathrib and Mecca, which lay inland from Jidda on the Red Sea, the Quraysh Arabs had long commanded the incense, cosmetic and spice trade from Aden and the Hadramaut on the Indian Ocean, and the commerce in slaves and ivory with Abyssinia and the Sudan. In the sixth century AD they were already an astute people, in contact with the Byzantines and the Sassanian Empire in Iran ; more worldly than the desert Bedouin, who had periodically descended on the settled lands since the dawn of history. Mecca was also the sacred city of the Ka'bah, the Black Stone, a fetish respected by all the tribes of western Arabia, from time immemorial an object of pilgrimage. The city was also a centre for fairs, where tribal poets declaimed *qasidas*, as well as of moon worship – for here the sun was an enemy. And the Quraysh had long been familiar, for there were many Jews and Christians in their territory, with Judaism and Christianity, the two Semitic religions of a Book.

In AD 571 the founder of the third great Semitic world religion was born in Mecca. Muhammad, unlike Jesus or the Buddha, combined religious genius with warlike political finesse. An orphaned cadet of the already well-established Hashimite family, he was employed by Khadija, a rich widow, to manage her caravans to Syria. He married her ; they had two sons, who died, and four daughters ; it was not until middle-age that he heard voices 'like the reverberation of bells' and experienced the revelations 'in the name of Allah, the Beneficent, the Merciful . . . owner of the Day of Judgement', recorded in the Qur'ān. At this time also Muhammad is said to have visited the seventh heaven, carried by Al-Burāq, a supernatural creature which took off from a site near the dome of the Rock in Jerusalem, henceforward sacred in Muslim tradition. The prophet soon roused hatred in Mecca by denouncing pagan cults and, in AD 622, the year of the *Hijra* which begins the Muslim era, he migrated east to Yathrib, which became known as Madinat il Nabi (Medina), the city of the prophet. His *Ansar* (helpers) now attacked the Meccan trade route to the north, and consolidated their hold in Medina by expropriating the large colony of Jews. A counterattack was foiled, and in 630 the prophet captured Mecca, won over the powerful Umayyad family and made the Ka'bah a centre of Muslim pilgrimage. But Medina remained his principal stronghold until, after a triumphal entry into Mecca, now his religious capital, he died in the summer of 632.

His kinsman, Abu Bakr, elected caliph or deputy, now diverted his tribesmen from their vendettas by raiding Syria and Iraq. Armed with Indian sabres and bamboo lances, the swordsmen and archers of the desert camelry penetrated deep into the cultivated lands.* Forays turned to conquests: in 636 Khalid-ben-al-Walid defeated the Byzantines at the river Yarmuk and mastered Syria; in the next year, the Sassanians were defeated at Quadesija and Ctesiphon captured: the Arabs pressed on to another great victory at Jalula and invaded Iran. By 642, under the austere and gigantic caliph, 'Umar I, they had taken Alexandria.

These astonishing exploits were due to Bedouin fanaticism, lust for plunder and mobility, as well as to the hatred of the native eastern populations for Byzantine and Sassanian rule: ill-paid troops deserted; garrisons handed over whole towns. Within ten years of the prophet's death, the Muslim Arabs had conquered, and were beginning to exploit, the most ancient civilizations of the world and change the face of the Near and Middle East.

This Semitic triumph was the prelude to an expansion to the Indian Ocean and the Atlantic. In the eighth century the Muslims swept along the entire coast of North Africa, crossed the Straits of Gibraltar in 711, conquered Spain and penetrated to the Loire, until they were defeated in 732 by Charles Martel. Their sphere of influence also spread east into southern Russia and central Asia, while, as already recorded, Muslim invaders were to overrun much of northern India. Arab commerce came to dominate the Indian Ocean and spread south to Mombasa, Zanzibar and into the interior of Africa; the Arab-exploited Near and Middle East, at its climax in the tenth century, far surpassed western Europe, for it was the heir to Egypt, Mesopotamia and Iran. Damascus in Syria became the first centre of Arab power, which was then patriarchal, the caliphs living merely as very important sheiks. In 661, following the murder of the wise and chivalrous Ali, the fourth and last of the 'rightly guided' or orthodox caliphs, who had married the prophet's daughter, Fātima, the formidable and worldly *Malik* Mu'āwiyah (661–80) was elected the first Umayyad caliph. His highly sophisticated family retained a secularized office until 750, when they were ousted by the Abbasids of Baghdad. The cult of Ali's

---

* No, not for Paradise did though the nomad life forsake;
  Rather, I believe, it was thy yearning after bread and dates.

Abu Taman; see P. K. Hitti, *History of the Arabs* (New York 1958), p. 144.

sons, the martyred Al-Hasan and Al-Husayn – the one poisoned, the other slain at Karbalā – who descended through their mother from the prophet, formed the nucleus of the Shi'ah sect of Islam, to be prevalent in medieval Egypt, over much of Iran and Iraq and parts of India. In opposition to Sunni Muslims, they recognized only the 'rightly guided' caliphs, not the Umayyads – a division, consecrated in blood, which still continues. Only the descendants of Ali, they were to insist, are the true Imāms, supreme spiritual authorities, where the caliphs were deputies.

The Umayyads of Damascus, a desert city in a rich oasis, where their celebrated mosque remains, represented the original conquering Arab aristocracy; sheiks accustomed to no boundaries save grazing grounds and tribal areas, who formed a privileged class, exempt from taxes, and who imposed a fairly tolerant overlordship, reinforced by garrison towns.

But when, in 750, Abul-'Abbas, a descendant of one of Muhammad's uncles, and known as Saffāh, the Blood Shedder, massacred most of the Umayyad family and became the first Abbasid caliph, his power was based on Khorasan in Iran, and his capital became the newly founded city of Baghdad on the Tigris. The Abbasids claimed to restore the old orthodoxy, but they represented a new interest, the *mawali*, or 'clients' of Islam, converts mainly of Iranian and Mesopotamian background; and they established an oriental despotism on the Sassanian model with all the elaborate etiquette of the Shahanshahs. The powerful bond was religious: in comparison with the Roman Empire, the conquests were superficial, poorly administered; often, through the tyranny and debauchery of the rulers, unstable. But the climax of this opulent, culturally Iranian, and luxurious civilization was reached under Harun al-Rashīd (786–809), and under the great caliph al-Ma'mūn (813–833), when Hellenistic learning was popularized and science and medicine flourished. In the Muslim East, as in Byzantium, there had been no 'dark ages'.

This Baghdadi Abbasid caliphate was stifled by its own guards. By the later tenth century, Turkish mercenaries had it in their control, and in 1055 Tughril Bey, a Seljuq, became the first sultan (*the Power*), leaving the caliph a figurehead. His successor, Alp Arslān (*Hero Lion*), defeated the Byzantines at Manzikert in 1071, and Malik Shāh and his vizier, Nizam-al-Mulk, overran most of Anatolia and threatened Byzantium. Their incursions provoked the first crusade.

While these events determined the main stream of Muslim politics, the outlying provinces hived off. Westward, in Cairo, a Shi'ite Fatimid dynasty was established, to be superseded by the brilliant Kurdish prince, Salah-al-Din (1171–1193), 'Saladin', who defeated the crusaders at Hattin. But his descendants succumbed to Turkish Mamlūks, who ruled Cairo until the early sixteenth century and formed the third focus of Muslim power. When the Mongols under Hulagu Khan sacked Baghdad (1258), wrecked most of Mesopotamia, finished off the last Abbasids and conquered Iran, the formidable Mamlūk sultan, Beybars (1260–77) – like Saladin, in leisure moments, an expert polo player – was able to hold Egypt. Meanwhile, a ferocious refugee Umayyad and his descendants long ruled most of Spain, and the Berber Almoravids and Almohades fought the crusaders of the *Reconquista* in campaigns strategically decided by the Christian victory of Las Navas de Tolosa in 1212. Eastward, in the ninth and tenth centuries, the native Iranian Safavid and Samanid dynasties were overcome by Turki invaders: Mahmud of Ghazni, as already described, pillaged northern India.

Such, in brief, was the political background of Muslim civilization, the heir at once to Mesopotamia and Iran, as well as to the former Hellenistic-Roman territories of Palestine, Egypt, North Africa and Roman Spain.

## II

The religion of the conquerors was clearly defined, and flung like a net over the whole kaleidoscope of the Near and Middle East. The Qur'ān, revealed to Muhammad over many years, proclaimed a ruthless monotheism. As Yahweh had commanded Moses 'Thou shalt have none other Gods but me', so the Qur'ān commands 'Set not up with Allah any other God, O man, lest thou sit down reproved, forsaken.' Like St Paul, Muhammad despised the world: 'Know that the life of the world is only play and idle talk, and pageantry and boasting . . . and rivalry in respect of wealth and children; as the likeness of vegetation after rain, whereof the growth is pleasing to the husbandman, but afterwards it drieth up and thou seest it turn yellow, then it becometh straw' (*Sura* 57). Allah, alone, is 'the first and the last, the outward and the inward . . . knower of all things'. The God of the Jews had asked Job: 'Gavest thou the goodly wings unto the Peacocks?'; the Qur'ān demands:

> Have ye observed the water that ye drink,
> Is it ye who shed it from the rain cloud or are we the shedder?
> Praise the name of thy Lord, the Tremendous.

But if Allah was omnipotent, he was merciful. Paradise, automatically attained by those who died fighting the infidel, was described in memorable detail. Reclining on 'lined couches', the faithful, served by 'boys of everlasting youth', enjoyed cups 'from a pure spring, whereof they get no aching of the head nor any madness':

> And fruit that they prefer.
> And flesh of fowls that they desire,
> And [there are] fair ones with wide, lovely eyes,
> Like unto hidden pearls.

For the guilty, on the other hand, there would be:

> Scorching wind and scalding water
> And shadow of black smoke . . .
> Ye will drink boiling water
> Drinking even as the camel drinks.

To this prospect, universally intelligible, Islam added brotherhood among Muslims – since all human distinctions are insignificant before God – and intolerance of all infidels. Pre-Muslim blood-feuds, endemic in the desert, had been merged in the *Jihad*, the Holy War. The Jews, said Muhammad, had betrayed the faith of Abraham, and the Christians had founded monasteries and eaten pig. Both must be destroyed; still more, pagan idolaters.

These general principles were reinforced by habit. Summoned by the Muezzin from his minaret, the devout Muslim prostrated himself towards Mecca five times a day. He must observe the ritual of the Mosque, give alms, fast from sunrise to sunset during Ramadan and, once, at least, in his lifetime, he was enjoined to make the *haj* to Mecca. Sober, forswearing alcohol, upright, just to his co-religionists, he often embodied the patriarchal Semitic virtues – sententious, imperturbable, urbane. He was sometimes a murderous fanatic.

His veiled and secluded women were the chattels of their husbands, who could divorce them at will. Muslims might have four wives and many concubines – hence atrocious dynastic feuds. 'Men have authority over women,' said the Qur'ān, conclusively, 'because God has made one superior to the other'; disobedient wives might be beaten and 'banished to bed apart'. 'Here,' writes Ibn Battutá, the fourteenth century Moroccan traveller blandly, 'my wife was attacked by severe pains and wished to go back, so I divorced her and left her there.' Women often played a decisive part in politics, but since they were confined to harems, much Muslim social intercourse tended to be exclusively male. Like the Christians, the Muslims soon split into many sects. Besides Sunni and Shi'ah, there were Ismailis and their sub-sect, the Assassins, who originated in the Elburz mountains at Alamut in northern Iran,* and whose western leader, the Sheik al Jabal, the Old Man of the Mountain in Lebanon, sent his followers, maddened by 'hashish', to 'assassinate' his enemies during the third crusade. Until obliterated by the Mongols in the thirteenth century, they provoked horror in the Near East. The Druses of Palestine had also evolved their mysterious religion by the tenth century, and Dervishes and Marabouts, with their Turkish Shamanistic background, were flourishing by the end of the twelfth. These enthusiasts, who happily chewed glass,

---

*In pursuit of their ends they made free and treacherous use of the dagger, reducing assassination to a fine art. Their motto was 'Believe nothing and dare all.' Hitti, *History of the Arabs*, p. 446.

swallowed fire and whirled to the sound of flutes and the thud of drums, explored strange states of consciousness, like the Indian ascetics.

Islam, 'submission' – the context is the story of Abraham's attempted sacrifice of Isaac – if a very practical and persistent way of life, was sometimes fatalistic. Squalor, arbitrary power, famine and disease were accepted as the will of Allah; an inert conservatism often reinforced the Bedouin aristocrats' contempt for toil. The Hellenistic-Iranian civilization which the Arabs overran was extremely rich, its enterprise far-flung, its literature and learning elaborate, but after the brilliant creative period of the ninth, tenth and eleventh centuries, a relative stagnation set in over much of the Muslim world. The way of life, hypnotized by so potent a spell and interpreted by Turks surfeited with conquest, became elaborately lethargic.

# III

This aspect of Islam did not affect the commerce which flourished under the Abbasids from the Persian Gulf to Spain, from Turkestan to the Gambia and which dominated the Indian Ocean and Indonesia until the advent of the Portuguese. Strategically placed athwart the trade routes of the Middle East to control the Persian Gulf and the Mediterranean – the Sea of Rūm – Muslims had the initiative in the Indian Ocean, in Sicily and southern Italy, in Spain and, until the eleventh century, in the south of France. While the West was crassly ignorant of geography, the Abbasid Muslims of the Persian Gulf, who had assimilated Hellenistic and Sassanian learning, made surveys, itineraries and maps; they exploited the east coast of Africa, the Far East and Indonesia. When, in the eleventh century, the Norman Roger of Sicily wanted a survey of the known world, he employed Al Idrisi, an Arab geographer, and in the fourteenth century the Moroccan Ibn Battutá, already mentioned, left a detailed and entertaining record of his travels to West Africa, Constantinople, Ceylon, India and China.

This observant traveller gives a detached account of the customs of the Hindus: 'When one of them comes to drown himself [in the Ganges],' he writes, 'he says to those present with him "Do not think that I drown myself for any worldly reason, or through penury; my purpose is solely to seek approach to Kusay", Kusay being the name of God in their language.'[1] Ibn Battutá much preferred the Chinese – the most skilful of all peoples in the arts: 'In regard to portraiture, there is none, whether Greek or any other, who can match their precision.' At Constantinople, as might be expected, he was impressed by the bells, a Christian sound striking to anyone fresh from the Middle East. Ibn Battutá is only the best known of many medieval Muslim travellers: it was mainly from Arab sources in translation that Columbus got his notion of the shape of the world.

For long the Muslim camel caravans traded with central Asia, with

Samarkand and Bukhara and Chinese Turkestan; across the southern Russian steppe, and over the Sahara with the ancient kingdom of Ghana, between upper Nigeria and Senegal. The Muslim influence on Europe is apparent from many names still current for textiles: muslin and damask, for example; and from such key words as cheque (*sakk*), tariff, traffic, *magasin* and *douane*, while the tabby cat gets his name from the watered silks made originally in the Attabiyah quarter of Baghdad. The Muslims also conducted a brisk slave trade with Kievan Russia and the Sudan. Over all the Near and Middle East, through political vicissitudes, their covered *suks* flourished; Arab humour and inconsequence blended with the wily enterprise and commercial method which came down from remote antiquity.

# IV

Muslim learning, like that of Rome, mainly derived from Hellas, though its literature was predominantly Persian. 'Islamic medicine and science,' it has been said, 'reflected the light of the Hellenic sun, when its day had fled, and they shone like the moon, illuminating the darkest night of European Middle Ages.'[2] Muslim philosophers were often doctors and mathematicians; 'Umar al Khayyam (d. 1123), a poet more celebrated in the West than in Persia, wrote, under Seljuq patronage, a treatise on algebra, not a science generally congenial to poets; reformed the calendar and anticipated Descartes in analytical geometry. In mathematics, indeed, the Muslims surpassed the Greeks, since they used numerals invented in the Gupta Age by the Hindus, who had hit upon the notion of zero and of indicating the value of numbers by their position. These Arabic signs gave the Muslims an advantage and in time superseded the clumsy Roman figures in Europe: by the fifteenth century, they had made European science, trade and administration more efficient.

Arabic, a lucid, practical and sonorous tongue, became the Latin of medieval Islam, and created a similar cosmopolitan learning. The two famous Muslim philosophers, Avicenna (980–1037) and Averroes (d. 1198), came, respectively, from Bukhara at one end of the Islamic world and Cordoba at the other. Avicenna (Abu Ali al-Husayn ibn 'Abd Allah *ibn Sina*), 'The Prince of Physicians', is buried at Hamadan; Averroes (Abu'l–Walid ibn *Rushd*), at Marrakesh: the famous Moses Maimonides, a Spanish Jew, lived at the court of Saladin in Cairo in the late twelfth century.

The first great centre of Muslim learning was at Jundeshapur in south-western Iran, where, in the sixth century, Byzantine pagan philosophers had fled from the persecutions of Justinian: Galen's treatises on medicine were here translated into Syrian, Persian and Arabic. In the early tenth century Rhazes, who came from the district of Tehran, was to write of smallpox and measles and to speculate on 'why frightened patients easily forsake even the skilled physician'. Al Hawi compiled a medical encyclopedia; Jabir, famous in medieval Europe as the alchemist 'Geber', attempted to transmute metals into gold. The world's greatest centres of mathematics and science in the ninth, tenth and eleventh centuries were no longer in Alexandria, but in Bukhara, Khorasan, and the colleges and hospitals of Abbasid Baghdad, with its famous Nizami university.

Under the Fātimids, Egypt again became important, and Al Hazem of Basra, who was summoned there by the caliph to regulate the Nile flood, and feigned madness to escape the tyrant's wrath when he failed, was a pioneer in optics. This learning spread to Spain and to the medical school of Salerno which flourished under Frederick II. Much of it derived from Aristotle, and many more of his works became familiar in the West through Arabic translations in the thirteenth century. Averroes interpreted Aristotle to deny immortality and free will, since deity was entirely conditioned by the medium of creation: he found a redoubtable adversary in St Thomas Aquinas, who interpreted Aristotle in a more optimistic sense. If Averroes was sceptical, there were more positive Muslim theologians – Al Ghazali, a contemporary of Anselm, a brilliant scholar at the university at Baghdad, renounced his career and wrote the mystical *Niche of the Lights*; and the Persian Sufis, Hallaj and Abu Said, as well as the Spanish Ibn Arabi, whose account of heaven influenced Dante.

In political theory, also, Aristotle's idea of justice and of the purpose of society was widely accepted by Islam; it blended with the view that the caliph, commander of the faithful, Amir al-muminin, was not a despot but *Wakil* – a trustee. Early Islamic political thought, like that of medieval Christians, distinguishes between the prince, who rules under God, and the tyrant, or *Malik*, who rules by force. The collapse of the Abbasid caliphate at the end of the thirteenth century, before a Turki sultan, may be compared to the decline of the papacy and the empire before sovereign dynastic powers, justified, only because law, however imposed, was better than anarchy.

Ibn-Khaldun (1332–1406) is the outstanding medieval Muslim philosopher of history. He was born in Tunis of a Yemeni family, originally from the Hadramaut, and, like Plato, he attempted and failed to find an enlightened prince. After exacting political and diplomatic experience, he retired to a castle in the Maghrib to write his *History of the Berbers, and the Muslim sovereigns of Western Africa.*\* He then became a judge in Mamlūk Cairo and ended his days in Damascus.

\*See Muhsin Mahdi, *Ibn-Khaldun's Philosophy of History* (London 1957), and C. Issawi, *An Arab Philosopher of History: Selections from the Prolegomena of Ibn-Khaldun of Tunis, 1332–1406* (London 1950). Of his *History*, Professor Trevor-Roper writes: 'It is a wonderful experience to read those great volumes, as rich and various, as subtle, deep and formless as the ocean, and to fish up from them ideas old and new. Sometimes he seems marvellously precocious, as when he deals with the division of

Like most Muslim writers, Ibn-Khaldun was dominated by Aristotle, but he anticipates Vico in psychological insight, Montesquieu in his sense of environment and Marx in understanding the movement of events and the influence of the means of production on culture. The basis of society, he points out, is an instinctive collaboration for survival. This creates the culture of primitive peoples, *'umran Badawi*: 'unlike city dwellers, they have not gone far in the practice of vice. They may be eager for vice . . . but because they have never had the opportunity to practise it, their original nature remains pure.'[3] They have *āsabiyya*, a solidarity made dynamic through religion, a more violent inspiration than ordinary biological needs. So inspired, they 'actualize their potentialities', and create *'umran hadari*, civilized culture. They then impose a State, *Dawla*, which animates the whole society. But after a brief phase of brilliance, decline sets in, and the collapse of the State drags society down with it. The desire of city dwellers for luxury leads them to self-destruction; there is poverty, unemployment, a bestial struggle for survival exploited by demagogues. Men of learning become an irresponsible and mischievous intellectual proletariat.

Ibn-Khaldun believes that this all-too familiar process is inevitable. Yet he admits 'an incurable desire for reform'. The 'virtuous city,' he says, 'is indeed hypothetical, but the statesman . . . who declares himself neutral about what is good and bad, noble or ignoble, is like the physician who abstains from calling a disease a disease'. Ruling remains an art enhanced by the study of the deeper causes of history. Like Hobbes, he thought that the State created law, which did not exist in its own right; the ruler alone can maintain *āsabiyya* against corruption.

These views were natural where so little independent civic spirit prevailed, and the use of capital and the promotion of trade so much depended on the ruler and his bureaucrats. As Professor Trevor-Roper points out, this totalitarian society was, in fact, superseded by the superior initiative, the *āsabiyya*, of Europeans.

Ibn-Khaldun is a great writer who repays study: he analysed the nature and causes of civilization, the city, the economy, the culture, when most historians were mere chroniclers. But he wrote deep in the decline of the creative phase of Muslim civilization. At its peak, at the Abbasid court, a romantic literature had flourished. Ibn Dawad, for example, a contemporary of King Alfred, began *The Book of Venus*, on the many aspects

---

labour, the social origins of wealth, the distinction between the form and substance of history. Often we are struck by his maturity, his capacity to see good and evil in the same thing.' H. R. Trevor-Roper, *Historical Essays* (London and New York [as *Men and Events*] 1957), p. 28. And Professor Toynbee enthusiastically concurs: he terms his *History* 'a piece of literature which can bear comparison with the work of Thucydides or the work of Machiavelli for both breadth and profundity of vision as well as for sheer intellectual power', and even writes of his *Prolegomena* as 'the greatest work of its kind that has ever been created by any mind in any time or place'. *A Study of History*, III (London 1934).

of love, at fifteen. But the most famous literature is Persian. That adaptable and ancient culture, coming down direct from the Achaemenids and Sassanians, assimilated Arabic influences but was never swamped. Firdausi in the early eleventh century wrote his long epic, the *Shahnama*, from which the tale of Sohrab and Rustum derives, and 'Umar al Khayyam is only one of many poets who wrote *rubai*, short verses which express the Persian flair for proverb and epigram. His disillusioned hedonism recalls that of Li Po, though he is a lesser poet. In Fitzgerald's translation he became very popular among late nineteenth-century agnostics, and was rather romanticized from the original. When Fitzgerald writes:

> I sometimes think there never blows so red
> A rose as where some buried Caesar bled.

'Umar says, literally:

> Every place where there has been a rose and a tulip bed
> It has come from the redness of some Prince's blood.

The lyrics of the great Hafiz, who died in 1389, the year, by western reckoning, of Sempach and Kossovo, are much more highly considered in Persia, although Sir William Jones, in the late eighteenth century, translated one of his poems in a saccharine manner.* *'Take wine . . . ,'* wrote this contemporary of Chaucer, *'And retail me no more legends of the doom of infidel tribes.'*[4] Jones can translate,

> Sweet Maid, if thou would'st charm my sight,
> And bid these arms thy neck infold;
> That rosy cheek, that lily hand
> Would give thy poet more delight
> Than all Bocara's vaunted gold
> Than all the gems of Samarcand.

But Hafiz in fact wrote:

> If that Shirazi Turk would take my heart into his hand,
> I would give Samarquand and Bukhara for his Indian (dark) mole.

> – agar ān Turk-i Shīrāzi ba-dast ārad dil-í-mar-ā
> bi-khāl-í Hinduyash bakhsham Samarqand ū Bukhārā-ra.

In their own country the mystical *Poems of Rumi* are also considered sublime. But the most celebrated Persian book outside Persia has always been the *Arabian Nights*, which derives from a lost Iranian original, and combines erotic appeal with adventure. It was first drafted in the tenth century, and reached its final form in Mamlūk Egypt.

Muslim literature was widely read, since by the early eighth century the

---

* A. J. Arberry (ed.), *The Legacy of Persia* (Oxford 1953). His poetry has at once an elaborate sensuality and mystical, sufic, content.

Arabs had learnt to make paper – not generally used in Europe until the later Middle Ages – from the Chinese in Samarkand, but Muslim architecture had a more direct influence both on Europe and Asia. The Gothic arch, usually considered a response to the climate of the north, came originally from the East, and Muslim Indian architecture was austerely different from that of the Buddhists and Hindus. The original Arab conquerors at once erected splendid mosques in the cities they subdued: the famous Dome of the Rock in Jerusalem dates from as early as 639, and combines a rotunda whose columns are Byzantine with a cupola probably of Iranian origin. The great mosques of Damascus, Qyruwan and Cordoba were all built in the eighth century. At the same time, the elegant pointed arch was already common in Mesopotamia, when Charlemagne was clumsily imitating the late Roman architecture of Ravenna. Eastern fortifications far surpassed anything in Europe outside Byzantine territories, until the crusaders learnt the art of machicolation, as they did that of heraldry, from their enemies. The oriental influence on the Doge's Palace at Venice or the cathedral at Pisa is obvious. The Renaissance dome, on the other hand, owed little to the East, though the more pointed oriental domes, developed in Iran, where brick-built mosques, covered with brilliantly glazed and enamelled tiles, reach their climax in the fifteenth and sixteenth centuries. A religion which forbids the representation of the human form naturally inhibits sculpture, and though their interior colouring could be magnificent, mosques were generally decorated in abstract designs and by Arabic texts.

All this wealth of great cities and exotic merchandise, of cool colonnades, of fountains tinkling in quiet courts, of silk and muslin and robes of honour under huge turbans; of negro executioners, eunuchs, veiled women and slaves, confronted the barbarous western crusaders with a civilization of apparently overwhelming opulence, ruthlessness and refinement. In its final phase, under the Ottoman Grand Turk, who was to unite all the lands from eastern Persia to Egypt and dominate the Levant, a Muslim conquest again threatened Europe. But it was the creative period in the eighth, ninth and tenth centuries which had so profound an influence on the countries they ruled and the enemies they fought, and which forms the background to traditional Muslim culture today.

## V

The peak of Muslim civilization had, indeed, been passed even when, in 1055, the Turki sultan, Tughril Bey, had seized Baghdad. Its creative aspects had been Arab, Hellenistic, Sassanian; now Turki political dominations began, to be followed two centuries later by the devastating Mongol incursion. Hulagu Khan wrecked the basis of its prosperity in Mesopotamia, though the Mongol Ilkhans in Iran soon became highly civilized patrons of the arts.

The Cairo of Saladin and the Mamlūk Beybars benefited by the decline of their economic rivals and long remained a rich metropolis, comparable to the old Alexandria, with similar commercial advantages, but its culture was an elaboration of the past. Anatolia saw the last and most formidable phase of Muslim political expansion. After Byzantium had been broken by the fourth crusade and the Seljuqs had been overrun, the Ottoman sultans invaded the Balkans, survived the assault of Timur Lenk, whose defeat of Bajazet I only postponed the drive to the West, and took Constantinople in 1453, capturing a decayed city much of which they had to rebuild. They also attacked the Safavids of Persia, took Syria and Egypt and brought the full weight of their power, based on the extraordinary *kullar* or slave household, to attack Vienna.

All four phases of Muslim power were thus militant. All – Damascene, Baghdadi, Cairene and Ottoman – had originated because the *āsabiyya* of the desert Arabs had been mobilized by a dynamic and enduring religion, and had overrun great territories which Mongol and Turki conquerors were afterwards to exploit.

# Ten

# BYZANTIUM: SOUTH AND EAST SLAVS

## I

The Roman Empire included parts of modern Hungary and Romania, and the Greek colonies round the Black Sea, but it never mastered central Germany or the Baltic, still less penetrated the wilds of Scandinavia and the southern Russian steppe. It was not until after its centre of gravity had moved to the shores of the Bosphorus, that a Byzantine Christian culture spread into what is today the western Soviet Union. Yet this influence was to prove decisive for an immense area, then vaguely termed Scythia, which stretched away into central Asia and the north-east.

Modern Istanbul still has none of the Levantine languor of Izmir or Iskanderun; with the current running swift out of the Black Sea, and a brisk climate, this large maritime city has a touch of the north. The great natural strength of its position for trade, sea power and the swift dispatch of armies, made it a bastion which, for many centuries, secured central Europe and the Levant from Asian attack. The culture of the Balkans, already part of the Roman Empire, was long to be dominated by Orthodox Christianity, and that of the Kiev Russian waterways by a blend of Swedish and Byzantine influence. If the West owes directly an overwhelming debt to Rome, indirectly, it owes much to Rome's eastern continuation in the Byzantine Empire. For when in AD 330, Constantine had moved the administrative capital of the Roman Empire to the Greek city of Byzantium which he rebuilt as Constantinople, commanding the trade routes of the Levant and the Black Sea, he had only confirmed a long shift of political and economic power. Diocletian had ruled the empire from Nicomedia, and the headquarters in the West was already not Rome, but Trier. As the northern barbarians overran Italy, North Africa and the West, Constantine's strategic insight was vindicated: civilization withdrew East, nearer to its origins.

The Byzantine imperator, in Greek *Autokrator Augustos*, was the only real *sovereign* in early medieval Europe, the direct successor of the orientalized rulers of the later empire; his people were *Romaioi* and his territory was known to the East as *Rūm*. So long as it could draw on the manpower of the Balkans and Anatolia and control the sea, Byzantium remained rich, highly organized and formidable. It converted the Serbs, the Bulgars and Kiev Russia, and set standards for the parvenu Carolingian and Ottoman empires, outclassing anything in the West until the thirteenth century.

The political history of Byzantium began with the still Latinized empire of Constantine and Theodosius. Justinian (AD 527–65) attempted to regain Italy and North Africa, but his dynasty ended with the murder of the Emperor Maurice in 602. After a series of defensive wars, when all North Africa and most of Italy were finally lost, and when Sassanians and fanatical Muslims attacked the very heart of the empire, the Muslims besieged Constantinople in 673, and again in 717. The city was saved by Leo the Isaurian, and survived with territories diminished but more compact.

The greatest and most characteristic period of Byzantine history now began. Basil I, a gigantic and illiterate Armenian, born near Adrianople, whom the Emperor Michael III had made Master of the Horse, and who murdered and supplanted his patron in 867, founded the 'Macedonian' dynasty which reached its climax under Basil II Bulgaroctonos, Slayer of Bulgars (963–1025). At this time came an official break with the Papacy (1054), whose claims the Byzantine Church was unable to admit and whose doctrines it regarded as heretical. The dynasty ended with the disaster of Manzikert in 1071, when the Emperor Romanus IV Diogenes was captured by the Seljuq Turks under Alp Arslān; the Byzantines lost command of Anatolia; and, in the same year, the Normans took Bari. These disasters are chronicled by Psellus, a racy and perceptive historian, who took a leading part in the events he described.

A new dynasty, the Comnenoi, now attempted to restore the situation, but the able Emperor Alexius Comnenos, whose exploits are described by his daughter, Anna Comnena, the first woman historian, had to contend not merely with their traditional enemies in Anatolia and the Balkans, but with the barbarous barons of the first crusade. The eastern empire remained rich but vulnerable, and in 1204 Constantinople was taken and plundered when the fourth crusade was diverted by the Venetians to destroy their rivals. This disaster was the beginning of the end. A ramshackle Latin empire did not last; the Byzantines still held Nicaea, Salonika and Trebizond, and in 1261 Michael Palaeologos regained the city; but by 1308 the Ottoman Turks entered Europe, and by 1357 they had outflanked the Byzantines by the capture of Adrianople. In 1397 they first besieged Constantinople itself: it held out until 1453, when the last of the Palaeologoi, the Emperor Constantine XI, fell fighting in the gate of St Romanus as the Turks stormed the city, and a dilapidated Constantinople became 'Istanbul' – an oriental corruption of the Greek εἰς την πολιν, 'to the city' – the centre of the vast dominion of the Grand Turk.

## II

'The Great Basileus, Autocrat of the Romans', as he came to be called in the ninth century, ruled a far-flung centralized State. It maintained a gold currency, the bezant, far superior to the crude silver coinage of the West, and it was administered by a bureaucracy of *illustres*, *spectabiles* and *clarissimi*, in direct descent from the empire of Hadrian, with the old titles and precedence. Justinian, the nephew of the Emperor Justinus who had been an Illyrian peasant, 'unable to tell one letter from another', and commander of the palace guards, was a revolutionary innovator of wide vision, much influenced by his consort, Theodora. According to Procopius,★ she had been a dancing girl of the versatile kind familiarly known as the 'infantry', expert in 'plying her trade'; she is described by the French historian Diehl as 'unscrupulous, perfidious, violent, cruel, implacable and adamant', and she had a powerful intelligence and will. Justinian married her when he was forty. He was fanatically Christian and persecuted those of his subjects who remained pagan: encouraged by Theodora, he imposed fierce penalties for breaches of morality, laws which were often useful for punishing political opponents. Together they attempted to make the empire once more a great power in the West, but Justinian's more permanent achievement was the codification of Roman Law. In 529, two years after his accession, his lawyers condensed the vast material of Roman Law into the *Codex Justinianus*, and, four years later, produced the *Digest*; the *Institutes* further simplified the law into a manual for students. The continuity of Roman law was thus never broken in the East.

It has been said that the Byzantines had no political theory, but their practice was steeped in it. From the beginning to the end of their history their conception of empire is clearly defined. 'Like the man at the helm of a ship,' wrote Agapetus, adviser to Justinian, 'the mind of a king, with its many eyes, is always on the watch, keeping a firm hold on the rudder of enforcement of the laws, and sweeping away by its might the currents of lawlessness.' Weighed down by the tradition of Greece and Rome, and by a fashion of elaborate rhetoric and grammatical complexity – for they wrote a Greek, as Professor R. M. Dawkins remarked, 'as classical as they could make it', different from the spoken tongue – the Byzantines felt the ideal ruler was 'steadfast, rooted, in the revolving wheel of human affairs'. They quoted from Aristotle, Cicero and St Augustine phrases familiar in the West, such as the comparison of tyranny to 'brigandage writ large'. Society

---

★Procopius of Caesarea was private secretary to Justinian's general, the young Belisarius, and an eye-witness of his campaigns. He wrote the official *History of the Wars* with a Thucydidian detachment, but got his own back in his *Anecdota* or *Secret History*, in which he blackguarded his employers, calling Justinian a 'stupid donkey' and Theodora much worse. See Procopius, Loeb edn, VII vols, ed. H. B. Dewing (London 1914); for the *Anecdota*, see VI.

is thought of as a 'colony planted out from heaven in this quarter of the universe', and the 'science of politics' as a means of man's occasional return to their mother city on high. The Basileus is at once a god-appointed trustee and the august symbol of the rational harmony of universal mind. 'Where the life of, the progress, and the claims of each man go unregarded – left loose, so to say, and untested – for want of a system of supervisory justice,' writes the late Byzantine Theodore Metochites, 'the consequences will as a rule be irrational.' The theory of monarchy is as clear in the sunset of Byzantium as in its dawn.

Along with this lofty conception of empire – the expression of the cosmic order, akin to the finer aspects of the Chinese theory of government – went a cult of extreme political cunning, As the tenth-century Emperor Constantine VII Porphyrogenitus, for example, wrote in his testament to his son: 'I seek to explain what are the nations that can aid or injure the Romans, and in what respects they can do so; which of them can be fought and conquered; how this is to be done in each case, and what other nations should be used for the purpose.'

## III

The political practice of Byzantium, of course, was often atrocious; a tale of blindings and usurpations, criminal rulers and illiterate adventurers who castrated their enemies, left them to rot in dungeons, or cast their strangled corpses into the Bosphorus. The crusaders considered the Byzantines, with their elaborate Romano–Sassanian court etiquette, their painted faces and scented beards, to be crooked and cruel, if the cool diplomacy and ruthless politics of Alexius Comnenos appeared to his daughter merely vigilant and humane. To her he was the ideal Basileus: 'On each side,' she writes, 'he had black eyebrows arched, and under them his eyes were set, with a glance at once awful and gentle, so that from the gleam of his look, the clearness of his forehead and the dignity of his countenance, men derived both fear and encouragement . . . for the personality of the man had beauty and grace and strength and unapproachable dignity.'[1]

The household of the Basileus descended from Rome, but by the tenth century the titles of the great officials were Greek – the Great Domestic of the East, the Great Drungary of the Fleet, the *Thalassocrator*. The palace guard were now 'axe-bearing barbarians', Scandinavians, and English exiles, some of whom had fled to Denmark in 1066 to offer the Danish king the English crown, and had fetched up in Constantinople. These fair-haired and extremely expensive warriors were much admired by the Byzantines: Bohemund of Otranto, the outstanding personality of the first crusade, whose laugh was like 'snorting in others', also fascinated Anna Comnena, though she complained that her father's gout had been exacerbated through standing to listen to garrulous crusading bores.

The imperial power was solidly based on a bureaucracy numbering at least ten thousand, which was independent of the fighting services, for military and civil authority were carefully segregated. The great prefectures were subdivided into dioceses, which in turn were made up of provinces: the *Magister Officiorum* and his subordinates, the *Agentes in Rebus*, the *Sekretikoi*, the *Logothetes*, directly depended on the Basileus, who symbolically and ceremonially paid them himself. This administration carried on beneath all the changes of dynasty.

Byzantine troops were elaborately equipped. The panoply of the Kataphracts included bow, sword and lance; Procopius remarks, rather smugly, that the Homeric archers were amateurs, who drew only to the chest. The general staff had good maps, and analysed the characteristics of their frightful variety of enemies. It was best, they considered, when fighting Franks, to shoot at their horses, not at the mailed riders, but Turkish horsemen should be tempted to charge and then surrounded. The Byzantine army, alone in their day, had a medical service, logistics and supply, and field engineering was completely organized.

The fleet of heavy dromonds with two banks of oars, and of pamphyli, faster, lighter, craft, relied on the celebrated 'Greek' or 'sea fire', probably a mixture of sulphur, naphtha and quicklime, which ignited on contact with water, and was siphoned through hoses, or solidified with charcoal and discharged by catapults and hand grenades. The crews were drawn mainly from the Ionian coasts and the Greek Islands. The fleet proved successful against the raiding Russian flotillas of *monoxyles*, little more than single-trunk war canoes, but, by the twelfth century, the Byzantines were losing their grip on the Adriatic and the Aegean, and, by 1204, the Venetians and Genoese had the advantage.

Though the fleets and armies were extremely expensive, in its great days Byzantium could well afford them. 'We have gold,' said Nicephorus Phocas, 'and with that we will break you.' But Byzantine wealth, though colossal to the West, was limited by guilds which inhibited private enterprise, though they guaranteed quality and kept prices stable, as well as by the Christian prejudice against 'usury'. The Byzantine silk trade, established under Justinian, when two monks brought back the secret from China, was challenged in the twelfth century by competitors from Sicily, though Byzantium long retained her supremacy in brocades, an imperial monopoly. *Cloisonné*, glass and ivories were made at Thebes, Corinth, Salonika and Trebizond, and the court, the rich magnates and the great cities long provided a steady export market. The wealth of the Hellenistic East had always been fabulous in western eyes, and no accessible government disposed of such revenues, save that of Abbasid Baghdad in the ninth century, at the peak of its affluence. Constantinople, with its deep, sheltered harbour, so prosperous that it was called the 'Golden Horn', and its rich fisheries, had an incomparable strategic position, the natural focus of the whole trade of its hinterland in Europe and Asia Minor.

Some Byzantine emperors were fierce warriors: as Psellus puts it, they had 'that wild beast look'. They would invite enemies 'who at dawn the next morning were destined . . . to undergo the most horrible tortures',[2] to dine 'the evening before, and to drink of the same cup'. But others were enervated by luxury, as was Constantine VIII, the last of the Macedonians, whose robust frame was:

. . . naturally adapted to assimilate all kinds of food with ease. He was extremely expert in the art of preparing savoury sauces, giving the dishes character by the combination of colour and perfume. Being dominated by gluttony and sensual passions, he became afflicted with arthritis, and, worse still, his feet gave him such trouble that he was unable to walk. . . . For the theatre and horse-racing he had an absolute obsession and devoted himself to the chequers and dice.'[3]

Self-indulgent emperors were often vulnerable, and in 1034 Romanus III, when 'swimming on the surface, and floating lightly, blowing out and refreshing himself', was easily drowned by the bath attendants. Naturally, these autocrats regarded good fortune as precarious: Isaac Comnenos (1057–59), coming in from victorious battle, and not even pausing to change his clothes before issuing directions to secure his unexpected success, remarked to Psellus himself; 'Philosopher, this amazing piece of good luck seems to me a fickle business.' And Psellus replied; 'Once you change your philosophic outlook . . . or become inflated with pride, divine justice will certainly oppose your plans, and quickly at that.' But divine justice was often tardy.

A calculated splendour, the 'pomp' of the autocrator, was kept up for visiting ambassadors. A curtain swept aside, and the Basileus, like a Sassanian monarch – the design of Theodora's diadem is Sassanian – was discovered seated in full regalia on an elaborate throne, with two mechanical lions roaring on either side, while artificial birds twittered in the branches of a gold tree and an organ played. This ingenious glitter greatly impressed the barbarians. But for all his grandeur, the Basileus was not a theocrat. He was supposed to show a general *philanthropia*, but the spiritual independence of the patriarch, and the near autonomy of some of the great monasteries, with their vast estates, limited his religious authority. It was not, in the main, the fault of the Byzantine Basileus that the schism with the West developed and worsened; rather the division came from the monks, popular fanaticism and, later on, from the hatred provoked by the sack of 1204 and the appointment of a Latin patriarch.

The art and architecture of this rich civilization were elaborate. The best mosaics at Ravenna are Byzantine, and they are paralleled by fine medieval mosaics in Haghia Sophia and at Kiev. Byzantine ikons began a new kind of painting, which had a profound influence on Italy as well as Russia, with designs in red, green and black on a background of old gold. The ivories are incomparable in European art, and the stiff jewelled robes of European royalty derive from magnificent Byzantine originals.

Architecture combined Roman engineering and design with Sassanian variety of shape, and nowhere in the world had a dome been set over so vast a space as in the great church of Haghia Sophia, built under Justinian, while the clustered domes and mysterious vistas of St Mark's in Venice are Byzantine, glowing in mellow colour. Within these great churches and monasteries, an elaborate recitative and unaccompanied choral music developed, from which derived the majestic singing of the Orthodox Church, well-suited to dim lighting and mosaic walls.

The quality of Byzantine historians has already been suggested; there was also a rather derivative, mainly twelfth century, literature of love lyrics and romances, descending from antiquity, which influenced old French writers and so all western Europe. But the most vigorous Byzantine poetry was based on popular ballads and folk tales, ancestral rather to modern Greek than coming down from the past. The *Epic of Digenes Akritas* – Digenes the Frontier Guard – was written in the mid-twelfth century about events in Cappadocia and on the Euphrates frontier in the tenth.

This great civilization, a direct continuation of the Roman Empire, was self-sufficient and extremely arrogant. The high-bred disdain of Anna Comnena, her pride in her own elaborate culture – 'I desire to expound in writing the deeds of my father . . . being not unversed in letters, nor unpractised in rhetoric, having well mastered the rules of Aristotle and the dialogues of Plato' – blends with an acute aesthetic sense of situation and character and an unmedieval refinement. Besides the studied calm, the wary suspicion of motives, the reluctance to believe that anyone means what they say, there is a wit and casualness comparable to the sensibility of eighteenth-century Paris or Vienna, if without their rationalist 'enlightenment'. And Byzantium is historically important not only for its own achievements; as already emphasized, it was the centre from which radiated the Slav civilization of the Balkans and Kiev Russia.

## IV

The Slavs originated round the Pripet marshes, between Lithuania and the Ukraine. The main weight of their settlement was to be in Russia, but they had early invaded the Balkans, and disrupted contact between Constantinople and the West; others spread into Poland, Bohemia, Moravia and Slovakia. These western Slavs became part of Catholic Christendom; the southern Slavs, cut off from the rest by the Magyars, a Finno-Ugrian steppe people, who were also eventually to become militant Catholics, took their civilization and creed, like the eastern Slavs, from orthodox

Byzantium. But it was the Bulgars, Turki invaders, Slavized and orthodox Christians by the ninth century, who first became predominant in the Balkans at the expense of the Byzantines.

Old Greece, long part of the Roman Empire, was least affected by these invasions and their sequel. Slavs penetrated even into the Peloponnese, but the country remained Byzantine and in close relation with southern Italy and Venice. Although Theodosius had discountenanced the Olympic Games, Justinian had closed the philosophy schools at Athens, Hellenes became *Romaioi*, Normans from Sicily were to sack Corinth and the French de la Roches were to be Dukes of Athens: the economic and cultural predominance of Byzantium remained. The fine, if over-restored, mosaics at Daphni are more representative than the incongruous *fleurs de lys* of the adjacent tombs of the de la Roches, or than the relics of the Catalans who ousted the French, brought in Aragonese princes from Sicily, and were superseded by Florentines. Long after 1204, the despotate of Mistra in Sparta witnessed an Indian summer of Byzantine civilization, commemorated by the frescoes of the Peribleptos, as well as by Gemestes Plethon, who inspired Cosimo de Medici to found a Platonic Academy in Florence. As Byzantine power waned, it was the Venetians who fought off the encroaching Turks: their fleet took Nauplion in Argos in 1389, the year of Kossovo, when the Ottomans broke the Serbs, and in 1684 the guns of Morosini blew up the Parthenon, used by the Ottoman commander as a powder magazine.

Such was the fate of old Greece. The scene of the brilliant classical civilization which had defied Darius and Xerxes and Hellenized most of the Near East, had become a land of poor peasants, ruined towns and Turkish domination. Yet the Phanariot Greeks of Istanbul long retained their commercial supremacy and beneath successive invasions the original Mediterranean stock survived. The dark profiles of classical vases are still commonplace in Athens.

The inspiration of Byzantium had been religious as well as commercial. Mediterranean civilization spread to the southern Slavs of the Balkans and the eastern Slavs of Rus through missionaries and traders. In 862 Rostislav of Moravia petitioned the Emperor Michael III: 'We Slavs,' he wrote, 'are a simple people who have no one to tell us which doctrine is true. Send us, we beg you, gracious sovereign, one who will teach us correctly, for from you derives the law which governs the whole world.'

The emperor dispatched Constantine and Methodius, two brothers from Salonika; as St Cyril and St Methodius, they became the apostles of the Slavs. Constantine had already converted the khan of the Kazars, and Methodius had been governor of Thessaly. Their arrival was resented by the German clergy, and they were summoned to Rome, where Constantine retired to a monastery. He died, as Brother Cyril, in 869, and is buried in the church of St Clemente; Methodius, vindicated, became bishop of Pannonia and converted the Bulgars. But St Cyril had devised a new *glagolitic* script (from *glagol*, word) out of cursive Greek to translate the scriptures for the Moravians; it was now adapted by a colleague of Methodius into the 'Cyrillic' script and became the alphabet of the Bulgars, Serbs and Russians.

The reception of Christianity did not assuage the ferocity of Balkan politics. The Bulgars had early overrun both the fertile southern plain of the Danube and the valley of the Maritza. These territories are separated by the Balkan mountains which extend from Sofia nearly to the Black Sea.

The Bulgars came originally out of the southern steppe. One branch, the Volga Bulgars, had settled near that river north of Kazan; the other, led by khans and *bagaturs*, had moved west. Krum Khan, a contemporary of Charlemagne, captured Sofia, beheaded the Emperor Nicephorus I, and kept his silver-mounted skull as a goblet. But Boris Khan, in terror, it is said, at a picture of hell painted by St Methodius' own hand, and doubtless, also, for good political reasons, became a Christian, massacred his pagan opponents and converted his people *en bloc*. Simeon the Great (893–927), the first Bulgar tsar, captured Nis and nearly took Constantinople, but the Bulgars were harried by Sviatoslav, the grand prince of Kiev, and later defeated in 1014 by Basil Bulgaroctonos at Cleidion.

The Āsen Tsars established a second domination. By 1205, Tsar Kalojan defeated and decapitated Baldwin I, the first and singularly incompetent Latin emperor of Constantinople, and even held sway to the mountains of Albania; but by 1330 the Bulgars were broken by the Serbs at Velbuzd on the Struma.*

The brief Serb hegemony was even more ambitious. A peasant people, ruled by clan chieftains or *zhupans*, they had spread over the plains of Serbia, and, like the Croats, into the mountains above the Adriatic coast, where originally Roman towns, ancestral to Dubrovnik, Trogir and Split, were now closely linked with Venice. Serb military power had first developed among the bleak pastures of Montenegro above Kotor, and between Mostar and Sarajevo: they soon took Nis and Skoplje: by the twelfth century the *Veliki zhupan*, Nemanja, had accepted Orthodox Christianity. King Stephan Nemanjic and his brother, St Sava (1196–1223), brought to heel the *bans* and *voivods* who led the armies and ruled the

---

*The Bogomil heresy also contributed to the empire's decline. Its founder, Jerome *Bogomil*, as he called himself (*Friend of God*), thought, like the Manichees, that the creation was the work of the devil and procreation a crime. He also denied the divinity of Christ and denounced the Church. His more ascetic followers withdrew from the world; others gave vent to the wilder forms of anti-social enthusiasm. Their doctrines of salvation through irresponsibility spread into Lombardy and Provence, where they provoked the Albigensian crusade, though they were often popular missionaries who healed the sick and 'conjured' evil spirits, and had an elaborate and highly sophisticated literature, which expressed ideas afterwards influential on the Anabaptists and on various heresies in Russia.

provinces. The defeat of the Bulgars at Velbuzd by Stephan Uros III was due in part to the exploits of his illegitimate son, the famous Stephan Dushan, who in 1331 supplanted his father. Dushan created the greatest of all the Balkan Slav empires: he tried to unite all the Balkan peoples against the Turks and to get to Constantinople first. He conquered Macedonia, Albania, Salonika and the Peloponnese; he brought his frontier east to the mouth of the Maritza: in 1346 he was crowned 'Tsar of Serbia and Roumania' and, three years later, promulgated a memorable code of laws, the *Zakonik Tsara Dushana*. Though the Venetians failed him, and the Turks anticipated him by seizing Gallipoli, he mounted, but never launched, a massive combined attack, for he died at the height of his power in the winter of 1355.

The tsar's empire, under a weak successor, at once broke up. The Turks defeated a combined Serb and Greek army on the Maritza in 1371; advancing on Skoplje, they finally destroyed the Serbian empire on the field of Kossovo, the Plain of the Black Crows, in 1389.

The outcome seems to have been inevitable. The Turks far outnumbered Tsar Lazar's army:

> Were we grains of salt [runs the ballad] instead of warriors,
> Yet we would not salt that army's dinner . . .
> Like a cloud their battle standards streaming
> And their tents like snow in winter.

But the Serbs died gamely. On the eve of battle Tsar Lazar had taxed the *Voivod* Milosh Obilitch, with treason; so Milosh, determined to prove his loyalty, swore to kill the Turkish sultan with his own hand.

And this he did. Crossing the Turkish lines, he declared himself a Muslim and demanded to kiss the sultan's foot. But 'in the very act,' writes a Turkish eye-witness, 'he drew a poisonous *hanjar* hidden in his sleeve and boldly thrust [and so] caused the illustrious Sultan to drink the Sherbet of Martyrdom.' Milosh was at once cut to pieces; Bajazet I succeeded Murad I. And the battle was lost; Tsar Lazar, his nine sons 'like grey-eyed falcons', and the flower of the Serb nobility, after an epic fight had been overwhelmed. All were beheaded in the dying sultan's tent. Thus the Serbs lost their ancient empire; it was not until 1912 that the Serb infantry were to liberate the field of Kossovo. Only in Albania George Castriota ('Skanderbeg') resisted the invaders in the Balkans; through John Hunyadi and Ladislas Jagello checked them in 1443 at Hish, they were themselves overwhelmed by the Turks in the following year at Varna.

## V

The Balkans, so much influenced by Byzantium, had long formed part of the Roman Empire: now Mediterranean civilization was to spread to northern peoples hitherto far outside its range. Great amorphous territories of forest and swamp extended across the Baltic–Black Sea isthmus and away to Finland and the far north; eastward the steppe lay open to the Mongol and Turki nomads who had moved, from time immemorial, under the hot sun and bitter cold of central Asia, over vast areas between the Carpathians and China. As already recorded, the Romans had thought the interior of Germany too sinister to penetrate, and were ignorant, save for the tales of a few traders in amber, even of the Baltic territories beyond. Yet, within two generations of the conversion of the eastern Slavs of Rus to Orthodox Christianity, civilization had grown up along the rivers which link the Baltic and the Black Sea. Novgorod, near Lake Ilmen in the north; Smolensk; Kiev, the capital of the southern region of the black earth, were its greatest cities. Rus, so called from the Finnish word for its Scandinavian rulers, reached its climax in the eleventh and twelfth centuries. It was then wrecked by Tatar invasion. Brutalized by Tatar domination, which drove the centre of Russian power back from vulnerable Kiev into the forests round Moscow between the head waters of the Oka, the Volga and the Dnieper, Russian civilization still carried on; and out of Muscovy were to come imperial Russia, the colonization of Siberia and the vast Soviet Union.

The eastern Slavs of the swamps and forests of the Pripet and the Upper Dvina, like those who had infiltrated down the great waterway of the Dnieper, had to pick up their first rudiments of culture from the Goths: they learned the words for sword and helmet, for vineyard and for plough. In the ninth century, by the time of the Macedonian Emperor, Basil I, they were dominated by Swedish Vikings – the *Varyagy* or Varangians. According to the official chronicles, these adventurers were 'invited' to rule the land: they found some prosperity and the prospect of more. The Slavs already had stockaded *Gordoriki*, tribal rallying points and trading posts along the rivers which were the sole regular means of uniting the country; the *Varyagy*, a tiny minority, exploited and developed the trade in wax, slaves and fur from a huge hinterland. 'The lure,' wrote Sumner, 'that beckoned the adventurous groups and then the Novgorod bands, organized by rich merchant-landowners and led by tough, experienced boatmen-pioneers, was above all fur – sable, marten and fox.'[4] Rurik, a contemporary of King Alfred, 'accepted' the lordship of Novgorod in 862; he had already conquered Jutland. Oleg, who extended his rule down to Kiev, had his eye on the Black Sea, and his successors, Igor and Sviatoslav, attacked Constantinople; failing conquest, they made trade pacts. So militant trading city states grew up, living off the river commerce and fighting the steppe nomads to keep the trade routes open. They looked both to the Baltic and Byzantium.

The Scandinavians brought their Nordic family feuds with them;

worsened since senior princes were succeeded by those from minor cities, and so all moved up a step. Soon, like the Bulgars, they became Slavized. Their war-bands became Slav *druzhinas*; they were not territorial feudal magnates, like those of the West, but *boyars*, more directly dependent on the prince, or, as in Novgorod, part of a merchant oligarchy. But they displayed the predatory flair of their kinsmen in Normandy, England and Sicily, and swiftly assimilated the culture of the south. Vladimir I of Kiev took the decisive step. A polygamous heathen, he had begun his reign, 'in an orgy of paganism. He put in front of his palace figures of the old Slavonic Gods: Svavog, the father of gods, Dashd-Bog, his son, the God of the Sun, Velas, the patron of Cattle, Stribog, the Wind God, and, chief of all, Perun, the God of Thunder, with a huge silver head and moustaches of gold.'[5] But he soon began to inquire into the major religions of civilization. Since, he decided in 988, Muslim intolerance of strong drink would make life insupportable in Russia; since the fate of the Jews was no recommendation for their religion; since his envoys were immensely impressed by the splendours of Constantinople; and since he desired to marry a Byzantine princess – he became a Christian. He had little difficulty in converting his subjects wholesale. The people of Novgorod were also converted by their rulers, and other cities followed; Byzantine clergy brought the scriptures, written in Old Slavonic in the Cyrillic script: a church of Sancta Sophia was built at Kiev in 1019. By the time of Yaroslav the Wise (1034–54), who defeated the Pechenegs of the steppe, the Grand Prince of Kiev was as famous as anyone in Christendom. One of his daughters married Harald Hardrada of Norway; another, Henry I of France; another, Andrew I of Hungary. His grandson, Vladimir Monomakh, whose mother was Byzantine, married a daughter of Harold Godwinson of England. This Vladimir Monomakh left an *Instruction* to his family which depicts the adventures of Kiev Russian royalty. 'Thrown by a bull, butted by a stag, trampled by an elk, bitten by a bear, borne to the ground by a wolf', the survivor of numerous campaigns against the Polovtsy and against his relations, Vladimir Monomakh might well exhort his children to fear neither battle nor beast.

The grand princes were, of course, backed by the Church, which linked their courts with Constantinople and the culture of the southern Slavs, and provided literate administrators. If heathen customs were tenacious among the peasants and lower clergy, the Church brought the prestige of Byzantine architecture, music and art. Already, amid the prevalent wooden buildings, a few brick and stone churches were being built, and the characteristic Russian 'onion' dome dates from the twelfth century. In the later Middle Ages, Russian artists produced ikons comparable to the best Byzantine work; great monasteries grew up; the Pechevsky monks of the 'Monastery of the Caves' at Kiev had compiled the first old Russian chronicle by the late eleventh century: 'no other country of their time possessed a more faithful record of its public life ... each individual district developed its own psychology in its chronicles; Kiev, radiant and many coloured; Novgorod, short and drastic; Suzdal, dry and plain'.[6] Little popular poetry has survived, save the twelfth-century *Tale of the Host of Igor*, familiarized by Borodin, but the heroes of Kiev Russia – Oleg, Igor, St Vladimir – are all an integral part of Russian folk tradition.

On this vigorous and martial urban minority culture, spread thinly on a shifting peasant agriculture and colonization and living mainly off riparian commerce, broke the hurricane of the Tatar invasions. Kiev Russian influence on the steppe, always precarious, was swept away; contacts with Constantinople, itself crippled by the Latin *coup* in 1204, were cut off, and the centre of Russian power moved back into the zone of mixed forest land where, by now, the grand princes of Moscow alone had the resources and manpower to survive. For while Novgorod and the northern cities had been under attack from the Swedes, routed by Alexander Nevsky on the Neva in 1240, and from the Teutonic knights, outmanoeuvred, two years later, at Lake Peipus on the ice, the Russians between the Oka, the Volga and the headwaters of the Don, had long been colonizing the East. They thus evaded both western pressure from the Baltic, the economic decline of the old waterways, and the worst of the menace from the steppe, since the Tatars were ill-equipped for campaigns in the forest. And though at first the Tatars sacked and subjugated Moscow itself, the grand princes of Moscow came to terms with them and even collected the tribute, until strong enough to defy them.

These Tatar horsemen out of central Asia, led by Mongols of the royal family of Genghis Khan, were the western wave of an expansion which extended from China deep into Europe, and which, as already remarked, swept down into Mesopotamia. In the West the invasion proved a reconnaissance, but in southern Russia the Tatars settled in. Archers adept in cavalry tactics, they had first defeated a combined force of Russians and Polovtsy on the river Kalka in 1223. In 1239 they sacked Kiev, and it was not until 1380 that Dmitri Donskoi, Grand Prince of Moscow, decisively defeated them at Kulikovo. Even after that, the Russians were long to pay tribute in furs, gold and slaves to the Tatars of the Golden Horde at Sarai, near the modern Stalingrad on the Volga, so-called from the Golden *Ordu* or tent which symbolized the descendants of Genghis Khan. What for thirteenth-century Europe proved a scare, for Russia proved a catastrophe; the wealth of Rus was extinguished. Toughened, in some degree orientalized, Muscovy survived. Its expansion belongs to the history of the later Middle Ages.

The civilization of Rus had been part of European Christendom, but already it differed fundamentally from the West. Western feudalism and its economic base, the manor, did not develop: rather Rus was a country of city states which ruled a shifting and colonizing Slav peasantry. Manpower, not land, was valuable. Further, the Russian Church, with its scriptures and liturgy in Old Slavonic, became cut off from its Mediterranean origins; it had a diminishing part in the inheritance of Roman antiquity. So in Muscovy there was to be no scholasticism, little contact with the superior Arab culture, and if the Church was part of the people, it was provincial, not cosmopolitan as in the West.

So great northern territories, in antiquity unknown, with all their resources and growing manpower, under a climate of terrible extremes – even Stalingrad is in the latitude of Newfoundland – were brought, by the ninth century, through Byzantine and Scandinavian initiative, out of prehistory into civilization. If, by the thirteenth century, the remarkable culture of Kiev Russia had been superseded, Moscow had begun to lay the foundations of a more massive power, the destined base not merely of resistance to Polish–Lithuanian, Swedish and Tatar attack, but of a vast expansion down the Volga, out to the Caucasus, and into central Asia and Siberia, comparable only in scale to the colonization of North America. All this future, and that of the southern Slavs, had been culturally determined by Byzantium.

# Eleven

# WESTERN CHRISTENDOM

## I

While the Byzantines had maintained the eastern Roman Empire and brought the Slavs into their orbit, China, Japan and Gupta India had been flourishing and the Muslims had altered the face of the Near and Middle East, the western Roman Empire had suffered singular decline. If the old basic skills were never lost, and the stirrup and horse collar came in from Asia, the wheeled plough from the north and the windmill from the Near East, intellectually the 'Dark Ages' were tedious, elementary and inept. Yet, by the twelfth century, there was a new and vigorous western culture: it included northern peoples unknown to Rome, and it was distinguished, at its zenith, by brilliant architecture, elaborate heraldry, a new cult of 'chivalry', an original 'scholastic' intellectual discipline and by fruitful notions of law and government. Though its main roots were in Mediterranean antiquity, this culture owed much to the north, to Germany and to northern France.

## II

The barbarians who had moved south into the late Roman Empire had known where they were going. 'Traders, raiders, and perhaps returning conscripts or mercenaries,' writes Sir Mortimer Wheeler, 'had already demonstrated the way to fortune'; and the Huns, striking in across the continent, had impelled others to face 'the mists of the North Sea'.[1] For centuries the empire had been softened up by the barbarization of the armies and by alien settlement; and by 406, when the Germans crossed the frozen Rhine, saturation point was reached; they got into Gaul, and could neither be evicted nor assimilated. The western empire began gradually to break down. In warbands often not more than three or four thousand strong, Goths, Visigoths, Vandals and Burgundians from round the Baltic now won vast kingdoms in the richest regions of the south. But, demographically, their fluctuating realms were not important: the reservoir of barbarian manpower remained in the north. Out of it came the Carolingian Empire and its German, Ottonian and Hohenstaufen sequel, the Capet kingdom of France, Anglo-Saxon England, and the far-flung

Scandinavian realms, native and Norman, and Rus as well. Many of the conquerors who crossed the Alps failed to understand the doctrine of the Trinity, and adopted Arian Christianity, but the Franks of Gaul took to Catholicism; Clovis, in 496, made an alliance with Rome. The invaders, whether Arian or Catholic, held the old civilization in awe and eagerly adopted the ancient titles of the empire and the trappings of a Mediterranean way of life.

It was long otherwise in the wilds of Germany and Scandinavia. Here, still prehistoric peoples remained irreconcilable: Harald Fairhair, the first Yngling ruler of Norway, was heathen in the time of Alfred. The Germans of the interior, whose Wagnerian behaviour, roaring into their shields before battle, dying for their leaders, and committing suicide if captured, had early impressed Tacitus, were still vowing their enemies to sacrifice, spoiling their loot and throwing it into swamps to propitiate Woden. Their weapons long remained primitive. The Anglo-Saxons, in the fifth century, though they fought with ten-foot ashen spears and five-foot bows, had little armour, and, for close fighting, only the scramasax, a crude knife. Their boats were horrible craft, about seventy by eleven feet, with no mast, and rowlocks so clumsy that the crews could row only forward. Yet, out of this brutish heathen background, came medieval Christendom. It emerged from the taming of the barbarians and the taming of the land.

This settling-in was decisive. Generations of forest clearing, colonization and peasant agriculture are behind the Carolingian and Ottonian empires, the Capet kingdom and Wessex. The Anglo-Saxons of the Low Countries, from the Scheldt estuary through Holland and Friesland up to the heaths of Jutland in Denmark, came to Britain for land. The pagan calendar they brought with them was already a barbaric record of the farmer's year.* It recalls the interests of all these Germanic peasants who colonized to the east, got into Bohemia, and helped to contain the Magyars in the south; of the Franks, also, of the Rhineland and Burgundy, of Meuse and Marne, of the Ile de France and the Loire.

But the survival and spread of Mediterranean culture in the north was mainly due to the clergy. If towns decayed, roads deteriorated, aqueducts collapsed, harbours silted up, meadows reverted to marsh, the Church carried on. Cassiodorus, who gives so vivid and depressing a picture of his time, served the Arian Gothic King Theodoric at Ravenna. St Isidore (560–635), a contemporary of the brilliant early T'ang Empire in China, transmitted his debased and garbled knowledge as archbishop of Visigothic Seville; the parishes kept the sub-Roman peasantry and converted

---

*The two climatic crises of the year were marked by the winter period of Giulu (Yule), which ran from the beginning of December until the end of January, and by Litha, the double moontide, which covered June and July, the climax of the summer. August was Weodmonath (weed month); September, the Holy Month of Harvest Festivals; October, Winterfylith (winter full moon); November, when the cattle were slaughtered, Blood Month.

barbarians in touch with the official cult. In monasteries, acclimatized from the East, gradually disciplined and humanized by the Rule of St Benedict, chronicles were kept and manuscripts preserved. Byzantine missionaries, as already recorded, were to go out to Khazars, Bulgars and Slavs; Gregory the Great, in 597, sent St Augustine to Kent, and St Birinius, who had come across Anglo-Saxon sailors at Genoa, evangelized Wessex. It was known that England was a promising field.

In Ireland Celtic Christianity had been revivified by St Patrick (432–61); St Columba, by the sixth century, converted the Picts of Scotland. The Irish monasteries had grown up in a tribal society in a country never occupied by Rome; in Dublin remain Celtic crosiers, bells and books, and the leather cases in which their owners hid them from Scandinavian pirates amid the bogs of Killarney or Connaught. At Clanmacnoise Greek was still known, and Irish missionaries evangelized parts of Frankish Gaul: in the early seventh century St Columbanus founded a monastery on the reed-girt peninsula of Reichenau near Konstanz and his tomb is in the northern foothills of the Apennines. The Irish supplemented the drive from Rome – witness the elaborate decoration of the Celtic books, still exhibited along with the neat red Roman scripts at St Gallen.

In time Anglo-Saxon missionaries also helped to control the continental pagans. St Boniface of Crediton, the apostle of the Germans and the first Archbishop of Mainz, founded monasteries in Bavaria, and the great house of Fulda. He was martyred by the Friesians amid the polders at Dokkum in 754.* Such dangers were courted by many missionaries. The cumulative result of their labours, in royal halls and peasants' huts, was the conversion of northern and central Europe. For Catholicism spread among the Poles, the Czechs and the Magyars, while the Slavs and Bulgars looked to Byzantium. By the tenth century, Micsko I of Poland was Christian, the 'good' young Premyslid Duke Wenceslas is still remembered, and the able Magyar ruler, Vajk (985–1038), was canonized as St Stephen.

# III

In the eighth century this expansion of Christendom could hardly have been foreseen. The Saxons of the northern German plain were still militant heathen, the Scandinavians were soon to launch their ferocious and comprehensive attacks, and the western Mediterranean and its islands were

---

* '*Ecce*,' writes his biographer in rudimentary but expressive Latin, '*furens paganorum multitudo cum gladiis omnique infesta armatura super eos irruit eorumque corpora felici caede cruentavit.*' *Vitae Sancti Bonifatii.* ed. W. Levison. Scriptores Rerum Germanicorum (Hanover 1905), p. 210. 'Behold the furious multitude of the heathen, with swords and weapons levelled from all sides, overwhelmed them and massacred their bodies in a fortunate death.' St Boniface defended himself only with a Testament, which was cut clean through; miraculously, though the Saint attained martyrdom, not a letter was destroyed. His assailants, disappointed of booty, and overcome by drink, were soon butchered by the converts of the district.

controlled by Muslims who had overrun North Africa and Spain, and raided to the Loire.

As already observed, they were defeated in 732 by the Frank, Charles Martel, near Poitiers, and the rise of this Frankish power marked the turn of the tide. The Merovingian Clovis had first made Paris his capital and collaborated with Rome: his degenerate and sacred dynasty was supplanted in 751 by Pepin III, whose family came from Metz, Burgundy and the Ardennes. His son, Charlemagne (768–814), created a vast, if ramshackle, empire, and revived the imperial title in the West, calling himself '*Imperator*' and '*Augustus*'.

This empire was to set the political framework of western and central European history. Based on the Rhineland, the Ardennes and northern France, with its main capital at Aachen, it extended across the Alps and the Pyrenees. Charlemagne conquered the Lombards, subdued the Czechs and the Avars, dominated the northern Adriatic. In gruelling campaigns he crushed and converted the Saxons: he first harnessed the might of the Germans for Christendom and his paladins were to be commemorated in the famous twelfth-century *Chanson de Roland*. The titles of his household officials – Seneschal, Constable, Chamberlain, Chancellor – were to be the models of subsequent European courts, and if his dominions lacked the common citizenship and bureaucracy of the old empire, they had a common and militant religion.

Charlemagne's way of life was at once Frankish and sub-Roman. He was a mighty hunter, wore the Frankish tunic, cross-gartered hose and barbarian moustache, but he also followed the Roman cult of warm baths, and the basilica at Aachen is copied from San Vitale at Ravenna; among his treasures is a magnificent cameo of Augustus. His patronage of Alcuin of York, of the Italian Paulus Diaconus, of the Spaniard Theodulphus, of Hrabanus Maurus and Walafrid Strabo created the Carolingian revival. At the palace school at Aachen, Latin grammar and the rudiments of classical and patristic learning were eagerly conned; in the lucid Carolingian script the ancient texts were preserved. 'Devoutly searching the pantries of the holy Fathers,' writes Alcuin, 'I let you taste whatever I have been able to find in them.'

Charlemagne dominated his huge empire through polyglot armies, their nucleus the heavy cavalry, long decisive in battle; coinage was rare and debased, for only Byzantium retained a gold currency, and so they were paid in land. The great magnates became *vassals*, holding *benefices* or *fiefs*; as lesser men *commended* themselves, a complex *feudal* pattern grew up. Only knights, trained from boyhood, could afford the expensive armour, the war horses and skilled retainers. They made up the feudal host, often riddled with the jealousies of arrogant and illiterate barons, but with a heavy, if intermittent, striking power; and it was not for centuries that kings could raise standing armies to enforce the new authority of a 'State', a term unknown to the feudal world. Charlemagne's age saw the rise of a European fighting aristocracy, long powerful and destined to persist, even in its political decline, with all its punctilio and privilege, until the French Revolution and beyond. The *Almanach de Gotha* originated among upstart and barbarous Carolingian Franks.

Charlemagne thus gave a political framework to the settlement of the barbarians and the taming of the land: he towers over western Christendom in the dawn of the Middle Ages. And when on Christmas Day 800, Leo III suddenly, and probably to Charlemagne's annoyance, crowned him 'Emperor of the Romans', the Pope inaugurated a new epoch. The western empire, of course, was regarded as a vulgar imposture in Constantinople, and increased the tension between Byzantium and Rome which was to create an official breach in the middle eleventh century,* but, in spite of latent internal and external conflicts, Charlemagne's military empire, like the original authority of Constantine, had obtained an added prestige.

# IV

The Carolingian dominance soon collapsed into the major divisions of northern Europe. The Strasbourg oath of 842, taken before their respective armies by Charlemagne's grandsons, Louis the German and Charles the Bald, in uncouth German and primitive French, marks 'the first symbolic appearance of the French and German nations. Charles swore: '*Pro Deo amur et pro Christian poblo et nostro commun salvament, d'ist di in avant*'. Louis: '*In Godes minna ind in thes christianes folches ind unser bedhero gehaltnissi, fon thesemo dage framordes*'.[2]

Together in 843, they forced the treaty of Verdun on their elder brother, the Emperor Lothair. Louis took the German territories east of the Rhine; Charles those west of the Meuse, the Saone and the Rhone; Lothair retained a 'Middle Kingdom' which contained the two capitals, Aachen and Rome, and stretched from the duchy of Benevento over the Alps to Burgundy and Provence, and through Lorraine, the Rhineland, and the Low Countries to the sea. But Lotharingia soon dwindled: these rich, but geographically incoherent, territories were to be fought over for generations.

It was with the German inheritors of Charlemagne's eastern dominions that predominance in northern Europe long remained. In the tenth and eleventh centuries, as Sir Richard Southern observes:

. . . the future of Europe might reasonably have appeared to lie in the hands of the kings of Germany. . . . For two hundred and fifty years there was a series of emperors who, whatever their lapses and failures, had no rivals among the secular

---

*The Byzantines objected to the supremacy of Rome, denounced the compulsory celibacy of the clergy, the shaving of beards, instrumental music, and the inadequate western baptism. Only total immersion, they declared, was sufficient.

rulers of Europe for largeness of designs, personal grandeur, and the respect paid to them by their contemporaries. The failure, if it was one, lay in the fact that having too much to hold on to, they slowly lost what they had.[3]

He notes a 'misfiring' of German leadership.

The beneficiaries of this decline, hastened by a conflict of empire and papacy that crippled both institutions, were the French kings; but it is necessary to follow in outline the fortunes of the Germans before turning to the rise of the French, English, Spanish and Scandinavian realms.

The first phase of the empire, under a Saxon dynasty, derived from the exploits of Duke Henry the Fowler against the Magyars. He defeated them on the Unstrutt on the southern borders of Saxony; his son, Otto the Great, so crushed them at Lechfeld near Augsburg in 955 that only seven Magyars escaped, and they had their ears cropped. In the same year he crushed the Wends in Mecklenburg. Elected *Dominus Imperator* at Aachen, he was crowned in Rome in 962 with the great octagonal imperial crown made at Reichenau for the occasion, since known as 'Charlemagne's' and which is still, in all its splendour of well-matched gems, in the Hofburg at Vienna. Like Charlemagne, Otto had to rescue the pope from the vendettas of Rome, and regarded himself, as well he might, as the custodian of the Church.★ Otto II was recognized by Byzantium and married a Byzantine princess, and the youthful Otto III, who was half Greek, in a mood of mystical antiquarianism, opened the tomb of Charlemagne, whom he found 'seated in a certain chair as if he lived'. A romantic idea of empire thus distracted the German rulers from their most pressing task – the creation of a strong realm in Germany. The Salian emperors were also deeply involved in Italy; Henry IV came into conflict with Gregory VII, the great reforming pope inspired with a new conception of a universal papal power. During the notorious 'investiture' struggle, the pope undermined the emperor's ecclesiastical authority in Germany, essential to a government faced by the disaffection of the big tribal duchies. But the excommunicate emperor, after some successful moral blackmail of Gregory VII at Canossa in 1077, forced the pope into a disastrous alliance with the predatory Normans of Sicily.

Under the glamorous Hohenstaufen emperors, when the empire attained its most spectacular prestige, the basic weakness increased. Frederick I Barbarossa (1152–90) attempted to settle Germany with some success. But he, too, was preoccupied with Italy, where he was defeated in 1176 at Legnano by the Lombard League, based on rich, well-irrigated,

★The young Pope John XII hunted, wenched, diced and fought. '*Habebat consuetudinem sepius venandi*,' writes the Chronicler, Benedict of Monte Soracte, in dog-Latin, '*non quasi apostolicus sed quasi homo ferus. . . . Tanta denique libidine sui corporis exarsit quanta nunc [non] possumus enarrare.*' 'He was often in the habit of hunting, not like an apostle but like a wild man of the woods . . . finally, his bodily lust burnt so hot as to beggar description.' Migne, 138, col. 46, Patrologia Latina (quoted by Henry Osborn Taylor, *The Medieval Mind*, II, p. 189).

strong territories and towns. He left his son, Henry VI, whom he had married to the heiress of Norman Sicily, even more deeply involved in the south. His grandson, Frederick II (1211–50), *Stupor Mundi*, the last and most brilliant of his line, was a cosmopolitan Mediterranean tyrant, brought up under Greek and Arab influences, the most versatile, civilized, and interesting ruler of his time. But his genius could not achieve the impossible: in conflict with Innocent III, the greatest of the medieval popes, and with Gregory IX, who destroyed him and lived to be a hundred, even Frederick II failed. By the mid-thirteenth century the first German Reich was a political fiasco.

The French heirs of Charlemagne had slowly consolidated a more manageable realm. Louis VI, in the early twelfth century, based on the Ile de France and the Loire, had been crowned at Rheims in 1131: Philip Augustus (1180–1223) had defeated the Angevins who, based originally on their keep at Angers, striped black and grey, smooth as steel, the most sinisterly functional fortress in the West, had dominated most of western France and Aquitaine: he took Château Gaillard whose white ruins tower above the Seine at Les Andelys, and captured the rich duchy of Normandy. In 1214 he won a great victory at Bouvines over a German, English and Flemish coalition, and gained control of rich towns in Flanders. He left this legacy to St Louis IX (1226–70) who realized a new pattern of monarchy by divine right. He was, at first glance, 'the sort of king who might have stepped out of a stained-glass window'. He was also a shrewd politician. In default of emperor and pope, he became the moral arbiter of the West.

In England, Spain and Scandinavia the pattern of national realms was also set. When King John, the heir to Duke William's conquest of England and to Henry II's consolidation, lost the Angevin dominions in Normandy, along the Loire and in rich Romanized Aquitaine to Philip Augustus, he in fact strengthened the English throne. Edward I concentrated on subduing Scotland and Wales, used his parliaments for administration, buttressed the King's Law. Politically, if not legally, superseded over much of Europe by the fifteenth and sixteenth centuries, in England medieval representative institutions were to survive.

In Scotland the heavy hand of Edward I provoked a dynastic resistance from Robert the Bruce, and popular resistance led by William Wallace: at Bannockburn, in 1314, the independence of the country was achieved.

In the Iberian Peninsula, meanwhile, a Christian counterattack had been launched. Muslim Spain was far more civilized than the hard-bitten kingdoms of Leon and Castile, but Alfonso VI of Castile had reconquered Toledo by 1085; Lisbon was taken in 1147 and the realm of Portugal consolidated; at Las Navas de Tolosa in 1212 came the turning point of the *Reconquisita*, though the Moors long held Granada.

New Christian kingdoms were also formed in Scandinavia. Save in timber and fish, in iron for the axes so important to Scandinavian life, they were comparatively poor, the springboard of far-flung Viking raids and settlements. These countries were now converted, if not pacified, from England and Rus. Haakon of Norway was brought up by Athelstan; Olaf Triggvasson at Kiev.* St Olaf the Stout, converted in England, organized the Norwegian Church. He was slaughtered by the Danes, who emerged into history under Gorm the Old and Harold Bluetooth. They controlled the outlet from the Baltic; Canute of Denmark and England created an empire. Though it proved ephemeral, Waldemar the Great (1157–82) founded Copenhagen, and Waldemar Sejr – the Victorious – defeated the Esthonians in 1219, when the Dannebrog standard fell from heaven on to the battlefield, an auspicious event commemorated by the oldest Danish Order of Chivalry. Roskilde Cathedral, the burial place of the Danish kings, dates from the twelfth century. The Swedes, or Svear, long held to paganism. In 829 the Frankish Ansgar, later bishop of Hamburg, had visited the country, but his mission had failed; and, although, by AD 1000, Olaf Scötkonung, 'the first Swedish king about whom anything is known',[4] was a Christian, when Adam of Bremen (c. 1070) described the country round lake Maleren, nine-yearly human sacrifice was still being perpetrated at Uppsala – 'as well as men, dogs and horses are strung up in that place'.[5] The main Swedish initiative was to the East: King Sverker was campaigning against Rus in 1130, and in 1167 Knut, the son of Eric the Saint, built a. fort on the site of Stockholm. Adam of Bremen depicts a flourishing country; 'the Swedish contempt for ostentation, and their moderation in all matters save that of their numerous wives; and he praises, too, their lavish hospitality'.[6] There was already an ancient tradition that the will of the folk expressed in the *Ting* was decisive: by the Västergötland law 'the Swedes may take a king but they may also depose him'. By 1250 the Ericsson kings were replaced by the Folkung dynasty, who were to rule until 1363, ten years before the death in Rome of St Birgitta, Sweden's most famous and attractive saint, founder of the Birgittine order. Scandinavia and the Baltic shores thus became Christian; Poles, Czechs and Hungarians, as already observed, were converted, and German power consolidated in Vienna, when Henry Jasomirgott, the first Babenberg Duke of Austria, obtained his Charter of Privilege from Barbarossa. While Byzantium, until 1204, remained incomparable, the western peoples had reasserted, and greatly extended, the Christian culture of the south, created the political framework of new realms and launched counterattacks in Spain, along the Baltic, and even in Palestine.

---

*When he brought Christianity to Nidaros, 'the heathen men said, it was no wonder they had ill weather that autumn; it was all the King's new fangledness and the new law that had made the Gods angry'. W. P. Ker, *Epic and Romance*, p. 378.

Of these crusades the most famous were the least fruitful. While Spain and the Baltic were held, the feudal realms of Outremer never took proper root. In the long run the Palestinian crusades were politically a failure; they had at first succeeded only through the conflict of Seljuqs and Fatimids. As already described, in 1204 the crusaders wrecked Byzantium and let the Turks into the Balkans; at best, along with the Mongol threat to the Ottomans, they proved spoiling attacks. But they brought the West into closer touch with the superior civilization of Byzantium and Islam, enriched Venice, Genoa, Pisa and Amalfi, and if most crusaders, save those few who went native, were indifferent to eastern culture, the Palestinian crusades left their social mark in the 'gothic' arch, heraldry, military architecture and civil dress.

This stimulus was only one aspect of a wide expansion of horizons. By the twelfth century the beginnings of the main nations of Europe had emerged out of sub-Roman decadence, all with their royal folk heroes, still remembered, and with a new economic and intellectual life.

# V

Carolingian society had been almost entirely rural. The turn of the seasons dominated all men's lives and, until the Industrial Revolution, the vast majority of Europeans were peasants. Cut off from North African granaries by the Muslims, scarified by Viking pirates, battered by Hungarians who penetrated even to Burgundy and Provence, western and central Europe had been reduced almost to a subsistence economy. By the twelfth century, not only had many ancient Roman cities revived, but new towns were flourishing in northern Italy, in the Rhineland, in France and Flanders, along the Baltic and on the Atlantic seaboard. This transformation had come about since the agricultural basis of society had proved invulnerable. The Iron Age barbarians of Germany had at least invented the *caruca*, the wheeled ox-drawn plough, or *pflug*, able to work the heavy soils of the north. Peasant villages, where yearly one of the great common fields lay fallow, housed a growing population which spread out as local woodlands were cleared and drained, or as new lands were opened up in the northern German plain beyond the Elbe. On this village life, which went back time out of mind, the manor, the economic basis of feudalism, had been superimposed. The peasants were often glad of a protector on any terms; without manpower the lords could not exploit their demesnes. Whether in the huge scattered possessions of a rich abbey or barony, or in the poor holding of some knight of Brittany or Auvergne, agriculture was deeply conservative, but by the tenth century a greater surplus was coming in. In the Mediterranean countries vine and olive cultivation had continued: on terraced slopes every inch of soil was still cultivated. Here, always, had been wealth and manpower: the barbarians had not gone south merely for the climate.

So, by the tenth century, the population of western Europe had begun to increase: it went on increasing until the end of the thirteenth. The process which had ruined the towns of the later empire and depressed the rural cultivators into serfdom on huge estates was now reversed. The peasants began to break out of the conservative framework of the manor, which had grown up under an almost subsistence economy. The reclamation of the land between Meuse and Loire, the draining and dyking of the polders of the Low Countries, the spread of planned colonization beyond the Elbe, meant, in time, more labour. Old cities revived, and new ones were founded. In the south many ancient towns had preserved the crowded life of antiquity, and the northern Italian plain, in particular, had remained relatively prosperous. Venice, originally founded for refuge among the lagoons, had early traded with Constantinople; the routes over the Brenner, and over the Semmering through Carinthia and Styria, carried luxuries between Venice and southern Germany, Salzburg and Vienna. The trade route into Burgundy through the passes of the western Alps, led, by Dijon, to Rheims and the great fairs of Champagne, long the greatest focus of commerce in western Europe. The Rhineland was always a highway, in spite of the predatory barons, whose turreted castles still dominate the river. Genoa, Pisa and Marseilles profited from the crusades, while Naples and Palermo felt the Norman stimulus. The wine trade through Bordeaux and La Rochelle to Southampton and Flanders, and the wool trade from the Cotswolds, Lincolnshire and Yorkshire met the trade in corn, tar and timber, cordage, fur and herrings out of the Baltic at Bruges, then a great sea port where Italian bankers were established.

In the north fortunes were made in ivory, seal-skins and salt fish.* Ship-building flourished at Hamburg, Lubeck and Southampton, as well as in Venice and Genoa. Their ocean-going ships were already more seaworthy than Mediterranean galleys.

By the twelfth century there were also great centres of commerce and manufacture not only in northern Italy but in Flanders, where the new textile industries of Arras, Ghent and Ypres exploited English wool and exported their cloth over most of the continent; the tenuous luxury trade of the early Middle Ages gave place to commerce on credit. The Jews at first supplied it, since their chances of salvation were not compromised by usury, and kings could squeeze them 'like sponges'; but they were now

---

*One way of getting a trading ship was to present some great king with a polar bear or a falcon. 'It is not generally known,' writes T. J. Olson, 'how eagerly the princes of Europe desired to possess polar bears, nor that the Icelanders, and their compatriots in Greenland, trapped these animals and, by presenting them to kings, gained royal favour.' Many of these bears, together with the American white falcon, came from Arctic America. Rulers competed in lavish generosity in return for them. It was a good speculation to sell out to get a bear, if in return one got an ocean-going ship. See T. J. Olson: 'Polar Bears in the Middle Ages', *Canadian Historical Review*, XXXI (1950), p. 47ff.

increasingly displaced by Florentine, Genoese and Lombard money-changers, who kept cash on a bench (*in banco*) and financed, at necessarily exorbitant interest, the heavy risks of medieval commerce, the adventures of insolvent kings, and the vast building projects of the Church.

# VI

It was long before the bourgeois could compete with the Church – the other traditional centre of order. Monks and missionaries had done their work; the rudiments of civilization had been preserved and the heathen brought into Christendom; now the canalized impulse of the northern peoples was behind the clergy. By the eleventh century the authority of Rome had greatly increased. Christianity, like Buddhism and Islam, crossed all boundaries; the popes claimed a wide spiritual authority. 'Mine is the God-given power to bind and loose,' said Gregory VII; for Innocent III, the great administrator and statesman, the papal power was a 'two-edged sword, sharper than any other, which flashes from sea to sea as the eye sweeps over the sea at one view'. Innocent IV even claimed to be *Dominus naturalis* in things temporal as well as spiritual. Rome, too, became the ultimate court of appeal in canon law, the best-conducted centre of legal business in the West – not simply a place of pilgrimage, as it had been for King Alfred, or even Canute. Under the old empire, all citizens had been subject to Roman law; since its disintegration, the barbarians, subject to their own tribal customary law, had broken this union; but the Church had restored a universal law for the clergy long before the revival of Roman law penetrated into lay society.

The popes also became immensely rich. Behind them stood the whole hierarchy of archbishops, abbots and bishops, based on broad lands and accumulated wealth, and sanctioned by excommunication and interdict. This grandeur was in part based on terror. Medieval religion was sombre, obsessed with hell; nothing else could have induced barbarous feudatories to endow the clergy and thick-headed peasants to work for them. The lurid windows at Strasbourg, the writhing sculpture at Autun, innumerable frescoed Dooms in churches up and down Europe, appalled the laity; the clergy were reminded of the penalties of sin by St Bernard's terrifying and sonorous eloquence.*

The Church monopolized knowledge. Though most kings and barons long despised learning, and thought it beneath them to write, regarding the literate as low-born technicians paid to do a sedentary task, the Church, like the Chinese bureaucracy, provided careers for talent. Men of humble family might rise to be great bishops and abbots; the clergy, officially

---

* '*Paveo Gehennem, paveo judicis vultum . . . contremisco ab ira potentis, a facie furoris ejus, a fragore ruentis mundi, a conflagratione elementorum, a tempestate valida, a voce archangeli, et a verbo aspero.*' A passage worth reading aloud. Henry Osborn Taylor, *The Medieval Mind*, II, p. 197.

celibate, were recruited through new universities. The command of colloquial Latin – a vivid language in its own right, different from that of the upper classes in antiquity – was the passport to a cosmopolitan world of formal disputation, leisured study and artful intrigue.

By 1158, the students of Bologna, next to Salerno the oldest medieval university, were sharpening their wits on Roman law; the universities of Paris, Naples, Oxford, Salamanca, Cambridge and Coimbra, in that order, were incorporated by the thirteenth century. By 1362 Cracow was inaugurated; four years later, Vienna; Heidelberg and Cologne in 1386 and 1388; St Andrews in 1412. They were organized in *faculties* of Arts, Theology, Canon Law and misguided medicine. Universities, all over the world, have been modelled on these medieval institutions: they became the centres of a vigorous intellectual life, sometimes brilliant within its strange convention. Abelard (1079–1142) had used a new '*dialectic*': not content with merely citing the Fathers, or drawing far-fetched analogies from them, he would set one authority against another – *sic et non* – and incite 'young readers to search out the truth . . . and render them the sharper for the investigation. For the first key to wisdom is called interrogation.'

The Cluniac revival of the eleventh century and the Cistercian order, launched by St Bernard, had put new life into many monasteries. The Franciscan friars, founded by the most attractive of medieval saints to combat the wealth and pride of the clergy, and the Dominicans, founded to combat heresy, stimulated the universities. St Thomas Aquinas (1226–74), who came of German nobility settled in southern Italy, was a Dominican. He assimilated newly discovered works of Aristotle into Christian thought in vast *Summae*, covering systematically all aspects of life. He was, and remains, the master mind of the Catholic Church.

The strictness and clarity of scholastic discipline – different from the half-baked piled-up quotations and allegories of the Dark Ages – was reflected in an elegant new architecture. The Romanesque of the Rhineland and of southern and western France, had been diversified, as at Poitiers, by pointed turrets and novel sculpture; and the massive columns of Durham, Norwich and Winchester had their own magnificence; but the barrel vaults and the round-topped, deep-set windows were still Roman. The sharp-cut Gothic arches, the flying buttresses, the immense height, the reduction of the walls to a framework for the blaze of stained glass, as in the Sainte Chapelle in Paris, are original. The size and virtuosity of these cathedrals, the most obvious memorials of the more brilliant phase of medieval civilization in the West, are fantastic in relation to the rustic society which produced them; and the superb glass and sculptures of Chartres are comparable to the best work of the Greeks, the Indians or the Chinese, having the simplicity and calm of the greatest art. This fine taste is also apparent in the blue-enamelled Limoges chalices, in ivories and illuminated manuscripts.

# VII

The laymen remained fiercely martial. The division of classes into those who fight, those who pray and those who till the soil, though not as rigid as the caste system of India, long remained strict, though ability in war and learning could break it. But the brutality of William the Conqueror's knights, their heads crew-cut at the back to take the conical helmets, had given place by the time of St Louis to a cult of chivalry within the knightly class. This custom, paralleled most vividly in Japan, derived in part from the barbarian practice of ceremonially investing a young warrior with arms, now consecrated by the Church. Knighthood was not then hereditary, but won by prowess. Practice fell far short of the ideal, but excesses were mitigated; prisoners held for ransom, not massacred; and the ferocity of the barons in the brief periods between wars was sublimated in tournaments, general organized mêlées, which became formal jousts in the later Middle Ages. The ideal ruler, as among the Muslims, was extravagant, courteous, impeccably brave. Impulsive acts of generosity were much admired.

The education of a baron was almost entirely practical; the art of managing a war-horse, charging with a heavy lance, and handling a great cutting sword when encumbered with thick leather, ringed steel and a kite-shaped shield, needed early training and constant practice. They had plenty to do: when not making war or carousing, they could hunt.

The Teutonic peoples also had a very ancient tradition of epic poetry, recited in the mead-hall on winter nights:

> Over the ale he speaks, seeing the ring,
> The old warrior who remembers all.

The epics were monotonous, rambling, with flashes of high poetry. The most ancient recalled a whole Nordic mythology, since neglected for Mediterranean myths, and glorified loyalty and endurance. The grand, if hackneyed, lines of the Anglo-Saxon *Song of Maldon* sum up this morality:

> Thought shall be the harder, heart the keener,
> Mood the more, as our might lessens.

Out of the same pagan background as the ninth century German *Hildebrandslied* and the Anglo-Saxon *Beowulf*, were to come the romantic Christian Old French and Spanish *Chansons de Gestes* and the grim Icelandic sagas.

The *Chansons* became fashionable in the early twelfth century, sung to the rhythmic notes of a primitive violin. The two most famous are the *Chanson de Roland*, and *El Cantar de Mio Cid* (*c.* 1140). The former, which commemorates events three centuries old, is a tale of Carolingian battle and tragedy, of '*la duler pur la mort de Rollant*'. The Spanish epic records the exploits of the Lord (*Sayid*) Rodrigo de Bivar, a Castilian knight of the early *Reconquista*. Both glorify muscular Christianity, and the former is touched with a feeling for landscape.

The Icelandic sagas, on the other hand, are entirely matter of fact. They express, writes W. P. Ker, 'clear intelligence applied under a dry light to subjects that are themselves primitive such as have never before or since been represented in the same way . . . the record is that of dispassionate observers'.[7] The earliest Scandinavian literature is contained in the twelfth century *Poetic* (or *Elder*) *Edda*; in the thirteenth century Snorri Sturlasson collected the prose *Edda* and compiled the *Heimskringla*, lives of the early Norse kings. The most famous of the sagas are the *Njala*, the *Laxdaela* and the tale of *Egil Shallagrimson*. They are prose epics about real people, written down in the late twelfth and early thirteenth centuries. They showed shrewd insight into character: 'Fair enough is this maid . . . but I know not whence thief's eyes have come into our race.' There is also a laconic fatalism: 'What broke there so loud?' said Olaf, as his best archer's bow was split; 'Norway, King, from thy hand.'[8]

The *Chansons de Gestes* were recited by wandering *jongleurs*. The troubadours of Aquitaine and Provence, who invented French lyric poetry, were dandified, rather precious, courtiers. They devised the *ballade*, the *aubade*, the *rondel*. By the thirteenth century the *trouvères* of northern France were popularizing a cult of courtly love, unknown in antiquity, which was gradually to filter down through society, to make the status of European women different from that usual in most other civilizations. The most elaborate and influential poem which popularized this romantic cult was the *Romain de la Rose* of Guillaume de Lorris (1237):

Ci est lo Romanz de la Rose.
Où l'art d'amor est tote enclose.

The German court poets took up the theme, which they embellished with much sentiment: by 1170 the Austrian Dietmar von Aist was writing:

Dû bist beslozzen
In mînen herzen;[9]

and the celebrated Walther von der Vogelweide announced the theme of many a *lieder* when he wrote:

Under der linden
An der heide
dâ unser zweier bette was,
. . . Schône sanc diu Nahtegal.[10]

Another aspect of Teutonic life was expressed by the thirteenth-century German-Swiss poet, Steihmar, who sings:

Minen Slunt ich prise
Mich würget niht ein grozin gans
So ich slinde.★

In Italy vernacular poetry began at the splendid court of the Emperor
Frederick II, who wrote verse himself as well as his famous treatise on
falconry. Salimbene describes his entourage at Pisa: 'A crowd of young
people playing harps and violins, while the others danced and sang to the
music and the rest stood looking on, holding on leash leopards and other
strange beasts from across the sea.'[11] 'The illustrious heroes, Frederick
Caesar and his noble son, Manfred,' wrote Dante, 'followed after elegance
and scorned what was mean, so that all the best compositions of the time
came from his court.' The emperor's illegitimate son, Enzio, a prisoner at
Bologna, wrote one of the earliest lyrics in Italian:

Salutemi Toscana-quella ched è sovrana
in cui regna tutta cortezia.
e vanne in Puglia piana-la magna Capitana
là dov'è lo mio core notte' e dia.†

The French cult of *la gloire* and *l'amour*, Spanish martial pride, Anglo-
Saxon tenacity and moralizing, Scandinavian realism and gloom, German
sentiment and grossness, Italian elegance and observation – all these are
recognizable by the thirteenth century, with the dawn out of the Dark
Ages, through the Carolingian revival, and the twelfth-century renaissance, of vernacular national cultures in the West.

★'I am proud of my gullet: I could swallow a goose without choking.'
†Salute for me Tuscany, who is queen of all
  Where courtesy reigns,
  Go to the plains of Puglia – the great Capitana
  There where my heart is, night and day.

# Twelve

# THE HEARTLAND OF ASIA: CHINA: INDIA

## I

When, in 1228, Dmitry Donskoi had been defeated by the Mongols on the Volga and, twelve years after, Kiev had been sacked, the Russians met a new version of a familiar menace. But when, in 1241, the Polish and German knights were routed at Liegnitz in Silesia and the Hungarians at Mohi, and when, that winter, the Mongol cavalry crossed the ice on the Danube and threatened Vienna, there was panic in western Christendom. The Mongols, through spies, knew a good deal about the West; save for vague memories of Attila, the Catholic Christians did not know what had hit them. Then, in 1242, the Great Khan, Ogatai, son of Genghis Khan, died at Karakorum, and Batu Khan who commanded the horde in Europe, returned to base. Though the results of the invasion were serious for Muscovy, for the West it proved a flick of the tail.

The steppe which stretches into Asia from the Hungarian plain beyond the Carpathians into southern Russia and, between the Urals and the Caspian, to Turkestan, extends onwards to the Kazakh uplands between lake Balkash and to the mountains of the Altai. It then rises through Zungaria between the Altai and Tianshan, and sweeps north-east above the Gobi, through Mongolia, to the western tributaries of the Amur, which curves south into Mongolia and on to the Pacific near Sakalin. From Samarkand and Tashkent, across the Pamirs to Kashgar, a more southern route leads from Turkestan to the Tarim basin and the plateau of Sinkiang. In this belt of steppe, with its vast prospects and fierce extremities of climate, between the northern coniferous forest and the immense mountains which rise to Tibet, lived the Mongols, the Tatars and the various tribes of Turks.★

Out of what Palaeolithic and Mesolithic hunting cultures they emerged is still mysterious. They were nomads who periodically abandoned their

---

★The term 'Tartar' is medieval. 'The name *Tatar,* borne by one tribe of the Mongol confederacy, reminded the Christians of *Tartarus,* the hell of classical mythology and they referred to the whole diabolical brood as *Tartars.' The Travels of Marco Polo,* trsl. and introduced by R. E. Latham (Harmondsworth 1958), p. xi. The Asian name is, therefore, *Tatar*; the Christian version means, roughly, 'Hellhound'.

seasonal, and circular migrations over tribal pastures to irrupt into the civilized lands. Here they would loot and massacre, and sometimes found great or petty dynasties which became acclimatized to the native culture, Confucian, Muslim or Hindu. They could best attack China from Mongolia through Kansu in the north-west, down the valley of the Yellow River; they could invade India by Kabul and the Khyber, and swoop down on Mesopotamia through Iran; they could assault Byzantium through Syria, whence they could strike at Egypt, or, as the Seljuqs in the campaign of Manzikert, and the Ottoman Turks after them, direct through Anatolia. And the way into southern Russia and the Hungarian plain was easy.

But China was the main Mongol objective. To nomads who spent most of their lives in the saddle and who could devote years to a campaign, great distances were no deterrent. Only two things stopped them: northern or tropical forest and the sea. They never entirely wrecked Muscovy; they failed to subdue Cambodia and Java, and, as already observed, Kublai Khan's attack on Kamakura Japan was a fiasco.

Attila's assault in the fifth century had been their earliest recorded deep invasion of the West, part of their first great wave of expansion, as Batu Khan's raid to the Elbe and the Danube was to be part of their second. It will be recalled that the Chinese emperor, Shih Huang Ti, in the third century BC, had built the Great Wall of China, 'to keep out the Tatars'; that the Han emperors had 'lit beacons of war' far into Sinkiang to outflank the nomads, and even sent an army to the 'Parthian Sea'. In spite of this counteroffensive, the Hsung Niu ('Huns') had overrun northern China, and had only been prevented from conquering the south by their defeat at Fei Shui in AD 387. In northern India the White Huns had smashed the most creative phase of Hindu civilization when they broke the Gupta Empire, which had produced the writings of Kalidasa and the best Ajanta art. At the other end of Eurasia, the Huns had invaded Transylvania and, two generations after, Attila had threatened Orleans and had only in AD 451 been held at Troyes. He even invaded northern Italy, sacked Padua and drove the Venetians to the lagoons. But with his death his domination had collapsed.

Attila had invaded Europe when the western Roman Empire was in dissolution; seven centuries later, when the second major upheaval took place in Eurasia, thirteenth-century civilization was at its height; yet the invaders still had the advantage, and the feudatories put up less of a fight than the Romanized Gauls, Franks and Visigoths.

The superior Mongol strategy and tactics were due to the organizing genius of the most successful artist in destruction in medieval world history. Genghis – the Inflexible – Khan (1162–1227), the son of a petty chieftain in Outer Mongolia, had fought his way to supreme power through frightful vicissitudes.★ He had founded a dynasty which was to conquer the whole of China, subjugate central Asia and southern Russia, raid India, devastate Mesopotamia and rule Iran. Nor was the Mongol aggression the end of the assault from central Asia. It was followed by the Turki invasion of northern India by the Muslim Timur Lenk (Tamberlane) in the late fourteenth century; by the conquest of Byzantium and the Balkans by the Ottomans; and by the foundation of the Mughal Empire in India by the Turki Babur, a descendant both of Tamberlane and of Genghis Khan. Add to this the Seljuq domination of Egypt and much of the Middle East, and the Turki sultanates in Mesopotamia and Iran, and it will be apparent how decisive for the surrounding civilized peoples were these experts in war out of the heartland of Eurasia.

# II

Of all the central Asian nomads the Mongols were the most ferocious. Alien to Europe, as Europeans to the East; flat-faced, slant-eyed, with shaven heads and sparse beards, their hair coiled behind their ears, they wore felt, skins, and armour of tanned and lacquered hide. The primitive Mongols refused, on principle, 'to wash or bathe from the cradle to the grave';[1] they were 'extremely addicted to alcohol',[2] and kept wives by the dozen – Genghis Khan had five hundred. These customs might be taken, in the central Asian Middle Ages, for granted, but their blood-lust horrified peoples hardened in the normal vicissitudes of conquest. They would destroy whole towns since it annoyed them to see buildings; they despised all agriculturalists as vermin: 'Who would want,' they asked, 'to support themselves on top of a weed?' Genghis Khan was only dissuaded from massacring the entire peasantry of northern China, so that the land could return to pasture, by the intervention of Yelu Chu' Ts'ai, a Sinified Khitan in his employment, who, at some risk, explained that, if the Chinese were left alive, they could pay enormous tribute in kind.

The Mongols were professional soldiers: they were not allowed to do any other work. Their armies were not the chaotic hordes of popular imagination, but well-disciplined cavalry, skilled in manoeuvre. Their

---

★ His original name was Temujin, and his title is spelt by various authorities in various styles – Jenghis, Genghis, Gencis, Chinqis, or Cingis-qan. His background was entirely pastoral and nomadic, and he would use hunting as an occasion of diplomacy. For example, when seeking alliance with the Taiciuts, the line of the beats of the two tribes happening to coincide, he had the game driven towards them 'et leur en laissa capturer une grande quantité, jusqu'a satieté'. This initiative proved vain, but in general, his rise was extraordinarily rapid, vanquished or outmanoeuvred tribes submitting 'like horses without pastures'. See P. Pelliot and L. Hambis, *Histoire des Campagnes de Gencis Khan, Cheng-won Ts'in – Tcheng Lou* (Leiden 1951), p. 141ff. The Mongol armies were organized on the decimal system, their *Toumans* running from 10,000 to 10. They had arrows suited to different ranges in separate quivers, and never charged home until their opponents were demoralized by their fire, which could be supplemented by pack artillery – light catapults and mangonels. Since they were all mounted, the problems of coordinating cavalry and infantry tactics did not arise, and their mobility far surpassed that of their enemies: hence their successes, often against superior numbers.

standards, or *'tughs'*, were triangular black and white pennants hung with yaks' tails, used for signalling in battle. Before action they would sprinkle them with ritual *kumiz* (fermented mare's milk), rattle their drums, raise their war shout and then encircle the enemy in sinister silence, racing in to loose their arrows at full gallop; drawing off to renew the attack. The most honourable post was on the right wing, and each contingent had its coordinated objective. They learnt siege warfare from the Chinese and if, Genghis Khan decreed, any city, summoned to surrender, offered the slightest resistance, it would be razed and all its inhabitants, men, women and children, massacred. These instructions were faithfully carried out; the Mongols particularly liked to make a fine pyramid of skulls.

On the other hand, like the Goths and Vikings, they fell greedily on the luxuries of civilization. By the mid-thirteenth century the nomadic life of the leaders had become opulent. They soon became adept in collecting taxes, and in organizing swift communications throughout their dominions. They owned enormous herds of cattle, sheep, camels and goats, and their tents were of white or black felt, the former sometimes treated with white soil or powdered bones to make it shine. The Tatar magnates wore furs and brocade, and their households moved slowly over the steppe after the pasturing herds, with long trains of ox carts which transported their tents and goods.[3] If the tents of the ordinary wolfish tribesmen – the reservoir of the armies – were as squalid as those in other nomad encampments, the arrogant chieftains who served Ogatai and Mangu Khan already disposed of great wealth. The habits of nomad predation, with its alternating austerity and surfeit, continued to haunt the highest circles, even at the court of Kublai Khan. Observers recorded 'the constant drinking, both in public and in private, which kept Kublai in a constant state of alcoholic inebriation. It was the national vice of the Mongols. Chingis Khan, the dynasty's founder . . . had attempted to curb its excesses; but Ogudai, his son and successor, and a world conqueror, too, came at last to *delirium tremens* . . . and Chingis' grandson Mangu, his brother, led a life *inter pocula.*'[4]

In spite of these habits, when the Mongols achieved their supreme objective, the conquest of all China, it took only three generations of settled, centralized power to transform the royal family of Genghis Khan into sophisticated aesthetes, the centre of a vast palace bureaucracy, ruling the greatest empire on earth. The Mongol peace also enabled Europeans to travel widely in Asia, and their tolerance permitted many Christian trading ventures and missions.

## III

It will be recalled that in China the brilliant T'ang regime had been succeeded, after a phase of confusion, by the Sung dynasty (960–1127), founded by the astute Chao Kuang-yin. The powerful Sung emperors had become the most pacific and civilized of rulers. Chen Tsung, the son of the founder, reinforced his authority not by the sword, but by obtaining 'messages from heaven': though disbelieved by the *literati*, they were widely accepted by the populace. Shen Tsung (1068–85) had even tried to alleviate the condition of the debt-ridden but prolific peasantry. His adviser, Wang An-shih, unpopular with the conservatives, was relegated during most of his career to provincial sinecures (officials thus rusticated were known as 'sleeping dragons'), but Shen Tsung imposed new laws. By the Law of the Green Shoots peasants could borrow from the government, rather than from money-lending landlords, on the security of the spring crops: by the Law of Remission of Services forced labour could be commuted for a tax; by the Law of Exact Measurements cheating over landmarks was mitigated; state pawnshops and a capital gains tax on the value of property were devised: the emperor even declared that 'he regarded the welfare of the masses as more important than the profit of the gentry'. Further the militia was better organized; every two families had to provide a spearman; in the north, each family a horse, for only cavalry could resist the nomads. These measures failed to defend the empire from the Ch'in, but in 1124 the population of Sung China was probably a hundred million.

Intellectually, too, the age was remarkable. In face of stiff opposition, an elaborate neo-Confucian orthodoxy was formulated which was to shape Chinese thought until the thirteenth century. Chu Hsi (1130–1200), using the ancient Confucian text, the *I Ching* (Book of Changes), gave the old teaching a more exact content. The new Confucianism was austerely ethical: if there was 'no Man,' said Chu Hsi, 'in Heaven judging sin', there was still a valid moral law. For man is by nature superior: evil is the result, not of original sin, but of an *Interruption of Harmony*.

The Sung Empire also saw the development of a famous old Chinese industry, already established under the T'ang. A monochrome, pale blue Kuan porcelain was first made in the imperial factories in the reign of the artist-emperor, Hui Tsung, who spent much time tea-tasting and judging art competitions, in the days, by English reckoning, of William Rufus and Henry I.

These amenities were rudely interrupted. In 1125 Tungus Ju-chen tribesmen from the north defeated the Khitans who had been encroaching on the empire, and drove them westward, far into Turkestan. Here some of them became Nestorian Christians and gave rise to the first legend of Prester John, afterwards transferred to Abyssinia. Having disposed of the Khitans, the Ju-chen, who called themselves the Ch'in (golden) dynasty, overran much of northern China. They captured the tea-tasting emperor and, in 1130, invaded the valley of the Yangtze. But the Sung now rallied; they recaptured the vital Yangtze territories, and in southern China their prosperous and pacific empire carried on. 'The foundation of the new dynasty,' writes Eberhard, 'was a relatively easy matter . . . for the south had already been economically supreme, and the great families that had ruled the state were virtually all from the south. . . . Thus the transition . . . was not of fundamental importance.'⁵ Southern Sung China, or Nan Sung (1127–1279), always had a teeming population, rich agriculture, good communications and great cities; it traded with Malaya, Indonesia, India and the Arabs of Aden, the Yemen and Zanzibar. But the Northern Chinese Empire had been softened-up before the Mongol attack.

In 1210 Genghis Khan struck. By 1215, the year of Magna Carta, he began to destroy the Ch'in domination; then Peking was sacked, the northern and most ancient areas of Chinese civilization in Honan were so devastated that they took centuries to recover; Kansu and Shensi, the centres of the Han and T'ang, were wrecked. By 1234 the Mongols had conquered the Ch'in empire. In 1273 the Mongols moved into the south; they systematically invaded and mastered the rich and massive southern Sung territories. By 1279, Kublai Khan (1260–94), had brought the old dynasty to an inglorious end. He became emperor of all China and moved his capital down from Karakorum to Peking, the first foreign conqueror to rule the whole of China. Peking in the north, at the expense of the Sung cities, now became the centre of a gigantic and united empire, of a cosmopolitan bureaucracy, of commerce and religion, for the Mongols took the Buddhism and Taoism to which they were converted more seriously than did the neo-Confucian Chinese élite. Temples and monasteries were endowed; Peking was transformed, by forced labour, into a city of unprecedented wealth and splendour. All this apparent prosperity masked grave economic decline; the currency was soon debased, and excessive taxation and the demands of the privileged classes – as well as of about a million Mongols – fell hard on the peasantry, and gave rise to a series of proletarian revolts during the fourteenth century, which undermined the Mongol régime.

But to Marco Polo, Kublai Khan appeared a tremendous potentate, living in splendour in a five-gated palace, behind white, battlemented walls. It had a fine, columned gallery; inside, it was covered with gold and silver and 'decorated with pictures of dragons and birds and horsemen and various breeds of beasts and scenes of battle'. Its great hall could contain six thousand persons, and the roof was 'all ablaze with scarlet and green and blue and yellow and all the colours that there are, so brilliantly varnished that it glitters like crystal, and the sparkle of it can be seen from far away'. This palace was also an arsenal, with buildings which housed each kind of munition. 'Thus, one contains saddles, bridles and stirrups. . . . In another are bows, bow strings, quivers, arrows and other requisites of archery. In a third are cuirasses, corselets, and other armour of boiled leather.'

The Mongol conquest was not without some immediate benefits. The Sung Empire, ruled by bureaucrats recruited by elaborate examinations in the Chinese classics, had become more than usually conservative. The invasions at least created social change: foreigners were admitted to the administration; there were new openings for talent; to the court of the Great Khan came travellers and envoys from all over the East. There was a widening of horizons. It is significant that the anonymous Yüan plays, which first made the stage so important in China, became popular in the mid-thirteenth century. Written in vernacular idiom, without scenery, but with elaborate conventionalized make-up and costume, enlivened by acrobatic ballets and with the female characters played by boys, these plays began a lasting tradition. China in the thirteenth century was still a united and creative civilization, and besides being the Son of Heaven, Kublai was paramount Khan over the largest land empire in world history, extending from the eastern Mediterranean to the China Sea, from Siberia to the Persian Gulf.

His descendants, the Yüan emperors, soon became enervated and there were widespread popular revolts. Great famines struck the population; an increasing surge of Chinese national feeling was aggravated by class hatred. By 1368 the dynasty came to an end, when the Emperor Togan Timur was hounded from China by Chu Yüan-chang, a peasant-born adventurer who had seized Nanking and attempted, with conscious archaism, to revive the T'ang Empire. Having mastered the south, his armies struck northwards, destroyed Karakorum, and founded the Ming Empire which included both northern and southern China and, by the early fifteenth century, again had the capital at Peking. Like the Han, which had first created a centralized empire, the Ming dynasty was founded by a native Chinese of peasant origin. Here the Ming emperors built the famous Forbidden City in the early fifteenth century, by English reckoning in the reign of Henry v. The Ming dynasty was to last until 1644, a rich and elaborate period of Chinese culture. The Mongol régime had centralized the empire through a network of garrisons and couriers; the native Ming dynasty inherited the organization, and the Chinese, having again absorbed their conquerors, remained the dominant fact of the Far East.

# IV

In 1239 the Mongols had attacked a country hitherto understandably immune from invasion. At an average height of more than 15,000 feet – even the valleys are seldom below 12,000 – they found the enormous Tibetan plateau, which its peculiar inhabitants called Bod. They were mainly descended from tribesmen who had originally been sheep breeders in the region of modern Szechwan on the upper Yangtze, and related to the Tunaguts, with Turki and Mongol affinities. These ancestors had played an important part in the fluctuating politics of western China before the establishment of the Han, so that from very early times they had influenced and been influenced by Chinese civilization. The nearest thing to a government was the Sa Skya Pandita, abbot of the Sa Skya lamassary.

Tibet had long been a refuge of Indian Mahayana Buddhism. Back in the seventh century, Srong bTsan sgampo had established a paramountcy over the tribes. He had conquered parts of western China, northern Burma and Nepal, married both a Chinese and a Nepalese Buddhist princess, and introduced Buddhist missionaries, who combated the animistic native religion known as Bon. On his death in AD 650 the Chinese had taken Lhasa, but, in the next century, the Tibetans had heavily counterattacked. Under Khri Srong lDe bTsan (755–95), who exacted tribute from China and raided Shensi, the Indian Padmasambhava, still venerated in Tibet, had founded the lamassary of Bsam yas: a script based on Sanskrit had been introduced and Buddhist scriptures translated. Atíśa (982–1058), a holy man from Bengal, long to be commemorated in Tibetan art, had also reinforced the Buddhist influence. By the eleventh century the monks had overcome the lay rulers; the only organization in the country, through which it could be taxed, was theocratic, and so vigorous was Tibetan religion – a version of Buddhism now combined with native beliefs – that the lama 'Phags-pa won much reputation at the court of Kublai Khan, where he was appointed ruler of all Tibet and invited to devise an alphabet for the Mongolian language. It proved impracticable.

By 1380, a reformer, Tsong ka-pa, whose symbols are the book and the sword, established the dGa' Idan, a lamassary still extant. The Mongol incursion, though it again brought Tibet into closer contact with China, had thus only confirmed the old trend to theocracy, and increased the advantage of the lamas over the nobility. In colourful robes, wadded garments and sheepskin coats, living on yak-flesh, mutton, cheese and salted, buttered tea, the tough weather-beaten lamas and landowners ruled their peasants and herdsmen. Nowhere in the world, since early antiquity, not even in the nascent contemporary Andean Inca empire of Peru, its nearest equivalent, had so elaborate, comprehensive and lasting a theocracy appeared. Religion, now strongly coloured by the propitiation of demons and of the dead, and conducted through constant prayer assisted by prayer wheels and paper flags on which religious phrases were inscribed, permeated the entire people, who were obsessed with the doctrine of reincarnation. By the seventeenth century the Grand Lama Ngawang Lobsang Gyatsho was declared 'Dalai' Lama – the fountain of 'Ocean Wide' wisdom, and the highest incarnation of the Buddha. He built the Potala palace at Lhasa, and laid down the custom that future Dalai Lamas would be sought, incarnate, in a child. But the regents' wives were apt to kill the Dalai Lama in boyhood and choose another child and so perpetuate their power. At the same time, the office of Panchen or 'teaching' lama was instituted. Tibetan relations with Mongolia and China were destined to be belligerent, if sometimes culturally close, and the Chinese, under both Ming and Manchu dynasties, attempted to assert their suzerainty over Tibet. Few Europeans got to Tibet: the Jesuits were there in 1661; Warren Hastings sent an envoy in 1774 and Thomas Manning described it in 1811. In the 1860s the British sent spies there as part of the 'great game' to keep the Russians out.

## V

Kublai Khan had ruled directly only over Mongolia, China, and its spheres of influence in Tibet and South-East Asia. At his death, the rest of the Mongol power divided into the Khanate of Jagatai, extending from the western Chinese border through Turkestan to the Oxus, with its capital city at Samarkand, into Khazakstan, Crimea and southern Russia, the territory of the Kipchak Tatars of the Golden Horde; and into the Ilkhanate of Iran, to which the Seljuq Turks of Anatolia, old enemies of Byzantium and the crusaders, were subordinate. This division was accentuated by the clash of religions. The Far Eastern Mongols became Confucians or Mahayana Buddhists; those of Turkestan and Iran, like the earlier Turki conquerors of India, Mahmud of Ghazni and Malik Shah of Baghdad, became Muslims.

Samarkand and Bukhara in Jagatai, both, as already observed, vigorous centres of Muslim commerce and culture, had been overrun and devastated at the height of the Mongol expansion by Hulagu Khan. He had destroyed Herat and invaded Iran; he sacked Baghdad in 1258, ended the Abbasid caliphate and wrecked the irrigation of Mesopotamia, though the culture of Iran, like that of China, was also to absorb its conquerors. As already observed, only the ruler of Egypt, the redoubtable Mamlūk sultan, Beybars, advancing into Anatolia, defeated them.

In the western part of Jagatai, the Seljuqs, now highly civilized, were ousted by new nomads out of central Asia: by the late fourteenth century, the Osmanli or Ottoman Turks, as already recorded, dominated Asia Minor and had all but encircled Byzantium. They had followed up their conquest of the Balkans at Kossovo by a resounding victory when, seven years later, in 1396, Bajazet I routed a great force of French, German, Hungarian and Polish knights at Nikopolis. He captured Jean sans Peur, the heir of Burgundy, and told him, when ransomed, that he would like to fight him again; he staged a great hunt with falcons and cheetahs, to impress his captives, and sent the king of France a drum and some bows strung with human skin, while keeping a few knights for exhibition in their 'iron armour' to other Near Eastern potentates. The less important captives were massacred.

Bajazet might well have taken Constantinople and invaded Europe, but he met his match. Timur Lenk (1335–1405) – the Lame – the next central Asian world conqueror, was the son of an obscure emir of the Barlass Turkis of Samarkand. His early adventures compare with those of Genghis Khan: he rebelled against the Jagatai Khan, took to the mountains, gathered about him a devoted band. By 1369 he was sultan of Transoxiana, and a fanatical champion of orthodox Islam. Soon he had captured Kashgar, conquered Khorasan and turned on the Kipchak Tatars of the Golden Horde, indirectly helping the Russians to defeat them at Kulikovo. He destroyed Toktamish, the ruler of the Crimea, and even briefly occupied Moscow. He then moved south and subdued most of Iran: he crushed the Baluchis, defeated the Afghans, who had dominated north-western India and, in 1398, launched a *jihad* against the Tughluq sultanate of Delhi. The city was sacked and its inhabitants massacred.

Timur now returned to central Asia, but he soon moved west, routed even the Mamlūks of Egypt at Aleppo and stormed Baghdad. Ibn Khaldun, in 1401, encountered him at Damascus, 'upright on his horse, while the bands played round him till the air shook with them'. 'Highly intelligent and very perspicacious', he commissioned the historian to write an account of the Maghrib, 'so that he could actually see it'. 'His right knee, as he told me, is lame from an arrow which struck him when raiding in boyhood. He dragged it when he went short walks, but when he would go long distances men carried him.'

Timur sacked Damascus, and deported its craftsmen to Samarkand; next year he laid siege to Ankara, determined to settle accounts with Bajazet. There was no room for them both in western Asia.

Bajazet's smaller host included a contingent of mercenary Serbs, and of Janissaries (*Yeni Cheri*, the new troops), its *corps d'élite*, recruited from the sons of the toughest of his subject peoples. But at the sight of Timur's central Asian standards, many Seljuqs and Kharasmians deserted: Bajazet was totally defeated, though not, as Marlowe declares, caged. He was most ceremoniously treated; the conqueror even spared the only survivor among his five sons. But Bajazet died of rage. Three years later, Timur, now aged seventy, perished on a great expedition, beyond the borders of Jagatai, against Ming China.

The Ming Empire was spared; in the West, also, there was respite. The two worst Asian predators of their time had neutralized one another, and the remnant of the Byzantine Empire staggered on for another half century. Timur's tomb still exists; 'The Gur Emir,' writes Sir Fitzroy Maclean, 'remains to my taste the most beautiful and the most enthralling building in Samarkand. Nothing else can quite equal the severe majesty of its great blue ribbed dome. And . . . it would be hard not to be moved as one stands looking down at the plain narrow tombstone of dark green jade from Chinese Turkestan which marks the tomb of Timur the Lame.'[6] The conqueror was a man of taste.

# VI

When Timur attacked northern India, the country, as already observed, had long been under Muslim domination. The villagers who were the vast majority of the population over all the subcontinent, who practised their varied and bizarre religions and spoke an extraordinary variety of languages, possessed little for an invader to plunder. But their manpower could be harnessed; the small surplus which they contributed to the money-lenders and landowners had made some of their rulers rich. Underneath the wealth of this minority, the people, indifferent to their changing rulers and resigned to wars which merely added to the risks of famine and disease, accepted their privations and prayed for a punctual monsoon. The system was, none the less, self-supporting, indestructible; against this unchanging penury and routine must be set the political adventures, luxury and culture of the rulers of medieval India. 'The state itself was an instrument of dynastic and oligarchic ambitions, an estate rather than a patriotic entity. This prevented any sense of unity against a possible invasion.'[7]

Since the invasions of Mahmud of Ghazni (998–1030) in the early eleventh century, the Punjab had become the springboard for wider Muslim campaigns. Alien Muslim rulers, with a predominantly Persian culture – Mahmud had been a patron of the poet Firdausi – settled on the massive but relatively ill-organized Hindu civilization. The Hindus, though often employed in the administration, withdrew behind the barriers of religion and caste. This did not prevent a growing economic enterprise in manufacture and commerce; in textiles, cotton and rice, which was to make medieval India the greatest exporting country in Asia.

Only the Rajput clans continued to put up a fierce resistance, based on Kanauj, Delhi, Ajmer and Chitor. These elegant and martial aristocrats had a passion for war, hunting and hawking: 'courageous and adventurous in the extreme (the Rajput) was frequently haughty, stubborn and wilful. But as a rule he spared the vanquished, respected the womenfolk and was generous to his followers and even his enemies . . . the Rajput warriors reveal striking resemblances to the medieval Knights of Europe',[8] save that some of them were highly educated. Like the medieval nobility, they were incapable of sound organization, fighting for precedence and honour:

their haughtiness, impetuosity and clannishness, fanned by bards, scholars and poets alike, rendered a common national effort difficult. . . . The gallant resistance of these swordsmen to the Turko-Afghans was further handicapped by old-fashioned tactics, and a reliance on war-elephants, now obsolescent before the Muslim cavalry, so that Babur was to say of the Rajputs that they 'knew how to die but not how to fight'. They were also patrons of literature and connoisseurs of building, military and civilian. *Ghats* and *Chatris* (tombs) were also constructed by the Rajput rulers with commendable skill in engineering and architecture, both of which are still living traditions in Rajputana.[9]

After the decline of the Ghaznavids, Afghan conquerors dominated the Punjab and moved east. Muhammad of Ghor, a contemporary of Richard Coeur de Lion, advanced deep into Hindu territory: he defeated the Rajput King Prithviraja at Tarāin in 1192; two years later he captured Ajmer and Delhi: in the next year his viceroy, Kutub-ud-din Aibak, took Benares. The famous university of Nalanda was destroyed, and the Muslims overran Bengal. When, in 1206, Muhammad was assassinated during his siesta, probably by a Muslim heretic, he left a realm more extensive and better organized than any Muslim conquests before. Kutub-ud-din now became the first sultan of Delhi, but he was killed playing polo and his line did not last; it was a Turki usurper, Ala-ud-din Khalji, who next fought his way to power at the end of the thirteenth century, and imposed a tributary empire over most of India. He defied the Mongols in the north – then a threat to all southern Asia – and subdued most of the Deccan. This vast suzerainty began to disintegrate under Muhammad Tughluq (1325–51), of whom Ibn Battutá remarked that he above all men delights most in giving presents and shedding blood; and the Turki sultanate of Delhi, as already observed, was destroyed by Timur Lenk.

Timur's invasions had been devastating but brief; out of a welter of conflict between Turkis, Rajputs and Afghans, a new power arose at Delhi – the Afghan Lodi Sultans. But they were unable to resist the mightiest of all the conquerors. Sehir-ed-din Muhammad Babur, the highly intelligent founder of the Mughal Empire, had been born at Ferghana near Tashkent. After twice taking Samarkand in desperate campaigns, he conquered Afghanistan and became king of Kabul. From this strategic vantage point, in 1525, he descended into northern India. Ibrahim Lodi, sultan of Delhi, deployed an enormous polyglot army at Panipat. In 1526 Babur totally routed him, and occupied Delhi and Agra: 'By the munificence and liberality of God,' he wrote, 'there fell beneath my blows an enemy as formidable as Sultan Ibrahim, and I gained the vast empire of Hind.' In the following year, he destroyed a huge Rajput army at Khanua, a victory won over 'pagans' which entitled him to the style of *Ghazi*. He died in 1530, master of northern India, the founder of an empire to be consolidated and extended by his grandson, Akbar.

Such in outline, was the political background of late medieval northern India, from which, in the times of the Tudors, the Mughal Empire emerged. Babur, the last and greatest of the Turki conquerors, thus completed the Muslim occupation, first established in the north-west by Mahmud of Ghazni and Muhammad of Ghor: from the twelfth century the Hindus had been increasingly overwhelmed. Two different societies now came to coexist. The one derived its culture and court language from Iran and its way of life from the hills. It was monotheist and intolerant 'at the threshold of the magnificent mosque at Ghazni, were buried the fragments of the Siva Lingam of Somnath'.[10] The other society was immensely old, indigenous to the plains and the peninsula, caste-ridden, but with an inextinguishable vitality, deriving from the India of the Guptas, Aşoka, and Mohenjo Daro. Though there was to be much cultural fusion, this medieval division is today expressed in the barrier between Pakistan and India.

# VII

The Muslim domination was adverse to the development of Hindu culture. Few early or even medieval Hindu temples in northern areas survived. But in peninsular India, far from any overwhelming influence from central Asia, the Hindu Dravidian civilization flourished in tropical luxuriance. And the ancient Kalinga oceanic trade and colonization, which had been going on for many centuries into South-East Asia and which had increased under the Guptas, was extended and consolidated during the Middle Ages. The Tamil Cholas of Tanjore dominated the eastern Coromandel coast by the tenth century; Rajaraja Chola I (c. 985–1014) ruled all peninsular India below the Tungabhadra and conquered Ceylon; Rajendra Chola in the early eleventh century sent famous expeditions to Burma and Sumatra, though he was expelled from Ceylon by the Sinhalese Vijayabahu, whose descendant Parakramabahu (c. 1153–86) was the most powerful medieval ruler of the island. Both kingdoms were to be eclipsed in the fourteenth century by the highly militarized realm of Vijayanagar, which was to reach its climax under Krisnadevaraya in the early fifteenth century and was only broken by a coalition of Muslim princes at Talikota in 1565.

The temples, the sculpture and the bronzes produced in medieval Hindu India derive from Gupta traditions. In Orissa, south-west of Calcutta, the twelfth-century Jaganath (Juggernaut) temple at Puri, with its enormous two-hundred-foot cylindrical tower, and the fiercely erotic sculptures of its Black Pagoda, compare with the most sophisticated building and sculpture of contemporary Europe. The gigantic image of the Jain saint, Gommatesvara, at Bellura in Mysore, is comparable to the largest statues of ancient Egypt. At Madura there is a riot of exuberant and massive temple architecture, and westward too, in the cities of the Malabar Coast, as well as in Ceylon: at Tanjore, the massive temple of Siva was surrounded by enormous walls. But the most brilliant achievements of Tamil artists were their bronzes. The famous bronzes of dancing Siva (Nataraja, Lord of the Dance), made in the tenth and early eleventh centuries, are contemporaneous, by English reckoning, with Athelstan and Canute. Surrounded by lambent flames, the four-armed deity swings to a serene, exultant rhythm.

The greatest intellect of this high civilization of medieval southern India was the Tamil theologian Sankara (fl. 820), who gave Brahmanism a new inspiration, thus reinforcing the old Hinduism and combating Muslim influence. He was a great organizer and a poet. The mystic Ramanuja (*c.* 1047–1137) also made Hinduism more dynamic, stressing the cult of *bhakti* – an active charity which can even transcend the barriers of caste. Like Sankara, he undertook missionary journeys to the north, so that his influence ramified through India.

Tamil mysticism is expressed in ardent poetry to Siva:

> You are family, friends and Home
> You are lord, Rider on the Bull,
> You are bliss.

This cult and the practice of *bhakti* could even combine with Sufi mysticism to bridge the gap between Muslim and Hindu, as in the famous poetry of the eclectic Kabir:

> I am neither in temple nor in mosque
> I am neither in Kaaba nor in Kailsa.
> If thou art a true seeker, thou shalt seek me at once . . .
> Thou shalt meet me in a moment of time.

These high manifestations of religion went along with a welter of Tantric cults, grossly sensual and promiscuous. But in spite of a basic incompatibility, Muslim and Hindu thought sometimes enriched one another and, with the waning of the prestige of Sanskrit, new vernacular literatures developed.

The rulers, if not the teeming peoples, of these Tamil kingdoms were rich, profiting by their position between the Arab world, Malaya and Indonesia; even Marco Polo's vocabulary was beggared to describe the wealth of the privileged castes.

A flourishing trade, conducted by the Arabs, went on with the southern Sung Empire, Malacca, Aden and the Red Sea. Leather, pearls and precious stones; ginger, indigo and spices; cotton quilts and incense, prayer mats and buckram were shipped to Arabia; gold and silver poured in. The environment was tropical; the swarming inhabitants ate coconuts and drank rice spirit; brilliant parakeets abounded – 'no lovelier sight in the world'; even the kings went naked, save for the ropes of pearls and 'a handsome loin cloth . . . set with rubies, sapphires, emeralds and other brilliant gems, so that this scrap of cloth is worth a fortune'.[11] As for the Hindu-Dravidian popular religion – 'Most of them worship the ox because they saw it is a very good thing.' Temple maidens 'pirouetted before the images' and thoroughly tested would-be monks for any sensual disposition. But Marco Polo thought little of the slender peoples; they made ritual ablutions twice a day, but did not regard any form of sexual indulgence as a sin. Further, the tarantulas were a nuisance, and the Hindus would insist that 'all the saints are all black and the devils all white'. The memory and the shrine of the apostle St Thomas were still extant; he had been martyred, the people said, by mistake, by a shot intended for a peacock.

East of peninsular India, across the ocean beyond Burma in Cambodia on the Mekong, the cult of Siva and Vishnu had inspired a majestic art. By the late twelfth century Angkor Thom, the gigantic Khmer temple city, square built with five gates and balustrades in the form of snakes, had been erected by King Jayavarman VII. Suryavarman II (1112–52) had built the Angkor Wat, with its towers, lakes and cloisters, the most splendid of all these monuments. But, by the thirteenth century, Thais of the alluvial plain of the Menam came to dominate Cambodia; they also pushed south into Malaya. Ayuthia, north of Bangkok, was founded by 1350.

In Sumatra the Hinayana Buddhist kings of Sri-Vishaya ruled from Palembang over most of the Malay peninsula as well as western Java. The Javanese in the early ninth century created the famous stupas of Borobudur, and in the fourteenth built up the powerful kingdom of Madjapahit. By the later Middle Ages many of these peoples, who owed much of their culture and religions to early Mesopotamian contacts and to the Kalinga expansion from southern India, came under Muslim domination from Aden and the Hadramaut. The Arabs gradually monopolized the spice trade, and their religion took root in Malaya and Indonesia: Madjapahit, the last Hindu kingdom, fell to them in the fifteenth century, and even the distant Moluccas and Philippines came under their rule.

Thus the Hindu-Dravidian civilization of southern India and the culture of most of South-East Asia, all based on great populations living off rice in a tropical climate, flourished during the Middle Ages in a luxuriant setting. It contrasted sharply with the deserts, steppes and mountains of Arabia and central Asia, the homeland of the Arabs, the Mongols and the Turks; but as in northern India, many native cultures came to be dominated by Muslim conquerors; in Malaya and Indonesia they were exploited by Muslim traders coming across the Indian Ocean. They were all, like other civilizations of that age, minority cultures, living above a mass of poverty, illiteracy and inefficient toil. Yet they produced advanced religions and theology, as well as great art. North-east of them, massive and ultimately invulnerable, was China, which contained the greatest civilized population in the world, temperamentally more solid and industrious, fixed with tenacity on practical objectives, firmly unlike either medieval Europe or Hindu India.

# VIII

The panorama of medieval Asia, extending, in all its cruel grandeur and swarming poverty, from the coast of Anatolia to Java, from Manchuria to Cape Cormorin, and dwarfing Byzantium and western Europe, presents the greatest example of the interaction of the nomad and the agriculturalist, of the Desert and the Sown. Again and again the land-bound peoples of central Asia swept down on the rich cultivated lands; in spite of frightful destruction, they were absorbed and civilized. It is the story of the invaders of Sumer and Egypt, of the northern Europeans and the Mediterranean, but on a greater scale.

In this interaction of the peoples of the heartland of Eurasia with the two greatest centres of population in the world, land power had hitherto had the advantage. Now, in the late fifteenth century, the picture was to be radically changed. The centre of Asian dominion had long been in central Asia, in Samarkand or Bukhara, the base of the Mongol and Turki empires. This power ranged from southern Russia to the Deccan; from North Africa to Manchuria and Indo-China. Now, when in 1498 Vasco da Gama's Portuguese fleet reached southern India, the ocean-going western Europeans outflanked the land powers of the steppe.

# Thirteen

# EUROPE IN THE LATER MIDDLE AGES

## I

Out in the west of the Eurasian continent, the distinctive culture of Catholic Christendom had been well-established by the thirteenth century. It differed greatly from the classical Mediterranean civilization on which it was based. But in the world picture it was not yet particularly important; China was far more massive, the wealth of southern India seemed dazzling to Marco Polo, and the Mongol invasion had not been defeated; it had been called off.

Only two centuries later, Europeans were beginning an expansion which was to bring them the mastery of the planet and, by the seventeenth century, creating a scientific revolution which was to transform the status of man. It is not the most familiar side of medieval civilization – chivalry, the monasteries and cathedrals, scholastic theology, or even the vernacular literatures, that were to be of world significance (all have parallels in other cultures) – but European technology and political and economic institutions. The romantic aspects of the Middle Ages give place, in the widest perspective, to ostensibly more ordinary achievements, which were to make Europe the spring-board for an enterprise of which the Portuguese appearance off the coast of India on the fringe of Babur's Empire, was the first portent for the East, and Columbus' landing in the Bahamas in 1492 for the Americas.

Western Europe was no longer a rustic society supporting a feudal and clerical élite: it was already the scene of decisive economic progress and inventions. The prehistoric skills, which even the outer barbarians possessed, had been supplemented by some new devices in antiquity, but they had not been much exploited. As Dr A. C. Crombie remarks, inventions, considered 'toys' in the old slave-owning society, were now put to industrial use.[1] The basis of this technical advance has already been touched upon – the taming of the western lands, the colonization along the Baltic; by the fourteenth century most of the Continent had been occupied and tamed. Sluices, dykes and sand dunes, osier and pine belts on shifting soils had been established in the Low Countries; the complex irrigation of the Lombard plains was in being. The *Ruralia Commoda* of Piero Crescenzi of Bologna, written about 1306, treats of hops and rice and mulberries as well as of traditional crops. His book, embellished in the original edition with revealing woodcuts, deals systematically with the best sites and ways of building; with plants and how to grow them; with arable, vineyards, fruit trees, gardens, meadows and woods; with tame animals and birds and game, and concludes with a calendar of 'What is done in each month'.* Wells, cisterns and aqueducts; fish ponds and the netting of birds – *qualiter aves rhetibus capiuntur*; hawking, how to trap wolves and foxes; fungi – *quidam sunt boni, quidam mortiferi* – all are minutely described. It is already a landmark in method and observation.

The early medieval Europeans, generally thought unpractical, had often been more efficient than the Greeks and Romans. 'To judge by sculpture, vase painting and medals,' writes Dr Crombie, 'horses [in antiquity] were harnessed in such a way that the pull was taken on a strap passing round the neck, so that the harder they pulled the closer they came to strangulation. The modern horse collar appeared in the West in the late ninth or early tenth century, introduced perhaps from China.' The nailed horse-shoe, deep saddle and stirrups, which together gave the knights supremacy, were all early medieval inventions; and it was not the aesthetes and savants of Hellenistic or Antonine times who devised spectacles, but della Spina and Salvino degli Armati in northern Italy in the early fourteenth century – major, but generally unknown, benefactors to the human race.

Even in the Dark Ages, flour, saw and water mills were common, and windmills had been early acclimatized in north-western Europe: the Flemish cloth industry, which was the basis of the wealthiest cities in the north, depended on rudimentary mechanized spinning. It is well known that Caxton in the reign of Edward IV introduced printing into England, but by the time of Dante block printing off wood was practised at Ravenna, and, as already recorded, paper had early been introduced from the Near East. Perhaps the most psychologically important invention was the mechanical clock. By 1350 the hour had been divided into sixty minutes, and the novel notion of punctuality began to take on in parts of Europe, an idea still not universally accepted.

Another original medieval achievement, destined to spread far outside Europe, was the theory and practice of constitutional government. Its pedigree is in part classical, but the institutions which embodied it owed much to the Middle Ages. Over most of the Continent they were to be swamped in the seventeenth and eighteenth centuries by despotic monarchies; but they persisted – most vigorously in England – and took root in North America to become the political framework of the United States;

---

*Petri de Crescentiis civis Bononien: in Commodŭ ruralium cum figuris libri duodecim. The author, who explains that his city is called Bononia because it is *Bona per omnia*, was trained in logic, medicine, natural sciences and law. 'Nothing,' he says, 'is more worthy of a free man than the practice of agriculture.'

revived in continental Europe after the French Revolution, and were transplanted with varying success to Asia, Africa and Australasia.

The Greeks had invented civic constitutions, deliberately contrived, and the idea of the rule of a law existing in its own right, since, they argued, no one could be trusted with absolute power; and the Romans had formulated the idea of a universal law, applicable to all civilized men. With the breakdown of the Roman Empire, this idea declined in the West, though, as already emphasized, it was maintained in Byzantium: the barbarians practised their own various tribal customary laws. But the Church always retained the concept of a universal order, and the distinction between *princeps* and *tyrannus*. This theory, combined with barbarian assumptions that rulers often held sway only by election, or the feudal notion that it was legitimate to 'defy' a defaulting or tyrannous lord, gave rise to the concept that *dominion* resided, ultimately, not in the person of a monarch but in the community or 'commonwealth'. This *communitas*, in medieval times, was often thought to be represented by the estates of a realm; these estates met in a *parliament*, a *Cortes*, a *Landtag*, a *Riksdag* or a *Diet*. And in England the 'Commons' gradually began to gain economic power.\* When, in the sixteenth and seventeenth centuries, monarchs claimed the right of arbitrary taxation, medieval precedents were cited. The House of Commons in England appealed to the medieval notion of commonwealth, claimed that the ruler was a trustee who could be deposed for misgovernment, and asserted that the newly defined *sovereign* power of the community resided not in a monarch by divine right but in a king-in-parliament.

Such ideas ran clean contrary to the arbitrary rule often predominant in Asian empires, though they are paralleled, in a different idiom, in some Chinese and Muslim political theory, and reflect the habits of many primitive societies all over the world, where the elders or wise men 'declare' custom, and tribal laws are more powerful than the fiat of temporary leaders. While, therefore, western Europe has no monopoly of the notion of the rule of law, of the trusteeship of power, and of the right of individuals to participate in political and social decisions, it was in western Europe, and in European-descended nations overseas, that such ideas were embodied in formidable institutions and in elaborate laws, and that the idea of self-government under law ultimately became predominant.

Both the technical knowledge and the political procedures which were to spread outside western Europe and make Europeans pioneers of a world society, owed much to antiquity, but more to the Middle Ages.

---

\*These institutions also existed in eastern Europe, though they failed to develop. In Muscovy the *Duma* of the Boyars was paralleled by the more widely representative *Zemsky Sobor*.

# II

Although by the late fifteenth century Europeans were set upon expansion, the brilliant civilization of the age of St Louis and Frederick II had suffered a tragedy. The Black Death, bubonic plague brought by rats out of Asia, had wrought appalling havoc. From 1348 population steeply declined; there were peasant revolts, *jacqueries*, *Bauernkriegen*. In Germany and the Low Countries the plague particularly demoralized the people who took to self-flagellation and massacred the Jews, whom they accused of poisoning wells. Pessimism infected much thought and literature. During the Hundred Years' War some of the richest areas in France were plundered and wealthy towns sacked, while that model of late medieval chivalry, Edward III of England, many of whose subjects had profited by the contest, defaulted on his debts. The Hussite religious wars in Bohemia, an occasion for revolutionary tactics which gave pikemen and artillery in *lager* the advantage over armoured knights, were a prelude to the seventeenth-century Thirty Years' War in Germany; and the eviction of the *Moriscoes* by the bigots who consolidated the *Reconquista* did no good to the Iberian Peninsula. The decline of empire and papacy, the increase in religious schism, the commercializing of war beneath a romantic veneer, the rise of classes better qualified for long-term calculating self-interest and the elaborate scepticism of many late medieval scholastics must have appeared a moral retrogression. The contrast between the world of the early Pastons in late fifteenth-century Norfolk, wary realist upstarts consolidating a local influence, equally apt in legal chicanery or violence, and that of the aristocratic and chivalrous entourage of St Louis described by Joinville is symbolic. The clear-cut certainties of St Thomas contrast with the scepticism of William of Ockham, as the arches of Chartres or Salisbury with the elaborate profusion of late medieval buildings, where design had no further to go. If the economic recession, endemic plague, war, and social dislocation which struck so much of northern Europe in the fourteenth and fifteenth centuries led to the rise of monarchies and cities on a more business-like foundation and to a greater appreciation of economic interest, the immediate prospect of late medieval society was discouraging.

The old European institutions were breaking down. By the late fifteenth century new dynastic centres of government were established. In alliance with a new unfeudal kind of administrator they set the pattern of the European nation-state, a form of polity still predominant. The two poles of dynastic power were to be the French monarchy, consolidated by Louis XI, which ruled the most heavily populated and potentially the richest country in the north-west, and the Habsburg interest, consolidated in Vienna, and made more formidable when Maximilian I, the descendant of Rudolf I, the first holy Roman emperor of that house, made his spectacular marriage to the heiress of Burgundy. This Habsburg power was to extend over the Low Countries, much of Italy, over Spain and Portugal and the Americas. The French–Habsburg dynastic conflict was to be the main theme of continental power politics until the mid-eighteenth century; and against it the subsidiary dynastic and national conflicts are set.

Attempts were made to reorganize the great cosmopolitan institutions. The papacy was 'captive' at Avignon during most of the fourteenth century in the hands of French kings and, after the 'great schism', the 'conciliar' movement tried to rehabilitate it. But the holy see sank into the political welter of Renaissance Italy, the papacy of the Borgias and Medici. Similarly, the empire survived only as part of a new order. The Czech emperor, Charles IV, tried to regularize the ancient institution: in 1356 his Golden Bull defined the functions and status of the Electoral *Kurfürsten* – the archbishops of Mainz, Cologne and Trier; the king of Bohemia, the dukes of Saxony and Bavaria, the markgraf of Brandenburg. But though he preserved the formal relics of Charlemagne's empire, Charles IV's attempt to keep the peace 'through the concord of the Electors' in fact contributed to the disunion of the Germans.

Significantly, he was far more successful as a national ruler, one of the more attractive of the new type of kings, of whom he may be considered an early example. The son of John of Luxembourg and Bohemia, the blind warrior killed at Crecy (*nichilo-minus tamen sic cecus bellum interesse voluit*) – 'who although he was blind, wanted to be in the battle', and descended from the Premyslids through his mother, Charles was brought up at the brilliant French court and married a French princess. When, in 1333, he returned to Prague, he found his inheritance a wilderness. Not a single castle, he wrote, but was in pawn; 'for a dwelling I had nothing but a burgher's house'.[2] In an adventurous life – he escaped from Venetian pirates by jumping into a dinghy and covering himself with nets, and from the king of Poland by putting his horse at a wide moat – he set himself to create a Bohemian realm. He persuaded his wife to learn Czech, brought in French architects to build the Karlstein palace and the Charles IV bridge at Prague, developed mines and canals, reformed the currency, released his subjects from debts to the Jews, founded an archbishopric and a university – for a time the main focus of central European learning.* 'When he died he left one of the finest capitals in Europe, every means of transport improved, the manufacture of paper, glass, pottery and dyes flourishing.[3] Bohemian beer was famous and Bohemian villages prosperous. When Richard II of England married one of his daughters, he made a grand and profitable alliance.

* Bookish and austere, liable to psychic visions, he warned his successor – in vain – against the pleasure of the table. '*Nolite crapulari,*' he wrote, '*a cibo et potu, sicut faciunt hii quorum Deus Venter est.*' J. F. Boehmer (ed.), 'Vita Karoli Quarti Imperatoris ab Ipso Karolo Conscripta, 1316–46', in *Fontes Rerum Germanicarum* (Stuttgart 1843), p. 232.

The future was with such methodical and intelligent monarchs. But in eastern and central Europe only the Habsburgs consolidated a permanent power; the new monarchies succeeded better in the West. The empire itself survived as part of the Habsburg inheritance: Bohemia, after the Hussite wars, again flourished under Georg Podiebrad in the mid-fifteenth century, but politically it was absorbed in the Habsburg dominions. Poland, under Kasimir the Great in the fourteenth century, achieved much, symbolized by the university of Cracow, founded in 1364, and became in 1386, by a dynastic marriage, part of a large Polish–Lithuanian realm created by Ladislas Jagello of Lithuania, who defeated the Teutonic knights at Tannenberg in 1410 and dominated most of the territory between the Baltic and the Black Sea. But the Jagellon kingdom was handicapped by an uncontrollable nobility; by the notorious *liberum veto*, any one member of the Polish diet could paralyse the government. If national consciousness and military power were well-established in eastern Europe, they were not, in spite of the sixteenth-century cultural achievements of the reign of Sigismund I, embodied in viable institutions.

Similarly, in Hungary, the Angevin Louis the Great (1342–82) made a formidable kingdom which reached its widest power under the Hunyadis. Mathias Corvinus (1458–90) was one of the ablest princes in Europe; but all was to be overrun by the Turks.

In the West, on the other hand, the alliance of the kings, the more adaptable magnates and the bourgeoisie began to create nation-states. Louis XI (1461–83) asserted his supremacy over all the Loire country and Brittany; over Provence; and above all, over Burgundy. Henry VII, the first of the Tudors, revived and consolidated the strong monarchy for which, after the Wars of the Roses, England had desperate need. The Portuguese Aviz dynasty, which had won power after the battle of Aljubarrota in 1385, was soon to launch an epoch-making overseas expansion. Ferdinand and Isabella of Aragon-Castile (crowned 1474) controlled Spain and the western Mediterranean, including Majorca, Sardinia and Sicily. After the union of Kalmar (1397) Denmark and Norway were united, and Queen Margrethe (d. 1412) was also sovereign of Sweden. Though the Swedes soon broke the union in 1448, the Danes became a formidable Baltic power.

By the end of the fifteenth century, western and Baltic Europe had seen the rise of centralized monarchies, with new standards of administration, generally backed by standing armies with artillery and siege trains, and by rudimentary systems of finance. Already Fortescue in his *Governaunce of England* could depict a reorganized royal council which could decide 'how the going out off the money may be restrained, how bullyon may be brought into the lande, how also plate and jewells and money late borne owt may be geyten ageyn': their procedure, he wrote, should be 'putt in a boke and that boke kept in this counsell as a register or an ordinarye, how that they shall doo in everything.' Clearly he spoke for a more methodical kind of government.

In eastern Europe, by contrast, where town life was not so far advanced, where the social pattern was still overwhelmingly agrarian, the nobles ruling vast estates and hordes of peasants, and where, as in Poland, the main urban middle class were alien Jews, the new monarchies could not thrive. Hence a fateful contrast between east and west.

# III

In the West there were now two great centres of urban development, the Low Countries and Italy. Here a new variety of culture flourished, first and most brilliantly in the south. The Italian cities had a classical pedigree, but the northern towns were nearly all medieval. Save for the old Roman centres along the Rhine, and Roman–Merovingian Tournai, they represent native enterprise founded on maritime commerce and cloth manufacture. In Bruges and Damme there had long been merchants from all the major districts of Europe from Portugal to the Baltic: as the Zwin silted up, Antwerp inherited their supremacy, the greatest centre of commerce in the north. Ypres and Ghent in Flanders; Maestricht and Dinant on the Meuse; Leyden in Holland; Brussels and Louvain, developed a cloth industry mainly dependent on English wool. Population greatly increased: by the fourteenth century Bruges and Ghent had at least sixty thousand inhabitants. Urban oligarchies arose, *gildebroeders* who employed skilled workmen on a large scale, and who came to canny decisions at conclaves in the gothic guildhalls which still dominate the cities of the Low Countries. In all this area from the Rhine to the Somme were rich, competitive bourgeois, keeping accounts, watching the markets, aware of European events, far more alert and efficient than the old feudal magnates and their dependants. And below them were prosperous artisans, as well as a seething, uprooted populace at the mercy of their employers and the markets, even if, in good times, they enjoyed a prosperity undreamt of in their villages. They could make savage revolts; sometimes they created democratic communes at the expense of the oligarchy; sometimes they were driven into chiliastic revolution, led by fanatics, of whom John of Leyden at Munster in the following century was to be the most notorious. This restive proletariat was ripe for mischief; and ripe for enterprise.

The cities fought against their lords and against one another, linked sometimes, as in Italy, only by a chain of alternate animosities: often, like the Hansa towns, they would collaborate. Generally the artisans who broke down the old oligarchies, as in Ghent and Liège, enjoyed only a brief success, and in time all the cities had to come to terms with the princes whom dynastic chance or policy set over them. Charles the Bold of Burgundy ruthlessly asserted his authority in this rich part of his dominions, and his Habsburg heirs profited from his heavy hand: the cities were involved in wider political and economic interests, and commerce came more to depend on bankers who had new methods of book-keeping and transferring funds, and whose interests and power were cosmopolitan.

This vigorous urban life was lived, by modern standards, on a small scale, in huddled, insanitary towns, whose civic towers and cathedrals rose above the polders of Flanders, Zeeland and Holland, or along the winding Meuse, as those of Milan, Pavia and Mantua commanded the Lombard plain. From the spiked gothic belfries of the north, the bells of guildhall and cathedral chimed through the mist, from the Zwin over the Scheldt into Holland and Friesland, to Hamburg and Scandinavia and the Baltic. The reek of tar and fish, the cry of gulls, the tang of the sea, the snug interiors, the foresight, the tenacity of the Low Countries, are behind the oceanic enterprise, in which, along with the nations of the Atlantic seaboard, they were to play a decisive part.

This late medieval northern culture was recorded by artists and writers. The realism of Van Eyck and Memlinc is at once delicate and robust, and this art was reinterpreted by the Portuguese Nuno Gonçalves. Maerlandt, a contemporary of Chaucer, wrote satire in the Flemish tongue; Boendale, chronicles; the chronicler Commines came from Flanders. Developing from the French style, the brick-built gothic of Ghent cathedral and of the lower part of the belfry at Bruges, the elaborate town halls of Brussels and Ypres, express the wealth and confidence of a vigorous culture.

Beyond the Burgundian plateau and the Jura, the Swiss cantons also formed a new kind of community. On 1 August 1291, in the time, by English reckoning, of Edward I, the free peasants of the forest cantons of Uri, Schwytz and Unterwalden on Lake Lucerne, commanding Altdorf and the Gotthard (their struggle is symbolized in the legend of William Tell), concluded an alliance against their Habsburg overlords. In 1315 they destroyed the army of Leopold of Austria in the valley of Morgarten. The city states of Lucerne, Zurich and Berne now joined the alliance: by the mid-fourteenth century the collective term 'Sweintz' appears, and the final victory at Sempach in 1389 secured the union (*unser Eydgnosschaft*), defined in the *Sempacherbrief* of 1393. The Swiss pikemen soon mastered the Aargau, pushed north-west to the shores of Lake Konstanz; later, the important Rhine city of Basel joined the union. They defeated the Burgundians at Grandson and Morat, and killed the great Duke Charles the Bold at Nancy in 1477. They mastered Bellinzona and Lugano; at Novara they defeated a large French army; their career of victory was stopped only when Francis I overwhelmed them at Marignano in 1515. But he gave them generous terms; bought up the Swiss as mercenaries whose prowess was the talk of Europe. In the heart of the Continent, guarded by the mountains, a republic of city states and free peasants had been established.

South of the Alps, the ancient cities of Italy had never lost their vitality. From the Lombard plain and Venetia, over the Apennines to Florence and the maritime Alps to Genoa, and along the coast to Pisa; down the spine of the peninsula to Perugia, Siena, Orvieto and Rome itself, the life of antiquity, never broken, had taken on a new style. The city states prospered; they employed professional *condottieri* in mutual wars, and often made Italy too hot for German and French invaders. The celebrated families who mastered the city states became brilliant patrons of the arts: they emerged during the later Middle Ages – the Visconti and Sforza in Milan; the Scaligeri at Verona; the Gonzaga at Mantua, the D'Este at Ferrara, the Medici in Florence. Long the most efficient, because it was impersonal, was the republic of Venice, whose Doge and Council of Ten supervised the conquest of the Adriatic and the economic domination of the Levant. It is often forgotten how far back into the Middle Ages run the causes of the 'Renaissance': Dante, the first great writer of Italian, and Giotto, the greatest of the early artists, were both born, by English reckoning, in the reign of Henry III. If neither had the Renaissance obsession with antiquity, they both had a new creative genius.

This force made Italy the dominant cultural influence of Europe. The earliest vernacular literature, as already remarked, came out of the Sicily of Frederick II: the next movement came from Tuscany. Dante (1265–1321), the greatest of Italian poets, ranged over cosmic themes; but he used metres adapted from Provençal forms and the homely similes of the vernacular: if his theology is medieval, his idiom enriched a native literature. Petrarch (d. 1374) sought out classical manuscripts, attempted to write Latin in the manner of Cicero, regarded the medieval language as barbarous. He was an individualist, concerned not with great cosmic themes, but with himself. Boccaccio's *Decameron* revives the bawdy narratives of Hellenistic antiquity with a new flavour. All three writers were to influence not only Italy but the whole of Europe.

In the following century, the cult of Plato, imported into the Academia at Florence from the Byzantine Peloponnese, was developed by Pico de Mirandola under the patronage of the Medici: neo-Paganism, often implicit in the paintings of Benozzo Gozzoli and Botticelli, was creeping in: and the cult of Greek led to a new interpretation of the sacred texts which might lead anywhere. The full tide of this movement, which was not so much a rediscovery of antiquity as a deeper sympathy for it, did not set in until the High Renaissance of the sixteenth century; but already Italy – long the battle ground of popes and emperors and harried by warring factions and brigandage, as witness the hill cities and villages of Tuscany and Umbria, sited, not for the view, but for defence – had become a European influence. This vitality came out of city states, based on ancient intensive agriculture of vine and olive, on the commerce of Venice, Genoa and the cities of the Lombard plain. It was older, more sophisticated, if in kind similar to the equally unfeudal urban culture of the north, but set against cypress and ilex, the blue Mediterranean and Adriatic and their cicada-sounding, thyme-scented shores. Its civic pride and the wealth of its princes were to be expressed, not by high-pitched parti-coloured roofs and elaborate gothic, as in Dijon, or by gargoyles and flying buttresses, as in the Ile de France, or by the complex decoration of cloth hall and belfry, but in the clean-cut colonnades, marble stairways, dramatic domes and façades of southern architecture, reinterpreting the ancient Mediterranean way of life.

The vernacular literature, of which the Provençals and Italians were pioneers, also developed in France, England, the Germanies, Scandinavia and the Iberian peninsula. The wealth of late medieval architecture, sculpture, stained glass and manuscript illumination are well-known. If court life was precarious, it was elegant. The rich, elaborate, plate armour; the tight fitting hose and pointed shoes setting off turbanned or cylindrical hats; the long, close-waisted coats, reminiscent of Persia, attest a fine taste among the tiny privileged minority. The courts of the kings of France and England, of the dukes of Burgundy and the Avignon popes, were centres of a very articulate culture. Charles d' Orléans in the mid-fifteenth century, could write:

> Le temps a laissié son manteau
> De vent, de froidure, et de pluye,

and, looking across the Channel, *à Dovre sur la mer'*, long for his own country,

> De veoir France, que mon cueur amer doit.

The Parisian Villon could ask:

> Dictes moy où, n'en quel pays
> Est Flora, la belle Romaine;
> ... Semblablement, où est la royne
> Qui commanda que Buridan
> Fust gecté en ung sac en Saine?
> Mais où sont les nieges d'antan!

Already both express a Gallic sensibility and wit.

In England, Chaucer (1310–1400), the first great vernacular writer of profound influence, was writing of

> Yonge fresshe folkes, he or she
> In that love up groweth with your age.

He created the Canterbury Tales, with their shrewd observation of character; and Hoccleve could lament him:

> my worthi maister honorable
> This landes verrey tresor and richesse.

Dunbar could now apostrophize London as '*the flour of cities all*'. These writers, with their roots in the Middle Ages, show a new outlook. And Chaucer could already translate Boethius' *O Stelliferi conditor orbis* into recognizable prose: 'O Thou Maker of the whole that bereth the sterres, which that art y-fastened to thy predurable chayer, and tornest the hevene with a ravishing weight', while Wycliffe's translation of the Bible has already the cadence of famous later versions.

The Germans, too, were developing their idiom, both in trite and simple piety, as in Tauler's:

> Es Kumpt ein schiff geladen
> rech uff sin hochstes port
> es bringt uns den sune des vatters
> das êwig wôre wort;*

as, also, in the roistering sentiment already foreshadowed in the earlier Middle Ages:

> Wein, wein, von dem Rhein
> Lauter, klar und fein
> . . . Du gibst medizein.

All this vigorous and increasingly popular culture, along with a more secularized learning, was now diffused by a decisive invention. In Mainz by the mid-fifteenth century, printing by metal movable letters had been invented, giving far greater freedom than the block woodcut. The art spread to Holland and Flanders, Paris and London and, by the end of the century, Aldo in Venice began to print beautiful and convenient editions of classical writers in Greek as well as Latin. The circulation of the translated scriptures and a spate of pamphlets, mainly on theology, formed the background to the work of Erasmus and, less fortunately, of Luther and Calvin.

If, north of the Alps, this new invention was most widely used to disseminate theology, it also gave technical treatises of all kinds a far wider circulation. The financial operations of the Fuggers of Augsburg or of Jacques Coeur of Bourges, of the Venetians and Genoese and Catalans, demanded an intelligence service provided by skilled agents. They also demanded maps: the room in which the Florentine Council deliberated was lined with them. The Catalan and Majorcan cartographers who served the

---

* A ship deep laden is coming right into port; it brings us the son of the father, the eternal veritable word.

Infante Henriques of Portugal were far superior to most of the map makers of the thirteenth century, and navigation had been greatly improved by the invention of hinged rudders and lateen sails to give greater speed and manoeuvre. The hulls of the ocean-going caravels were now more seaworthy, and the swinging magnetic compass in its marked card was now common. Dr J. A. Williamson wrote:

By the mid-fifteenth century the foremast and foresail had arrived, together with the mizen at the after end, and the three-masted ship was complete. . . . They had a decisive advantage over the single masters in that they could, in good conditions, work to windward, although that ability must not be exaggerated . . . and it is no mere coincidence that a new age of oceanic voyaging set in with this invention. One cannot imagine Drake going round the world in a cog.[4]

The hinged rudder, set in the sternpost, had also superseded the vulnerable steering oar, set in a projecting pivot, from which the word 'starboard' derives. By the last century of the Middle Ages Atlantic Europe was ready for expansion. But this initiative did not, as often suggested, first come out of overflowing vitality and enterprise; it was forced on the West.

While the North used printing mainly to disseminate theology, elsewhere it publicized technical knowledge. Maps became much better and more widely diffused. Moreover the Ottoman Turks were engulfing the remnant of the Byzantine Empire, the instability of the Mamlūk regime in Egypt had long been stifling the luxury trade with the East, and pricing such goods as came through out of the market. By 1450 there was also an increasing shortage of gold, replaced by silver currencies minted from the Bohemian mines. The Portuguese, who were best placed to exploit the west coast of Africa and the Atlantic islands, began to push further south, in the hope of rounding Africa, then thought far smaller than it was, and getting to the East.

The Infante Dom Henriques, the third son of Dom John, the first king of the House of Aviz, and a grandson of John of Gaunt, established an observation post on the cliff at Sagres, and lived there. One of his ships, blown off course when exploring the coast of Africa, discovered the island of Santos. Madeira was clearly visible, and in 1420 the Portuguese, under João Gonçalvas Zarco, crossed over to this magnificent island which they colonized. Vines were imported from Cyprus, sugar-cane from Sicily: Dom Henriques was better employed than his cousin Henry V, trying to hold down France after Agincourt. Soon after the mid-century, the Portuguese were off the Gambia, then the Guinea, coast. Here they found slaves and ivory, sugar, gold dust and pepper: the exploration had paid off. It is not surprising that by 1487 the Cape had been circumnavigated, and that Vasco da Gama in 1487, on his way round the Cape coast beyond Mossel Bay, encountered rudimentary African music. 'On Saturday [appeared] about two hundred negroes, large and small. They at once began to play on four or five flutes, and some of them played high and others played low, harmonizing together very well for negroes, in whom music is not to be expected; and they danced like negroes. The Commander-in-Chief ordered the trumpets to be played, and we in the boats danced and so did the Commander-in-Chief . . . we traded a Black Ox for three bracelets.' Da Gama went on to land in South East Asia and dominate the Indian Ocean and beyond.

Christopher Columbus (Christopher Colón 1451–1506) also knew the west coast of Africa. Bred to the sea in Genoa, he knew the Ligurian coast from Savona to Chiaveri; after many adventures, he fetched up in Lisbon, now the greatest centre of maritime enterprise. Columbus became well-versed in geographical speculation and had long been obsessed with Marco Polo's account of the riches of the East. He set himself to 'find a shorter way of going by sea to the land of spices than that which [the Portuguese] are making by Guinea'.[5] After long frustration, his plan was sanctioned by Ferdinand and Isabella. Since Cadiz was full of emigrating Moriscoes, Columbus put out from Palos. In September 1492, three well-found caravels, the *Nina*, the *Pinta* and the *Santa Maria* – the first two provided by the municipality of Palos who had incurred a fine – ran south to the Canaries. Then they sailed before a brisk trade wind for thirty-three days: technically, it was an easy voyage, Columbus records '*el gusto de las mañanas*'. 'On October 12th at 2 a.m., as the *Nina*, under full sail, cut through a lively sea, Rodrigo de Triana, looked out on the *Pinta* forecastle, saw something like a white sandcliff gleaming in the moonlight on the western horizon, then another, and a dark line of land connecting them.'[6] They had sighted the coral island of Guadahaní in the Bahamas.

Next morning, through dangerous reefs, they entered a calm bay. 'Presently they saw naked people, and the admiral went ashore . . . with the royal standard displayed. . . . And all having rendered thanks to Our Lord, kneeling on the ground embracing it with tears of joy for the immeasurable mercy of having reached it, the admiral arose and gave the island the name of San Salvador.' Afterwards the Neolithic natives, not, as had been expected, black, but with light-brown skins and straight hair and good physique, brought parrots, darts and cotton thread to the invaders, whom they thought, wrongly enough, came from heaven. Columbus, in return, gave them the routine baubles provided for the negroes of West Africa, red caps and hawksbells. He had expected to find blacks with crinkled hair.

Convinced that he had arrived at the outposts of his objective, which was the Far East, Columbus set sail south-west to find Japan. He would never admit that he had come upon a new world; his geography remained firmly medieval. 'In his cosmographical ideas,' writes his biographer, 'Columbus remained stubbornly and obstinately, to the end of his life, absolutely and completely wrong.'[7]

# IV

So the late medieval Western Europeans circumnavigated Africa, outflanked the great Asian land powers by sea, and brought modern arms and commerce into the Indian Ocean and Malay Archipelago; while across the Atlantic – 'the Ocean Sea' – they discovered a huge continent, hitherto unknown to Europe or the Far East. The whole aspect of world history was changed. The first, most decisive phase of this expansion developed naturally from the commercial needs and technical skill of medieval Christendom; the discoveries were to be exploited by the more dynamic and formidable Europe of the sixteenth and seventeenth centuries.

# Fourteen

# PRE-COLUMBIAN AMERICA

## I

The amiable Tainos 'Indians' encountered by Columbus on Guadahaní were remote descendants of the hunters who had wandered into the Americas from Asia across the Behring Straits in Palaeolithic times. These Amerindians had infiltrated a vast wilderness; from Alaska and the far north down into British Columbia, the Rockies and California; out into the plains of the Middle West and eastward to the Hudson Valley and Virginia; down into Arizona and Mexico, Central America and the West Indies, the Andes, the Brazilian jungles, the Pampas and Paraguay.

In some favoured areas they made their own peculiar Neolithic revolution; others, still hunters and gatherers, developed elaborate but primitive societies. The Eskimo went their own specialized way. Most Indians of the Plains remained Mesolithic (they had no horses until the Spaniards imported them); the *Pueblos* Indians of Arizona settled into solid communities; and the most highly developed North American cultures were in what is now British Columbia, on the Pacific coast. In the huge tropical forests of Brazil, still lurk tribes expert with blowpipes and poisoned darts: in the cold of Tierra del Fuego, Palaeolithic scavengers went naked until the nineteenth century. So various was the environment; so sparse, scattered and unrecorded the expansion, that a total survey is impracticable. Two aspects are clear: in areas with easy soil and inferior hunting, the Amerindians made their own elaborate cultures, and warrior tribes outside them preyed upon their wealth.

There were three main civilizations: the Maya in Guatemala, Honduras, and, later, in Yucatan; the Toltec and ultimately Aztec culture of the valley of Mexico; and the highly organized empire of the Incas of Peru. Though often culturally advanced, none of these peoples used iron; none invented the wheel; they had no cattle, pigs or sheep; their only beast of burden, and that only in South America, was the llama. In general, it was man. On the other hand, they had maize, beans, gourds, squashes, tomatoes and tobacco; and in the Peruvian highlands, potatoes. If they had no silk, they wove the finest cotton fabrics in the world, and for cloaks and headdresses used the feathers of exotic birds. Gold was not currency but ornament.

Through at least twenty centuries, almost unknown to the rest of mankind, complex, teeming, and entirely original civilizations had been going on. They centred, as did other ancient cultures, on some very odd religions.

## II

The archaic Maya – a linguistic term – had achieved a shifting forest agriculture contemporary with the Augustan Principate in Rome in the tropical *Tierra Caliente* of Guatemala and Honduras. By the time of Constantine, they were building elaborate ceremonial cities, since swamped by a riot of vegetation. About the time of Charlemagne these cities were abandoned, and some of their inhabitants migrated to the relatively arid plateau of Yucatan. Here, in the early Middle Ages, there was a revival, mainly under the rule of invaders from Mexico.

The priests of the classic Maya culture were obsessed with time. They devised an accurate solar year and superimposed on it a sacred calendar which came round independently of the sun.* They thus became involved in calculations fascinating to mathematicians and they measured enormous stretches of time, running into millions of days. These operations presumably marked the routine of agriculture, but in the tropics this is not much determined by the seasons; probably they were anxious to keep the cosmic process going and avoid ill luck, and they let their fantastic system run away with them. They thought the day marking the lapse of fifty-two years particularly dangerous: 'They counted in terms of elapsed units, which kept the priests constantly looking forward to a date which could close the current period; not backward to a date which had already passed. Their conception of time was such that they were always planning ahead.'[1]

Fifty-ton monoliths, dragged into position on logs, and manhandled with liana ropes, were erected to mark the passing of *notuns* of five, *lakuntuns* of ten, and *katuns* of twenty years. Deep into the monolith, with stone implements, they would cut the likeness of a thick-set, heavily featured man, wearing a short tunic, a great head-dress and cascades of jewellery, looking out at the passage of time. Or they would inscribe, in a frame of radiating convolutions, the glyphs which are not, as in Egypt, pictures of common objects, but artificial symbols of great complexity. 'The fantasies of Gothic decoration,' wrote Aldous Huxley, 'seem pedestrian by comparison . . . but however rich and strange, the extravagance is always rigidly disciplined, each hieroglyph is contained by, and completely fills its appointed square.'[2] They generally signify the movements of the sun, moon and stars and the recurrence of eclipses. The Maya also propitiated a tapir-headed rain god, and 'expressed the idea of

---

* The difficulties of collating the Maya with the Christian calendar are daunting; experts disagree by a couple of centuries. Most modern opinion inclines to the later dates adopted here.

death, with a penetrative force only surpassed, in all the history of art, by the Aztecs'.[3] At the height of their culture, which coincided in Europe with the Dark Ages, in India with the Guptas, and in China with the T'ang, the Maya built huge pyramidal temples, altars and observatories, with staircases and colonnades. They produced fine sculptures in jadeite as well as stone, and bright pottery with brisk designs often depicting their ritual ceremonies. They could also carve in low relief – as when a throned high priest, crowned with nodding toucan and parakeet feathers, accepts an offering with nonchalant dignity. Their language may be indicated by some names still current in the sixteenth century: *Ah-moo Chan Xin*; *Ahtz – 'un Chinab*; *Napoot Cupul*.

By the ninth century their cities were left to rot. It may be that their method of agriculture was suicidal, since they continually burnt off the vegetation and, in time, turned the ground into a savannah of matted grass. This creeping disaster may have coincided with some hysterical climax in religion. When all failed, perhaps the priests, like other philosophers, lost their faith and their prestige. Such a run of bad luck may have been too much for them: perhaps, as one authority suggests, they just became plain crazy.

The archaic Maya civilization is unique. It was developed quite independently; it shows what ingenuity can do, and it stands behind the central American civilization of the Toltecs and Aztecs in Yucatan and Mexico.

## III

The Mayas in Yucatan were overrun in the ninth century by the Itzas, a warlike, Nahuna-speaking tribe from central Mexico, who may at first have been brought in as mercenaries. They worshipped Quetzalcoatl, the feathered serpent, whose likeness appears in the sculptures of Chichen Itza, a ceremonial city which blends Maya and Mexican architecture, and at Mayapan, a fortress which dominated the Yucatan peninsula in the Middle Ages.

Up in Mexico itself, the Zapotecs of Oaxaca and Tehuatepic in the south-west, and the people of Teotihuacán in the high valley of Mexico near the Acolman River, had early created ceremonial cities in more favourable surroundings than Guatemala.

About the time that the Maya centres were abandoned, the Toltecs, originally a nomadic warrior tribe from the north, and now based on the city of Tula, conquered Teotihuacán and began to make it the imposing centre of a warlike Mexican civilization, which prospered from the tenth to the thirteenth centuries. They had 'armour' of quilted cotton, shields and clubs, and worshipped the plumed serpent, a rain god and a frog goddess. They also worshipped the sun and moon, and built gigantic pyramidal temples adorned with glaring serpent heads with obsidian eyes. They made *pulque*, a powerful intoxicant, from the agave; invented steam baths; exploited their manpower to create the monstrous temple of Quetzalcoatl, where they buried captives at the corners of the foundations. 'Once,' writes G. C. Vaillant, 'we found a great red and yellow bowl . . . it contained the remnants of the *pièce de résistance*, the upper legs and hips of a human being, the most succulent portions for festive consumption.'[4]

Alongside this ceremonial city, the Toltecs also built the town of Azcapotzalco, which outlasted them. Together these cities realized the 'classical' phase of Toltec civilization, which flourished, by English reckoning, roughly from the time of King Alfred to the reign of William Rufus. There followed a period of war and political breakdown, from which the Aztec domination of the later Middle Ages emerged, culturally an elaboration of the basic Toltec society. The Tenocha Aztecs worshipped Huitzilopochtli, the 'Wizard Humming-Bird'; and by 1325 they had founded Tenochtitlán on an island in the salt lake of Texcoco in the great valley. Like Rome, it was a refuge for desperadoes, and the rise of the Tenochas is marked by ruthless war. Under Itzcoatl (1428–40), they built causeways connecting their city to the shore and organized an administration to exploit their conquests. Montezuma I brought in a good water supply and constructed a dam to control the flooding of the lake. His successors extended their power as far as Oaxaca and Guatemala and constructed a huge temple to Huitzilopochtli. The dynasty ended with the unfortunate Montezuma II, who perished during Cortez's conquest of Mexico in 1519–20.

Aztec civilization was one of tribal city states, among which Tenochtitlán became dominant. It derived mainly from the previous Toltec culture, which in turn, was influenced by the Zapotecs and even the Mayas. Religion obsessed the Aztecs, as it did the Mayas, but where the Maya religion was comparatively harmless, the Aztec religion was horrid.

At seven thousand feet, the salt lake of Texcoco and its adjacent fresh-water lagoons, were swarming with wild fowl and rich in alluvial soil on which maize, beans and cotton could be cultivated. They were protected by high mountains and surrounded by well-timbered hills. It was a much more stimulating environment than the tropical rain-forests of Guatemala, and its civilization was equally ancient and more dynamic. The Toltecs had principally exploited the valley of Teotihuacán; now the Tenocha Aztecs established a political domination on the main lake itself. They solved the most pressing economic problem by creating artificial islands (*chinampas*) made of reeds and mud, anchored to the bottom by tree roots and with the top dressing regularly renewed. These immensely fertile islands were linked by canals and provided harvests as rich as those of Sumer, Babylon and Egypt.

With this economic background, the Tenochas developed their own handicrafts and bartered their produce – for they had no money – in regular markets. Like the Chinese, they particularly prized jade, which they valued much more than gold, and it was not until after the Spanish conquest that the gold and silver mines of Mexico were all too fully exploited. The rich consumed 'chocolatl' from cocoa beans, and smoked cheroots in reed holders. They devised a ritual game, probably surpassed in complication only by the wall game at Eton. In a court the shape of a capital 'I', a rubber ball was propelled through a hoop by the players' hips and thighs; the winners, in the very rare event of a goal, were apparently entitled to the losers' clothes. They ate green and red peppers, avocado pears, pineapples and tomatoes, as well as turkeys, plump little dogs, and fish and wildfowl from the lake. Their cooking is alleged to have been elaborate.

Tenochtitlán, like Venice, was a city of canals and causeways, dominated by imposing temples (*Teocalli*). The steps which led up to the shrines and altars were cunningly contrived to promote awe. 'Pomp and panoply,' writes Vaillant, 'dominated their costume. On the barbaric splendour of high civilian dress was superimposed the fantastic garb of the priests and priestesses in their impersonation of the complex and ornately represented divinities of the Pantheon.'[5]

But the Tenocha Aztec's main business was war. Since they believed that the sun was swallowed up by the earth at night, and rose famished and thirsting for blood, they thought it a logical and paramount duty to provide victims for sacrifice. They therefore systematically raided their neighbours for captives. Their warriors called themselves 'eagles' and 'jaguars', and wore the skins of beasts or cotton garments woven to look like them. Armed with obsidian-edged clubs, with round, painted, leather shields, and with javelins propelled by throwing sticks (*atl-atl*), bedizened with huge feather head-dresses supported by wicker frames, the warriors advanced into battles in which 'the howling mob which represented the collective strength of one tribe tried to route the yelling horde of its adversary, and the first to run lost . . .'[6] War was a kind of ritual, in which the main object was to take prisoners, and in the rare intervals of peace, they staged ceremonial 'wars of flowers' between the fighting élites, which also provided the necessary prisoners for sacrifice.

The fate of captives was considered enviable. Like warriors killed in battle, they would go straight to heaven. They mounted the steep stairs of the *teocalli* and, deftly thrown on their backs across the stone of sacrifice, were ripped open by an obsidian knife. Then, with an expert twist, the priest snatched their hearts out and displayed them, pulsating, to the sun. It was all over in a few seconds; the sun was appeased, the victim became immortal; the cosmic order went on; the tribe was victorious. The priests, to set an example, lived in the atmosphere of a charnel-house, with matted hair and bloodstained robes. These revolting customs added a sinister note to a culture which oddly combined great sophistication and luxury with the most elementary incompetence. Without effective metals save beaten copper; without wheels; without the plough; terrified by the horses of the Conquistadors and utterly defeated by their cold steel, discipline and tactics; their fine poetry memorised only by picture writing, the Aztecs of Tenochtitlán, who represent the climax of a barbaric civilization paralleled in many other cities and deriving from the earlier cultures, administered a highly complex, artificial and amphibious way of life. Their rule cannot be termed an empire: it was a short-lived, if far-flung, supremacy over cities which turned against them, but it was one of the most original in history. It went down, fighting to the last, before the Spaniards, and much of it survives in the society of modern Mexico.

# IV

Down the western coast of South America runs the immense *cordillera* of the Andes. It contains some of the highest mountains in the world, its topmost peak running to 22,000 feet, and it descends eastward into the Amazon forests; westward it falls steeply to a narrow strip of now predominantly desert coast along the Pacific. Here, first in the coastal lowlands and, later, high above the clouds in valleys and plateaux at 8000 to 11,000 feet, overlooked, as Prescott puts it, by the 'precipitous steps of the Sierra, with its splintered sides of porphyry and granite and its higher regions wrapped in snows which never melt under the fierce sun of the equator',[7] other barbaric cultures were established, which culminated during the later Middle Ages in the highly organized empire of the Incas of Peru.

So famous has this empire become for its dramatic overthrow by a handful of adventurers led by Pizarro in 1530–3 that it has swamped the memory of much more ancient cultures on which it was based, and whose brilliant pottery and textiles are the finest in the Americas.

The tawny desert of the Peruvian coast had little rainfall, sometimes none. In winter the cold Humboldt current, drifting north, creates the fog which often envelopes Lima; in summer the tropical glare is unrelieved. But in the valleys of Huaylas, Cuzco and Titicaca – with its icy lake at 12,500 feet on the Bolivian border – there are well-watered valleys and broad pastures, the country of the llama, the alpaca and the potato. It was the extraordinary achievement of the Incas to combine such a fantastically difficult area under one rule, but it was from the peoples of the coast that the earliest and basic civilizations emerged, originating about 200 BC.

Behind the late medieval Inca domination there was a very ancient culture. By 1300 BC they had been growing maize. As early as 650 BC there was a large Neolithic ceremonial city at Chavin de Huántar on the flank of the northern highlands, and at Chupinisque in the Chicama valley north of modern Trujillo. Stone-carved jaguars, condors and snakes already state themes afterwards elaborated. By the time of Alexander the Great these Neolithic coastal peoples had further developed. At Moche near Trujillo and in the Nazca valley, south of Lima, elaborate cultures were established. The Moche society (*c.* 300 BC–AD 500) had most of the characteristics of the subsequent Peruvian empire, with irrigated, terraced cultivation, aqueducts and canals. They drank *chicha*, maize-beer, still a popular intoxicant, fertilized their fields with guano from the adjacent islands and chewed *coca* leaves, which had a soothing effect. They made pottery and realistic portrait heads, and vividly depicted hunting and ceremonial, as well as more intimate aspects of life. Their consecrated maces and axes are of almost Cretan splendour.

The contemporary Nazca culture is famous for its brilliant textiles, which the dry coastal climate has preserved – great cloaks, in exquisite colours, of cotton or alpaca wool. Superb polychrome ware, depicting fishes, birds and insects, was created at a time coincident with the Roman Empire and the Han. All this was achieved by a people without ploughs, with no domestic animals save the llama, alpaca and guinea pig, and without even bronze implements. These coastal cultures are related to the highland civilization which appeared at Tiahuanáco near Lake Titicaca in Bolivia by AD 500 and, at 13,000 feet, had left the most impressive Megalithic monument in the Americas. Carved out of one great block, in aspect reminiscent of Stonehenge and the Lion Gate at Mycenae, the Gateway of the Sun is dominated by the out-thrust head of a puma-like god, to which, each in their frame, worshippers do reverence. One monolithic idol is twenty feet high, and all form part of a ceremonial centre on a great scale. The pottery is particularly distinguished, painted with naturalistic flowing designs, in glowing and subtle colours. This influence spread down from the highlands, and is reflected in the coastal cultures of the early Middle Ages. It is likely that the Tiahuanáco culture was at its height about the tenth century.

During the European Middle Ages, until 1438, when the Incas first established a far-flung power, Chimu peoples on the coast near Trujillo and Lima built large, rectangularly planned cities, no longer ceremonial centres but the scene of considerable prosperity. When the small but ferocious and well-organized Inca tribes began their enormous conquests in the thirteenth century, they had long-established societies to exploit. Their legendary history, with its tales of Manco Copac who was descended from the sun, and of the miracles which attended his career, centres on Cuzco and the grim site of Machu Picchu in the eastern part of the southern highlands of Peru. The latter is perched among gigantic wooded cliffs, with clouds drifting below them, and surrounded by higher peaks. Much of its well-wrought masonry remains menacing and intact, with bastions, doorways and steep, well-cut, stairs. At Cuzco, smooth, beautifully coursed walls are curved and sloped for defence and, above it, reach their climax in the cyclopean fortress of Sacsahuamán.

The Incas were the only Amerindian people who created an empire. At its sudden climax, it extended from northern Ecuador to Chile over the most impossible variety of terrain in the world, from tropical rain forest to enormous mountains; from the cold *altiplano* round Titicaca to the hot deserts and rich valleys of the coast. By the mid-thirteenth century the Incas had conquered Tiahuanāco: they now proceeded to subdue the urban coastal peoples. But their first historical ruler was the Inca Pachacuti, who came to the throne in 1438. He was a ruthless conqueror, and his son, Topa Inca Yupanqui (1471–93), extended the empire northwards to Quito, and south to Bolivia and northern Chile. In a few decades the Inca Empire expanded over thousands of miles. Topa Inca Yupanqui was the greatest of all the Incas, and is said to have dispatched an expedition to explore the Pacific. It is possible that they discovered the Galapagos Islands.

He was succeeded by his son Huayna Capec (1493–1525); but his grandson, Huascar, was ousted by the illegitimate Atahuallpa, who massacred him and his family, and was himself captured by Pizarro in 1532. Although he provided a ransom by heaping a large room to a man's height entirely with gold, the last of the Incas was soon garrotted by the Spaniards for polygamy, incest and idolatry – a hard fate, since all these practices were obligations for the Incarnate Sun.

The death of the pious Atahuallpa enabled the Spaniards to take over the Inca Empire as a going concern. They found it elaborately organized, and held together by complex communications. Roads were a foundation of their power; through the highlands from Columbia as far as northern Argentina and, parallel, along the coast; connected, transversely, with the more important cities. There was no wheeled traffic and mountain roads were narrow, sometimes stepped, and connected by pontoons, or by suspension bridges of fibre, swaying over deep ravines.

Along this tenuous but comprehensive road system the Inca armies, messengers and administrators could move swiftly over an enormous area. In a curtained, gold-plated, litter, or under a state parasol, the Inca himself, carried by his highest nobles, led swift campaigns, or proceeded, from his mountain strongholds, to his more luxurious residences on the coast or in the eastern valleys of Ecuador. On this god-king centred the whole life of the State:

The royal throne was a low stool of red wood, only about eight inches high and covered with a rich cloth; this was placed on a raised platform. A small square, stiff, painted cloth pennant was the royal standard, but the emperor personally carried a war club or mace with a star head of gold. Two similar ones on long poles were carried to flank the royal standard.

Like the simplest of his subjects, the ruler slept on the floor . . . he ate from the most ornate containers of gold, silver or pottery.[8]

The royal Incas were much inbred, since, like some of the Pharaohs, they were too sacred to marry anyone but their own sisters, though they possessed, of course, numerous inferior wives, by whom they had large families. These morganatic descendants formed an important part of the aristocracy, the nucleus of the court and of the armies.' So holy and efficient were the royal Incas that usurpation was seldom attempted. Beneath this semi-royal class were the *curacas*, an aristocracy of officials, who ruled the *ayllus* or clans. They were supplemented by the *yanacona*, youths selected, like the Janissaries, from the clans for outstanding qualities, who often rose to high positions. The training of the Inca élite was exacting: they were drilled to fight with bows, slings and clubs, and 'expected to preserve an aspect of insensibility during flogging'.[9] They were drawn up in line and a captain would wield a spear or club 'dextrously among the novices, sometimes close to their eyes, and at others seeming to aim at their legs to break them. If, unluckily, any novice showed a sign of fear, either by winking his eyes or drawing back his foot', he was disgraced: 'They were expected to stand as immobile as rocks beaten by sea and wind.'[10]

The royal Inca, says Garcilasso, who as one of their descendants wrote the most authentic account, set off the broad gold fringe and great golden earplugs (Inca means, literally, 'big ears') which framed his dark countenance, by generally dressing in black, more harmonious 'because a black beast was black all over, while a white one always had a black nose'.[11] All the high aristocracy wore golden earplugs, and the 'knights of the blood royal', like the Japanese or West European fighting aristocrats, were supposed to observe a high code of chivalry, and 'endure the toils of war' without complaint. These formidable and remote rulers administered a static and communal society; 'as they had neither letters for writing nor figures for ciphering, they kept their accounts by means of marks and knots'.[12] In this primitive way they registered elaborate statistics of population, age grades and liability for public work. The cultivated land was divided into three parts, one for the priests of the sun, another for the Inca, the third for the peasantry: all belonged to the State. The peasants had to 'sow the lands and reap the crops of the Sun', and their overseers 'flogged the lazy farmers with ozier wands'. The mass of the Indians were thus immobilized; the roads and bridges were only for the rulers, their messengers and subordinates, and for the transport of their supplies.

But the government stored up the produce and insured its subjects against famine; supported the old; supervised a rudimentary and communal welfare state. Even the llama herds were public property. Work was, of course, compulsory; only monstrous toil could have built the cyclopean buildings of Machu Picchu and Sacsahuamán.

This sombre and static society was geared to war and religion. The peculiar Inca weapons were slings six feet long, and the 'bolas' of six strings, a stone on the end of each, flung and wrapped round the prey. They had pole-axes with stone heads and two-handed wooden swords, wood or cane helmets adorned with the feathers of toucans and macaws, quilted armour and hide shields. Their fortresses were well-sited and skilfully designed; in their tactics they were superior to the Aztecs; they planned far-flung campaigns based on swift, sudden marches, and kept their armies well supplied.

They worshipped Inti, the sun, and Kon Tiki Viracocha, who made the world, and, naturally, in their tropical mountain setting, a god of thunder and storm. In general they sacrificed llamas rather than humans, but on very important occasions they would select particularly fine boys and, after a great ceremonial dance, strangle them, drunk on *chicha*, to appease the gods. They would thus invoke the deity:

> Viracocha, Lord of the Universe!
> Whether male or female,
> At any rate commander of heat and reproduction, being one
>    who, even with his spittle, can work sorcery.

Sun temples (*Wacas*) were built in all the cities, and smaller shrines in the villages. The high priest, or *Villac Umu*, chosen from the imperial family, ruled a complex hierarchy, from the aristocratic higher clergy to the peasants who tended local cults. All were under strict surveillance: church and State were one. The sacred virgins of the sun were vowed, like the Roman vestals, to perpetual chastity; the almost equally holy 'chosen women' were reserved solely for the Inca himself. The priests practised divination, sometimes by watching the interesting behaviour of large spiders. Doctors specialized in trepanning skulls; with *coca* and *chicha* at their disposal, as well as a wide range of drugs, they even anaesthetized their patients. Their art compared well with medieval European surgery, since they actually washed the sick and cleaned the room before operations. Tobacco was taken as a prophylactic, as snuff.

The empire of Topa Inca Yupanqui extended over vast and various territories and over cultures as ancient as any in the Americas. It was far better organized than any other Amerindian society, and relatively benevolent. The ruling class practised an austere chivalry; the royal Incas were able and vigorous, and the phlegmatic subject peoples, toiling in their rudimentary agriculture, were seldom, unlike most medieval people, at the mercy of famine or external attack. The Inca aristocrats ruled docile peasants whose routine was enlivened by religious observances, by the consolations of the *coca* leaf and of *chicha* beer.

# V

The pre-Columbian Americans, in their three principal centres of civilization, Guatemala, Mexico and Peru, were to be pulverized by the impact of European conquest and decimated by European disease. All were subjected to the Spanish Catholic conversion and achieved a new kind of culture, based on a mixture of races and religions. Their subsequent history belongs to that of Latin America.

In the north, while the *pueblo* Indians of Arizona had achieved a settled urban culture, Mesolithic hunters, in various stages of development and adaptation, ranged the enormous wilderness. The biggest concentration of settlement was on the Pacific; 'Fittingly enough,' writes Dr Brebner, 'the rainy, lowering, Pacific coast, reared the most accomplished societies, the most subtle artists and accomplished craftsmen and the gloomiest religion . . . their poetry mirrored the pessimism, the rank violence, the sharp social graduations and the cruel glory of their lives.'[13] Here the Haidas – 'arrogant seafarers' – who lived off salmon and teeming game, who built fine cedar lodges and sea-going canoes, and practised the curious convention of the '*potlach*', whereby anyone who accumulated wealth gave it away in a lavish hospitality, which put inescapable obligations on the recipients, established the most sophisticated of the northern societies. In Ohio the Amerindians were building elaborate tombs and earthworks by the time of Augustus, and as early as the first millennium BC they were using Eurasian-looking pottery. The Iroquois in Ontario had 'long houses', and rudimentary agriculture. Snow shoes, moccasins, toboggans, canoes and pemmican, without which the white settlers could never have explored the continent, were all Indian inventions.

The losing struggle of these tribes in North America with the encroaching Europeans will later be described. Their fate was to be severe: where Latin America is based on a pre-Columbian population, the Indians of North America were to be swamped. French missionaries and *coureurs des bois* might mix with them, but the Puritan Anglo-Saxon settlers generally preferred, under fierce provocation, to exterminate them. Today, in the mid and far west, their descendants survive, mainly in state-subsidized reservations, the merry copper-coloured children recalling Asian affinities. And the 'Red Indian' remains a romantic memory in the folklore of North America.

# Fifteen

# MEDIEVAL AFRICA

## I

The interior of most of tropical Africa remained unknown to Europeans until the nineteenth century. But from earliest times Africa, unlike the Americas, had been important in world history. In the south the earliest humans had emerged: in Palaeolithic times the then fertile Sahara carried a considerable population which ranged north into Europe and, as already observed, the paintings of the Bushmen, who now represent the last remnant of a numerous and widespread race, are the only direct continuation of Palaeolithic art into modern times, a natural sequel, since the Saharan art surpasses even that of Lascaux. In Egypt a civilization of almost comparable antiquity to that of Mesopotamia flourished for millennia, and from it Mediterranean culture heavily derived. Carthage long dominated the trade routes of antiquity; the entire North African coast and its Berber hinterland formed an integral part of the Roman Empire. And when these territories, long fought over by Vandals and Byzantines, were overrun in the seventh century by the Arabs, they were absorbed into a Muslim culture which extended from Morocco to the Far East. The northern half of Africa was never a dark continent, though it was a strange one. The Africans exported gold, ivory, skins and slaves from both East and West Africa. It was the Negro peoples of the tropical rain forest, the high savannahs and the great lakes, and the Bantu-speaking warriors and pastoralists of the south who had remained mysterious.

## II

By the late Middle Ages much of North Africa was in touch with the Muslim world, and the western coast with the Christians of western Europe: certain barbaric and old-established cultures were described by the Portuguese and, later, the Elizabethans and Dutch, when they discovered the Guinea Coast.

Far to the south of the predominantly Berber Maghrib, and reached by caravan across the Sahara, were the sultanates which fringed the desert and extended south to the borders of the tropical forest kindoms of the coast. These sub-Saharan peoples of the Upper Niger were ruled by Muslim horsemen, who wore chain or quilted armour and built fortified cities, of which Kano, the Hausa capital between the Niger and Lake Chad, is a well-known survivor. The earliest of these Negro empires was Old Ghana, 775–900, between the head waters of the Gambia and Senegal and those of the Niger. It was conquered by the Muslim Almoravids from Morocco in 1076, revived by the Soninke and later taken by the Malinke of Málli. By 1307 their ruler, Musá Mansa, dominated Timbuktu, all the Upper Niger and far out into the Sahara to the territory of the veiled Touareg. Ibn Battutá visited Málli and vividly described it.

South of this Muslim-dominated area lay the pagan kingdoms. In physique, mentality, social order and surroundings, the Negroes were very different. They had a rudimentary agriculture of millet and sorghum and yams; kept poultry and goats. In their sweltering jungles, and along their mangrove-fringed rivers, they practised sacramental *ju-ju* in secret societies, the witch doctors impressive apparitions in magic masks. By the late Middle Ages many of their rulers were rich, their authority symbolized by golden stools and ceremonial umbrellas. These kings had great pride of ancestry, and lived in open-handed, despotic splendour; their artists made superb ivories and bronzes and their musicians haunting and thunderous jungle rhythms. Their people, dressed in bark-cloth, palm fibre and gaudy cottons, used gold, not for exchange, but for ornament. Benin was the most prosperous state; further west lay Ife and Ashanti, powerful by the seventeenth century.

Down the tropical coast, below the bight of Benin, past the mouth of the Congo, late medieval Africa remained unexplored, the forested interior the home of many tribes. Further south the Bushmen and Hottentots of the Kalahari and the Cape were harried by the Bantu expansion from the north which had been going on since late Roman times, but undisturbed by Europeans, save for casual contacts as with Vasco da Gama in 1496.* But by the sixteenth century the Portuguese, having rounded the Cape, were penetrating south-eastern Africa up the Zambesi; the missionary friar João dos Santos, met and described the Monomotapa, paramount chief of a well-organized Bantu state in what is today Rhodesia, representative of the warrior peoples whose depredations were to culminate in the kingdoms of the Zulu and the Matabele. An earlier and higher phase of Bantu culture was represented by the elliptical ruins of the Zimbabwe (*zi-mabwe*, great stones), which may date, by western reckoning, from about the time of the Norman Conquest of England.

The walls of the 'Temple' at Zimbabwe are 35 feet high and 15 feet thick, perfectly smooth, built . . . without lime, and of small stones, not vast Megalithic blocks. The mortarless walls have stood for centuries . . . and whereas the visitor to

*The term Bantu is a linguistic classification, covering peoples of mixed origin; it applies to those Africans who use the termination 'ntu', meaning, with a varying prefix, 'man'.

Baalbek, Stonehenge, or Luxor stands in wonder at the quarrying and engineering of the Cyclopean masonry, at Zimbabwe he is astonished rather at the craftsmanship involved in building walls to such a height, to stand so long without mortar, the outer surface so neatly ordered. The place is like nothing one has seen in Europe or Asia. . . . There is nothing of the geometrical precision to be seen in the ground plan of Stonehenge; one could hardly suppose that the builders had any knowledge of mathematics or astronomy . . . they do not seem to have known the concept of measurement at all. . . . But they must have had a high degree of political organization and a disciplined body of intelligent workers.'[1]

The ruins are a Bantu temple-stronghold, recognizably similar in design to Bantu royal kraals; they are only indirectly connected with mining and have nothing to do with King Solomon.

North, beyond the Zambesi, the Portuguese discovered Muslim merchants long established along the East African coast, trading up the Red Sea and with southern Arabia, India and Indonesia. By the twelfth century their principal depots were already Mogadishu and Kilwa. In the interior, among the highlands of modern Kenya, austere pastoral peoples, of whom the most warlike and untamable were the Masai, remained unknown to Europeans, and beyond, the highly organized kingdom of Buganda remained mysterious until 1862, when Speke visited the court of Mtesa, that temperamental Kabaka, who represented an ancient and sacred royalty.*

North of the great lakes lay a much larger, civilized, kingdom, long sought by Europeans: the Christian state of Abyssinia, now termed Ethiopia.† At an average height of 8000 feet, this odd, literate and basically Hamitic civilization was ruled by an originally Semite aristocracy, the only African society comparable in scale to the contemporary Christian and Muslim states. And beyond Abyssinia, cutting it off from the Mediterranean, were the now Muslim peoples of the eastern Sudan. Ancient Napata had been closely linked with Egypt as far back as the third millennium BC, and the kingdom of Meroë, flourishing north of Khartoum in Roman times, had become Christian, with links with Byzantium. But by the late fourteenth century the Muslim tide had swamped them: the Abyssinians, in their fastness, were the only Christian state in Africa.

So, from the Maghrib over the Sahara to tropical West Africa, round the Cape to the Zambesi and Zanzibar, and north to Abyssinia and the Sudan, vigorous African cultures at different stages of development had long been established. The interior of tropical Africa remained an enigma, but there,

*So sacred that the Kabaka 'loaded one of the carbines I (Speke) had given him with his own hands, and giving it full cock to a page, told him to go out and shoot a man in the Outer Court, which was no sooner accomplished than the little urchin returned to announce his success with a look of glee such as one would see on the face of a boy who has robbed a bird's nest. . . . The King said to him "And did you do it well?"' Perham and Simmons, *African Discovery*, p. 197.

† The name is geographically misleading, since, for antiquity, Ethiopia (in Greek 'the land of the dark faced people') lay in the Sudan.

also, elaborate settled communities must have already existed, as well as the nomadic pastoral peoples and the forest tribes. The picture of Africa now being revealed is not one of chaotic barbarism, as popularized in the nineteenth century, but one of a long-established variety of cultures, generally ruled, like the Egyptians, in terms of elaborately organized divine kingship. By the later Middle Ages and the sixteenth century African art provides evidence of these cultures, and the early explorers a glimpse.

# III

First-hand evidence for western tropical Africa dates from the fourteenth century: we are long dependent on the accounts of travellers, often prejudiced, as the Africans were illiterate. When Ibn Battutá set out, as he puts it, 'for the Negrolands' of Mállí across the Sahara in 1352, he came first to the salt mines of Taghaza, where the Massufa – in modern terms Sanhaja – carried on an already ancient trade with the Negroes. After ten days of waterless, 'demon-haunted' desert, without visible road, 'nothing but blown sand', the caravan came to Walata, the first outpost of the south.[2] Here 'the womenfolk of the blacks sold millet, milk, chickens, pulped lotus fruit, rice, *funi* . . . from which *Kuskusu* and gruel are made, and pounded haricot beans.' At Mállí, the 'Capital of the King of the Blacks', Ibn Battutá found Sultan Mansá Sulayman (1336–59), great-nephew of the Malinke conqueror, Sunjata. He was a magnificent potentate, enthroned under a silk umbrella on an ivory bench surmounted by an arch of tusks. 'On his head he had a golden skull cap, bound with a gold band which had narrow ends shaped like knives, more than a span in length . . . the Sultan is preceded by his musicians, who carry gold and silver [guitars] and behind him come three hundred armed slaves. He walks in a leisurely fashion, affecting a very slow movement.'

This contemporary of Edward III, like most African rulers, commanded a total obedience. Ibn Battutá wrote:

> The Negroes are of all peoples the most submissive to the king and most abject in their behaviour towards him. They swear by his name, saying '*Mansá Sulayman Ki*' . . . If anyone addresses the king and receives a reply . . . he throws dust over his head and back, for all the world like a bather splashing himself with water. I used to wonder how it was they did not blind themselves.

The sultan's armour bearers bore swords, ornamented with gold, in silver scabbards; gold and silver lances and crystal maces: 'at his head stood four Emirs driving away the flies'.

The king imposed strict discipline. Those out of favour might be exiled to the country of the cannibals in the south. One *quadi*, guilty of embezzlement, had lived there for four years, but 'the heathens did not eat him because he was white, for they say that the white is indigestible, because he is not "ripe", whereas a black man is "ripe" in their opinion'. When a party of Negro cannibals, suitably known as '*Nyam-Nyam*', arrived at the sultan's court, they had caused some embarrassment by eating the slave girl presented to them: 'The choicest part of women's flesh', they had remarked, 'are the palm of the hand and the breast'.

Ibn Battutá, wisely, did not venture further south. From Mállí he crossed the mosquito-infested Upper Niger, and proceeded by dug-out canoes to Timbuktu and Gao, the capital of the ancient sultanate of Songay. He returned north through Tugadda, with its copper mines, and on through the country of the Touareg, 'who wear face veils and are a rascally lot'. Fortunately it was Ramadan, when even the Touareg refrained from attacking caravans. The traveller finished his journey at Fez. He had found a rich country, trading across the Sahara, eastward across the Sudan, and with the pagan Negro states of the south and of the coast, using salt and cowries as a medium of exchange.

These coastal kingdoms were first discovered by the Portuguese in 1472; in 1539 de Barros wrote the earliest thorough European account; and in 1553 an Englishman, Thomas Windham, risked the fevers of the Guinea coast in search of pepper and gold. It was to be a disastrous enterprise; less than forty out of a crew of 140 survived, for the men exceeded in palm wine and fruit, in 'smothering heat and close and cloudy aire and stormy weather of such putrifying qualitie that it rotted the coates off their backs'.[3] But they came upon the kingdom of Benin. The Oba was a wealthy potentate, 'a blacke Moore (although not so blacke as the rest) . . . in a huge hall long and wide', He was keen to trade, and sent for pepper from the interior.

A century later Old Benin was a large, well-organized city, protected by a stockade reinforced by red clay. The Oba's palace now had long wooden galleries, under palm thatch, 'decorated with turrets ending in a point on which birds [were] standing, cast in copper with outspread wings'.[4] The Oba offered slaves, and the trade was not without its benefits for the Negroes; captives now fetched a good price, and fewer were sacrificed.

Swathed in bright cottons and checked calicoes leaving one shoulder bare, the rich in Benin wore coral or hair ornaments, anklets and arm bands: cheeks and foreheads were cicatrized with tribal marks. The poor went about all but naked. There was a teeming population: 'Every man,' wrote an eighteenth-century Dutch observer, 'has as many wives as he likes . . . the negroes are very libidinous, which they ascribe to their [palm] wine and good eating, which invigorates nature.'[5] Unwanted children were exposed in earthenware vases to be eaten by ants.

The religion of Benin was based on terror. Maluka, the fetish of the big water, Shango the thunder god, the Oba, himself a fetish with miraculous powers, were regularly propitiated by human sacrifice. The *Egugus* – medicine men – would prance, intoxicated, before the altars and, at the climax of their orgy, split their willing victims' skulls. These accumulated in mildewed heaps. Or men and women would be crucified between tree trunks and left as offerings to the god of rain. Hell, they thought, was in the sea. The masks and bronzes, now so popular in Europe, from which Epstein drew inspiration, had a sinister and entirely functional purpose. They show a great sense of form – solid and severe; others are frozen in a grin of terror. Enormous elephant tusks, matted with human blood, curved on either side of the altars, rich with carvings of cat-fish, elephants and snakes. One of the best ivory masks is decorated, in miniature, with a fringe of bearded European heads: leopard masks are notable for 'the clean way in which the teeth are depicted'.[6] Young women with cone-shaped head-dresses provide more attractive themes: the sculptors of Benin also eagerly portrayed the armoured Portuguese, wielding matchlocks and hung with pistols and swords. These strange beings made an indelible impression.

It is clear that the Negro societies in this western part of tropical Africa were much richer, more populous and better organized than those of the eastern Bantu or the Nilotes; they practised trade on a large scale between considerable and permanent cities and produced not merely for subsistence, but for markets. They therefore accumulated surplus wealth in a way which the improvident and primitive Bantu failed to do, and their standards of building, and in particular the art of Nok, Ife and the Yoruba, were the highest in Africa south of the Sahara.

# IV

The Portuguese had discovered the mouth of the Congo by 1482, but they sailed on south. Having rounded the Cape they explored the eastern coast, as well as reaching India. Gradually they also penetrated East African territory. In 1590 Friar João dos Santos, from Sofala, explored the Zambesi to Tete, south of Lake Nyasa. Sofala was already a rich country, with 'Indian figs as great as cucumbers, yellow when they are ripe'; sugar cane and palm trees yielded 'infinite cocos and palm wine'; salted lemons were exported to India. The Bantu *Quiteve* was a despot, with an immense harem. When the 'Great Lion' emerged from his sacred kraal, three hundred guards and executioners preceded him, crying '*Inhama, Inhama*', 'Flesh! Flesh!'[7] He had jesters, poets and musicians with horns and drums, who, plied with *pombe* (beer), played and danced before him. The Kaffirs,* as dos Santos calls them, grovelled to their ruler, prostrating themselves and crawling into his presence with averted eyes. They worshipped the royal ancestors, assembling on a hill top at the September full moon in their best finery, and feasting for eight days. They vaguely believed in a high god called Molungo, but thought that the *Quiteve* controlled the fertility of the

* An Arabic term for 'infidel', applicable also to Christians.

land. They held, too, that the monkeys were formerly men and women, and called them 'the old people'.

The subjects of the *Quiteve*, observed the friar, were all 'black as pitch'. They wore their hair in 'horns' piled one above the other – 'as male wild beasts have horns, which the females want, so do these savage beasts also.' And though their chiefs wore gaudy cotton, and even silk, the ordinary people went stark naked, save, sometimes, for a monkey skin. Most of the work was done by women.

Up the Zambesi, in modern Mashonaland, reigned the Mambo, the paramount chief, or Monomotapa (supreme conqueror), of the most extensive Bantu kingdom. He carried a gold pointed assegai, but, like his subjects, lived in a round thatched wooden hut. His warriors, dos Santos recorded, spoke not, like the Moors, in their throats, but pronounced their words 'with the end of the tongue and lips . . . in a whistling accent wherein they place great elegance'. Execution was by assegai, justice by ordeal – by poison, licking a red hot iron or by an emetic, cast up by the innocent, on which the guilty choked. Through this prejudiced but detailed account a highly organized tribal society can be discerned. Mambo was doubtless representative of other great chiefs of the Bantu in that part of Africa and further south. They embodied a lazy and predatory way of life, but one based on fairly substantial agriculture – on the coast, comparatively rich – and with iron weapons and elaborate tribal ritual. They must have already been much less primitive than the Masai pastoralists of the highland interior further north, who were ruled not by great chiefs but by tribal elders, and they had considerable wealth through trade with India, southern Arabia and the Far East.

## V

Very different from the Bantu were the peoples of the Abyssinian highlands. In Saba in the Yemen, in the early first millennium BC, had lived a tribe called the Habash. They had crossed the Red Sea and, penetrating into the north-east of modern Ethiopia, had established a kingdom at Axum in the present province of Tigre. They had exchanged the desert for strange surroundings: rising steeply from the Red Sea coast behind Massawa and Eritrea, the Abyssinian plateau is furrowed by deep gorges and intersected by mountains that run to 15,000 feet. Out of Lake Tsana, south of Gondar, the Blue Nile sweeps round Debra Markos and north to Khartoum to meet the White Nile from the Uganda lakes. Southward, the country is divided by the valley of the Hawash, running seaward between Addis Ababa – at over 10,000 feet – and Harar. Although in the latitude of southern India and Ceylon, the Abyssinian highlands have a good rainfall and a bracing climate; the precipitous valleys are well-timbered, with tropical vegetation; the rich fauna include lion, civet cat, ostrich and hyena.

The Habash of Axum, in Greek *Abbasenoi*, lived in their fastness for many centuries. It was a country difficult to govern; the truncated cones of the mountains, known as *ambas*, were natural strongholds, some even broad enough for self-sufficient communities and their cattle. But gradually the authority of Axum extended south over the provinces of Gojjam and Shoa, as well as of Amhara and Tigre. In Roman times, influenced by the civilization of the Sudan – the Ethiopia proper from whom they took their official language, Geez – they were converted in the fourth century AD by St Frumentius of Alexandria to Coptic Christianity. He became the first Abuna of the Abyssinian Church. The rulers of Axum also claimed a more ancient Hebraic contact. The Queen of Sheba, or Saba, they believed, had been the mother of Menelik, the eldest of Solomon's sons.* Menelik had refused the succession in Jerusalem, and made off to his mother's country with the Ark of the Covenant, leaving a substitute under the sacred coverings in the Temple. The royal line of Abyssinia thus descended from King David himself: the emperor of modern Ethiopia, through a female descent, was styled Lion of Judah.

The Christian gospels were soon translated into Geez; during the centuries an extensive literature grew up, theology, chronicles and hymns. The Chronicles of Axum record the reign of King Amda Seyon (1314–44); unlike most medieval Africans, the Abyssinians had an ancient written culture behind them. They formed a bastion of Coptic Christianity. It was isolated, save for a tenuous export trade in ivory, gold, slaves and coffee, of which the original plants came from Kaffa in their territory. Their memory lived on in the West in legends of Prester John, formerly applied to the Nestorians of central Asia.

By the late fifteenth century the Portuguese had found them. In the reign of Lebna Dengel, a contemporary of Henry VIII, a Portuguese expedition was helping them against the Muslims, and Francisco Alvarez described the country and its people. The Negus, whom Alvarez calls 'the Prester', he found encamped on a wide plain. Among innumerable white tents was a great red one with a series of red and white-bound arches leading up to it.[8] Before the Negus stood men cracking whips to clear the crowds. There were mace bearers in silk shirts, with lion skins over their shoulders and round their waists, and adorned with coarsely set jewellery. Four saddled horses, caparisoned in rich brocade and with plumed diadems, waited near

---

*She had arrived at Jerusalem with 797 camels and vast quantities of ivory and gold. Impressed by her beauty, Solomon obtained her favours by a trick. A highly spiced dinner made her parched with thirst, so that she was constrained to take a jar of water from the king by force, thus breaking a mutual contract that neither would do violence to the other. Once the oath was broken, Solomon felt free to act in the interest of his dynasty and Menelik proved the finest of his sons. The legend, which dates from the eleventh century, and was given its final form in the thirteenth, proved a great asset for a dynasty and a people fighting heavy odds. See A. H. M. Jones and Elizabeth Monroe, *A History of Abyssinia* (Oxford 1935), pp. 10–21. This work is the standard history.

the richly carpeted tent: four unfortunate lions were tethered with massive chains. The Negus, fascinated by the Catholic ritual, at once demanded of Alvarez whether he obeyed 'Constantinople in Greece or Rome in Frankland'? They spent hours discussing the nicer points of ceremony, and the friar presented a complete set of vessels for the mass. The country, indeed, swarmed with priests, monks and nuns. The Abuna, seated on a bedstead under a curtain, in a 'white cotton robe of fine thin stuff', and a hooded upper garment 'like a good cloak for rain', had a beard 'like white wool'. Like the Negus, he was guarded by men with whips, and he had two tremendous state umbrellas 'big enough to cover ten men'. Behind another magnate hung four swords, each on a pole, and two great books, similarly suspended. The monks wore yellow habits of coarse cotton, or garments of tanned goat-skin 'like wide breeches'. The heavily bearded priests chanted their liturgy to the sound of drums and cymbals. In contrast to the lion-skins, brocades and 'Mecca velvets' of their rulers, the populace wore dirty white cotton or strips of moth-eaten oxhide. They had wine and mead, but their agriculture was primitive. Horses were rare and unshod: mules and donkeys were better suited to the country. Dynastic politics were complicated, since the Negus normally had six wives: all the royal relations, if not blinded, were, therefore, shut up for life on an *amba*, a 'cold and extensive mountain'.* Such was the impression given to an early sixteenth-century Portuguese of the extraordinary civilization of Abyssinia.

Ancient Ethiopia itself lay north below the mountains in the heat of the Sudan. Long ago the Ethiopians of Napata had provided guards for Minos and had briefly conquered Egypt in the eighth century BC. 'The Ethiopians who dwelt in that part of Syria which borders upon the southern seas,' Herodotus remarked, were the 'tallest and handsomest men in the whole world.' They defied Cambyses, for their king sent him a great bow, saying: 'When the Persians can pull a bow of this strength thus easily, then let them come with an army of superior strength against the long-lived Ethiopians . . .'[9] Herodotus may well have heard of the Dinkas, a particularly tall Nilotic people, then perhaps living in the northern Sudan, now pastoralists in the territory between the great lakes of Uganda and the papyrus swamps of the Sudd, the country of the Nuer.

By the late Middle Ages the Shilluk were also established round modern Malakah and Fashoda. All these Nilotes, and the elephant herds of the southern Sudan, were to be exploited by Arab traders in slaves and ivory. Further north, towards Egypt, Napata had been succeeded by iron-bearing kings of Kush, then by old Meroë, on the curve of the Nile between Khartoum and Dongola. Here a Christian kingdom had held out until the

---

*Hence the legends on which Dr Johnson, who read Alvarez in *Purchas His Pilgrims*, based *Rasselas*.

eleventh century; but by 1182–3, when Renaud of Chatillon, lord of Oultre Jordan and of Krak des Chevaliers, launched his reckless crusade down the Red Sea to strike at Mecca, the heart of Islam, and plundered the port of Aidhab on the way, no Christian kingdom survived in the Sudan.*

# VI

From the late Middle Ages to the end of the sixteenth century, Muslims and Europeans were thus in touch with the more advanced societies of Africa; but the Congo hinterland, Uganda, most of Tanzania and the Kenya highlands, the Rhodesias, the Transvaal, the Kalahari and the Karoos, remained unknown to Europe.

In the absence of indigenous written records, most medieval Africans can thus be seen only through alien eyes. The societies discovered were in many aspects barbaric, if socially very ancient and stable. In black Africa they were technologically primitive. The Bantu, who used iron for weapons, never invented the wheel or the plough, and their thatched, beehive huts were all of a pattern, the chief's being merely larger than the rest. They practised primitive, shifting, hoe cultivation and, in contrast to peasants in Europe or in most of Asia, their lives did not centre on villages, administered by headmen or elders, but on clan kinship and age groups. Kinship went by both patrilineal and matrilineal descent, and the land belonged to the clan, not to individuals. Marriage, too, was not so much a personal partnership as an arrangement to carry on the lineage; polygamy was general, and the position of women often degraded. On these close-knit clan relationships was superimposed, in the more warlike societies, division by age groups and, in particular among the Zulus, by regiments. The tradition of the clan was embodied in its oldest members, who were treated with deference as the representatives of the ancestral spirits, and in the chiefs, who were at once the guardians, the mascots and sometimes the scapegoats of their tribes. They were more powerful among the predatory peoples, Matabele, Barotse, Zulus, than among their victims, the Mashona, and the matrilineal Yao.

Since, outside the rich West African territories and Abyssinia, agriculture, in tropical Africa, was generally for subsistence, not aimed at producing a surplus to sell, there were no great differences in wealth, no large cities, and little permanent building, save at Zimbabwe and a few similar strongholds, which appear to be relics of a time of exceptional activity, which coincided with the climax of Arab maritime trade in the eleventh century. Since the land was owned in common, the tribesmen,

---

* For a vivid account of the attempt see Sir D. Newbold, 'The Crusaders in the Red Sea and the Sudan', *Antiquity*, 80; (December 1946). Within a day's journey of Mecca, the adventurers were killed or captured. Chained to camels, facing the tail, they were led to execution to the sound of cymbals and drums. Finally Renaud, refused ransom, was cut down by Saladin himself.

though extremely poor, had no anxiety over employment and, save in times of famine or devastation, could count on subsistence. By European, Chinese, Indian or Inca standards they were improvident, lazy and feckless, with no idea of technological improvement or personal enterprise. On the other hand they were enmeshed in a most elaborate system of custom, taboo and ritual, psychologically well-adjusted to a limited but easy-going and even satisfactory way of life, which encouraged endless discussion, fine manners and the more subtle nuances of social intercourse. Among the Lozi of Barotseland, for example, there was a complicated system of parallel royalty, male and female, with councils and committees and a kind of umpire-executive, the *ngambela*, who represented the people against the king, and a *natamoyo*, or sanctuary. Their laws, though unwritten, have sometimes been compared in principle to the English Common Law:

The conception of justice and equity, the idea of the reasonable man and what he may reasonably be expected to do, the need to hear both sides of a case and to cross examine thoroughly, the idea of a body of precedents among which there is likely to be a parallel for every given dispute – all these are highly developed from their own native institutions.[10]

This respect for law and custom, however, was often overshadowed by the power of the paramount chiefs, who at once embodied the ancestors, luck and tradition of the tribe, and leadership in war. The chief, indeed, did not exist in his own right, but only as a kind of tenant for life, dependent not so much on organized force or even on individual ability, as on religious sanctions, prestige and the support of his council. Yet his power was exercised through secret messengers and executioners, always at the ready; he could murder on impulse, and wholesale massacres of men, women and children were normal in the course of political and clan feuds.

In contrast to Europeans and Muslims, often more individual, more enterprising and efficient, the Bantu were part of close-knit self-sufficient communities, callous and conservative, but undemanding and, save in times of war and famine, set in a routine which gave them a kind of liberty. But seldom the liberty of individual responsibility and choice, or the initiative of personal ambition. The rhythm of their lives was slow, and their interest lay in cheerful idleness and inconsequent conversation.

It is significant that, of all people, the Africans, both Negro and Bantu, are most susceptible to music. As Lord Hailey in his masterly *An African Survey* remarks: 'The growing body of literature devoted to African music is unanimous in pointing to the exceptional position which it occupies in the life of the African people. Music infuses all the activities of the African from the cradle to the grave . . . it is the only constant factor which permeates the very fibre of African social and personal life.' Quoting from an official report, he concludes: 'The African sings about work, about hunting, about money, about women, about canoeing, about planting, about war.'[11]

The resilience was a desirable contrast with the sombre fatalism sometimes found in Asia, for, in black Africa at this stage authority was generally ferocious. Since all peoples are descended from barbarians, the facts do not prejudice Africa's future, but many Christian, Muslim, Buddhist and Confucian rulers, heirs to ancient civilizations, often paid at least lip service to humane ideals, and even acted on them. Yet if there was a basic social strength and solidarity among many tribes, the Bantu chiefs, in particular, were often hailed as the embodiment of force – as 'Mighty Elephant', 'Devourer of the People', 'Great Wild Beast'. These leopard-skinned warriors, a link with Palaeolithic savagery, were the nearest human equivalent to the major carnivores, comparable in ferocity only to the primitive Mongols.

The population was sparse for the immense area. African physique, customs and culture were extremely various; the people illiterate, excitable, volatile, untamed. Yet their societies, well-adapted to their different environments, had survived through millennia. Mysterious in its past, enigmatic for the future, the huge African continent lay brooding on the threshold of world history, to enter it fully only in the nineteenth century.

# Sixteen

# THE FAR EAST
# AND THE PACIFIC

## I

When, in 1497, Vasco da Gama had encountered negro musicians at the
Cape, he had sailed on up the coast of East Africa and, crossing the Indian
Ocean, appeared off Calicut on the Malabar coast in south-western India.
In 1500 the Portuguese sent a powerful fleet to break the Arab trade
monopoly and, by 1510, they had already established themselves at Calicut,
Goa and Bombay. They pressed on to Malacca, to Java and Sumatra, even
to Celebes, and by 1516 had arrived at Macao near Canton. A quarter of a
century later, they got to Japan. Spectacular as were the contemporary
exploits of the Spanish Conquistadors, the Portuguese first achieved the
original objective. When, in 1520–1, Spanish ships, under the Portuguese
Magellan, rounded South America, crossed the Pacific and discovered the
Philippines more than fifty years before Drake, the Iberians had circumnavigated the globe and foreshadowed a European world domination which
was to last until the twentieth century.

The civilization of China, by European standards, was fabulously rich,
and the spices of Malaya and Indonesia brought the Portuguese enormous
wealth to which the architecture of Lisbon and Coimbra still bears witness.
But the strange foreign traders were not considered at all important by the
arrogant rulers of China and Japan, if accorded the usual tolerance shown to
Malay and Arab merchants, and soon abused. Their fanatical and
rapacious brutality soon earned them the name of 'ocean devils', and their
trade, though lucrative to all concerned, was soon rigidly circumscribed.

The Ming dynasty in China had now been long established: founded in
1368, it was to continue, in terms of English history, until the first Civil
War. In 1644 it was overthrown by the alien and ferocious Manchus from
the north-east, whose dynasty, the Ch'ing, or 'Pure', was to last until 1911.
The Mongol Yüan dynasty had continued for only a hundred years; but it
had united the whole of China, and the Ming emperors inherited the
administration. The Confucian élite of scholar gentry, recruited by
examinations, still ruled the empire: complacent, conservative, worldly
and astute, they had no competitors, save the imperial eunuchs and court
women. Even when the Manchus became masters of China, they were

soon tamed by the cunning, the prestige, the indispensability and inertia of the civil servants. Though the Manchus subjected the Chinese to the humiliation of wearing 'pigtails', and socially held aloof, the dynasty, like others before them, was absorbed by the establishment.

## II

The founder of the Ming dynasty, Chu Yüan-chang, who had reigned as the emperor T'ai-tsu or Hung-wu from 1368 to 1398, came from the humblest origins. The son of poor peasants in the middle Yangtse valley, he had fought his way to supreme power, being distinguished from other bandits by his strategy and foresight. Since he had no territorial title, he called his régime the Ming – 'Brilliant' – and ruled all China from Nanking, inland from the Yangtze estuary. The city was better placed than Peking: in the thirteenth century the élite of northern China had migrated before the Ch'in and Mongols into the territory of the southern Sung, and the empire's economic centre of gravity, unlike that of the Han and T'ang, was now, of course, firmly in the south. Chu Yüan-chang's family had not possessed his strategic insight; politically the 'brilliant' period of the Ming empire was brief. His grandson was driven from the throne by a ferocious uncle, the Prince of Yen, who reigned from 1403 to 1425 and was known – to use his reign title – as the Emperor Yung-lo.* He moved the capital back to Peking, and built the vast Imperial Palace – the 'Forbidden City'. A formidable warrior, like his father, he had rebuilt the Great Wall, refortified many of the key cities of the empire and expanded his dominions. But by the mid-fifteenth century, short-lived emperors and long minorities had given the palace eunuchs their chance. A young emperor, Chêng T'ung, was dominated by a sinister eunuch, Wang Chen, whose military incompetence led to disaster. The Son of Heaven himself was captured by the Mongols within fifty miles of Peking; henceforward the Ming empire, with its vulnerable cities, was to remain on the defensive in the north. In spite of the depredation of the Mongols and of Japanese corsairs, its rulers carried on in affluence; but in 1592, in the reign of Wan-li the Japanese, under their warlord, Hideyoshi, invaded Korea and started a gruelling war; then, in the early seventeenth century, the alien Manchus stepped up their attack.

Finally, an internal rebellion against the last Ming emperor gave them their chance. In 1644 the rebels took Peking and the emperor committed suicide; but a fresh Chinese dynasty was not established. The rebel would-be emperor could not control his followers. One of his generals, in command against the Manchus, negotiated with the enemy, hoping with their support, to win the succession. The Manchus then entered the capital;

---

* The Ming restored the ancient custom of having only one reign name for each emperor. Hence Ming and Manchu emperors are generally known by these styles, which in fact, denote a period of time.

the rebel emperor was evicted and killed, the general discarded and the Manchu dynasty established. In spite of violent palace intrigues, it was somehow to last.

The Manchus now overran all northern China. They took longer to subdue the rest of the empire; and it was not until the reign of the Emperor Sheng-tzu (reign name K'ang-hsi), who crushed a dangerous rebellion in 1673, that they mastered all the south. Alien and unpopular, the Manchus and their northern officials harshly exploited their new territories: all the Manchu tribesmen lived off their subjects, the new emperors planting out strategic garrisons of 'banner men' over most of China. Gradually, this idle minority lost its prowess.

On the frontiers Manchu fighting qualities had more scope. The new dynasty extended the boundaries of China as never before; west into Sinkiang and Tibet and even to the Himalayas and Nepal; north far beyond the Great Wall, over Mongolia and Manchuria; south, intermittently, into Indo-China and Burma. The grandeur of the eighteenth century reigns of Yung-cheng and Ch'ien-lung was unsurpassed. But in the nineteenth century, before the European challenge, their vast, intensely conservative and self-sufficient régime proved an anachronism. In the later Middle Ages and the sixteenth century, Chinese civilization had been the most formidable in the world; by the nineteenth it lay helpless before western exploitation.

The early Ming period has left the most imposing palace and military architecture in China. The Forbidden City, with its courts, ceremonial gates and pavilions, their sweeping roofs tiled in yellow and turquoise porcelain, was to witness five centuries of imperial luxury and intrigue. Well-proportioned, massive yet elegant, it remains one of the masterpieces of the world. Military architecture in northern China now reached its climax in moated, rectangular, towered fortifications.

But, in the West, the Ming dynasty is more famous for its porcelain. Under the Sung, exquisite monochrome ceramics had been made, with a novel crackle in the glaze. In Honan a particularly fine lavender pottery was produced, though, during the Mongol invasions, this delicate industry naturally fell into decline. The Ming emperors made the manufacture of porcelain a state enterprise, and Sung monochrome ware was imitated; but the characteristic Ming court porcelain, made at Ching-te-chên in Kiangsi in the south, was quite original – brilliantly coloured in 'red, green, turquoise, yellow, aubergine and brown . . . sometimes supplemented by under-glaze blue. Gilding was added, either in leaf form, or applied with the brush.'[1] In the political decadence of the Ming, these superb ceramics were popular, and under the Manchus the industry was further developed, in part for export to Europe. The delicate *famille rose* and *famille verte* porcelains were made in the early eighteenth century; in

Europe the sequence of this development is perhaps best apparent in the great collection in the Rijksmuseum in Amsterdam.

In the seventeenth and eighteenth centuries the Chinese also made incomparable lacquer screens and wallpapers, with designs of pheasants and peonies and knowing, ornate, ducks. They were exported in quantity, and advertised to the world the wealth and virtuosity of the Far East.

During the Ming period there also developed a Chinese vernacular literature, which continued under the Manchus. In the fifteenth century, in contrast to the formal compositions of the scholar gentry, oral romances, long an entertainment of the people, were written down. Three books are particularly famous; the fifteenth-century *San Kuo Chih Yen I* or *Romance of the Three Kingdoms*, an historical novel set in the second and third centuries during the decadence of the Han; the mid-sixteenth-century *Shui Hu, The Story of the River Bank*, a long tale of romantic outlaws which covertly satirized the established order; and the highly sophisticated eighteenth-century *Hung Lou Mêng*, the *Dream of the Red Chamber*. The emotional adventures of the hero, Precious Jade, are set against the rigid conventions of Chinese family life. Adolescent as well as mature characters are cleverly delineated.

By the eighteenth century, if Chinese society was overelaborate and overripe, it still presented a magnificent façade, the culmination of a culture rooted in immense antiquity, deriving, socially, without any major cultural breakdown, from the revolution made by the Han, and, culturally, from even older Confucian and artistic traditions. The most creative phase of this civilization, rooted in the north, had been the T'ang; the most peaceful and artistic, the earlier and southern Sung; in colourful ceramics and architecture the most memorable had been the early Ming, and the most elaborate and far flung the period of the eighteenth-century Manchus. China has always been the dominant fact of the Far East, and such are the main landmarks of its pre-industrial past.

The secret of the duration of this great society was the cause of its nineteenth-century decline. The neo-Confucian scholar gentry who manned the administration were immensely able; but they were often narrow, complacent and corrupt.* The system, self-perpetuating by examinations and unique in the world, was inflexibly conservative and totally indifferent to technological advance. In technology the medieval Chinese had been ahead of Europe: by the seventeenth century they had been hopelessly outclassed, and they continued to regard the gadgets of foreign devils with contempt. That contempt has now been abandoned.

---

*Under the Ming the field of recruitment had widened, but it was very expensive to attend the examinations, which sometimes took a long time. On occasion one had also to bribe the examiners, and successful candidates having attained official status, had to set about recouping themselves from the taxes at once.

## III

When, in 1542, Portuguese adventurers first landed in Japan, the country had long been subject to a caste of feudal warriors and tormented by war. In 1185, it will be recalled, the Shogun Minamoto Yoritomo had established a military régime at Kamakura in Eastern Japan. This *Bakufu*, or 'tent-government', had superseded the ancient, august and ineffective authority of the imperial court at Kyoto, which retained only religious and ceremonial prestige. Japan had not, like China, developed a scholar gentry: her government was by the sword. For centuries the great provincial magnates, the *Daimyo* and their *Samurai*, fought one another, practising an elaborate code of honour, termed *bushido* in the seventeenth century. They fought at the expense both of the powerless court aesthetes at Kyoto and of the peasant farmers and fishermen, the majority of the population. After the death of Yoritomo, his wife, known as the Ama Shogun, or 'Nun Generalissimo', and the Hojo family, her relatives, had established a regency. The Emperor Toba II had played into their hands. Exasperated since the *Bakufu* had both confiscated the family estates of two of his favourite boys and cheated his particular dancing girl over some property, he devised an incompetent conspiracy which led to his own exile and the confiscation of his intimate courtiers' lands. The Hojo regents not only made the Shoguns decorative puppets, but the emperors, puppets of the Shoguns, became even more ineffectual. Like Chinese boxes, one within the other, the court, the Shogunate and the *Bakufu* at Kamakura held the ceremonial, the apparent, and the real power of Japan.

The warriors of Kamakura attempted to preserve the austerity and thrift of Yoritomo's régime against the luxury and idle elegance of Kyoto. It was well that they did. In 1274 Kublai Khan's Mongols, based on Korea, landed at Hakozaki in Kyushu, the northern island: they were driven by the local swordsmen to their ships and dispersed by a storm. In 1281, like the Persians against Hellas, they tried again. They came ashore at Hakata Bay, 150,000 strong, and they fought the Japanese for five weeks. Once more, they were driven into the sea and wrecked by a worse tempest; a typhoon, the *Kamikaze* or divine wind.

This double triumph, the equivalent in Japanese history of the defeat of the Armada in English, did not secure the position of the Hojo regency. By 1333, Emperor Go-Daigo II, taking advantage of the general anarchy, captured and burnt Kamakura itself and all the Hojo committed suicide. Five years later, the Shogunate was revived by Ashikaga Takauji, a military magnate who had supported, but turned against, the emperor. Based on the Muromachi quarter of Kyoto, the aristocratic Ashikaga Shoguns were to remain paramount for more than a century, when their power collapsed in a general civil war known as 'the Age of the Overthrow of the Higher by the Lower'. The wars of Onin, in part contemporary with the English Wars of the Roses, raged from 1469 to 1477 and continued sporadically into the sixteenth century. The *Daimyo*, the *Samurai*, and the *Ashigaru* mercenaries fought up and down the island; the court was bankrupt; successive Shoguns, enervated by luxury, abdicated.

The Portuguese now profited by this anarchy. They supplied firearms to the Japanese and established a lucrative silk trade between Macao and Nagasaki. They also brought a new religion: in 1549 the Jesuit, St Francis Xavier, arrived in Japan. But his initial success was to have a tragic sequel. At first, the prospects of Christianity seemed promising. Japanese aristocrats, 'lavish patrons of the arts, connoisseurs of exquisite tea kettles, consumers of Chinese silk', welcomed the Portuguese carrack that sailed annually from Macao. 'After the grace and favour of God,' wrote a Jesuit Father, 'the greatest help we have had in securing Christianity is that of the Great Ship.'[2] But when the monopoly was broken and the Japanese began to possess their own silk, a religion which implied that all their revered ancestors were in hell became less popular.

The change in policy also reflected a social revolution. In the late sixteenth century, the old aristocratic Shogunate was transformed into a centralized, if feudal, government. Oda Nobunaga, who came of obscure provincial gentry, and his henchman, Hideyoshi (1582–98), originally a peasant soldier of fortune, subdued all the great barons of the West. The last Ashikaga Shogun committed suicide in his burning palace, and a more realistic and formidable régime came in. By 1590 Hideyoshi had established a new centre of government, and away from Kyoto, at Yedo, eastward along the coast from Kamakura, on the site of modern Tokyo. As already recorded, he promptly invaded Korea, intending to conquer the decadent Ming government of China. He died, frustrated of megalomaniac ambitions, in 1598. After a great battle at Sekigahara in 1600, Tokugawa Ieyasu, Hideyoshi's ablest commander, destroyed his superior's entire family: by 1615 he had subdued Osaka and attained supreme power. The Tokugawa Shoguns were to rule Japan until 1868.

The new, and more efficient, régime soon decided to extirpate the Christians. It held that they had abetted aristocratic anarchy, and about 300,000 were massacred. The Japanese were now forbidden to travel abroad, and in 1639, the Portuguese were expelled; in the following year Europeans were forbidden the country, only the Dutch keeping a foothold, soon lost. By the middle of the seventeenth century, the Japanese rulers, determined that potential rebels should get no foreign help, had deliberately and efficiently turned their backs on the outside world, a policy maintained for nearly two centuries.

The new Shogunate was still a *Bakufu* 'tent government' – the centralized, highly elaborate rule of the sword. The development of Japan was stereotyped and held; the benefits of nascent western science discarded, trade restricted, the country subjected to repressive laws. But, for the first time in centuries, there was peace.

The history of Japan had thus run clean contrary to the contemporary development of important states of western Europe, where feudalism had been superseded by monarchs in alliance with the bourgeoisie and the administrators, and even to that of China, where, in principle, military had been subordinated to civil power. Though the government was more centralized and less aristocratic, the position of the *Samurai* remained exalted: they had the right, if insulted by 'persons of low degree such as townsmen and farmers', to 'cut down and leave.'[3]

Religion and literature contributed to their supremacy. The basic pessimism of Buddhist beliefs, without hope for a world of illusion; the code of personal honour common to warrior peoples, as among the pagan Norsemen in the West, focused in Japan on the sword; the diversion of deeply held Confucian principles from the service of the State to that of a feudal overlord, and the Shinto cult of ritual personal purity and intense aesthetic perception, combined with the excitability of a partly southern people to encourage at once a stoical and belligerent ideal. Many Japanese monks, far from contemplating eternity, were notoriously turbulent: often whole monasteries attacked one another and 'bellicose Buddhist monks, after ravaging the countryside, retreated to hilarious potations in the heavily fortified "monastery of the Original Vow"'.[4] The new government brought them under better control.

Already, by the thirteenth century, patriotic feeling was apparent. The religious reformer, Nichiren, had thought contemplative Buddhism enervating, and proclaimed himself the 'pillar' and 'eyes' of Japan: his lotus sect survives. Zen Buddhism encouraged an austere self-mastery, a refinement of aesthetic sense. The culture of medieval Japan, like that of contemporary Europe, was aristocratic and religious. Yoritomo founded rich monasteries and imported Sung artists and architects. The picture scrolls of legends and romances, vividly illustrated the life of thirteenth-century Japan.[5] Yoritomo himself is portrayed, in all his watchful ruthlessness, close-up, on silk. Many *Daimyo* and *Samurai* were illiterate – their clerks recorded their transactions – but they patronized the writers of martial romance; vernacular epics, the *Heiji* and *Heike Monogatari*, intoned to a lute, glorified their exploits.

The Japanese even throve on feudal warfare. Flimsy houses, built with an eye on earthquake and pillage, were swiftly reconstructed; paddy fields, unsuited for encounter between crustacean-armoured *Samurai*, often undisturbed. The competing *Daimyo* outbid their rivals in calculated profusion. And when the parvenu Hideyoshi and the early Tokugawas established their new deal, they became even more lavish patrons of the arts. Hideyoshi himself gave enormous receptions, 'tea-ceremonies' and 'flower viewings', attended by the highest nobility. Sensibility and swordsmanship were equally acute. As in the contemporary late Ming Empire, furniture and building became more ornate; as the country was cut off, more specifically Japanese, though tobacco was smuggled in as 'Life-prolonging Tea'. Silk screens and wall paintings reached a new splendour: they depicted 'blue-eyed tigers' (blue eyes were sinister) 'prowling through groves of bamboo, or multi-coloured *shishi* – mythical beasts like lions, amiable and curly-haired, that gambol among peonies against a golden background'.[6]

In the seventeenth and eighteenth centuries peace encouraged a new middle class. The merchants of Yedo – the population was half a million – became rich: they prospered at the expense of the ancient military caste; nobles ran into debt; inflation hit all the old classes and peasants escaped from feudal estates to swell the population of the towns. In the end the new interest broke even the policy of isolation.

In Yedo and Osaka during the Genroko period in the late eighteenth century, the big merchants, prosperous shopkeepers and artisans developed their own amusements. The urban Japanese devised the night life for which they are still celebrated; geishas, elaborately trained, combined politeness with allure, and to the formal ululations of the antique Noh theatre more vivid entertainments were added. Puppet theatres became popular, even with the government, since live actors caused so much scandal. The most brilliant of the Japanese eighteenth-century playwrights was Chikamatsu Monzaemon. He wrote of pirates, courtesans and palace intrigue: his famous *Chusin Gura*, still performed, describes the vendetta of the forty-seven Ronin (retainers) of the *Daimyo* Asano, who avenged their master at the price of their own ritual suicide – a classic example of loyalty, much admired. 'In the history of the Japanese,' observes Sansom, 'little part is played by a personal sense of sin':[7] it was offences against loyalty and good form that were considered deadly. The political theorists, Yamaga Soko, an advocate of *bushido*, and Ogyu Sorai, a seventeenth-century economist, 'held authoritarian views which might have been stated by Hobbes in his *Leviathan*'. The family, the clan, the feudal overlord, came before the individual. Manners, the Japanese sages believed, made man.

The elaborate, highly perceptive, cultures of the military caste and of the richer bourgeoisie thus attained a peak of insular vitality. Beneath them toiled the peasant majority, as had their ancestors, time out of mind: when famine and oppression drove them to revolt, they were ferociously suppressed, beheaded, cut to pieces with bamboo saws, crucified upside-down. Yet they admired the prowess and elegance of their superiors, and still venerated the politically powerless emperors. After the revolution of 1868, that primeval loyalty flared up again.

While the ancient culture of Japan had been taken mainly from Han and T'ang China and deeply influenced by Confucian ideas, by the time of the Tokugawas it was national. The contrast may be symbolized by the appearance of Chinese and Japanese magnates; the former enthroned, in florid, civilian, garb of embroidered silk, their rank indicated by a coloured button on a round hat; the latter, cross-legged in austere simplicity, the whole composition subordinate to the high-peaked cap of nobility, and, unobtrusive but handy, the long hilt of a sword.

# IV

South of China and Japan, the civilization of the Indo-Chinese peninsula focused on three great rivers, the Irrawaddy in Burma, the Menam in Thailand and the Mekong in Cambodia. Here were predominantly Mongoloid peoples; those in the lowlands had long achieved an elaborate and colourful culture; in the mountainous jungles of the interior, primitive tribes remained untamed. As already observed, Hindu Khmer temples in Cambodia were in being by the twelfth century, and the Thai capital Ayuthia had been founded by 1350. In Burma, on the other hand, divided from India by the Arakan and from China by the mountains of Yunnan, Hinayana Buddhism was early established: swamped in India by Hinduism, in Burma it flourished. By 1054 King Anawrahta ruled most of Burma; he was an ardent Buddhist and his dynasty is commemorated by the great Ananda Pagan pagoda, built about the end of the eleventh century. In spite of Mongol incursions in the thirteenth, Shan kings of Pegu in Lower Burma built the fifteenth-century Shwe Dagon at Rangoon, with its gold-sheathed, pinnacled, pagodas. In the sixteenth century, when the Portuguese had entered the country, a new dynasty under Bayinnaung (1551–81) took the Thai capital, but failed to hold it. By the eighteenth century, the Burmese capital was at Ava, on the Irrawaddy, north of its junction with the Chindwin.

Against this changing political background, the casual subjects of martial kings cultivated their rice-fields, mined jade and silver, felled and carved teak. They were not, any more than the Thais, afflicted by the Indian caste system, though their culture was mainly derived from India, and they followed Indian religions; Hinayana Buddhism, in particular, which derived from the *Theravada* formulated in the days of Ananda, the Buddha's disciple. It was practised, ideally, by Arhants 'translucent in mind': in spite of the bloodthirsty and endemic vendettas conducted by the champions of Ava and Pegu, the life of the common people, and of the saffron-robed monks they supported, placidly went on.

In Thailand a similar blend of culture is apparent. Among the ancient population of the south – Sakais, Was, and highly sophisticated Khmers whose civilization centred on Cambodia – the Thais of Yunnan had long penetrated. By the mid-thirteenth century the Thai kingdom of Nanchao had been broken by the Mongols: some Thais went south to form the confederation of Pong, whose boundaries are unknown;* others consolidated Thai influence over the Menam estuary and founded the kingdom of Suko-t'ai. Ancient Nanchao had been a considerable kingdom, fighting and negotiating with T'ang China. Thai warriors had leather armour and rhinoceros-hide shields, and the king 'eight white-scalloped standards of greyish purple carried before him, also two feather fans, a hair plume, an axe and a parasol of kingfishers' feathers . . . the chief dignitaries wore a tiger skin'. Suko-t'ai was founded in 1240 by K'un Bang Klang; under Ram K'am-heng the Great (1283–1317), the first king to possess a sacred white elephant,† a new alphabet was adopted, embassies sent to Yüan China, Chinese influences assimilated. By the mid-fourteenth century, Buddhism had modified traditional spirit worship. The Thais were deeply influenced by Indian Pali literature, and their complex coronation ceremonies are basically Hindu. Four decades later, Rama T'ibodi I, prince of U'tong, had founded Ayuthia; his successor, Boromoraja I, controlled all Suko-t'ai and invaded Cambodia. It was his descendant, Rama T'ibodi II, now paramount over the whole area, who received the Portuguese in 1511.

The political history of Thailand presents an intriguing mixture of violence and finesse. The Thais had refined sensibilities: when murdering their royalties, they put them in a velvet sack and beat them to death, untouched by profane hands, with sandalwood clubs. Dynastic succession was sometimes determined by single combat on elephants, creatures here still often decisive in battle, and even out of it, as when Laos sent spies into the Thai victor's camp, who cut off the tails of the captured animals, so that they stampeded among their captors and put them to flight. In the intervals of war, the Thais amused themselves with betting on boat-races and on fighting fish. Their art and architecture were delicate under the tropic sun.

## V

By the late Middle Ages the immense area now termed Malaysia and Indonesia, which extends for three thousand miles from the western promontory of Sumatra through Java, Borneo and Celebes, north-east to the Philippines, and east through the Moluccas to Amboyna, the islands of

---

*This early history is particularly obscure, since most of the records were destroyed in the sack of Ayuthia in the eighteenth century, and mid-nineteenth-century versions are unreliable. 'The chief peculiarity which strikes the student of all these versions for the *P'ongsawadan*,' writes one authority, 'is that starting from about the year 1370 almost any date is given wrong . . . they invented a complete system of chronology for themselves.' W. A. R. Wood, *A History of Siam* (London 1926), p. 24. Prince Damrong's *History of the Wars between Burma and Siam* (Bangkok 1920) is the most reliable.

† These animals, which lived in great splendour and luxury, were sacred because they were incarnations of the Saviour of the World.

the Timor Sea and New Guinea, had developed, on the basis of paganism, rich versions of Hindu, and later of Muslim, culture. As already recorded, since the time of Aşoka, the Kalingas from peninsular India had been colonizing in South-East Asia. Java was being settled by the first century AD, and the Pallavas had followed up this enterprise. By the eighth century the kingdom of Sri-Vishaya was flourishing in Palembang, and the first Brahman kingdom had been established in Java at Mataram. A century later, Buddhists had built the masterpieces of Borobudur.

The predominantly Malay population, who had mingled in very early times with a negroid stock, lived in bamboo palm-leaf huts and 'long-houses' built on piles. Central Asian paganism, the cult of *shamans* and spirit worship, had blended with a rich Hindu civilization from India. In 1292 a Mongol conquest had been attempted. The armies of Kublai Khan had crossed the Java Sea and landed at Surabaya in eastern Java. They had failed, and the prince of Madjapahit, who had led the resistance, had established his influence over the Moluccas and even Mindanao in the southern Philippines. This wealthy maritime empire marked the final political phase of Hindu influence.

By the late fifteenth century, it had been superseded by the traders and missionaries of Sunni Islam, who had long penetrated Indonesia both from southern Arabia and from India. In 1478 the rulers of Madjapahit withdrew to the isle of Bali where an elaborate Indian-Malay culture was to persist. Most of the rest of this great area was now ruled by Muhammadan rajas; in Malaya there was a strong sultanate at Johore; in Java a second kingdom of Mataram. But Chinese influence was also powerful. In 1407 the Ming Emperor Yung-lo, the former Prince of Yen, sent a fleet to Manila in Luzon in the northern Philippines, and to Brunei in North Borneo. Chinese traders would lay out silk, beads, metals and pottery and declare their presence by beating gongs. Emerging from their jungles, the inhabitants would collect the goods and leave spices, resins and rattans in exchange. But it was only in the wake of European enterprise that the Chinese settled in large numbers, though they had early exploited the tin mines of Malaya. In the seventeenth century Formosa was still in the hands of its Malayan aborigines.

When in 1511 the Portuguese took Malacca, they had a base on the Malayan mainland from which to seize the famous 'spice islands', the Moluccas. But they never systematically colonized. The Spaniards in the Philippines made a more lasting settlement: by 1564 Legaspi and the missionary friars were converting the pagan Philippinoes; Spain was to hold the islands, the only predominantly Christian territory in Indonesia, until they were taken over in 1898 by the United States. In the rest of the area the Dutch East Indian Company had a free hand. The English were preoccupied with India and, by 1619, the Dutch were established in

Batavia, the modern Djakarta. After the Amboyna 'massacre', they drove the English traders from the Moluccas, and by 1645 they dominated Mataram, whose degenerate sultan, Hamangku Rat II, became their puppet.

The mainly southern Mongoloid peoples of these large and diverse islands had common characteristics. They were generally villagers who practised hoe agriculture and lived off rice, fruit and fish; their dialects derived from the Malayan–Polynesian languages. They had little political organization beyond the village and the tribe; in their tropical environment they were an easy-going people, casually tending their rice-fields and their ubiquitous water-buffaloes in sweltering heat.

Over a thousand miles long, Sumatra, its eastern swamps rising to the central plateau and the volcanic peaks which confront the Indian Ocean, harboured matriarchal tribes whose term for a husband was *orang samando* – 'borrowed man'; Java, the richest and most thickly populated country, saw the most elaborate Indian–Malay medieval civilization, already established while western Europe was barbarous. In Bali, a picturesque miniature version of their culture flourished into modern times; its pagoda shrines, glittering head-dresses, and subtle temple dances are still celebrated.

Borneo was the most primitive of the larger islands: some of the interior is still little explored, hidden under matted jungle and haunted, until recent times, by sea-Dyak head-hunters. Armed with parangs and krises, blowpipes and poisoned darts, they emerged from their tepid estuaries, intent on collecting human heads. Smoked, dried, shrunk and set in the place of honour in the great partitioned long-houses, these prizes would ensure the fertility of the crops and the luck of the fishing.

North of Borneo, the Philippines harboured a variety of peoples. The Ifugao of northern Luzon built enormous rice-terraces, which dwarf even the irrigation of the hillsides of Peru; like the Dyaks, they were man-hunters, who whisked the severed heads of their enemies out of the mêlée with the speed of a scrum-half, and raced back to their village with the trophy to set it up. The Tiguans tripped their enemies with double-pronged shields, also useful in decapitation. The Bontoc Igorot practised trial marriage and still today, observes one authority, 'youths may go singly or in groups to visit the Olag [the girls' dormitory], or if a girl takes a liking to a young man, she may steal some article belonging to him thus giving a direct invitation for him to meet her at the Olag and recover it.'

In Mindanao, the southern island, under the sulphur-capped peak of Mount Apo, the Bogobo, who still 'file and chip their upper incisors and blacken the lower teeth', were the most elegant of the Philippinoes. Today 'two belts are worn, one to support the trousers, the other to support the . . . knives, and the men confine their long hair in headkerchiefs . . . decorated with beads and tassels.' These people were eclipsed in ferocity by the Moro of Sulu, Muslim slave-owning pirates, who long resisted the Spaniards with all the fiendish ingenuity at their command.

Thus by the late fifteenth century, in a great arc from Sumatra and the Malay peninsula to the China Sea, in a luxuriant tropical setting, with its spices, sugar-cane, minerals and timber; its fruits, durian, mangosteen, pineapple and guava; its teeming animal life, orang-outang, gibbon and tapir; tiger, deer and wild pig, dragon lizards and swarming fisheries, a wide range of cultures had grown up. The older derived, above its Malayan foundation, from Hindu India, the more recent from Islam: both had been assimilated and reinterpreted by a gifted and self-confident people, in part a branch of the Mongoloid race who dominated the Far East.

# VI

Eastward, in the wastes of the Pacific, the peoples of Melanesia, Micronesia and Polynesia were scattered over an even greater area, more than ten thousand miles, across the biggest of all oceans, covering a third of the globe. Melanesia, inhabited by a predominantly negroid race, included the great island of New Guinea, the Solomon Islands, the New Hebrides and Fiji. Micronesia, between Melanesia and Japan, included the Marianas, the Carolinas, the Gilbert and Marshall Islands. Polynesia extended in a huge triangle from Hawaii to New Zealand and Easter Island; it included Samoa, Tonga, Tahiti, the Society Islands and the Marquesas.

The Melanesians were in part descended from the Negritos, in part, probably, from an Australoid stock akin to the *Vedas* and Dravidians of Ceylon and southern India and to the Australian aborigines, as well as from an admixture of early Malay immigrants. In Micronesia, which was next colonized, the proto-Malayan element was dominant. Polynesia was settled many centuries later, by brown-skinned peoples of more massive physique, with a Caucasoid strain. Samoa, then Tahiti, seem to have been early centres of their culture: from Tahiti during the twelfth and the thirteenth centuries, New Zealand and Hawaii were colonized. The origins of all these peoples are Indonesian; ultimately, Asian. In spite of Heyerdahl's voyages, there is no conclusive evidence to link the Polynesians racially with the Americas.

When, in the first century AD, Indian influence reached Indonesia, all this oceanic world was Neolithic: it remained so until the advent of Europeans. The most primitive and stay-at-home Melanesians were the Negrito–Australoids of Papua; in Fiji they were more sophisticated, addicted to magic, secret societies, ritual masks and tattooing; they had outriggers and double canoes. The Polynesians, more advanced, had an elaborate art and culture, an oral literature and a superb skill in navigation. By the fourth century BC, they had begun to emigrate from Indonesia; their ocean-going canoes, seventy or eighty feet long, rode the long Pacific rollers and breasted the Pacific surf. They were ruled by hereditary paramount high chiefs who were supported by tribute in kind, and they fought, in coconut husk helmets, with slings, wooden war clubs and wooden spears. As they moved east, they discarded the loom and pottery: with hibiscus fibre and palm and pandanus leaves, they could make matting, and coconut shells and gourds served their turn.

Originally the Pacific was divided into relatively small areas of navigability, 'a number of little worlds, inaccessible except by accidental migration'.[8] Within these areas, off-shore voyages of two or three hundred miles were possible, when winds and currents were favourable: as the generations passed, greater one-way chance voyages occurred, covering immense distances. They were followed up, if contact was maintained. If not, the survivors multiplied, or died out, on their own. Polynesian ocean-going canoes were:

. . . equipped with mast, sails, paddles, bailers and stone anchors. Some vessels had as many as three masts. The sails were made of plaited pandanus mats sewn together in triangular form with wooden yards and booms to strengthen the long sides of the triangle. They were rigged as sprit-sails with the apex at the base of the mast, or as lateens with the yard slung from the mast and the apex forward at the bow . . . Polynesian paddlers faced forward towards impending waves and ever receding horizons.[9]

The steering paddles had names:

> Behold my paddle, Te Roku-o-whiti,
> See how it flies and flashes,
> It quivers like a bird's-wing.[10]

'The Arawa Cance, which sailed down to New Zealand in AD 1350, had two stone anchors named Tokaparore and Tu-Te-rangiharuru.'

These far-flung migrations were not romantic enterprises. They were occasioned by pressure of population on limited food supplies, and 'the weaker peoples with the least food must have left first and the strongest left last. . . .' Hence 'the distinction between chief and commoner is due not only to breeding and selection but to the food supply that accompanies rank.' All crews were skilled deep-sea fishermen, well-versed in the lore of winds and currents, capable of transporting women and children, animals and plants – young shoots of bread-fruit, banana, yams and the taro, the sweet potato, which much have been brought in originally by daring adventurers who had reached Peru. Pigs and poultry survived some voyages, not others. Both were unknown in New Zealand: there only the dog was acclimatized.

From the complex and rich mythology of the Polynesians, with their long genealogies, it would seem that by about AD 450 they had long been settled in Samoa in western Polynesia. The Tui Tonga, the high chiefs of the neighbouring Tongan islands, traced their descent back to the tenth century. From western Polynesia they colonized Tahiti and the surrounding islands of central Polynesia, and from there, during the European 'Dark' Ages, probably by accident when blown off course, reached Hawaii, then New Zealand and the islands of the East. In Hawaii they found a rich country, where they built great temples and images of their gods and devised ceremonial from which the Hula dances derive. These people were not 'noble savages'; they were sometimes belligerent cannibals, but their achievement is astounding.

> The fame of your canoes [runs a Maori lament]
> can never be dimmed,
> The Canoes which crossed the ocean depths
> The purple sea, the great Ocean-of-Kiwa.

# Seventeen

# THE WESTERN CENTURIES OF GENIUS

## I

Far to the west of the oceanic world of Polynesia, Europeans were also exploring new horizons, intellectual as well as maritime. As already observed, the dynamic qualities which were to make western Europe a springboard for a world-wide expansion, and for a scientific and industrial revolution which gave rise to the first potentially world-wide culture, were already apparent in the late Middle Ages. At bay on the Danube, the Balkans and the Levant, and politically incoherent in much of central and eastern Europe, the sixteenth-century western Europeans launched out into the oceans, outflanked the great land powers of central Asia, India and the Far East, circumnavigated the globe and began the settlement of predominantly European nations in the Americas. By the early seventeenth century, moreover, the Russians, having established a massive State in the central, forested, zone of their vast territory, began their expansion across Siberia and their drive south-east across the steppe to the Black Sea and the Caucasus.

If the initiative came from the Atlantic peoples, who, following the Turkish attack, had succeeded the Italians as the pioneers of western economic enterprise, the ideas and the political structure which were often to make Europe different from the rest of the world came mainly from the Mediterranean, and were reinterpreted in the north. It was long fashionable to decry the term 'Renaissance', since it is well known how far back run the origins of this movement into the western Middle Ages and Byzantium, and because the reinterpretation of classical learning was conservative, even pedantic, while the original scientific movement which made the seventeenth century, and not the sixteenth, the main 'century of genius' owed little to antiquity. But the conventional term symbolizes a new outlook on life, centred, like that of pagan antiquity, on humanism, not on Catholic or Orthodox Christianity. But Europeans now determined to take hold of the world and change it. This revolutionary idea, expressed by Francis Bacon when he wrote of the use of knowledge 'for the betterment of man's estate', and by Descartes when he claimed that his new *Méthode* would make men 'lords and masters of nature', is already expressed in the writings of Leonardo da Vinci; the new cosmology of Bruno and Galileo was developed in ways already foreshadowed by Copernicus. While it will be convenient to describe first the Renaissance, and then the scientific movement of the seventeenth century, they are two aspects of one movement which made Europe decisive and original in world history.

For it was in Europe alone that this change of outlook developed. Why it did so is mysterious: through a unique combination, perhaps, of native aptitude, environment, stimulus, social pattern; the rise of independent city states and of rudimentary capitalism, along with the administrative efficiency of the new great state. Suffice it that countries, in which no Renaissance or scientific revolution occurred, present to this day a fundamentally different aspect, only now being changed. In the sixteenth century there was no comparable movement even in Russia; and while, as already emphasized, the Ottoman Empire, Mughal India and China were all larger and richer than the states of Europe, all were, as will be seen, swiftly outclassed, and to be helpless before the West – for Muslim, Hindu, Buddhist and Confucian beliefs all reinforced a conservative outlook. Since the decline of the Roman Empire and the disruption of Christendom into Byzantine and Catholic territories, Europe had not been comparable in power and wealth to the great Eastern cultures: now, after a phase of relative weakness, Europeans were long to dominate the planet.

## II

The revolutionary ideas and inventions took on within a novel political and economic structure. The most vigorous economies in late medieval Europe had been the cities of the north Italian plain, of the Netherlands, Flanders and the Baltic; the most promising centres of government the new monarchies, with their continuity of dynastic interest. These civic and monarchical centres of power had long been thrusting aside the ancient cosmopolitan institutions of empire and papacy, at their climax in the twelfth and thirteenth centuries.

These new dynastic great states were best exemplified by the Habsburg and the French monarchies. The first, by judicious marriages, came to control, besides their original Austrian territories, the Burgundian Netherlands, Milan, Spain and her possessions in the Americas and, for a time after 1580, Portugal and her colonies. And when, with the abdication of Charles V (1520–56), these vast dominions were divided, the central European areas and the empire were assigned to Ferdinand I (1556–64), and Spain, the Netherlands, and the American possessions to Philip II (1556–98), the Habsburgs tended to maintain a common front, in particular in promoting the Catholic Counter-Reformation.

The French monarchy, already very formidable under Francis I (1515–47), was based upon the most populous and favourably situated country in the West, and inherited the predominance of the French medieval kings, reasserted under Louis XI. The Habsburgs, their hands full to maintain the defence of central Europe against the Turks on the Danube and in the Mediterranean, managed to contain the first French attack, but the contest was to continue: by the mid-seventeenth century France had become the strongest military power.

Against the background of overriding European dynastic conflict, the sixteenth-century monarchies of the West and the Baltic consolidated the new kind of polity of which France was the leading example. The nation-state, today the normal unit of political organization, was beginning to emerge. Its original nucleus was dynastic, its structure modelled predominantly on the 'estate' or personal entourage of Italian despots. In France, Spain and Portugal, Tudor England, Denmark and Sweden, stronger governments grew up.

In central and eastern Europe, the picture was more chequered. In Poland, the kingdom of Sigismund Jagello (1506–48), which under his successor, Sigismund II, harnessed Lithuanian and native resources, had become a great military power. Under Stephen Bathory and the Vasa kings, who transferred the capital to Warsaw from Cracow, it dominated much of western Russia and the southern steppe. But the Polish monarchs never achieved the centralized administration of the new western great States. Elective, not hereditary, handicapped by the notorious *liberum veto*, already described, whereby the vote of a single nobleman could paralyse government; without a substantial middle class, and with territories generally devoid of natural boundaries, the Polish–Lithuanian kings could not compete with the centralized power of Moscow, Vienna or Berlin. In Hungary, the flourishing late-fifteenth-century kingdom of Mathias Corvinus – as brilliant as anything in Europe – went down before the Ottomans at Mohacs. Prosperous under Charles IV, Bohemia, after the burning of John Hüss in 1415, had asserted its independence under Zizka, but after the reign of Georg Podiebrad, it came, through dynastic chances, into the Habsburg net.

In Russia, on the other hand, cut off from western Christendom and little touched by Renaissance influences, the Grand Princes of Moscow had survived after the fall of Kiev Russia. Ivan IV (1462–1505), who married a daughter of the last Byzantine emperor, first proclaimed himself Tsar. Commanding great resources of manpower and unlimited territory, Muscovy, massive and centralized, heavily affected by Tatar influence, became extremely formidable under Ivan the Dread (1533–84). After a phase of internal strife and Polish invasion, it proved the foundation of the imperial Russia of Peter the Great.

Meanwhile Germany was divided by the interests of the electoral princes, haunted by the mirage of the empire, rent with religious strife, and exploited by the new great States; the Germans had no part in oceanic expansion. Afterwards they determined to make up for lost time.

The decisive political theatre remained the West. In the French–Habsburg conflict, the Emperor Charles v emerged predominant. By the treaty of Cateau Cambresis (1559), the Habsburgs consolidated their power in Italy, and at Lepanto Don John of Austria checked the Turkish sea power in the Levant. But the imperial Habsburg Austro–Spanish hegemony, which now acquired new wealth and discharged immense new responsibilities in Central and South America, was attacked from within. The Lutheran and Calvinist 'Reformation', or Schism, came to dominate most of northern Europe, and often became a conflict between the northern and the Mediterranean peoples. Philip ii of Spain undertook an ideological crusade against the heretic English and Dutch, as in central Europe the Austrian Habsburgs persecuted their Protestants. This 'Counter-Reformation' grew into a great clash of political and economic interests, surpassing that of the Arian and Catholic Christians in sub-Roman times, and in which even the wealth of the New World proved insufficient to bring about a Catholic victory.

In the conflict two new and vigorous sea powers emerged. Henry viii (1509–47) made England independent of Rome and imposed a religious revolution without a religious civil war; he also created the English navy. Under his famous daughter, Elizabeth i (1558–1603), the English defeated the crusading Spanish Armada (1588) and broke the Spanish mastery of the Atlantic. The Dutch, too, conducted an even more ferocious conflict with Spain. Driven from much of their territory by the Spanish pikemen, they endured horrible sieges, flooded the polders, took to the sea. After the union of Utrecht (1570), they became the most enterprising maritime power.

France, long divided by religious warfare, was reunited by Henry iv (1589–1610), the first of the Bourbons. Under Louis xiii, Richelieu became the architect of the most efficient centralized great State and his work, consolidated by Mazarin, became the basis of Louis xiv's attempt to dominate the Continent. For the policies of Philip ii had fatally overstrained even the resources of the Spanish–Portuguese overseas possessions: in 1640 Portugal broke away. In central Europe, also, the Habsburgs had now to meet a more searching challenge. Following the defiance of the Protestant elector palatine – a new phase in the perennial Czech-German conflict – the Thirty Years' War (1618–48) devastated the empire. The Swedes under Gustavus Adolphus Vasa, killed at Lutzen in 1642; the Protestant princes; the Dutch; and French diplomacy combined to weaken the Austrian Habsburgs, whose grip, after the treaty of Westphalia in 1648, relaxed over the Germanies, and remained close and predominant only on the Danube, in Tyrol, Bohemia, northern Italy and the Austrian Netherlands.

By 1648, political and economic power had, indeed, shifted away from the Mediterranean and the empire, first to the Iberian Peninsula, then to the north-west Atlantic states. England and Holland became the greatest powers at sea; France, also formidable on the ocean, the dominant continental State in the West. This Atlantic predominance was new, decisive for the whole world.

# III

The mainspring of these Atlantic powers was a commercial bourgeoisie, already important by the late Middle Ages. These rudimentary capitalists were urban, methodical, close-knit in a ramification of economic interest. Italian bankers had financed the political adventures of the late medieval kings: Jacques Coeur (1395–1456), of Bourges, had pioneered French trade with the Levant and financed the expulsion of the English from France. He reformed the French currency; ennobled and employed as an ambassador by Charles VII, he disposed of enormous wealth. Victimized by the intrigues of the French court, he escaped to Rome, where he was appointed to command a fleet for the relief of Rhodes. No financier had ever before played such a part in high politics. Jakob Fugger, descended from weavers near Augsburg, also built up a rich business in the mid-fifteenth century. Jacob II became banker to the Habsburgs, and financed the development of the silver mines of Tyrol. Under Anton Fugger (1493–1560), these financiers arranged the election of Charles V to the empire, and extended their grip on the Habsburg possessions outside Europe. Landed millionaires, patrons of the arts, they were munificent portents of a new age.

Less spectacular, but cumulatively important, were the merchants of London and Amsterdam, who financed the trading companies to Muscovy, India, the Far East, North America and the West Indies. The dissolution of the monasteries in England under Henry VIII, and the dispersion of much of their property not only to the established magnates but to new men, lawyers, sheep farmers, cloth merchants, court officials – ancestors, like the Spencers, Russells and Cecils, of a new aristocracy – accelerated this shift of power away from the old feudal magnates. The new great states could be financed only with the support of the urban merchants, which was founded no longer only on the cloth industry of Flanders and on the luxury, wine and wool trades of Europe, but on new oceanic connections and the disposal of resources of capital which made long-term enterprise possible. It was this change of mentality, of political and social influence, which challenged the prestige even of the high feudal nobility. It made kings dependent on bankers, and left the country knights and squires of Gascony, the Welsh borders and La Mancha in social backwaters, relics of a past age. The alliance of the new dynastic great State, its officials, of regularly enforced law and standing professional armies, with landed and mercantile capitalists, with their new methods of book-keeping, skilled clerks and auditors and far-flung network of intelligence, laid the economic foundations of modern Europe. By building up further resources they also eventually made the Industrial Revolution possible. The concurrent changes of mentality, systematic, far-seeing, went along with the new humanism, anthropocentric, empirical and observant, it was to merge into the scientific outlook first elaborately defined by Bacon and Descartes. This mentality even triumphed in the long run over the ideological fanaticism unloosed by the breakdown of medieval Christendom into Protestant and Catholic camps and, in spite of official censorship, produced a new tolerance which enabled novel ideas not merely to be formulated, but to be widely discussed through the new medium of print.

# IV

In the Italian cities the life of market-place and colonnade, of crooked streets and dilapidated purlieus behind the public splendour of Piazza and Duomo, formed the setting of unmedieval ideas. The political structure, the household or gang of the self-made prince, was something contrived; not inherited and taken for granted. Filippo Visconti, the early fifteenth-century tyrant of Milan, lived closely guarded in the great brick citadel which still dominates the older part of the town; he travelled, for security, by preference, in a canal barge. The Baglioni of Perugia conducted their vendettas all over the town, and terrorized the beautiful country between Assisi and the city. The Sforza of Milan, the Gonzaga of Mantua, the d'Este of Ferrara, the Medici in Florence, held their positions, like Byzantine rulers, through astute force of mind. Needing fame, they competed for the services of writers, artists and musicians. The vulgarity of the new men, with their cortèges of hired ruffians, buffoons, bastards and sycophantic humanists, had early disgusted Dante. 'What mean their trumpets,' he had written, 'and their bells, their horns and their flutes, but "Come hangman – come vultures"?'[1] The sharp Italians could not, as Burckhardt pointed out, understand the motives of Charles the Bold of Burgundy, that belated pattern of medieval chivalry. 'The Swiss,' they observed, 'were only peasants, and if they were all killed, that would be no satisfaction for the Burgundian nobles who might fall in the war. . . . If the duke got possession of all Switzerland without a struggle, his income would not be 5,000 ducats the greater.'[2] Nor could they understand the hereditary prestige which enabled him to strike his nobles with impunity.

The basis of usurped power was a firm grasp of finance, of statistics, of intelligence. As well as buying up living writers and artists, the tyrants encouraged a cult of dead civic celebrities. This patronage was reinforced by native Italian taste. When Leonardo da Vinci (1452–1519) had designed the altar piece of the Santissima Annunciata in Florence, 'his cartoon representing the Virgin, St Anne, and Christ filled all artists with wonder, and was viewed for two days by crowds of people as if attending a solemn festival'.[3] But Leonardo was, of course, most valued by his patrons, Ludovico il Moro, Cesare Borgia, and Francis I, as a military engineer; though when he devised a plan for a submarine, he refused, unlike modern scientists, to divulge his inspiration, 'on account of the evil nature of men who would practise assassination at the bottom of the sea'. For his age, this universal genius was primarily an inventor. 'All knowledge,' he insisted, 'has its origins in our perceptions.'

On a more ordinary level, Benvenuto Cellini (1500–72) best evokes in his autobiography the rough-and-tumble of the Renaissance, with its respect for force as well as art. He admired Torrigiano, not only for his sculpture but for his 'consummate assurance, having rather the air of a bravo than of a sculptor . . .', for his 'tremendous appearance', and for 'continually talking of his great feats among the bears of Englishmen'. Cellini's life was packed with work, carousing, love affairs, graft; and he knew how to 'stab when occasion serves'. His impatient, exacting, patrons, also knew precisely what they wanted and a good thing when they saw one. Cellini, with his passion for beauty and money, telling the pope 'that good cats mouse better to fatten themselves than merely through hunger', collecting from the peasants ancient medals, topaz *intaglios* and a 'dolphin head in emeralds' when shooting pigeons among the ruins in the Campagna, and picking off the Constable of Bourbon with a lucky shot in the defence of the Castello St Angelo, recalls the sentiment, the gusto, the violence of his times. Baldassare Castiglione, too, whose '*Courtier*' ('verie necessarie and profitable for young gentlemen and gentlewomen abiding in Court, Pallace or Place', says his Elizabethan translator) was written to inculcate more civilized behaviour, treats also of 'merry [and elementary] jests and pranks'. The qualities celebrated by Verdi were already apparent in the Renaissance Italians – inseparable from their genius.

Out of this welter of vendetta, intrigue, comedy and crime, the artistic legislators of modern Europe emerged. Leonardo, Michelangelo, Raphael, Titian, are only the most famous names. The sculptor Donatello, the architect Alberti, could compare with the masters of antiquity. Palladio further developed the architecture of humanism into a cosmopolitan influence. Inigo Jones, in England (1573–1645), set new standards in the north. For artistic genius was reflected beyond the Alps. Here the courts of the new monarchies and the rich cities of the Low Countries and northern Germany provided patronage. In Flanders, besides the van Eycks, Memlinc and the Breughels, Dürer and Holbein could compare in technical skill and design with the southern masters; but it was Rubens, reproducing in his Antwerp studios the architecture of Italy, who proved, in the early seventeenth century, the greatest master. He was profoundly influential for northern painting; particularly in France, where the court painters of the later Valois, though competent in the old Flemish manner as miniaturists and portrait painters and able to provide the court of Francis I with the Italianate work they admired, had not yet created a native idiom. Under the liberating influences of Rubens, and of Poussin (1594–1665), who assimilated in Rome the best the Italians could give and interpreted it with a new French *finesse*, and of Claude le Lorrain, the first major French master of landscape, French painting first came into its own. Rembrandt, too, was as great an artist as the first masters of Italy. In Spain, where there had long been a fine tradition of religious painting, El Greco, influenced by Titian, produced his strange and dramatic masterpieces, and Velasquez his magnificent effects. The more macabre aspects of the age were depicted by the weird genius of Hieronymus Bosch. In the later seventeenth century, Dutch landscape, seascape and interior painting was at its best in the works of Vermeer, de Hooche, Ruysdael and the van der Veldes. These painters are only a selection of the most famous masters who now made European painting splendid, dynamic and original.

In literature the harvest of the Renaissance was just as rich. Some of the greatest vernacular masterpieces were now written. The Italians adapted the old romances to a colourful description of life: Ariosto (1474–1533) in his *Orlando Furioso* treated the tale of Roland in a more realistic way; Tasso, in the later sixteenth century, in *Rinaldo* and in *Gerusalemme Liberata*, tried to interpret old themes with a more complex understanding of character. In France the court poet Ronsard (1524–85), by origin eastern European,

> (Or quant à mon ancestre, il a tiré sa race.
> D'où le glacé Danube est voisin de la Thrace),

was diverted by deafness from action to learning. He became a classic master of formal French, as in the familiar

> Quand vous serez bien vieille, au soir, à la chandelle,
> Assise aupres du feu, devidant et filant,
> Direz, chantant mes vers, en vous esmerveillant,
> Ronsard me celebroit du temps que j'estois belle.

Rabelais, that entirely original genius, at once glorified and mocked the elaboration of contemporary scholastic learning.* He found his best translator and amplifier in Sir Thomas Urquhart, an eccentric Scot; the high spirits and rumbustious satire of this masterpiece are still topical.

In Spain, as in England, great dramatists arose. Lope de Vega (1562–1635), immensely prolific, sprung from the people, ranged over a vast field of social comedy and adventure. He wrote an epic in which Drake

---

*'Quaestio subtilissima, utrum Chimaera in vacuo bombinans posset comedere secundas intentiones.' Dr Francis Rabelais, *Lives, Heroic Deeds and Sayings of Gargantua and his son Pantagruel* (London 1921), II, VII, p. 215, q.v.

was the villain, and he took part in the expedition of the Armada: Calderon (1600–81), technically a more accomplished dramatist, plumbs depths of introspection in a setting of formal melodrama. But it was Cervantes who created the greatest book in Spanish literature. *Don Quixote* is untranslatable, 'for no other language can capture the underlying fluidity, the humour, the strength, the echoing cadences of Cervantes' prose', but it has become one of the masterpieces of the world, expressing an insight, a pity and an irony which transcend frontiers. In Portugal Camoens's *Lusiads* were the first epic of oceanic discovery and colonization.

It is superfluous to stress the impact of the Renaissance on England. Marlowe's bold romantic vision leads to Shakespeare, the greatest writer in the English language. Milton, the master of sacred epic, was Italianate, while a whole prose literature came into being, rooted in the speech of the later Middle Ages, now tuned to a new flexibility and range. John Aubrey, whose work was all but unknown in his own day, has survived as the first of the English biographers capable of hitting off a character in a few lines.[4] In Holland, Joost van der Vondel, who was born in 1587 and died only nine years before William III came to England, was at once a great dramatist, a lyric poet and a master of satire. As Renaissance turned to baroque, whole new fields of complicated and original experience were to be expressed. All originated from the impact of the southern classical influence on the vernacular writings of the north.

If that influence was originally neo-pagan, and often remained so, it also took on religious forms beyond the Alps. In the brief, halcyon, time of the new learning, before rival religious fanatics had trampled toleration in the dust, Erasmus, the most celebrated of the northern humanists, enjoyed a cosmopolitan fame. He was the first great publicist, whose *Colloquies* and *Praise of Folly* found a lay public. Sir Thomas More, his friend, part of whose *Utopia* was written in Bruges in 1515, depicted an ideal bourgeois republic whose inhabitants detested 'warre and battel as a thing very beastly'. His fantasy was the forerunner of many others; of Campanella's *City of the Sun*; of Bacon's *New Atlantis*, of Harrington's *Oceana*, and of their later counterparts.

The humanists, who hoped to use the New Learning in the service of a reformed Catholic Church, were soon superseded in the ideological conflicts provoked by Luther and Calvin, and persecuted by the Jesuit opponents of the Reformation. For the scepticism of the New Learning deriving in the north in part from Ockham's attack on superfluous scholastic terms – had not only liberated men's minds; it had led many to gloom and terror, through its apparent alienation of reason and religion. Obsessed with sin, with the awful danger of being 'wrong with God', many religious minds, in fear, loneliness and guilt, were driven to 'justification by faith', or to a compensating conviction of 'election through grace'. These depressing, and at the time predominant, aspects of the time are less interesting than the original, scientific, achievements; the new confidence and method of systematic enquiry.

That sense of order is well expressed in the new European music, so different from anything in the rest of the world. Palestrina (1525–94), papal choir master in Rome, created the classical forms afterwards perfected by Haydn and Bach; Monteverdi, in early seventeenth-century Venice, was the first famous creator of opera: Lully, a versatile Florentine, Master of Music to Louis XIV, and Purcell, organist to the Chapel Royal under the later Stuarts, both derived their clear, disciplined idiom from the Italians. Their music, with its verve and confidence, is an expression of well-ordered, high-spirited, practical intelligence.

# V

Brilliant and many-sided, European art and literature of the Renaissance and the seventeenth century was not qualitatively different from that of other civilizations. But in one thing European culture was unique and original – in the formulation of scientific method and techniques. The scientists of antiquity had made considerable discoveries, but they had not often followed them up; the Chinese had great scientific knowledge, coordinated in massive encyclopaedias, but not systematically and widely applied; the Muslims had gone a long way in medicine and geography, and medieval Europeans, as already pointed out, had made important inventions. But never, and nowhere else, had mankind set themselves systematically to observe, to classify, and to record the facts of nature in order to exploit and control them.

The nominalist attack on late medieval Thomism had brought home the limitations of mind, often with tragic consequences for theologians and their partisans. It had also encouraged the exploitation of mind as an instrument. Experiment and induction proved, in Francis Bacon's phrase, 'a key to open nature'. As Whitehead, in his classic *Science and the Modern World*, insists:

A brief and sufficiently accurate description of the intellectual life of the European races during the succeeding two centuries and a quarter, up to our own times, is that they have been living upon the accumulated capital of ideas provided for them by the genius of the seventeenth century. . . . It is this one century which consistently, throughout the whole range of human activities provided intellectual genius adequate for the greatness of its occasions.[5]

The background to it all was a revolution in cosmology. Copernicus, a Pole educated at Cracow, studied in Italy for ten years and fought in the wars against the Teutonic knights along the Baltic. He revived the heliocentric hypothesis of Aristarchus of Samos, and in 1543 published his

*De Revolutionibus orbium Coelestium*: he died the same year and thus avoided direct criticism. Another Baltic savant, Tycho Brahe (d. 1601), for whom the king of Denmark built a fine observatory, made many novel observations: he destroyed the theory of separate heavenly 'spheres', since comets, he pointed out, passed *between* the planets. When he observed new major stars, he insisted that the heavens were not immutable; his assistant, Kepler, went further; he discovered that the planets move in ellipses. Giordano Bruno, a Neapolitan monk, meanwhile, fated to be burnt by the Inquisition in 1600, published his dialogues *De L'infinito Universo e Mondi* in 1584. He scrapped the relatively cosy orthodox apparatus of crystalline spheres circling a stationary earth, and launched out into the boundless space of modern cosmology. This queer heretic canvassed ideas, horrifying to his contemporaries, with which modern man has learnt to live. But it was Galileo, a Florentine (1564–1642), who, with primitive telescopes – originally a Dutch invention – proved these theories by experiment and drew together the accumulated new knowledge. He observed the lunar mountains, the moons of Jupiter, and the difference in kind between the planets and the stars. Since Venus had phases, like the moon, it was clear that the planets revolved round the sun. In his *Dialogue on the Two Chief Systems of the World* he marshalled unanswerable evidence for the theory of Copernicus. Newton, born in the year of Galileo's death, the son of a Lincolnshire farmer, now read Kepler on optics at Cambridge: by 1666 he had formulated the law of gravitation and, until 1687, kept it to himself. He then published his famous *Principia Mathematica*. The whole cosmic system now fell into apparent order: the wild hypotheses of the pioneers were clinched. This vast, awe-inspiring, but ordered, background was entirely revolutionary in the history of mankind.

In the more intimate field of medicine, where misleading theories had run riot since antiquity and been elaborated during the Middle Ages, much more gradual change occurred. The hoary and ancient theory that the four 'humours', concocted by the liver under the influence of the stars, determined health, had for generations held the field. Now in 1543, Vesalius, a Belgian, who had studied like Galileo at Padua, published his *De Fabrica Humani Corporis*. It was based, not on the works of Galen of Pergamum, but upon dissection; and it was elaborately illustrated. Paracelsus (Bombastus von Hohenheim), a German-Swiss, the son of a doctor who discovered the still popular hot springs at Villach in Carinthia, studied in Vienna and Ferrara; he travelled over most of Europe and much of the Levant. He lectured in German instead of Latin; called himself *Monarchus Medicorum* and so became much disliked in his profession. But his remedies often worked. The greatest advance was made by a native of Folkestone, William Harvey, of St Bartholomew's in London and Physician in Ordinary to Charles I. He discovered the circulation of the blood and published his proofs in his *Exercitatio Anatomica de Motu Cordis et Sanguinibus in Animalibus* (1628). The concluding chapter-heading runs: 'The circulation of the blood established by means of observations which may be made on the heart and by those which are quite obvious in dissection.' Helpless though they remained before plague, smallpox, and the consequences of appalling sanitation, without antiseptics or anaesthetics; unaware of whole fields of essential knowledge, the doctors by observation and experiment had made a new move.

This practical bias, apparent already in Leonardo, and mainly deriving from the peculiar Italian setting already described, was formulated in terms of philosophy, and reflected in the theory of the State. Descartes (1596–1650) created the dominant conventions of philosophy for three centuries. He pared down consciousness to the apparent certainty *Cogito ergo sum* – 'I think, therefore, I am' – and from that hopeful basis built up, by inference, a knowledge of the external world, although, as Lord Russell wittily remarks: 'Oddly enough it was very like the world in which he believed before his excursion into scepticism.'[6] Descartes, on principle, refused to believe anything to be true which he did not 'clearly know to be such' through systematic observation and analysis. By accepting severe limitations on mind, he greatly encouraged the development of useful knowledge, and his *Discours sur la Méthode* (1637) became immensely influential. Artificial, oversimplified, his *Méthode* proved a powerful instrument, as he meant it to be, in the mastery of the physical world. Men no longer despised experiment and technology. Spinoza (1632–77), who sought 'not to laugh at men or weep over them or hate them, but to understand them', and attempted, by demonstration, to maintain a synoptic philosophy more comprehensive than Cartesianism, lived by making lenses and optical instruments. In the tiny Spinozahuis near Rikinsburg his instruments and his leather-bound books may still be seen: unpretentious, but entirely set on his own purposes, indifferent to persecution or fame, he went his own fruitful way.

Hobbes, whose *Leviathan* (1651) is the first elaborate treatise justifying the new great State in terms not of morality but of usefulness, attempted to create a science of politics, based on what he held to be the rationally ascertained facts of human nature. This powerful, magnificently phrased, baroque, and artificial construction, riddled by the criticisms of men of affairs, is a landmark in the modern fashion of defining the politically undefinable.[7] This kind of speculation, indeed, has led to much 'ideological' conflict, but Hobbes's objectives, like those of Bacon, Descartes and Spinoza, were practical: peace, order, wealth – not fanaticism and glory. He spoke for the new urban civilian interests, now increasingly coming to power: his practical aims, and conception of the State as an artifact, are similar to those long before defined by Machiavelli in his Florentine civic setting. But where Machiavelli studied the facts of power in the small field of Italian politics, Hobbes assumes the existence of great sovereign states, standing to one another in a 'posture of warre'.

# VI

So western Europeans emerged from the breakdown of the medieval order, which had still looked to the Mediterranean for economic and intellectual initiative, to a new age of sovereign States with world-wide, oceanic horizons. Many of their philosophers and scientists now accepted a new and practical view of the world. Dangerous as well as powerful, it reflected the humanist and experimental bias of the Renaissance in a more professional, systematic and formidable way. Within the framework of great States and mercantile capitalist enterprise, accepting the metaphysical limitations of mind, but avid for its scientific achievements, the western Europeans had become, by the mid-seventeenth century, the most dynamic and technologically competent peoples in the world.

# Eighteen

# MUGHAL INDIA: IRAN: THE OTTOMAN TURKS

## I

While Europeans were displaying dynamic enterprise, the massive civilizations of the south and west Asian continent were still dominated by Muslim conquerors from Central Asia. In India the Mughal Empire, founded by Babur, reached its climax under Akbar, a contemporary of Elizabeth I, and began its decline under the fanatical Aurangzeb. By the mid-seventeenth century, the Maratha princes of the Deccan challenged the Muslim supremacy and, during the eighteenth, the decadent Mughal Empire was fought over by Marathas, Sikhs, Rajputs, and Persian and Afghan invaders. Finally, the Maratha confederacy was defeated by the Afghans at Panipat, and the last bid for Hindu political supremacy in the north was over.

The Marathas remained powerful, since the Afghans failed to consolidate their success, but the victors of this internecine struggle were European. The British and French had long penetrated the subcontinent, intent primarily on commerce; but their manoeuvres developed into a contest for empire. By 1757 Clive, at Plassey, had won the whole of Bengal, and determined that the British would be paramount in India. The outflanking of Asian land power by sea-borne Europeans, begun by the Portuguese, had been a prelude to the British Raj and the Dutch exploitation of Indonesia.

## II

Babur, the descendant of Timur Lenk and Genghis Khan, had invaded India and defeated the Afghans and Rajputs in 1526-7. He was a brilliant soldier; in the Persian tradition in which he was brought up, he was also a poet. In his famous autobiography he writes; 'In the neighbourhood of Peshawar during the spring, the flowers are exquisitely beautiful'; in another context he records, 'here we erected a pyramid of heads'.[1] During a ferocious siege of Samarkand, he diffidently composed *rubai*, and wrote of a young favourite; 'such was the impression produced upon me by this encounter that I almost fell to pieces'.[2] A great hunter of tiger and leopard, he proved one of the most brilliant tacticians in the history of central Asia and north-western India, for he used wagons chained in *lager* to reinforce his infantry and guns, as well as the traditional cavalry manoeuvres of envelopment. He established his capital at Agra, but died in 1530, aged forty-seven. His son, Humayun, an indolent but attractive character, was unequal to this inheritance. In 1540 he was driven out by an Afghan ally, Sher Khan, governor of Bihar. This able administrator, who reigned under the style of Sher Shah, created the first properly centralized bureaucracy and fiscal system in the Muslim occupation. When, after his death, Humayun's general, Bairam Khan, restored his master, the Mughals benefited from this innovation which became the basis of their rule.

The wealth of the Mughal regime is famous, and the plunder which enriched Europeans who exploited its decline well known. This surplus came from large-scale specialized manufactures which had long made India the greatest centre of exports in Asia. This export trade in handloom products – calico, muslin and yarn – was supplemented by raw cotton, rice, sugar, pepper and luxury goods. By the sixteenth century Indian techniques of manufacture, finance and distribution had long been more advanced than the nascent commercial capitalism of Europe; hence, in spite of endemic famine and poverty among the peasants over vast areas of rural India, the fabulous wealth of Indian princes and great merchants which so greatly impressed Europeans. The Mughal Empire at its height was thus administratively and economically massive.

Only thirteen at his accession, Jalal-ud-Din Akbar became paramount from the Indus to the Bay of Bengal, from beyond the Khyber to the Deccan.[3] By 1562 he had asserted his personal rule; in middle age he abandoned Sunni Muslim orthodoxy to create a new religion to unite Muslims and Hindus. 'This prince,' wrote a Jesuit who knew him well, attempted to convert him, and tutored one of his sons, 'has broad shoulders, somewhat bandy legs, well suited for horsemanship, and a light brown complexion. He carries his head bent towards his right shoulder. His forehead is broad and open, his eyes so bright and flashing that they seem like a sea shimmering in the sun.'[4] Affable and accessible, he generally wore a turban to please his Indian subjects, not the Mongol cap. He dressed in silk embroidered with gold, and, in private, sometimes wore European clothes: he drove 'a two horse chariot, very striking and dignified'. His palaces were domed and lofty, unlike those of many Hindu rulers, and he passionately loved hunting. 'A great athlete, a magnificent shot, his control of unruly elephants is legendary and he was a first rate polo player.'[5] He hunted with cheetahs, for 'hounds such as those of the Gallia or Alan breed are unknown'.[6] He preferred water to wine: sexual offenders were beaten or strangled. He was a great pigeon-fancier, and would work with his artificers at mechanical crafts. He was illiterate, but well versed by ear in Persian poetry and in theology; a great patron of learned men. His religious opinions were tolerant, and doubtless tuned to policy, for politically he was a realist – 'a pike in a pond'. He said that 'he found in all religions something to offend his reason'; boggled at the niceties of Christian doctrine and told the Jesuits that he could hardly give up his harem. He inclined most, perhaps, to fire-worship, since he once ordered a lamp lighter to be thrown off a roof for showing the sacred element 'disrespect'. 'Although I am master of so great a kingdom,' he remarked, 'with what satisfaction . . . can I undertake the sway of empire? I await the coming of some discrete man of principle, who will resolve the difficulties of my conscience.'[7]

Probably the richest Indian ruler for centuries, he had a huge secretariat to administer his empire and his finances, kept a monopoly of banking and, unlike most contemporary rulers in the West, maintained his currency undebased. His household was regulated by a large water clock, which struck the time on bronze gongs, and trained runners kept him well informed. But his court was most impressive when on campaign, in acres of elaborate tents, after the Mongol fashion. On the march, all were supposed to be silent, 'save one who sounds his drum at short intervals, perhaps at every tenth pace, with a slow and dignified rhythm'. His official consorts followed on elephants; the treasury, appropriately enough, on mules. Logistics and supply were well organized, discipline strict. In battle the army kept the old Mongol half-moon formation, light cavalry in front, then the infantry and the armoured elephants. These feared no other animal, save the rhinoceros; maddened, apparently, by cat's flesh mixed with their food, they could charge to catch the enemy in their trunks, tread them underfoot or split them in two. They even carried artillery, and did not bolt when the guns fired. Though docile to the mahouts, they could be dangerous to both sides, and were in fact kept more to terrify the enemy than for close combat.[8] The main brunt of the battle was borne by the light cavalry, with their steppe tactics of feigned flight.

Such was the personality and entourage of Akbar, the most powerful ruler of India since Aşoka. Foreign to the Hindus in background and religion, he fought and hunted in the old Mongol-Turki way, but commanded a great and rich centralized administration.

Akbar's son, Jahangir (1605–28), was an indolent aesthete, dominated by his wife, Nur Jahan. His court, also, is described in curious detail by Sir Thomas Roe, an English ambassador: 'I went to court' (at Ajmer) he writes, 'at four in the evening and to the *Durbar*, which is the place where the Mogull sitts out daylie to see and be seene. The King hath no man but Eunuchs that come into the house . . . his women watch within and guard him with manly weapons.'[9] 'He sat in a court set above like a King in a play': all business was done in public, 'as all his subjects are slaves, so is hee in a kynde of reciprocall bondage, for he is tyed to observe these houres and customs so precisely that if he were unseene one day and noe sufficient reason rendered, the people would mutinie'.[10] Jahangir was extremely polite and amiable: though he would watch criminals being elaborately executed, he liked 'delicate' horses, and asked for mastiffs and Irish greyhounds. Under his successor, Shah Jahan (1628–58), who killed most of his near relations to secure the throne, the Mughal Empire reached its cultural climax and began its financial decline. In his reign were built the Pearl Mosque at Agra and the Taj Mahal, the tomb of his consort, Mumtas Mahal; he possessed the famous 'Peacock Throne' and the Koh-i-noor diamond, and he overtaxed his often famine-stricken subjects. He brought the empire to the verge of bankruptcy.

In 1657 his son, Aurangzeb, took advantage of his father's illness and imprisoned him. He then murdered his own immediate rivals and, in 1659, seized the throne: he was to reign until 1707. An austere Sunni Muslim, he spent his life persecuting most of his subjects; on campaign on the north-west against Pathans and Afghans, in the Punjab against the Rajputs and the Sikhs, in the Deccan against the Marathas.

Having alienated his Shi'ah Muslim allies in the north, Aurangzeb now had new enemies to face. Among the Jats of the Indus valley and the Punjab, a people probably of Scythian origin, a new religion had taken root. The founder, Baba Nanak (1469–1538), who had been influenced by Kabir, had attempted to synthesize and transcend Hindu and Muslim beliefs; he wrote:

> I will not worship with the Hindu,
> Nor, like the Muslim, go to Mecca.
> I shall serve Him and no other.
> I shall put my heart at the feet of one Supreme Being.

His disciples, *sicshas* or Sikhs, had developed his doctrine. Ram Das, their fourth Guru, had founded Amritzar, the City of the Water of Life, and Guru Arjun (1581–1606) had completed the sacred pool and the Golden House, the *Hur Mandar*. Within, smothered in flowers, lay the *Adi-Granth*, the first book of the Sikh scriptures.

The Sikh leaders soon became rich; in face of Aurangzeb's attack, Guru Govind Singh (1675–1708) transformed them into a fighting, widely recruited, sect: he created a *Khalsa* of initiated *Singhs* (Lions), a title taken from the Rajput aristocracy; he composed supplementary scriptures, the *Granth Govindi*, and encouraged a cult of comradeship and the sword. Sikhs were forbidden to shave or cut their hair; where the Muslims and the Jews abhorred pork, they abhorred beef; only the flesh of ritually slain animals was lawful. Baba Nanak had taught the omnipotence of God, the illusion of life: 'Wealth, youth, and a flower,' he said, 'are guests for four days . . . I may be called a Khan, King, or Raja, but without God I am nothing.' But Govind Singh's maxims were more martial.

Aurangzeb's other, and even more dangerous, enemies were the Maratha horsemen of the Deccan. Sivaji, a leader of genius, laid the foundations of Maharashtra, the last great Hindu realm, in the hilly country east and south of Bombay. He is said to have revived Maurya ways of government; defied the armies of the Mughal and plundered his territories. Sivaji, insulted by Aurangzeb, in reply compared the Mughal generals to 'a pack of old women', and from 1674 to his death in 1680, established an entirely independent kingdom. His successors, based on a relatively barren *terrain*, continued their aggression against the declining Mughal Empire. These campaigns, together with Afghan incursions from the north, wore down the Mughal power, so that at the death of Aurangzeb in 1707, it was gravely undermined.

Aurangzeb's reign saw decline, but not disaster: it was not until the mid-eighteenth century that the Maratha confederacy came near to the conquest of India. Sivaji's descendants were soon ousted by their *peshwas* or chief ministers; in 1737 *Peshwa* Baji Rao I defeated the Nizam of Hyderabad, the principal Mughal ally in the south. Meanwhile, in 1736, Nadir Guli Beg – Nadir Shah – a Turki soldier of peasant stock, seized the throne of the Safavids in Iran and conquered Afghanistan. He advanced into northern India, and three years later, utterly defeated the old-fashioned armies of Muhammad Shah, the representative of the Mughals. He sacked most of Delhi, carried off the Peacock Throne and the Koh-i-noor, and deprived the Mughals of their territory west of the Indus and the Sutlej. They were thus helpless before the Afghan Amir Ahmad Shah Durani, who sacked Delhi in 1756.

Into this chaos, the Maratha *peshwa* struck from the south. He captured Delhi and most of the Punjab; but he was no match for Ahmad Shah. In January 1761, the Afghan trapped and annihilated the Maratha army at the traditional battlefield of Panipat. But the Afghans were unable to consolidate their advantage: although the Maratha confederacy was shattered, it was Mahadji Rao Scindia of Gwalior (1761–93) who dominated the puppet Mughal emperor when the British were consolidating their rule in Bengal.

# III

For nearly a hundred years after the death of Timur Lenk, Iran, culturally the France of the Middle East, had remained under Mongol and Turki domination. Timur had ruled his empire from Samarkand; his son, the Il Khan Shah Rukh, a great patron of the arts, from Herat, then in eastern Iran. But gradually the Timurids had been ousted by Turkoman and Uzbek princes; indeed, the latter had driven Babur, the last Timurid, into India.

By 1502, a new native dynasty had come to power, the first for seven

centuries. The Safavids, descendants of Sheik Safaid-din, inaugurated a remarkable period of Persian civilization. Shah Isma'il I, a fanatical Shi'ah, had
first established their authority. During the long reigns of Shah Tamasp,
called by the English merchant, Jenkinson, who visited him in 1563, 'the
Sophi Shaw Thamas' (1524–76), and of Shah Abbas I the Great
(1587–1629), Persia attained a new prestige. The Safavids fought off or
evaded successive Ottoman-Turkish assaults, provoked by Isma'il's attacks
on them as Sunni heretics. And Shah Abbas, in need of military aid,
encouraged contacts with Europeans. As a traveller wrote, 'the king
esteemed it an addition of lustre to his court to behold exotics in their own
country habit.'

One of the exotics was the young Thomas Herbert, who, in 1627,
accompanied the English ambassador to the court, and wrote a detailed
description of its curious splendour. 'Abbas, the Persian Emperour,' he
wrote, 'was of low stature (a gyant in policy), his aspect quick, his eyes
small and flaming . . . he had a low forehead, a high hawked nose; a sharp
chin; and in the mode of Persia, beardless; his moustachioes were
exceeding long, and thick and turned downwards.'[11] 'The King is *Iuppiter
in Terris*, and by panbasilay and forced will, equates the Duke and Peasant
in his Command.'[12] The 'Potshaw', in fact, 'could by the fulgar of his eye
dart 'em dead.'

At his palace at Asharoff near the Caspian, this terrifying potentate
received the English, who had come to conclude an alliance against the
Turks and 'aggrandise the traffic in raw silk'. Through a spacious
courtyard, with a few carpets spread round a white marble tank, they
entered a fragrant garden 'curious to the eye', from whose terrace they
viewed 'the Caspian Sea one way and another way the tops of Taurus'.
They then proceeded to a 'gilded chamber, spread with most valuable
carpets of silk and gold, with pools of crystalline water, an element of no
mean account in these torrid habitations': there were jewelled vases;
golden perfume goblets; wine and flowers. Finally, through a room with a
tank of jasper and porphyry, where a 'purling stream seemed to bubble',
they came to the presence chamber itself.

The monarch wore plain red quilted calico: 'cross-legged he sat; his shah
or turbant was white and bungie . . . his waiste was girded with a thong of
leather, the scabbard of his sword was red, the hilt of gold, the blade formed
like a hemi-circle and doubtless well-tempered'. About him were 'tacite
Mirzaes, Chawns, Sultans and Beglerbegs, above three score; who like so
many inanimate statues sat cross-legged, and joined their bumms to the
ground, their backs to the wall, their eyes to a constant object, not daring to
speak to one another'. Silently, the 'Ganimed boyes in vests of gold, rich
bespangled turbants and choice sandalls, their curld haires dangling about
their shoulders, rolling eyes and vermillion cheeks, with Flagons of most

glorious mettal went up and down, and proffered the delight of Bacchus to such as would relish it'.[13]

The Turks, Shah Abbas remarked, were a base people; odious and offensive; he had beaten them in fifteen battles. Having threatened, *en passant*, to cut a traitor into as many pieces as there were days of the year, and 'burn 'em in the market with stinking dogs' turds', he agreed to exchange ten thousand bales of raw silk for an equivalent amount of cloth. He even 'pulled the ambassador down' beside him, 'smiling to see he could not settle after the Asiatic sort'. The ambassador then raised his hat, the Shah his turban. The agreement, of course, was never carried out.

The great Shah was in truth an ugly customer. When his horse shied at a sleeping beggar, he had put an arrow into him: 'I did the man no wrong,' he said, 'I found him sleeping and asleep I left him.' So the courtiers made the victim a 'common mark'. He had done to death his three most promising sons and blinded another; he impaled and bastinadoed; his deaf-mutes strangled at a sign or 'ripped men's guts'. In winter the sensitive despot slept in sables, diverting himself with dancing girls, catamites and 'sundry representations of venerious gambols, painted by some goatish Appeles'.[14] For all that, he was a successful, in some ways an enlightened, despot.

The ambassador never had audience again. There were difficulties in taking leave; the party were 'tormented by heat and gnats and mus-ke-toes . . . they were biting us and we thrashing them like mad folks'. Why the wind of favour had changed remained mysterious: the English concluded that oriental princes were 'terribly crafty and mysteriously politicious'.

The Persian ruling classes, Herbert observed, were bold warriors, 'save that women, wine and music fatten them': they were 'generally big lim'd, strong, streight and proper; the zone makes them olive-coloured, the wine cheerefull, opium venerious. The women paint, the men love Arms, all love poetry'.[15] A French observer noted *'leur pente est grande et naturelle à la volupté, au luxe, à la dépense, à la prodigalité'*.

This disposition encouraged a cult of carpets, sixteenth-century Persia's incomparable legacy to the world. The craft was very ancient in central Asia. The richer Mongol and Turki nomads, with ample wool in a hard climate, had thickly carpeted their tents: the Chinese, influenced by the nomads, had early evolved their own splendid patterns, mainly in yellow, blue and red, with central medallions and swastika and key-pattern frames. The Turkis of Bukhara designed in red and terra-cotta, with parallel octagons within chequered and diapered borders: the Ottoman Turks and the Arabs preferred prayer rugs with heavy angular lines and deep colouring; the Baluchis, hair rugs, with latch hook patterns, glowing in copper and dark blue. All these derived from central Asia and most were woven with the Turki, Ghiordes, knot.

Persian carpets were the most elaborate; woven with the Farsi or Sehna knot, often of silk with silver or gold thread intertwined, or mixed with cotton or camel's hair. The classic patterns were created under the Safavids; Shah Abbas himself established a court-factory at his new capital of Isfahan. The carpets of Kirman, Sarouk, Shiraz, Feraghan and Isfahan, of Sehna and Kashan, were coloured with lasting vegetable dyes of great beauty; the best Persian carpets were miracles of subtly contrasting colour, in rose, peach and indigo, pale green and tan. Flower designs predominated, but there were great hunting carpets as well. 'The influence of the designers,' writes one authority, 'whom the Safavid princes had gathered about them, was profound and permanent. They had copied, invented, adapted, and fixed for good a large variety of lovely floral and animal forms – Chinese, Arab and Persian – which appear time and again, in a thousand variations in the designs of their successors.'[16]

Only a few of these masterpieces found their way to the West, where Turkish carpets were easier come by. Further, until the mid-nineteenth century, the vicissitudes of Persian politics were to set back the craft: then, a substantial export trade was to develop, and encouraged sometimes inferior production.

Painting and calligraphy also flourished. By the mid-fourteenth century, Chinese contacts through the Mongols had influenced Persian miniatures, and, in the fifteenth, the Timurids had patronized book-binding superior to anything in contemporary Europe. Shah Tamasp and Shah Abbas had delicate porcelain, comparable in economy of line and in lustre to the Chinese. Textiles, in particular, reached a climax: robes of honour in silks, satins and superlative velvets, were decorated with arabesques of flowers, animals, and scenes from Persian poetry. Tents and hangings attained a great splendour.

All this luxury, and the peace of Persian gardens – walled oases in a windy, drought-stricken plateau – where water glided in blue-tiled sluices, and tulips, narcissi and carnations grew free among carefully placed trees, were the preserve of a privileged class. The peasants could 'call nothing their own', such was the rapacity of their rulers.

Shah Abbas is, indeed, best remembered as a brilliant patron of architecture. His Blue Mosque at Isfahan, writes Mr Sacheverell Sitwell, is the 'final blossoming or culmination of Persian art'; its 'cloister of sapphire and turquoise', its superlative dome, its entire design, are 'calculated to a marvellous nicety'.[17] The huge Maidan is splendidly proportioned, and the golden-plated dome of the Mosque at Meshed also commemorates his time.

Safavid power soon declined. The four last Safavids 'devoted the greater part of their lives to the pleasures of the harem and the table and to planning political murders. On every front the Persian armies suffered defeat.'[18]

Finally, the upstart Nadir Shah repelled the invading Pathans and Turks. In 1736 he took the throne and made the descent on India already recorded. In 1747 he was assassinated: his brief dynasty was succeeded by the Zends, who were ousted, at the end of the eighteenth century, by the Qajars, while the Persians came under attack not only from the Ottoman Turks, but from imperial Russia.

# IV

West of Iran, thrusting out beyond Asia into the rich, dynamic, but war-ridden European peninsula, the stolid and warlike Ottoman Turks now ruled from eastern Anatolia to the sea, from the upper Euphrates to the Danube. They were feared from Vienna to Agra, from Gibraltar to the Indian Ocean; the Grand Turk, or Grand Signior, was the terror of eastern and central Europe; for the West, the stock symbol of tyrannic power.

It will be recalled that already, by the late fourteenth century, the Ottomans had taken Adrianople and conquered the Bulgars and the Serbs; by the fifteenth, they had enveloped the remnant of the Byzantine Empire and clinched their success by the capture of Constantinople. The hawk-faced Mehmed II the Conqueror (1451–81) had ruled all the Balkans, the estuary of the Danube, Moldavia, Wallachia and the northern shore of the Black Sea; he had routed the Persians in 1473 and secured the eastern marshes of Anatolia. Selim the Grim (1512–20) won Syria and Egypt from the Mamlūks, became paramount in Arabia, Caliph of Sunni Islam and protector of Mecca, Medina and Jerusalem. He determined the future of Egypt until the time of Mehemet Ali, and of Palestine until the conquests of Allenby.

But it was Suleiman the Magnificent (1520–66) who furthest extended the empire. He took Belgrade, broke the Hungarians at Mohacs in 1526; nearly captured Vienna. He harried Shah Tamasp, and his fleets dominated the Levant. In 1523 the Turks captured Rhodes and drove the knights westwards, to settle in Malta.

The Emperor Charles V took Tunis in 1536 but, two years later, Kheyr-ed-din Barbarossa drove the Christian Admiral Andrea Doria from Corfu and threatened the straits of Otranto. The expulsion of the Moors from Spain also gave the Turks fierce allies along the whole North African shore; though they failed to take Malta, they combined with the corsairs of Algiers and Barbary to raid the coasts of the western Mediterranean and out into the Atlantic. Only in 1572, a year after the fall of Cyprus, did the Christians stem the tide, when the combined fleets of Venice, Genoa and Spain finally checked the Turkish sea-assault at Lepanto in the Gulf of Corinth.

The land attack continued; after a lull through wars in Persia and incompetent Sultans, Mehmed IV (1648–87) overran Transylvania: in 1683 he again laid siege to Vienna, and the Habsburgs were saved only by John Sobieski of Poland. It was not until over a century after Lepanto that the relief of the city marked the final failure of the Turkish land assault.

The Europeans now counterattacked: the Turks lost Belgrade, then Hungary and Transylvania, a loss confirmed by the Treaty of Karlovitz in 1699. But they still dominated the Balkans, the Levant, Moldavia and Wallachia, much of Galicia and southern Russia. It was only in 1774 that the treaty of Kuchuk Kainardji recognized Russian power over the southern steppe, and not until the treaty of Jassy in 1792, that the Crimea and the northern shores of the Black Sea were abandoned.

The Turks had, indeed, succeeded where the Persians in antiquity had failed. In the sixteenth and seventeenth centuries Asian armies outclassed anything in the West. For the Ottoman Empire was created and maintained by an odd and efficient system, the *Kullar*, or slave household. It numbered about eighty thousand men, mainly recruited from the conquered peoples. This sinister and formidable machine, whose discipline so much impressed the Christians, was in theory controlled absolutely by the Padishah: it came, in time, to control him. The sultans, indeed, were themselves part of it: they were bred from the slave girls of the harem, not, as in India, from royal princesses, and on accession they generally killed all their brothers and half-brothers in the interests of the state. There was thus no Turkish court aristocracy corresponding to the great nobles of the West, and less feminine intrigue. Save for the three hundred women of the harem, mainly Caucasians and Circassians, ruled by the Kizlar Aghasi, or 'General of the Girls' and given away after twenty-five, unless the sultan wished them kept, the Padishah's household was exclusively male. All the Turks, says Busbecq, the Flemish ambassador to the Sublime Porte, shut their wives away: 'If they go out into the streets, they are . . . so covered and wrapped up in veils that they seem to those who meets them mere gliding ghosts.'[19]

When the sultans were able rulers, the system worked. Suleiman the Magnificent, inscrutable and austere, who showed no change of countenance when his greatest victory was announced, was devoted only to one wife, Khourrem 'the Joyful', better known as Roxolana 'the Russian'. He kept great state: all granted audience were gripped by both arms as they approached, a precaution observed since the murder of the sultan at Kossovo.

The court was 'a sea of turbanned heads,' says Busbecq, 'wrapped in folds of whitest silk'. Ankle-length robes of splendid materials and uniform cut and great plumed turbans made their wearers imposing. Western Europeans, accustomed to the mixed formality and confusion of their own courts, were struck by the order, and above all, the silence of the Seraglio.

The crack Turkish cavalry, the Sipahis of the Porte, rode Syrian horses with decorated bow-cases on the right, arrow-cases on the left. They carried jewelled scimitars, maces and green spears: their turbans rose to a 'fluted' and feathered peak of purple silk, and the plumes of the marching Janissaries were like a 'walking forest'.[20]

The *Kullar* was recruited from captives taken in war and from renegades who had 'turned Turk'; from slaves bought in the open market, supplied at the rate of twenty thousand a year by the Algerine and Barbary pirates, and by the Krim Tatars in Muscovy; as well as from the *dershurmeh* or levy of Christian boys, imposed on the Balkans, Hungary, western Asia Minor and the northern Black Sea coast. Brought in droves to Istanbul, often with the eager concurrence of their peasant families, they were divided by officials 'more skilled in judging boys than trained horse dealers are in judging colts',[21] into an élite of *Ich Oglans* – Interior Boys – and ordinary *Ajem Oglans*, Alien Boys. The former, many of whom were Albanians and Serbs, were then segregated. They were highly trained in military, athletic, social and literary accomplishments: the ablest and best looking all-rounders even became pages of the imperial bedchamber. The *Salihdar*, who bore the sultan's weapons; the *Chokadur*, who carried his robes; the *Sharbdar*, his cup bearer, might become generals, admirals, governors and viziers. Selected, prized, they bore no taint of slavery. As the property of the Padishah, they were liable, whatever wealth and grandeur they attained, to instant execution.

Some of the *Ich Oglans* became Sipahis of the Porte, but the Janissaries were recruited from the best of the *Ajem Oglans*; the more doltish 'Alien Boys' became labourers on the sultan's estates. The Janissaries were, primarily, musketeers; they wore uniform – an innovation in the sixteenth century – and little armour, trusting to their disciplined fire-power.

The system of the *Kullar*, self-perpetuating, and based on a prosperous economy mainly conducted by Phanariot Greeks, began to degenerate by the seventeenth century. Under Ahmed (Amurath) IV, who shot at his gardeners with a carbine and drank, there was sheer terror. His servants, says Rycaut, 'observed his looks and every cast of his eyes . . . learned his nods and the meaning of every motion and gesture.'[22] And, indeed, promotion went capriciously:

It happened once that a paper floating casually from his hand out of the window, the Pages ran in all haste down the stairs, striving who should be the first to take it up; but one, more desirous than the others to show the zeal of his service, took the nearest way and leaped out of the window; and though with his fall he broke the bone of his thigh, yet being the first that took up the paper, he came halting to present it with his own hand; his bold readiness in his service so pleased the Grand Signior, that he was afterwards preferred to one of the most considerable offices of the empire.[23]

Ahmed IV executed his principal cook and his master of music, impaled tobacco smokers, and died at thirty-one of a surfeit of 'sweet Malvoisia, sometimes twisted and encouraged with the strong water called *Rosa Solis.* . . . This dissolute repast became fatal to the Grand Signior'. His successor, his brother, Ibrahim, who had been kept in close confinement for years, was naturally terrified when he heard the tramp of Janissaries coming to fetch him, and only after repeated reassurances ventured from his cell. He then made up for lost time, refused to fight the Persians, but, 'like a stout soldier of Venus waged another war in the Elysium of Cupid',[24] and led 'a life so lascivious as can hardly be imagined by a chaste fancy or described by a modest pen'. He called his principal mistress 'little sugar plum', and was strangled in 1648. Under Mehmed IV, on the other hand, in the later seventeenth century, as already observed, the Turks again became extremely formidable. As in other despotisms, all depended on the ruler.

The Turkish Empire thus displayed the strength and the weakness of an originally nomad horde, now settled upon vast territories, whose populations they regarded as nomads regard their flocks. The conquerors' aim was to live, without effort, on the labour of their subjects, on whose surplus they could subsist in affable dignity. Commerce and the details of administration were left to subordinates, and though great responsibilities were habitually conferred, the Turkish overlords regarded Greeks, Arabs and Balkan peasants with an equal contempt. Long accustomed, also, to the conservatism of Islam, they allowed their original technical superiority in war to decline before the increasing progress of the West.

Such a system could have but one end. During the eighteenth century, the Turks lost grip: the Janissaries became uncontrollable; the landowners worked their sons and relatives into the *Kullar*; the administration became inefficient and corrupt, with the usual symptoms consequent on arbitrary power. By the time of Kuchuk Kainardji, Turkey, long satiated, had become a waning power. The history of the long decadence belongs to the nineteenth century.

# V

Across the south and western areas of Asia, in India, in Iran, and in Ottoman Turkey, three empires thus came to their climax and to their decline. The Mughal Empire was the largest and richest; the Persian the most highly civilized, and the Turkish long the most aggressive and efficient. All lived off the toil of a multitude of poor peasants, and, in spite of the prestige and luxury of their rulers and a considerable commerce, all were technologically limited: none could compare in scale with the contemporary Ming and early Manchu empires of China, or with the initiative, oceanic sea power and technology of Europe. It has been shown how the Christians, though severely tested, flung back the Turkish attack, and how, during the worst times of the Turkish assault, they were discovering the Americas and mastering the oceans of the world. It is now necessary to examine why and how they did so.

# Nineteen

# EUROPE IN THE EIGHTEENTH CENTURY

## I

Although, against this vast Asian background, the rise of European scientific method was much more important than the power politics of the age, to western contemporaries their pompous and glittering panache of monarchs, courts and nobility seemed far more impressive. The dynastic rulers by 'divine right' had inherited a medieval glamour; they had emerged out of a warlike late-feudal world; they were supported by standing armies and artillery. The panoply of monarchy which survives was once real: the pikes, the axes, the armour, the jingle of armoured cavalry, were the equivalent of the apparatus of modern mechanized war. And the splendour of arrogant kings had its serious political purpose: it was supported by a bureaucracy, amateurish by modern standards, but at that time of unprecedented efficiency and scope; governments could exploit growing wealth both at home and overseas. The bourgeoisie of Lyons, of Amsterdam, of London disposed of far more monetary capital and resources in kind than their sixteenth-century forbears; great merchants drew their revenues from far outside Europe while, particularly in France, Holland and England, new agricultural and stock-breeding methods were paying off. The build up of mercantile capital from oceanic trade and the expansion of the coal and textile industries formed the background to the Industrial Revolution. The ocean-going ships of the late seventeenth century were already comparable in size and design to those that fought at Trafalgar: heavily armed with cannon, capable of keeping at sea for months. The eighteenth century was dominated by governments with intensely martial traditions, fighting at once for European prestige and far-flung economic objectives. Their conflicts on land and sea determined the fate of vast territories in the Americas and the East, and dynastic sovereignty set the national political framework of the nineteenth and early twentieth centuries.

## II

War was endemic: territorial ambitions involved Europe in perennial strife. England and Holland fought the Bourbons in the War of the Spanish

Succession, during which Marlborough, in 1704, defeated the French at Blenheim; the Treaty of Utrecht (1713) gave a respite; then came the War of the Austrian Succession (1740–8) involving Prussia under Frederick the Great. In the Seven Years' War (1756–63) Frederick was nearly annihilated: he defeated the French; he defeated the Austrians; but when great Russian armies advanced he seemed finished – and was saved only by a change of rulers, with the accession of Catherine the Great. Meanwhile England extended its colonial empire, then lost America in the War of Independence; in Russia, Ivan the Dread had consolidated a massive, centralized State, backed by a large, conscript army with efficient artillery and administered by 'service' nobles.

Peter the Great (1682–1725) became the first emperor of Russia. He looked westwards as well as south-eastwards. A giant who, on occasion, executed his enemies himself, he was passionately interested in the technology of the West, visiting England and Holland and working in the shipyards. He defeated the Swedes in the long Great Northern War; took Riga; created a Baltic fleet. Though he transferred the capital from Moscow to St Petersburg, against the opposition of the conservative boyars, he is said to have remarked: 'We need Europe for a few decades; then we can turn our backs on her.'

War, for its own sake and for economic advantage, was taken for granted, medieval ideas of royal trusteeship and peace in Christendom were discarded, arbitrary power made a cult.* Louis XIV was nearer in spirit to the eastern despots of his age than to St Louis; beneath his superb manners, charm and self-control, he had an insatiable lust for flattery and power, expressed in ruinous wars and a passion for building on unsuitable sites. His entire court, as Saint-Simon remarked, was yet another device to sustain the king's policy of despotism.† The stifling pomp and display, deliberately imposed on the great families of France, the spider's web of espionage and secret police, the king's own semi-divine aloofness, set the pattern for lesser dynasts. Although their power was in fact limited by *parlements* or law courts, even the ablest rulers became very odd indeed. With calculated coldness, the *Roi Soleil* himself preferred his servants and his setters to his subjects, whom he regarded, as did Akbar or Shah Abbas, as all equally in servitude. That witty, able and far-seeing monarch, Charles II of England, with his *seraglio* of official mistresses and young women brought in by the back stairs, well earned his nickname 'old Rowley' (after

---

* Voltaire expressed his opinion in *Candide*, the most scarifying satire on war ever written (1759).

† The memoirs of the time present an extraordinary picture of the monarch, consuming, in formal solitude, the gargantuan meals on which he throve: 'four full plates of different kinds of soup, a whole pheasant, a partridge, a large dish of salad, two great slices of ham, mutton served with gravy and garlic, a plate of sweet cakes, and on top of that, fruit and *hard boiled eggs*'. *Saint-Simon at Versailles*, selected and transl. Lucy Norton (London 1958), p. 235n.

a billy-goat in the Privy Garden) and Louis xv was similarly obsessed. Frederick the Great at Sans Souci tormented his male circle of cosmopolitan intellectuals, hankered for literary fame and detested his subjects: 'My chief occupation is to fight the ignorance and prejudices of this country which, by accident of birth, it is my duty to rule.' The people were what nature had made them; 'wicked animals'. And these eccentricities were tame, for all these rulers were remarkable men, compared with those of the often cretinous monarchs of Naples and Spain, mad about uniforms or the chase, or with Christian vii of Denmark or the elderly George iii, both actually insane. Probably at no time in European history since the Roman Empire had so many rulers presented such a spectacle, all the more peculiar, since the society they governed was becoming richer, more intelligent, more humane. This growing civility influenced some of them and produced the 'enlightened despotism' of the Emperor Joseph ii (1780), or the phases of reform which occurred under Spanish and Neapolitan Bourbons – though not, it is remarkable, in France, where the crash came.

# III

While the nations of Europe were at war, a contrasting political development took place. Although the predominant form of government had become absolute monarchy, in certain western states, as already emphasized, medieval institutions had survived. They were destined in due course to originate the vastly influential and far-flung structure of constitutional liberalism and social democracy. In medieval times the idea of sovereignty had been unfamiliar; authority had been vaguely and jointly vested in pope and emperor, who were supposed to preside over a cosmopolitan Christendom; but within the medieval realms, where the *communitas* or *commonwealth* was thought to have more authority than the king, certain representative and judicial institutions had grown up out of the remote past. As already pointed out, they were reinforced by ancient classical and medieval concepts of the rule of law, drawn from Aristotle, Cicero and St Thomas Aquinas, and by the vague notion of natural law – '*vera Lex, recta ratio naturae congruens*' – to which all citizens had a right of appeal. These ancient ideas were encouraged by the religious conflicts which grew up in the West during the Reformation and Counter-Reformation, when the combined front of Church and State was broken, when men refused, for the overriding sake of their salvation, to admit the authority of a monarch they held to be heretical.

Gradually, with the rise of the bourgeoisie, more utilitarian objectives were admitted. John Locke, the most influential of all the political theorists of constitutional government and critics of arbitrary power, held that the aim of government was simply to protect property, and 'defend the commonwealth from foreign injury; and all this only for the public good'.[1] 'The liberty of man in society,' he wrote, 'is to be under no other legislative power, but that established, by consent, in the Commonwealth; nor under the dominion of any will, and restraint of any law, but what the legislative shall enact according to the trust put in it.' Princes who exert irresponsible power are still 'in the state of nature', and 'no man in civil society can be exempted from the laws of it'. Peace, safety, the public good – these are the ends of government, and rulers who fail to promote them forfeit the right to command. Nor is it the business of government to control men's religious opinions, so long as the forms of law are observed, or to control education. It is not far from these ideas to the doctrine of Jefferson enshrined in the American constitution: 'that governments are instituted . . . to secure life, liberty, and the pursuit of happiness . . . deriving their just powers from the consent of the governed'. And that 'whenever any form of government becomes destructive of these ends, it is the right of the people to alter or abolish it.' So, out of the ancient distinctions between a prince and tyrant, between the rule of law and arbitrary power, there grew up a movement centred on England after the defeat of the Stuart attempt to rule by divine right. It contributed to inspire the revolutions in America and France, and in time undermined the imposing structure of dynastic power and gave rise to the liberal experiment and its sequel.

With this practice of self-government went an intellectual and moral liberty which was ready to accept innovation in a way new in history, and made the way easier for inventions which were without precedent to be accepted.

The rationalist bias of this culture made it original. The influence of Descartes continued to predominate, and his scepticism was carried further by Locke and Hume, who analysed the limitations of mind in apprehending reality, but glorified its power as an instrument. Vistas of potential 'progress' were opened up, and Europeans were stimulated by the discovery of alien peoples and ancient, long-established, cultures. Montesquieu (1689–1755), for example, in his *Esprit des Lois*, displays a new understanding of the effect of environment on institutions and ideas, and of the relativity of social standards. Diderot and d'Alembert, the encyclopaedists, marshalled the whole range of contemporary knowledge into a *Dictionnaire raisonné*: 'France,' remarked Voltaire, 'was becoming Encyclopaedist, and Europe too.' Condorcet, who lived on to perish during the French Revolution, was the most sensational prophet of the dogma of progress. He wrote a panorama of human history in which he sketched the cumulative effects of revolution, and looked out, optimistically, far into the future. Superficial and over-confident in the power of reason, he created a myth which deeply influenced nineteenth-century speculation. He had a vision of liberty, equality and fraternity, sustained by education extended to the mass of the peoples, and by a great expansion of applied science. D'Holbach, a rich German from the Palatinate, who had inherited his title from a relative who made his career in France, displayed a more systematic learning and a determined atheism. This spirited aristocrat was bitterly anti-clerical, and disbelieved even in the social utility of religion: good sense, a universal, humanist, morality of disinterested benevolence, he believed, could improve society. The abounding confidence in reason and progress, odd in so worldly a society as that of eighteenth-century France, with its wit, malice and social cruelty, seems naïve to those accustomed to reckon with the bestialities of mob-violence; with rabid demagogues and other manifestations of the sub-conscious and 'original sin'; yet, though the optimism of the eighteenth century often seems ridiculous and its knowledge superficial, its strategic objective of improvement was new and sound.

Against this background of social thought, the scientists were continuing the researches which had already proved immensely valuable. Newton had set in apparent order the cosmic background and physical laws of the world, and his *Opticks* had revolutionized that subject. Boyle, a son of the first Lord Cork, who had made his fortune out of Sir Walter Ralegh's confiscated Irish estates, had studied chemistry without the alchemist preoccupations which were to haunt even Goethe decades after. In Aubrey's words, he became 'peerless in a larger province, that of Unversall Nature, subdued and made obsequious to his inquisitive mind'.[2] Cavendish, another English aristocrat, first analysed the chemistry of water, isolated hydrogen and made key discoveries in magnetism. Joseph Priestley, the Yorkshire unitarian and radical, discovered oxygen. Lavoisier destroyed the hypothesis of 'phlogiston', a 'substance' that had long obscured chemistry, and further ordered the fundamentals of the science. Linnaeus (1707–78) – Karl von Linne, a Swede – was another pioneer scientist: he made an immense new classification of plants and animals and invented the nomenclature of *genus*, qualified by an adjective, to give a new, universal, vocabulary to biologists. Leuwenhoek's microscope revealed the existence of bacteria, an immensely important discovery, and the basis of propagation. These great names are only the most famous among a galaxy of discoverers; forerunners of the great professional scientists of modern times, whose discoveries were to affect the whole world.

In architecture the humanist outlook of the Renaissance, Italianate and ordered, now developed in luxuriance in the north as well as in its native Mediterranean setting. Space, coherence and proportion were combined with variety:

The emphasis of Renaissance humanism is less on order than on liberty. . . . It has learned the speech of architecture from Greece and Rome, but the Renaissance itself will choose what things their speech will say. Every value, every avenue of promise, it will explore, enjoy and express. Hence the insatiate curiosity, the haste, the short duration of its styles: hence the conversion of classic forms to the gay uses of baroque and rococo invention.[3]

From the Palladian villas on the Brenta to the massive yet lyric splendours of Melk, and from the palaces of St Petersburg along the misty Neva to the well-proportioned salons of Schönbrunn and the austere elegance of Holkham on the Norfolk coast, the same inspiration is apparent; exuberant in the immense façades of Spain and in the castles of Bavaria, pompous in the sweep of Versailles, discreet in the unobtrusive perfection of the Mauritshuis at The Hague. And along with this far-flung and confident building, went a new cult of landscape, contrived to create the vistas and horizons that a spirited age enjoyed. André le Nôtre (1613–1700) was the greatest of these designers.

From the earliest times, when lilies were grown in pots on the leads of the battlements, and when the herb and vegetable plot lay within the fortified walls, a garden had been something snatched from the surrounding wilderness and tamed, a plot of earth, no matter how small, subjected into a pattern, safe as a tapestry, a soothing background to an unsettled life. Every garden was a walled garden and for the most part, a utilitarian one. . . . As it was, the influence of Le Nôtre, like a strong gale from the east, blew down many hedges and for the magnifico, opened vistas that appeared to have no bounds.[4]

This refinement and elaboration of living extended also to the chase, which had its political overtones. The routine of courts was often determined by the hunt, formal and splendid, the hounds trained to an harmonious cry and the horns sounding their elaborate signals through the woods.

The German princes, in particular, asserted their rights against the empire by insisting on the royal privileges of the hunt.★

The eighteenth century also greatly refined the pleasures of the table, often, in western Europe, still more a matter of gormandizing than of taste. Brillat-Savarin (1755–1826), born at Belley in Savoy, at the southern foot of the Jura, was the first great prophet of gastronomy. 'Those who guzzle,' he wrote, 'or those who swill, do not know how to eat or drink.' This

★ 'Hunting was closely linked with the exercise of sovereignty . . . the rigid stratification of society until 1806 was reflected in the strict hierarchy of the game. The lower nobility was permitted to hawk as a pastime, but falconry was a sovereign pleasure. An immense social difference separated the wolves, hares and rabbits, the birds of prey (except eagles and eagle-owls), the wild geese and duck which fell to the guns of the lower nobility, and those stags, wild boars, bears, cranes, and pheasants, classed as *most noble*, to which was reserved the honour of being massacred by the Estate of the Holy Roman Empire. The Chase was not merely the sport of a German prince; it was . . . part of his princely function. One of the reasons for the progressive elaboration of the hunt, both in ceremonial and decoration, was that it took on at one point in the minds of its participants something of the character of an act of state.' H. M. Baillie, 'German Festival Hunts', *The Month* (May 1951).

revolutionary sentiment was backed by a whole complicated and subtle philosophy of cuisine, complete, in twenty-nine meditations, and reinforced by a variety of anecdotes, recipes and verse, exhorting, as Karl Marx was to exhort the workers, the gastronomes of the world to unite. His famous *Physiologie du Goût* concludes: '*Levez vers le ciel vos faces radieuses; avancez dans votre force et votre majesté, l'univers esculent est ouvert devant vous.*'*

Portrait and landscape painting now developed from the great tradition created in the sixteenth and seventeenth centuries. In France Watteau (1684–1729), in the lineage of Rubens, combined passionately observed detail with economy of line, creating an evanescent, lyrical beauty; Boucher and Fragonard also caught the gaiety and pathos of a privileged, and sometimes futile, society, while Chardin infused Dutch anecdote and observation with French wit. In Italy Tiepolo (1696–1770) painted his lavish compositions, full of light and life, a cheerful version of old mythology, while Canaletto, Longhi, and Guardi caught the luminous and changing moods of Venice. England was now producing fine painters; Reynolds, from the West Country, combined insight into character with harmonious colour and design; Gainsborough from Suffolk (1727–88), who remarked of his patrons, 'Now damn gentlemen, there is not such a set of enemies to the real artist as they are', and whose reputed last words were, 'we are all going to heaven and Van Dyck is of the company', shows a more suble technique. Both were well suited to record a great age in literature and politics, and to depict the sensibility of a privileged class, the seamier side of whose way of life, as that of their dependants, was described by Hogarth and Rowlandson. A tradition of landscape painting, which owed much to Holland, was created by Morland and Richard Wilson, to come to full fruition in Constable. In Spain Goya (1746–1828) proved as great a master as Velasquez, a painter of European fame.

European literature was still dominated by the French. The verve and lucidity of Voltaire (1694–1778), the fine prose and wide range of Montesquieu, the stately dramatic tradition created by Corneille and Racine, the wit of Molière, the arrogant certainties of sceptical writers of memoirs and maxims, combined in an overwhelming impact. It spread the cult of 'enlightenment' to Vienna, Berlin and St Petersburg, so that a cosmopolitan outlook grew up, more worldly and elegant than the old cult of Latin learning; including classes outside the pale of medieval chivalry, transcending the barriers of Catholic, Protestant and Orthodox Christianity. As one authority has it:

---

* See the admirably illustrated *Edition Karr*, p. 412. 'Lift up your radiant faces to the heavens; go forward in your strength and majesty, the edible universe is open before you.' Adam and Eve, he remarked, ruined themselves for an apple; what would they have done for a Turkey, cooked with Truffles?

Throughout the whole of the eighteenth century the figure of French culture ruled every court and salon claiming to be civilized.... In Russia, Poland, Prussia, it was light penetrating the darkness.... In the theatres of these capitals, as in those of the Netherlands, Denmark, Sweden, Austria and Piedmont, [French] was heard more often than the native language. The Russian aristocracy conversed in it even with their children.... When in the nineteenth century freedom and civilization reawakened in Greece, Rumania, Serbia and Bulgaria, the medium of the new found liberty was French.[5]

In England the baroque prose of Hobbes and Sir Thomas Browne gave place to the brisk lucidity of Dryden and Swift, while Defoe created a mode of fiction which developed into the more elaborate and subtle characterization of Richardson, Smollett and Fielding, whose *Tom Jones*, appeared in 1749. Gibbon, who at first contemplated writing his *The Decline and Fall of the Roman Empire* in French, achieved the greatest masterpiece of sustained historical narrative in the English language, while the eloquence of Burke and the resounding good sense of Dr Johnson vastly enriched an already great literature. In Spain the art of fiction had early developed: the *Life of Lazarillo de Tormes* (1554), an anonymous autobiography, is already a landmark in characterization; Aleman's *Guzmán de Alfarache* was an early picaresque novel of low life, and the poet Quevedo had further developed this form; but it was a German, Johann von Grimmelshausen (1622–76), who had brought this kind of knock-about, cynical, record of underdog experience (carried on in our own day in the Czech Hasek's *The Good Soldier Schweik*) to its most effective form in *The Adventures of Simplicissmus*. Klopstock was a pioneer of native German poetry, and Lessing, an exponent of the Enlightenment, wrote his *Laokoön*, one of the earliest works of literary criticism, as well as comedies; but it was Herder (1744–1803) who was the first great German romantic, with his cult of the folk and the land.

These are but a few outstanding names in the rich panorama of eighteenth-century European literature which was to influence many peoples in times and places far beyond Europe.

But it was in music that the age was supreme. In Protestant Germany J. S. Bach (1685–1750), a Thuringian, for thirty years *Kapellmeister* at Leipzig, brought contrapuntal fugues and chorales to perfection. A superb executant, this teacher and court musician calmly worked out the full intellectual possibilities of his idiom. The more worldly Handel (1685–1759) was a magnificent showman, who came to England with the elector of Hanover and achieved deserved success. In Catholic Germany, Haydn (1732–1809), of Croat descent in Lower Austria, became director of Music to the Esterhazys; influenced by Bach's son, Emmanuel, he brought symphonies and string quartets to a new level; a countryman, a good shot, he worked the folk tunes of his people into a more elaborate setting. Gluck (1714–87), a Bavarian, became the first important German composer of opera. But it was Mozart (1756–91) who was the greatest genius. Born at Salzburg, the young prodigy was knighted by the pope at fourteen and enjoyed a European *réclame*. It was otherwise in the provincial archiepiscopal court of his native town, but in cosmopolitan Vienna his genius came to its fruition. *Figaro, Don Giovanni, The Magic Flute*, symphonies, operas and operettas, the great final Mass – all showed the power of melodic shape and harmony of the most effortless genius of European classical composition. Beethoven (1770–1827), at once the last great classical composer and the first great romantic, was born at Bonn, but lived most of his life in Vienna, where he was, briefly, a pupil of Mozart, who saw his promise. His mighty symphonies, composed slowly, with effort, were well suited to the revolutionary, Napoleonic, age to which his main achievements belong.

# IV

The cultural vitality, the variety and the attack displayed by Europeans in the seventeenth and eighteenth centuries mark the rise of a civilization more dynamic than anything achieved since the days of ancient Hellas. It derived from Mediterranean beginnings but, by the eighteenth century, its mainspring was French, and it had been greatly enriched by the contribution of northern Europe. It was based on the economic and colonial expansion already indicated, which had brought European influence to the ancient civilizations of the East, to the fringes of Africa and the Americas. Further, when the new science of 'political economy', formulated by the Physiocrats in mid-eighteenth-century France, was defined in lucid and memorable form by Adam Smith, whose *Wealth of Nations* appeared in 1776, the year of the American Declaration of Independence, a most significant development had occurred. The commercial wealth of eighteenth-century England was already financing the beginning of the Industrial Revolution; now its theory was formulated. The surge of this development, which, along with the Romantic movement, the cult of liberty and popular sovereignty, proclaimed by Rousseau, and with the revolution which destroyed the *ancien régime* in France and transformed the political and social structures of much of Europe, now swept much of the old order aside. But the privileged, aristocratic and cosmopolitan society which it superseded had set standards which were to prove their value when the Romantic movement had run its course. Intellectually, as well as politically, the high eighteenth century was a rigorous and dynamic age.

# Twenty

# EUROPEAN EXPANSION
# OVERSEAS

## I

While these decisive political and social events had been going on, European traders and settlers had followed in the tracks of the early explorers. By the close of the eighteenth century, European societies were firmly established in the Americas; Siberia was being colonized; India and Indonesia were largely under European control, and commercial contact had been established, if not now directly with Japan, with Manchu China through Canton. Most of the interior of Africa remained unknown, but Bruce had revealed the source of the Blue Nile, and Mungo Park the course of the Niger. In 1768, a year before Bruce's expedition set out, Cook sailed on his first voyage to the Pacific; he was to survey the still unknown east coast of Australia: by 1788 Sydney was to be founded. New Zealand, first sighted by Tasman in 1642, when the Maori war canoes rammed and sank one of the explorer's boats, was also circumnavigated by Cook, and in the last decade of the century it was frequented by Australian whalers, sealers and lumbermen. For the first time in world history the outline of the entire inhabitable world came into view. Save for Antarctica, there were no more continents unknown. This achievement was due entirely to Europeans, whose expansion was the sequel to an intellectual, technological and economic development going on since the Middle Ages. Its sequel was also to be European – the Industrial and Technical Revolutions, which were to make the entire planet economically one, and create the potential basis of a world culture.

## II

The Spaniards now dominated South America; their government was strictly centralized, urban and Catholic. Protestant propaganda has grossly belittled the civilizing achievements of Spain. Atrocities there were, in particular the forced labour in the silver mines of Potosi; and the effect of European settlement on the native population was biologically catastrophic. They had no immunity to European disease, and the enormous Spanish cattle and sheep ranches swamped Indian agriculture and caused widespread erosion. But the aims of the Spanish government and of the

237

Church were humane. There was no apartheid: the Mexican and Peruvian aristocracies were encouraged to adopt Spanish ways. The Spaniards found closely organized and docile peasant societies, and even in the territories of the Andes, the more inaccessible parts of the Inca Empire, they took over a working administration. After the first violences of the Conquistadors, the vice-royalties were manned, if not very ably, from the home country, and the Franciscans and Dominicans, who brought Christianity to Mexico, were often picked products of Erasmian learning. The Indians, accustomed to a culture in which ritual pervaded life, took easily to the splendid ceremonial of the new religion, and Mediterranean cults blended with indigenous beliefs. Great baroque cathedrals were built on the sites of ancient temples, and over cloisters, modelled on those of Seville and Santiago, sounded the bells of Christian Spain.

In Mexico the ancient capital was retained and greatly enlarged; in Peru, Lima superseded Cuzco and the old Inca strongholds decayed. The population, even the Inca aristocracy, were more difficult to tame, and the Spanish culture remained concentrated on the coast. In Paraguay, the Jesuits had a free hand.

Thus, although Spanish domination was ruthlessly imposed, the Indian village economy often ruined, and the ancient religion overlaid, the conquerors interbred with the Amerindians; Catholicism was adapted to Indian minds, and Spanish civilization was modified, so that a mixed way of life, with its own flavour and qualities, emerged. When, in the early nineteenth century, the Spanish-American Empire broke away, a new, vigorous, often dynamic, if politically unstable, South America came into being, no mere imitation of Europe, but indigenous and original.

In North America the Spaniards spread slowly and sparsely from Mexico far into Florida, the south and even mid-west, exploring much of Ohio and Missouri by 1543: they traded horses with the Indians, and so revolutionized the Indian way of life in the great plains. But the main exploration and settlement was made by the English and the French.* As early as 1497–8 the Cabots had discovered Newfoundland, Nova Scotia and the New England coast, and in 1534, when Pizarro was completing the conquest of Peru, Jacques Cartier of Saint Malo, in search of the north-west passage to Asia, entered the St Lawrence. Two years later he penetrated to the site of Montreal, into territory he called New France, and developed a fur trade with the Huron-Iroquois. The first exploration of Canada and the closest contacts with the Indians were French.

The English came late to the exploitation of the northern continent. It was not until 1584 that Philip Amadas and Arthur Barlow landed at Cape

---

* When Charles v claimed all the Americas, Francis i had remarked that 'he much desired to see Adam's will, to learn how he had partitioned the world'.

Hatteras, off what is today Pamilco Sound in North Carolina, and sent Ralegh their glowing report;

The second of July we found shole water, where we smelt so sweet, and so strong a smel, as if we had bene in the midst of a delicate garden abounding in all kinde of oderiferous flowers, by which we were assured that the land could not be farre distant: and keeping good watch and bearing but slacke saile, the fourth of the same month we arrived upon the coast . . . we viewed the land about us, being very sandie and low towards the water side, but so full of grapes as the very beating and surge of the sea overflowed them.[1]

But the first colony failed. Then, by 1607, a permanent settlement was made on Chesapeake Bay. Jamestown, though in summer mosquito-ridden, was easy to defend. Under the leadership of Captain John Smith, the settlers survived the first privations, and the Virginia Company was finally incorporated in 1609.[*] The Jacobean-Caroline colonies, in an apparently genial but then treacherous environment – for the Chesapeake and Potomac areas were then haunted by fever – had desperate vicissitudes, apart from their conflicts with the Indians, their internal feuds, idleness, indiscipline. But the settlements survived, and, today, Williamsburg, its original architecture and way of life elaborately restored, recalls the importance of the Virginian settlement which acclimatized basic Anglo-Saxon political institutions, decisive for the whole North American future.

Northwards, by 1620, the Congregationalist 'Pilgrim Fathers' – mostly youngish people, small yeomen and artisans from Nottinghamshire, who emigrated to obtain toleration for their beliefs and to better themselves – had anchored, after a horrible two months' voyage, during which they had actually made a 'social contract' to form a civil society, off the sandy flats of modern Provincetown at the end of Cape Cod. They could hardly have timed their arrival worse, for they arrived in late November at the beginning of the New England winter. Settling across the bay at Plymouth, half of them managed to survive, for the Indians were at first not unfriendly, and many of them, by what the settlers considered a dispensation of providence, had been recently killed off by smallpox.[†] Their leader, William Bradford, an outstanding personality, governed the settlement and dealt with the Indians with firmness and decision.[‡] Their

---

[*] It is probable that the Indian King Powhatan's ceremonial mantle, now in the Ashmolean museum at Oxford, was given to one of the adventurers in 1608. It is 'made of deerskin and decorated with patterns of tiny shells, forming the figure of a man down the spine with an animal on each side, long ears and tail, in an attitude of supplication with outstretched paws. The rest has roundels of thickly encrusted shells disposed in rough symmetry. . . .' A.L.Rowse, *The Elizabethans in America* (London and New York 1959), p. 207, for a vivid account of the settlement.

[†] The 'Pilgrims' naturally, took some time to exploit their novel environment, being accustomed for ten years to the life of small artisans in Leyden. They were inefficient fishermen and inexpert at killing game, nor, unlike their descendants did they appreciate the clams and lobsters of the coast.

[‡] He died worth the equivalent of £50,000 in modern money, and his *Of Plimouth Plantation* (1630–50), ed. S. E. Morison (New York 1952), is a classic of its kind.

Congregationalist religion, which encouraged town meetings and local self-government, was much less intolerant than that of the Calvinist Presbyterians who later settled at Boston, further up the coast, and whose colony finally absorbed them. This Massachusetts colony had stronger backing, mainly from East Anglia and Dorset and the West – as witness the place names of the district – and many settlers had been educated at the Puritan colleges in Cambridge. They set up tenacious, well-found, communities. If they came, not to practise religious liberty, but to impose their own intolerance, their rugged determination served them well. The land they settled was rocky and wild, but with patches of good arable pasture; the winters were severe, but not so terrible as those later faced by the settlers of the mid-west and Canada; the summers better than those at home.

In the Far North, constant and often tragic attempts went on to find the north-west passage. It exists, but it baffled the explorers; nor could they have exploited it in the appalling climate. But huge sub-arctic areas were opened up. As early as 1576 Frobisher, in search for gold, had made his reconnaissance amid the ice and contacted the Eskimoes. 'They bee like Tatars, with long blacke haire, broade faces, and flatte noses, and tawnie in colour, wearing seale skinnes... their boates are made all of seales skinnes; with a keele of wood within the skin: the proportion of them is like a Spanish shallop, save only they be flat in the bottome and sharpe at both ends.'[2] Davis, in the 1580s, had sailed north into the strait between Greenland and Baffinland and afterwards explored far up the Greenland coast. Hudson, in 1610, entered the Straits between Labrador and Baffinland and emerged into the enormous Hudson's Bay. Here, after he had penetrated to its southernmost shore, his mutinous crew cast him adrift to perish.

Meanwhile the French, with the backing of Henry IV's government, had consolidated their position on the St Lawrence, striking down beyond the New England colonies towards the great lakes and the interior. By 1608 Champlain had founded Quebec. They pushed on west up the Ottawa, and south-west towards Lake Ontario, outflanking the English settlements behind the Hudson valley, and what is now the state of New York. Canada proved attractive to many young Frenchmen who had no prejudice against the Indians. In Canada 'they could hunt, as only aristocrats could at home; they could gorge themselves frequently and idle for considerable periods; a different set of sexual morals invited their endless indulgence; and their knowledge of lands and language made them courted by both Indians and Europeans'.[3]

It was through fur and fish that European settlements took root, though governments were still obsessed with a short cut to Asia. The Dutch, who commissioned Hudson to explore the great river named after him, founded

New Amsterdam on Manhattan Island. But their foothold was seized by the English and renamed New York after 1664, a more important event than the contemporary and notorious Dutch raid into the Medway, and the most abiding memorial to James Duke of York – afterwards James II.

Backed by the Company of New France, encouraged by Richelieu and afterwards by Colbert, the French pushed on. By the 1670s they had penetrated down the Ohio valley, by 1682 into the rich prairies of Iowa; la Salle explored the course of the broad Mississippi, named the new territories Lousiana after Louis XIV, and linked up with other Frenchmen who, in 1717, had founded New Orleans on the river estuary on the Gulf. It was an enormous exploit of pioneering, but the settlements were thin, and too much dependent on the State. As already observed, France was putting her main resources into continental wars. The enterprise ended, politically, in 1759, with Wolfe's capture of Quebec.

To European governments, the West Indies long appeared more important. Here, English, Dutch, and French had early challenged the Spanish monopoly, which had been early extended along the Pacific coasts, since in 1513 Balboa (not Cortez), the first European to see the 'South Sea', had observed it, not from a peak but from a hillock, in Darien. In 1568 John Hawkins, intent on selling West African slaves to the Spanish planters, was trapped by treachery during his third expedition in the Mexican port of San Juan de Ullao. After that, the English systematically attacked on an able strategic plan, ably countered. In 1572–3 Drake raided Panama; in 1585–6, after his brilliant circumnavigation of the globe, he was diverted from an expedition to the Far East again to attack the Caribbean. He took San Domingo in Hispaniola and Cartagena on the Main: his attack was an immediate cause of the expedition of the Armada. The Spaniards organized heavily armed convoys, and their treasure fleet was caught only once, in 1627, by the Dutch admiral, Piet Heyn: but the West Indies continued to be the scene of violence and piracy.

The English also colonized Bermuda, where, in July 1609, the expedition sent to Virginia, under Sir Thomas Gates and Sir George Somers, was cast ashore in a hurricane. To their surprise, they found the 'still vexed Bermoothes, otherwise called the Ile of Divels', a land of plenty. 'And fish is there so aboundant, that if a man steppe into the water they will come round about him; so that men were fane to get out for feare of byting. These fishes are very fat and sweet.' The place swarmed with wild pig, and 'great store of tortoises (which some call turtles) . . . all very good meate and yeeldeth great store of oyle, which is as sweet as butter'.[4] There were great cedars and 'Palmito trees', whose fruit was 'farre better meate than any cabbidge'. So fortified over the winter, the English made their own ship and pinnace and, in May 1610, reached Virginia in a fortnight, just in time to prevent the colony from being abandoned.

In the 'Carribee Islands', St Kitts was colonized in 1624; Nevis four years later; then Monserrat and Antigua. In the 1630s the French took Guadeloupe and Martinique. All these islands had chequered beginnings, since the fierce Caribs – the original 'cannibals' – unlike the mild natives of the Bahamas, put up an obstinate defence, and the Spaniards raided from the Main. Barbados, east of the Antilles, uninhabited and less accessible, was annexed for the Crown by Courteen, a Bristol merchant backed by Lord Pembroke, but ousted and ruined by the Earl of Carlisle, a court favourite of Charles I. Finally, the strategically important island of Jamaica, commanding the channel between Cuba and Hispaniola, was seized by a rather incompetent Cromwellian expedition in 1655, after they had failed to take San Domingo. Jamaica seemed, *de facto*, no one's property.

The area remained the haunt of 'buccaneers', so called from the masterless men who lived off hunting wild cattle for their hides and cured beef in strips over slow fires. The most notorious and successful desperado was Sir Henry Morgan, a ruffian who came out as an indentured servant to Barbados, and who was set on by the governor of Jamaica against the Spaniards. He totally wrecked Panama in 1668, and was knighted after a notable career of sack, arson and pillage.

In spite of these disorders, the West Indian islands became immensely rich. By the late seventeenth century the small tobacco plantations of the first settlers were abandoned, in face of Virginian competition, for the plantation of sugar on a great scale. Indigo and cotton were also raised. Much capital was put into these industries and it was not until far into the eighteenth century that the East Indian trade surpassed that of the 'Sugar Islands'. Hence their importance in the successive treaties of the time.

This prosperity, like that of the American plantations, was bought at a price. The slave trade, which went on steadily from the Elizabethan Age to the early nineteenth century, created a social problem of baffling scope. It was to cause, indirectly, the American Civil War, the most sanguinary conflict of the nineteenth century, and its repercussions continue. For in the West Indies, the cotton, rice and tobacco fields of Georgia, the Carolinas and Virginia, and spreading westward far beyond, a massive negro population settled in, its roots no longer in Africa, but planted, in-eradicably, in the Americas.

# III

The other great field of European expansion, though not of colonization, was the East. First the Portuguese, then the Dutch and English and then the French won footholds in India. Here, the Mughal emperor, Shah Alam (1759–1806), still nominally exercised the authority of his ancestors. At the mercy of 'rough Afghans, uncouth Mahrattas and rustic Jats',[5] the court of the Mughals was still the 'school of manners for Hindustan. From the time of Akbar it had much the same influence upon Indian manners as the court of Versailles upon Europeans. . . . Forms of address, the conventions of behaviour, and to a large extent ceremonial dress, approximated to the standard of Delhi. Even the Marathas felt its subtle and pervading influence.'[6] The successive rulers of eighteenth-century India always legitimized their authority in the name of the Mughals.

As already emphasized, after the failure of the Afghans to consolidate their victory at Panipat in 1761 the Mahratha Mahadji-Roa Scindia of Gwalior remained the most powerful prince in northern India and dominated the imperial court: but blinded after a palace revolution in 1787, Shah Alam, restored and subsidized by the British, long retained his nominal authority. His son, Akbar II, was to be succeeded by Bahadur Shah, the last of the Mughals, who died in 1853. To the end, the Mughals, in attenuated but distinguished state, were to remain patrons of the arts and retain the tradition of Persian civilization. Their court was 'the last refuge of a traditional culture whose tragedy it was to perish at the hands of political passion and misplaced alien benevolence'.[7]

Against this background, often ignored by western historians, the rise of the British Raj in India must be regarded. It was asserted in two phases: first, against the French; then against Indian resistance, and the process was devious and slow. It was not until 1819 that, save in the Punjab and Scinde, the British became entirely paramount. The beginnings had been tentative and entirely commercial. The European merchants found great opportunities, which always interested them more than the political responsibility which they were later forced to assume. As already observed, India – and in particular Bengal – in the early seventeenth century had long been a centre of flourishing small-scale industry, with a large export trade. This prosperity was to be diminished by the enormous exactions of the Mughals and their rivals, but, in spite of looting and political corruption, up to the mid-eighteenth century it was still considerable. Hence the wealth which the Europeans were to exploit. But with the British domination, Indian handloom weavers had to face an English competition which, after the Industrial Revolution, was to prove decisive. From an elaborately organized and prosperous centre of craftsmanship, with a great Asian export trade, the richest areas of India were to concentrate on the supply of raw materials and to become markets for the British manufacturers.

The conflict with France and the exploits of Clive are familiar. But these affairs appeared marginal to the main history of India; the failure of the last major Afghan invasion of the north must have seemed more decisive, but they determined the future. For, in fact, Clive and Warren Hastings, backed by superior sea power, laid the foundations of the British Indian Empire: the future of India was to be determined for over a century and a half by Europeans.

Their dominance was not, in principle, a new phenomenon in the country. One set of rulers was being superseded by another, and the British, six months' sail away from Europe, were often assimilated. They recouped themselves lavishly, as had other conquerors, and since they rarely brought out their families to India, they often took Indian mistresses and wives. Hastings and his entourage were deeply versed in both Muslim and Hindu culture, and the easy-going ways of the eighteenth century blended with Indian casualness and sensibility. It was not until the rise of Utilitarian political ideas, of Evangelical Puritanism, of the new kind of public schools, and, finally, the arrival of the *mem-sahib*, that the British began to form a caste of their own, aloof and self-consciously alien.

The English had developed their trade with India in cotton, indigo, saltpetre, as well as the more precious luxury goods, partly because the Dutch had forestalled them in Indonesia. As already pointed out, the spice islands, the goal of all the adventurers since Columbus, and originally exploited by the Portuguese, became largely a Dutch monopoly. Backed by a State which depended for its life on the sea, and had in part come into existence on it, the Dutch had expelled the Portuguese and thwarted the English. The Dutch East India Company had made Batavia in Java their main base, and they soon controlled the Moluccas. On the predominantly Malayan peoples, with their Hindu and Muslim cultures, they superimposed a new, European, régime.

The profits were fantastic. Since the early Middle Ages the European rich, dissatisfied with their native horseradish, herbs and garlic, had hankered for the more exotic flavours of the East. Venetian wealth had been built on this demand: pepper and cloves, mace and cinnamon, saffron, cardomum and ginger now made the fortunes of the Dutch. And when the market was glutted, coffee and tea from China came into fashion. Many opulent houses along quiet canals in Amsterdam were founded on the Eastern trade, and the Indonesians, like the Indians, were subjected to an alien domination.

# IV

Long before the Dutch had established themselves in the East Indies, the Polynesians had been spreading out across the vast spaces of the Pacific. Samoa, it will be recalled, had been colonized from Indonesia in about the fifth century AD, and from Tahiti, the Polynesians had colonized Hawaii, where their most elaborate culture had grown up; and afterwards New Zealand.

The sixteenth-century Europeans had missed most of the important islands of the central Pacific. Magellan, in 1523, had found the Philippines; the Spaniard Mendana, in 1568, discovered what he called the Solomon Islands, east of New Guinea; Drake, who landed in California as well as raiding the Spanish American coast, saw nothing until he came to the Moluccas. Mendana, in the last years of the century, also found the Marquesas. Quiros and Torres found the New Hebrides and coasted the southern shore of New Guinea; in the 1740s, Commodore Anson prospected for a southern continent; there was competition even for the desolate Falklands as a base. Then, in 1766, Samuel Wallis chanced on Tahiti, one of the main centres of Polynesia; a year later, Bougainville visited the island, and sighted the Great Barrier Reef of Eastern Australia.

Such was the patchy state of European knowledge, and so small the European impact, when the greatest British maritime explorer, Captain James Cook, finally dispelled the illusion of *Terra Australis Incognita* and cleared up the remaining mysteries of the South Seas. Even less was known about Australia than about Polynesia. That gaunt, sun-bitten, and enormous continent had lain cut off from the outer world since prehistoric times; geologically the most ancient of all lands, it harboured odd, primitive plants and animals, and its sparse inhabitants, racially akin to certain southern Indian peoples, were still Palaeolithic savages; gatherers and hunters, expert in bushcraft and in handling boomerangs and barbed spears, well adapted to their migratory, scavenging lives. They had wandered for untold generations over a continent nearly half of which was tropical and much of which was desert.

In contrast, a thousand miles beyond in the South Pacific, the temperate and mountainous islands of New Zealand contained a belligerent and capable people. The Maoris had begun to colonize the country from Polynesia about the mid-twelfth century.

The Dutch had discovered what was, so far, known of Australia: they had called it New Holland, and they had first sighted New Zealand. In 1605 Janszoon had explored the Gulf of Carpentaria; eleven years later, Dutch sea captains from the Cape had observed much of the western coast. In 1640 Van Dieman, governor-general of the East Indies, had commissioned Tasman to explore the southern ocean eastwards from the Cape. He had found Tasmania and New Zealand, but the entire east coast of Australia remained unknown and was thought to be continuous with New Guinea.

Over half a century elapsed before these voyages were followed up. In 1697 William Dampier, anthropologist, naturalist and buccaneer, won instant celebrity with his *A New Voyage Round the World*.[8] 'As to my stile,' he wrote, 'it cannot be expected that a seaman should affect politeness. . . . I have frequently divested myself of sea phrases, to gratify the land reader.' But his 'Mixed relation of Places and Action in the same order of time in which they occurred', is a classic of exploration, and contains the first English account of the Australian aborigines.

After trading rum and sugar, hats and axes, in Central America for logwood, Dampier, in company with some desperadoes under a Captain

Swan, had 'stood over the Southern Ocean for the East Indies'. They arrived at Guam, with only three days' provisions, and it was well that they got there, for the crew had planned 'first to kill the captain and eat him when the victuals were gone and afterwards all of us who were accessory to promoting the voyage'. 'Ah Dampier,' the captain commented, 'you would have made them but a poor meal.'

New Holland, reached in 1688, proved a desolate wilderness of sandy soil and gum trees, the inhabitants . . .

. . . the miserablest people in the world. The Hodmadods [Hottentots] of Manomatapa, though a nasty people, are Gentlemen to these; . . . and setting aside their human shapes, they differ little from Brutes. They are tall, strait-bodied, and thin, with small long limbs. They have great heads, round foreheads and great brows. Their eyelids are always half-closed, to keep the flies out of their eyes . . . they have great bottle noses, pretty full lips and wide mouths. . . . Nor have they any beards. They are long visaged and of a very unpleasing aspect. Their hair is black, short and curld, like that of the Negroe. The colour of their skins, both of the face and the rest of the Body, is coal Black, like that of the Negroes of the Guinea.[9]

They lived in small bands, fishing, gathering roots and shellfish, and armed with pieces of wood 'shaped somewhat like a cutlass' – in fact, boomerangs; they had fire and shared out their miserable diet. At first the men defied the invaders: when tamer, they stood 'like·statues without any motion, but grinned like so many monkeys'. They showed no interest at all in the ship, and at the sound of the ship's drum, they ran off crying, 'Gurry, Gurry! – somewhat through the throat'. Such was the first contact of the English seventeenth century with Palaeolithic Australia.

More than eighty years later Cook followed it up. This outstanding seaman, a Yorkshireman with Scots blood, the son of a farm labourer, had been bred to the sea in colliers plying between Newcastle and London. He had made his reputation by charting the St Lawrence for Wolfe and he was commissioned for his famous first voyage (1768–71) in the *Endeavour*, a Whitby collier, adapted for surveying dangerous coasts. The first official objective was to observe the transit of Venus from Tahiti, where Cook recorded the amiable characteristics of the islanders, already exploited by the French explorer, Bougainville. In their contrasting styles, the Frenchman and the Yorkshireman concur. With systematic, accurate and unadorned detail, Cook describes Tahitian physique, arms, food and animals, 'Hogs, fowls, dogs, the latter of which we learned to eat from them, and few there were of us, but what allowe'd that a South Sea Dog was next to an English lamb.'[10] The rulers were much taller and fairer than the common people. 'They have all fine white teeth and for the most part short flat noses and thick lips, yet the features are agreeable and the gait graceful, and their behaviour to strangers and each other open, affable and courteous . . . only that they are thieves to a man.' Both sexes painted their bodies; '*Tattow* it is called'; and their morals were shocking: 'The young girles . . . dance a very indecent dance which they call the *Timorodee* (To-miro-iti). Both sexes express the most indecent ideas in conversation without the least emotion.'* They lived on bread-fruit, coconuts, yams, and a variety of crustaceans and fish.

The Maoris in New Zealand, whom Cook called 'Indians', were much fiercer. When, in 1769, he landed on the eastern coast of *Eaheino Mauwe*, the north island, they at once attacked him – a 'sett of very obstinate and stubborn kind of people, and brave withall by endeavouring to gitt master of our boats, and fought as long as ever they had things to throw at us, even a parcel of fish, which they had in the canoe, they flung, and for all that there were two men dead in the canoe they did not seem the least Daunted or Frighted'.[11] They paddled round the ship in eighty-foot war canoes, shouting in a language easily intelligible to Cook's Tahitian interpreter: '*Haere mai, haere ki uta hei patu ake!*' 'Come here, come ashore to be *patued*! (knocked on the head).' Their banked, palisaded, and well-sited strongholds were visible as the ship passed the coast.

The Australian aborigines, on the other hand, seemed as primitive and ineffectual to Cook as to Dampier. When, on 19 April 1770, he first sighted part of south-western Australia – 'a round hillock very much like the Ram Head going into Plymouth Sound . . . the face of the country green and woody, but the sea shore is all white sand' – he observed the blacks and the smoke of camp fires.[12] At Botany Bay two natives with darts and throwing-sticks opposed his landing: their fourteen-foot canoes were the worst he ever saw. They wore bones through their noses, 'which the seamen call a sprit sail yard', and painted themselves in white spirals. They were quite indifferent to presents, would part with nothing of their own, and tried to get rid of the intruders by firing the grass: 'All they seemed to want was for us to be gone.' In their own interests, they were right.

Cook proceeded to explore most of the Great Barrier Reef. The *Endeavour* now struck on sharp coral, but was brought off; then she was nearly smashed against the reef by the Pacific swell, vast foaming breakers on a 'wall of coral rock rising all most perpendicular out of the

---

* Louis de Bougainville, who visited the island just before Cook, runs on in characteristic eighteenth-century clichés about their behaviour.

'As love is their only passion, the great number of women is the only luxury of the opulent . . . Jealousy is so unknown a passion here that the husband is among the first who persuades the wife to yield to another. . . . Wherefore should she resist the influence of the climate or the seduction of example? The very air the people breathe, their songs, their dances, all conspire to call to mind the sweets of love. They dance to the sound of a kind of drum, and when they sing, they accompany their voices with a very soft kind of flute. . . . Thus accustomed to live constantly immersed in pleasure, the people of Tahiti have acquired a happy and humorous temper which is the offspring of ease and joy.' But they found it very difficult to concentrate. L. Bougainville, *A Voyage Round the World*, trsl. J. B. Foster (London 1772), p. 257.

unfathomable ocean'.[13] By luck, judgement and discipline, the ship survived. They emerged into the Torres Strait, to round the northern tip of the new continent and return to England by Java and the Cape. 'The entire circumference both of New Zealand and New Holland had been revealed.'

In his second voyage, in the *Resolution* (1772–5) along the ice-bound fringe of Antarctica, Cook finally destroyed the legend of an inhabitable southern continent; on his third (1776–9), he discovered the Cook and Sandwich Islands, penetrated the Behring Strait between Siberia and Alaska, where he met Russian trappers, but where ice stopped him investigating the north-west passage. At Hawaii the priest-ridden inhabitants hailed him as a god, but tiring of their obligation to support the divinity and his shipmates, they hacked him to death in Kealakekua Bay. So at the age of fifty, perished the greatest of Pacific explorers.

His work was done. The Neolithic Polynesian society which had developed in isolation since late Roman times, was now exposed to the influences of the West. The Palaeolithic aborigines of Australia and the Polynesian Maoris of New Zealand were swept into a current which, with the expansion of Europe and the Industrial Revolution, was becoming world history. Meanwhile, in North America whole nations of European stock had taken root, and the native civilizations of Middle and South America had been transformed; in India the British had established their supremacy; in Indonesia, the Dutch. And, for the first time, the entire outline of the habitable world was known.

# EPILOGUE

# Twenty‑one

# PROGRESS: 'IMPROVEMENT': INDUSTRIAL DEMOCRACY

## I

The rich variety of civilizations hitherto surveyed had developed over millennia in different environments and in relative isolation. Now, by the end of the eighteenth century, European initiative had charted at least the outline of the entire globe: save for the wastes of the American Arctic and the corresponding desolation of the huge Antarctic continent, mankind, for the first time, could know where they were. Large areas of central Africa and South America and almost the whole of Australia were still isolated, but it was only a matter of time before these territories would become known to the rest of mankind.

Even the explorers did not anticipate how swiftly this would come about: in Anson's day it was thought improbable that a cure for scurvy, which came from 'bad air', would ever be discovered; Cook believed that no one would ever investigate Antarctica, and European exploration of central Africa appeared forbidden by the malign fevers to which there were then no answers. Yet within a couple of centuries, a mere flicker of time since *homo sapiens* appeared, the sudden cumulative impact of the industrial, technological and scientific revolutions had transformed the prospect, and dragged mankind, politically unprepared, into global interdependence, landed men on the moon and jeopardized the very existence of most life on the planet by nuclear weapons of escalating power.

Concurrently a swift political and social transformation had occurred: literate civilization, hitherto confined to minorities in the developed areas, had begun to include the mass of mankind, while in the underdeveloped countries governments were now desperately to try to satisfy their emancipated peoples' new demands. Along with this transformation of material prospects has come a population explosion due to modern medicine, while modern communications have made one half of the world know all too intimately how the other half lives or dies. The evils loosed by modern science and technology are the penalties of a new mastery, and it looks as if the progress vaunted by the nineteenth and twentieth centuries may even have been leading to catastrophe. Yet we cannot go back. And now, in the late twentieth century, we need to appraise how this promising but dangerous situation has come about and try to deal with it.

To an historian familiar with the slow pace and predominant and accepted poverty of all previous civilizations, the speed of the modern transformation has been staggering. Obviously its main causes demand analysis first; after that the consequences can be traced in political and social life as, with mounting speed and violence, they are transforming all the great civilizations hitherto depicted in this survey – that of Europe and of the countries of European settlement outside it; of India and China and of the societies deriving from them in South-East Asia and the Far East; of the Muslim world, and of the recently included peoples of black Africa. All this variety of peoples, whose pre-industrial history and cultural achievements have been already briefly described, are now being forced, whether they like it or not, into a global interdependence which may in time, saving catastrophe, produce a world civilization deriving from their many and diverse traditions and which will demand international organization and world management.

## II

The landmarks in the first or Palaeotechnic Industrial Revolution, which originated in Great Britain in the late eighteenth and early nineteenth centuries, are familiar. It began when textile industries were mechanized by water power, then by steam; and it was carried further, based on the juxtaposition of rich resources of coal and iron-ore, by steam power applied to bellows in blast furnaces to produce vast quantities of iron for machinery. The inventions of Crompton and Cartwright, who devised the power loom in 1785, exploited by the entrepreneur Arkwright, are behind the cotton mills; James Watt, who invented the steam engine (1781) and Trevithick (1804) and Stephenson, who invented the steam locomotive (1825), are behind the heavy industry and the railroads, and Isambard Kingdom Brunel (1806–59) behind the steamship (1830). These inventions created a new dimension of power and transport, and during the mid-nineteenth century, in a colossal feat of enterprise, they were spread over whole continents. Great industry gave rise to huge industrial cities, vastly increased the power of centralized governments and transformed war. The new technology also opened up and tamed huge areas in the Americas and even gradually altered the pace and outlook of the ancient peasant countries of the East, confirming the grip of European influence and, for the time, of European authority. During the long peace following the Napoleonic Wars, free-trading European entrepreneurs, bankers, industrialists and engineers exploited the new self-sustaining productivity of the mid-nineteenth-century railway age.

Such was the first revolution in industrial power and communications – the revolution of steam and iron: it dominated and transformed the times, and by the mid-century in Great Britain the population had already become more urban than agricultural. The millennia of peasant farming and of the minority cultures it had sustained were apparently being superseded, and it seemed that the Malthusian cycle of famine following overpopulation, had been broken. In Great Britain real wages rose by 25 per cent between 1800 and 1827, and the Industrial Revolution could not have taken off into its new dimension without an increasing work force with the purchasing power as well as the muscle to sustain it. It was not out of a ruined countryside but out of a relatively productive agriculture, unscarred by war, and out of an increasing rural population that the new industries developed, and although there was suffering in a strange environment, the picture of the whole process as a hideous degradation and exploitation is false. As great industry spread, it brought horrible evils and social and psychological malaise, but considering the condition of most of the peasantry in pre-industrial civilizations, it meant at least a new potential of well-being.

The second cycle of invention and of the exploitation of new sources of power did not occur until the late nineteenth century. It was made by exploiting gas, oil and electricity. The first, Palaeotechnic, Industrial Revolution had been made through coal, steam and iron – a comparatively wasteful, grimy and clumsy, if formidable, technology; the second, Neotechnic Revolution was made through mass-produced high-quality steel and by oil and electricity – more mobile and lighter forms of energy. The much-maligned internal combustion engine – the first practicable automobile was made by Benz in 1885 – generating power sparked off in petrol or gas vapour inside a small cylinder, is still relatively wasteful; but it is far handier than a boiler-driven steam locomotive, heated by external combustion from a furnace fed by a stoker, and belching coal smoke more pervasive than fumes from any exhaust. Electric power, generated by oil and coal and, best, by water power, had revolutionized lighting, heating and communications, industry and transport. The contemporary world with its jet aircraft, television, radio, and automobiles and electronic computers, has been profoundly changed even from that of the early nineteenth century, a mere hundred and fifty years ago.

All this enormous transformation has had one weakness: it is based mainly on the exploitation of fossil fuels – coal, gas and oil. Since the first transformation began mankind has been living on capital, and it is estimated that within, at best, a century oil supplies at the present rate of consumption may run out. Even that threat may now be evaded. Following the investigations of scientists from several countries into the structure of the atom, it was found that energy could be released by nuclear fission, and then that a chain reaction could release much more. Energy need no longer be tapped only by releasing it from fossil fuels, which have originally stored it up from the sun, but directly by a process that is going on in the sun itself – hence in principle a third technological revolution into a new dimension of self-sufficient power, different in kind from anything obtained from animal or manpower, from winds and tides and rivers, or from coal, gas and oil. Hence, too, its devastating and appalling effect when released in the atom and hydrogen bombs – a power out of all scale with human and animal life; capable, misused, of devastating the entire planet, but, properly exploited, of surpassing the achievements of the Palaeotechnic and Neotechnic revolutions and making them permanent. The expense and danger of exploiting nuclear fission for peaceful purposes has set back the hopes originally entertained for it, but the monstrous progress it has made in weapons, where cost is largely ignored, shows what it can do, and as the fossil fuels become more costly and begin to diminish, nuclear power in more sophisticated and safer forms is likely to become the main source of energy.

Such are the dominating technological facts that form the setting of the last two centuries of world history. From an agricultural and commercial economy, slow moving, traditional, geared to the biological responses of men and animals, and producing a surplus of wealth only for a tiny minority, the material side of the human condition has been transformed; and stimulated perhaps even more by wars than by prosperity and peace, the pace is accelerating so that the need for world management is becoming more urgently and obviously imperative. Such are the facts which have brought us where we now are, and of these the most externally compelling have been the three technological transformations emanating mainly from Europe and North America which have made all mankind, whether they like it or not, part of one world.

# III

This material and originally European influence was highly original, and it was paralleled by internally compelling and original European ideas. The concept of progress, first formulated by the 'Moderns' against the 'Ancients' in the controversies of the seventeenth century, had been alien to all previous civilizations; and while literate cultures had always been confined to minorities, now the ambition was formulated both to 'improve' and also to extend the benefits of civilization to the mass of mankind. The rise of experimental science, which in the nineteenth century became professionalized and enlarged the bounds of knowledge in a way hitherto unknown, encouraged these ideas. The confident rationalism of the eighteenth-century élites became the deepened knowledge of the professional classes of the nineteenth, in a widening range of subjects from medicine to archaeology; from biology and physics to classical scholarship, from geography to history and anthropology. The cumulative impact of this European initiative, concurrent with the spreading material might of the Industrial and Technological revolutions, had a tremendous impact on the entire world, and has even gradually changed the climate of opinion in the most massively conservative civilizations – not only among the adaptable Japanese, but in India and in China; while in Africa societies recently emerged from tribalism have taken within two generations to western-style improvement and to the western belief in progress. Ephemeral though the European colonial empires have proved to be, the assimilation and reinterpretation of western ideas, including western theories of progress, have been lasting.

To examine the whole range of European nineteenth-century ideas in all their variety and contradiction is impossible in a miniature context, but the most specifically original European ideas that have set the tone of a world-historical development far beyond Europe demand attention, for they radiated from Europe and America over the whole world. The most fundamental innovation of all, of which the Industrial Revolution is only one aspect, is the rise of modern scientific method and its consequences. It had been symbolized in the seventeenth century among the 'Moderns' by the empiricism of Bacon and the rationalism of Descartes, and its method of organized common sense had been systematically harnessed by the atheist Jeremy Bentham (1748–1832) to the task of 'rational social improvement', directed not to propitiate a transcendent God but by a rather naive 'calculus' of human happiness. Once this principle had been admitted, all institutions and beliefs stood or fell by a simple test: however venerable, awesome and mysterious, if they thwarted human happiness, Bentham declared, they ought to go. In various forms this principle of Benthamite 'improvement' has spread gradually over the whole world in both liberal-democratic and socialist societies, though the standards of human happiness whereby policies were judged, and the amount of misery they were thought to be worth, has proved variable. The idea of deliberate improvement, which implied accepting innovation and that governments ought to change rather than preserve, thus became taken for granted, and generated demands and expectations which have become insatiable.

The idea of improvement and innovation went along with that of popular democracy. When the first Industrial Revolution was getting into its stride a parallel social transformation had begun in Europe and in North America. Hitherto literate civilization had been confined to minorities; now for the first time the masses of mankind began effectively to claim their share of it, first in politics then in property. Liberal democracy, its demands made first for a limited franchise, then broadening down into the demand that one man – and one woman – should have one vote, implied, as its opponents foresaw, the socialist attack on private property and the demand for an egalitarian society very different from that implied by a restricted franchise in a liberal free-trading capitalist society. The aim common to both movements was to attack the old hierarchy of monarchs, established churches and aristocracy; the liberals launched the highly optimistic 'democratic experiment' gradually, hoping to extend their kind of culture to the masses; but the socialists endeavoured to abolish economic privilege either gradually by consent, in a still pluralistic society, or suddenly, following the theories of Marx and Engels as defined in the *Communist Manifesto* of 1849 by means of a dictatorship of the proletariat sweeping away the entire capitalist economic structure of the old civilization. At the sacrifice of individual liberties, they aimed to take a short cut to a civilization in which the means of production would be owned by the State and the mass of the people, were briefly disciplined by an authority which Marx and Engels optimistically predicted would wither away when its work was done – a hope singularly contradicted by the history of previous dictatorships and one hitherto unrealized.

Another original European invention, most fully developed in the United States, was the then revolutionary idea of systematic public sanitation and cleanliness. This concern with public health on such a scale was new. Though both the Roman and Arab way of life had been cleaner than that of the early modern Europeans, now a new initiative on a massive scale had been taken with a new technology behind it. And along with it, as the technology developed, went the novel idea of comfort rather than of luxury and display. Central heating, constant hot water, air conditioning that would largely discount extremities of climate, all became part of the worldwide impact of western civilization. These things, now widely taken for granted, created a novel way of life that is becoming assimilated among peoples of utterly different backgrounds, pushing at least the more prosperous minorities towards a common interest in maintaining such unprecedented standards.

Even more important than this advance – for advance it was – European medicine, which had so long been paralysed by dogmas inherited from classical and medieval times, so that with all his luxury and wealth to protect him even Louis xv had died of confluent smallpox, in the 1830s Hegel had died of cholera and, in 1861, the Prince Consort of Great Britain of typhoid, began to make a belated and epoch-making advance, with vaccination, aseptic surgery, primitive anaesthetics and, in the 1890s, with the control of yellow fever, and with Ross's discovery of the role of the anopheles mosquito in malaria.

The most pervasive, and in time worldwide, change in general outlook was due to the discovery by European scientific method of the vast antiquity of man and of his close relationship to the other animals. Many researchers contributed to and many hindered these conclusions: but in this field Darwin (1809–82) stands pre-eminent. It is hard now to imagine how radical a change was wrought in Europe when the Christian belief that the world had been called into being in 4004 BC precisely, and that mankind had been a separate creation apart from the other animals, was replaced by the proven fact that the world and the life on it are by human standards almost unthinkably old, and that man has gradually evolved by the natural selection of environment playing on genetic changes from a species which has branched out from immense antiquity, the nearest comparable descendants being the great apes. Hence, of course, the violent mockery and denunciation which greeted the discoveries of Darwin, an amiable and retiring but redoubtable discoverer, and the widespread despair and disillusionment which seized those who felt that their faith in transcendental religion had collapsed and, who had not yet, like most of their descendants, got used to more limited expectations.

Such were the most conspicuous and original ways in which the European scientific revolution of the nineteenth century influenced the outlook of the world and of subsequent generations. On the one hand a new confidence that, as Henri, Comte de Saint-Simon (1760–1825), had insisted, intelligence and economic enterprise, properly applied, could control and vastly ameliorate the lot of mankind. On the other that scientific method, while incapable of the total explanation that some of its pioneers expected of it, is able on an empirical basis to master many of the most daunting problems. Hence the belief, now widespread all over the world, that, given the vast expansion and deepening of sheer knowledge in the brief time of its professionalized existence, there is hardly a foreseeable limit to the transformation it has yet to make; not least, having launched man into space, next in prolonging the brief life span with which even the strongest and wisest and luckiest have so far had to be content. This originally European determination to take hold of the world and master it, and so to enhance the life chances not only of minorities but of the mass of mankind, is behind the determination now shown by all governments; both those that aim at 'welfare' by consent, and those that aim at it by discipline.

So in the nineteenth century man reverted to the practical aims of the rulers of archaic Mesopotamia, imposed in the dawn of civilization, and determined to make himself. By the early twentieth century European influence was thus becoming more secular, though the waning of Christian belief took a long time to undermine the impact of European missionary enterprise, which had reached its climax in the nineteenth century: in Africa and in Polynesia the missionaries of the various Christian Churches had attempted, and sometimes succeeded, to impose a totally different way of life on the relatively primitive peoples whom they had evangelized – though they had little success in converting either élites or masses in the ancient Muslim, Indian and Chinese civilizations and neo-pagan nationalism and quasi-scientific doctrines of historically determined class conflict proved easier for the poverty-stricken masses brought up in long-established civilizations to assimilate. In a global view the gap now appears to be widening between those who believe in any form of traditional religion, Christian, Muslim, Buddhist, Hindu or even the Confucian code of conduct, and those who are following the European agnosticism or atheism now radiating from the West, including the Soviet Union, with as much and perhaps more force as did Christianity in the nineteenth century.

The new professional research and the widening of sensibility following the European romantic movement also deepened knowledge and among the educated minorities made for greater understanding of societies, both within different civilizations and between them. For example, Europeans greatly increased their understanding of their own history and, in consequence, began better to appreciate that of other peoples. They developed the study of anthropology, comparative law and sociology, all sciences which, with greater depth and sophistication, were cosmopolitan in range and went far beyond the conventions of political history that was still mainly written and studied in terms of nation-states and very seldom related to other continents. The Enlightenment had dismissed what had come to be called the 'Middle Ages' as barbarous and grotesque; now among a widening European public, Herder's attempt to 'feel himself into' the Germanic past, and Goethe's (1749–1832) flair for a 'universal' appreciation combined with the romantic movement which mainly originated in Great Britain into a cult of history; romanticized and popularized by Sir Walter Scott. The anaemic doctrines of Benthamite 'improvers' were essential to the Age of Reform, but better research had also yielded a deepening of understanding. Similarly, the nineteenth century saw an analysis of society through the novel – the supreme literary form of the age; Dickens, Balzac and the major Russian writers, Pushkin (1799–1837), Dostoievsky (1821–81) and Tolstoy (1828–1910), the greatest of them all, mark a new self-consciousness in depth, which continued into the twentieth century. If man was making himself he also found himself more interesting; life, no longer dwarfed by prospects of eternity, became more important, and nature, as evoked in verse by Wordsworth and on canvas by Constable and Turner, and depicted in terms of light by the French Impressionists and Post-Impressionists, and in terms of form as well by Cezanne, seemed more significant for itself. This was the painting of humanism, not of other-worldly religion.

On the other hand, the new materialistic outlook, by depriving those who needed it of the sanctions and consolations of other-worldly religion, darkened the political and social prospect and opened the way for hideous and half-baked mythologies such as those that inspired Hitler. 'Exclude the idea of futurity,' wrote Pope Leo XIII, 'and the very notion of what is good and evil would perish, nay, the whole scheme of the universe would become a dark and unfathomable mystery.' Nietzsche (1844–1900) believed that once the people realized the implications of modern knowledge – in particular how it 'obliterated the distinction between man and animal' – there would be an age of barbarism. 'There will be wars such as have never happened on earth. Do we not feel the breath of empty space? Has it not become colder? God is dead. God remains dead. And we have killed him.'

Among European artists and intellectuals the romantic movement and the cult of personal relationships attempted compensation for this desolate prospect: and others tried to reconcile scientific method and humanism. Like the liberal democrats, who hopefully believed that in time the mass of the people, who vastly outnumbered them, would come to making the best of themselves in the middle-class liberal style, the more sanguine scientific humanists believed, like their eighteenth-century intellectual ancestors, that reason and good sense would prevail and that, accepting the premise that in the human condition everyone was in the same boat, the masses would come to collaborate in alleviating the lot of mankind rather than combine to plunder and so destroy a precarious civilization even if the grosser inequalities of exploitation were abolished. Others, perhaps with deeper insight, shared the disillusionment expressed by Kant, when, in a pessimistic moment, he remarked that 'out of the crooked timber of humanity nothing straight could be made', and strikingly argued by Joseph de Maistre in his highly readable *Soirées de St. Petersbourg*, and by Dostoievsky in his famous dialogues between the grand inquisitor and the returned Christ. Most people, they argued could not stand much freedom, the scientific humanists were as over optimistic as the exponents of the 'liberal experiment' in politics, so that the removal of the traditional sanctions for authority and of the expectation of other-wordly rewards and punishment would merely be followed by other authoritarian régimes, much more inhuman, being without the compassion of Christianity, and entirely materialistic and boring. This danger, that popularized scientific knowledge would make people behave not better but worse, was enhanced through the misinterpretation of Darwinism current in the late nineteenth century, when 'survival of the fittest' was interpreted not as the survival of the best adapted, but as of the most ferocious, and, transferred by a false analogy to the so-called 'social organisms' of nation-states and to the 'struggle for existence' between them. Nationalism was thus reinforced by a pseudo-biological sanction. The traditional sense of a cosmopolitan European order, inherited from the Roman Empire carried on in medieval Christendom, and still apparent among the élites of the seventeenth and eighteenth centuries, was thus increasingly diminished both by the ebbing tide of religious faith and by a neo-barbaric glorification of strife as such; and the vast opportunities created by the Industrial Revolution, which piled up wealth and raised living standards in a way unheard of before, were threatened by the decline of the sense of European order and the obligation of rulers to sustain it, or at least contain wars within bounds.

Indeed with the collapse of the old dynasties and the rise of the centralized nation-state, the old public law of Europe, which though never much observed, had been still in principle regarded, broke down in the competition of naked power, while the peoples, far from coming together in fraternity, identified themselves with the symbols and the martial traditions of their several states, inherited from the eighteenth century and the Napoleonic Wars. Nationalism proved far more powerful than the slogans of fraternity, and the doctrines of apparently scientifically determined dialectical materialism as set out in Marx's *Das Kapital* and by Engels, which in the tradition of Hegel claimed to reveal the 'inner go of things' but, unlike him, by scientific method, superseded the appeals of the intellectual 'Utopian' socialists since they had far more political effect. Further, no longer content, as in central Europe, to be part of the cosmopolitan Habsburg empire, Hungarians and Serbs, Czechs, Croats and northern Italians seethed with nationalistic fervour, and followed the doctrines of Mazzini (1805–72) idealizing the nation-state, destined, he foolishly believed, to bring peace to Europe in a 'sisterhood' of nations; while the Germans, following the doctrines of Fichte (1762–1814), Hegel (1770–1831) and Treitschke (1834–96), began to think of themselves as a master race, destined by the march of history to dominate Europe and the world. So liberalism, socialism, gradualist or revolutionary, and nationalism, idealist or militaristic, identifying a region, a people and a language with the recently invented national sovereign state, came to dominate the nineteenth century, and when in medieval times and in the sixteenth and seventeenth centuries men had murdered and tortured one another over religion, new secular dogmas now often roused a similar fanaticism, and in a new way, for the mass of the people were more affected by them through the new mass media, first in print, then on the air and by television. Thus misapplied Western science, by apparently destroying the old sanctions, contributed to political and social conflict as much as to improvement.

# IV

Meanwhile the unprecedented and immensely powerful technological developments that conditioned everything were proceeding in Europe and, after the 1860s, on an even more massive scale in the extrapolation of Europe in the United States. They confirmed Europeans in a political and economic mastery of the planet which gradually spread eastward over all Asia and westward over the Pacific to Australasia, south over the rest of the

Americas and finally over parts of Africa. But these contacts, cumulative since the sixteenth century, were not one-way only: the discovery of other and often highly sophisticated civilizations, as well as the exploration of exotic territories, greatly enriched the consciousness of Europeans over a whole range of interest, so that for the first time the prospect of a world civilization could be distantly discerned. But the reality in the foreground was the competition of European empires, commercial and political, and the impact on still conservative but massive and ancient civilizations, as well as on primitive peoples, of the astounding European initiative, an example which they, too, would soon set themselves to follow.

# Twenty-two

# A PROSPECT
# OF WORLD POLITICS

## I

Against this accelerating technological change, the unprecedented attempt to organize a mass civilization that included whole peoples was worked out. It was attempted in two ways: the first, following the ideas of the American and French revolutions, in terms of the democratic experiment through various forms of constitutional self-government, the rule of law and freedom of expression, broadening down into complete democracy; the second, through the dictatorship of a party controlling a totalitarian State, incoherent in aim and Fascist, or coherent in purpose and Communist.

The democratic experiment stemming from the French Revolution was unusually hopeful; it assumed that the mass of the people could take the challenge of liberty and were capable of self-government; and it accepted the idea of progress, alien to any previous civilization. The totalitarian experiment stemming from the Russian Revolution, though equally based on the novel idea of progress and inspired, in its Marxist–Leninist form by a secular religion which predicted an inevitable historical process, organized the masses into 'peoples' democracies' which were controlled by a close-knit party élite. The competition of these two ways of organizing the new mass civilization now divides mankind. It has arisen mainly through the historical circumstances of the societies concerned.

Inherited attitudes and institutions were often unpropitious to the democratic experiment. Constitutional self-government though it had Hellenic and medieval origins, was unusual even in Europe; and though the Napoleonic Empire had swept away the old régimes and inaugurated a new legal and administrative efficiency and new career opportunities, the centralized nation states and empires remained organized for war. Nineteenth-century liberal constitutionalists never managed to create an international order, the necessary corollary and guarantee of constitutional self-government within their own boundaries; nor, when constitutionalism was writ large in the League of Nations, did it prove viable. The United Nations has proved more effective, but its successes have been local and limited.

Constitutional self-government, the rule of law and liberty of thought and expression broadening down into full democracy did not at first imply an attack on property, and although, with complete popular franchise, the attack was bound to come, it came gradually, thus avoiding violent revolution and reaction. But such government was successful only where self-governing institutions had taken root, as in Great Britain, the United States, the British dominions of settlement, Holland, Scandinavia and Switzerland. In France, though the institutional changes consolidated by Napoleon proved permanent, and liberty of thought and expression prevailed, parliamentary democracy itself proved unstable; and while the British monarchy and parliament adapted themselves, and society was adjusted into liberal reform, then into the social democracy of a 'welfare state', the Bourbons had to be driven out and Louis Napoleon, as president of the Second Republic, turned it into a Second Empire. Virulent class conflict broke out in 1848 and 1871, and the history of the Third Republic showed how precarious was the democratic experiment in the country which had launched the revolution of 1789.

In central Europe the political climate for liberal democracy was much worse. In 1848 the liberal revolution was easily suppressed in Prussia; in Vienna it was quelled after a siege; Czechs, Hungarians and Poles were all put down and the Austrian Empire reorganized under Franz-Josef as a unitary State. And when, after the Austro–Prussian War, the Austrians were excluded from northern Germany and Italy, in 1867 the empire became the Dual Monarchy, *kaiserlich und königlich*, of Austria–Hungary, its rulers played their subject peoples off against one another, then, in a final attempt to prevent disruption by the Serbs, even set off the First World War. Meanwhile Bismarck's German Empire had been forged in blood and iron at the expense of the Danes and the French and, for all its administrative efficiency and social reforms, it would remain dominated by the army which led the country into the gamble for *Weltmacht* in 1914 when economic supremacy was already within German grasp.

The Iberian Peninsula was not propitious for liberalism either. The restored Bourbon régime had lapsed into civil wars, and when in 1868 Isabella II was driven out, the first Spanish republic lasted only until 1875. Both Alfonso XII and XIII failed to manage even conservative constitutional government in face of regional separatism, clericalism and anti-clericalism and disastrous colonial adventures in Morocco. In 1898 came defeat in a brief war with the United States, where Spain lost Cuba, Puerto Rico and the Philippines. After relatively prosperous neutrality during the First World War, the country fell under the dictatorship of Primo de Rivera, with whose fall in 1930 and the expulsion of Alfonso XIII in the next year, a second republic was inaugurated. By 1936–9 it had broken down into the civil war which ended in the dictatorship of Franco. Only between 1868–75 and 1931–6 were there democratic experiments in Spain.

In Portugal the Braganza monarchy, restored in 1821, lasted until 1912, when Manuel II, who had succeeded after both Carlos I and his heir had been assassinated, fled the country, and the first Portuguese republic was set up. But by 1926 that experiment too had failed: Carmona established a military dictatorship, followed in 1951 by the rule of Salazar. Such were the unhappy fortunes of the democratic experiment in central Europe and the Iberian Peninsula.

In Russia it naturally fared disastrously. Under Alexander I the stirrings of official liberalism in the early part of his reign had subsided by the end of it, and Nicholas I (1825–55) re-established a police-state. In 1809 Finland had been annexed; the traditional expansion, the traditional imperialism, continued into the Caucasus, central Asia and Siberia, and by 1832 Poland had been partitioned, Russia taking the main share, Prussia Pozen and Danzig, and Austria Galicia. Alexander II, relatively humane, partially emancipated the serfs; in 1881 he was assassinated; Alexander III and Nicholas II were both autocrats. By January 1905 revolution threatened: the tsar's troops killed a thousand demonstrators in St Petersburg, but the rising spread; at Odessa the crew of the battleship *Potemkin* – fortunate in not having been sent East against the Japanese – staged a famous mutiny. In May 1906, Nicholas II summoned a duma or legislative assembly, but by July dissolved it; Stolypin, the ablest exponent of constitutional government, was murdered. Then the economic and social strain of the First World War finished off the rotten régime: in 1917 the fourth duma refused to be dissolved and the social democrat Kerensky formed a provisional government; but by April Lenin had arrived in what was now Petrograd, and by October 1917 inaugurated the Bolshevik dictatorship, consolidated in March 1918 by the Peace of Brest-Litovsk. He had secured the first centre of Marxist-Leninist world revolution, an event of comparable importance to the French Revolution of 1789, the basis for the public ownership of the means of production and a direct attack on capitalism.

In the south-eastern extremity of Europe and in Italy liberalism was more successful, at least in terms of national liberation. The first Greek insurrection against the Turks in 1821 was backed by the Russians and encouraged by the British: in 1824 it was glamorized by the death of Byron; in 1827 an Egyptian–Turkish fleet was destroyed by the British, French and Russians at Navarino. In 1831 an independent Greek State was constituted, under the Bavarian Otto I; replaced in 1862 after a revolution by Prince William of Denmark who became George I. Two years later the British handed over the Ionian isles to Greece. National independence and the forms of constitutional self-government had been dramatically asserted in the original setting of European civilization.

In Italy in 1848, the attempt by Carlo Alberto of Piedmont to get rid of the Austrians had failed, and the short-lived Roman Republic had been put down by the French on behalf of the pope. So Cavour bribed Napoleon III with Nice and Savoy to join Piedmont against Austria and, in 1859, combined Franco–Piedmontese armies drove the Austrians from Lombardy. In 1860 Victor Emmanuel of Piedmont became king of all northern Italy, save Venice; then Romagna and Tuscany joined the new realm and, in the same year Garibaldi, having liberated Sicily and Naples from the Neapolitan Bourbons, acknowledged Victor Emmanuel as ruler of the south as well. An Italian kingdom was established with its capital at Florence: then, following the Austro–Prussian War, the Italians obtained Venice, and in 1870 during the Franco–Prussian War, they obtained Rome, which became the capital of a united Italy. Both in Greece and in Italy liberal democratic institutions were thus established; but Greek politics would often lapse into military *coups* and counter *coups*, and the Italian State, whose prophet had been the liberal Mazzini, lapsed in the 1920s into the Fascist régime of Mussolini.

Although the facts were masked by the containing oceanic power of the British Empire and the growing industrial might of the United States, nineteenth-century European civilization, for all its creative brilliance, had not, on the whole, proved receptive to the ideas of liberty, equality and fraternity or to working parliamentary institutions, in spite of the widespread fashion for them. The liberal bourgeoisie prospered, but they did not attain political power outside the West, and the great military empires of Germany, Austria–Hungary and Russia dominated central and eastern Europe, while that of Russia dominated Siberia and central Asia. By the end of the nineteenth century Great Britain had lost her industrial supremacy, the oceanic *Pax Britannica* had been challenged, and though the apparently predominant liberal democratic states took their immense progress and prosperity for granted, and the full horror of industrialized war was not understood, advancing technology was piling up armaments that were making the world singularly unsafe for the democracies and for everyone else.

## II

Meanwhile liberal democracy and its institutions had taken root better outside Europe; most powerfully in the United States – by the early twentieth century the only power capable of containing the bid for world domination by Wilhelmian Germany and, by the mid-century, the bid for it by the Soviet Union. The aims of the American Revolution of 1776 had been defined in the Declaration of Independence and its success had been consolidated by a written constitution balancing the power of Executive, Legislature and Supreme Court. The United States of America were the first example of a republic on a great scale in a world still predominantly of dynastic states – a sweep of territory from Georgia to Maine and destined to vast expansion to the west. Moreover the Federal Constitution of 1789 proved adaptable to mass parties and mass democracy and, for all its cumbrousness, it ensured the responsibility of government to the governed. Here was constitutionalism, rooted in the writings of John Locke and Montesquieu, writ large with enormous potential power behind it in a country that would become the richest and most powerful in the world.

For the North American continent was not parcelled up into sovereign states, but developed within a federal union. The Napoleonic Wars had been Jefferson's opportunity; in 1803 he had purchased the vast Louisiana territory from the French, and a brief second war with the British (1812–15) confirmed American independence; a principle extended in 1823 by the Monroe Doctrine over all the Americas in response to Russian claims on Alaska and to the threat of the European Holy Alliance to intervene in South America.

Having turned their backs on the old world, the Americans began to colonize their enormous continent beyond the Alleghenies, to the Mississippi and beyond. By 1820 there were already seven states added to the original thirteen: in 1846–8 the Americans went to war with Mexico and took over Texas, New Mexico and California, and by 1860 there were in all thirty-three states. This swift expansion put a heavy strain on the union; the rush of immigration into the west had changed the balance of population and the swift industrial development of the north accentuated the contrast, constant since the early settlements, between the northern way of life and that of the easy-going slave-owning south. The wealth of the south was now in cotton, and cotton meant slave labour: the economic need for it was generally admitted, but the north was determined that the 'peculiar institution' should not be sanctioned in the new states of the West. In 1860, with the election of the first Republican president, Abraham Lincoln, who was resolved to abolish slavery, eleven southern states seceded from the union. The resulting and sanguinary war was fought doggedly for four years, mainly to preserve it. It preserved the union, but at a terrible price; the southern states were crippled and, following Lincoln's assassination, reconciliation was slow. The business of the northern states had now become big business, as their factories had expanded to meet the demands of a war won partly by superior material resources; indeed, by 1870, railroads, shipping, mining, ranching and mechanized farming began to equal the industries of Europe: in the last three decades of the century to surpass them and dominate the whole union.

Long deliberately isolated from the old world and, following the massive immigration of large populations from central Europe, in 1917 the United States were forced only reluctantly into the First World War. But the intervention was decisive: President Wilson, with the might of the greatest liberal democracy behind him, had an unparalleled prestige; but he failed to commit the United States to a settlement that might have avoided the Second World War and given the League of Nations a better chance. The opportunity was lost, the world lurched into another conflict. All had to be done over again.

While the United States was developing a continental economic and political power, liberal democracies were also established in Canada, Australia and New Zealand, while in South America the peoples of the Spanish and Portuguese empires had won independence. Here, as in North America, the newly independent states followed a political pattern set by their own former rulers in Europe. Spanish American civilization was centralized and urban, imposed on the original Amerindians, and, as in the British North American colonies, the leadership of revolt came mainly from the upper classes. In Central America the going was hardest. In 1810 following Napoleon's eviction of the Bourbons from Spain, the original revolt in Mexico had been popular and led by a priest Miguel Hidalgo; it was put down by the wealthy creoles and the *peninsulares*. Mexico only became independent in 1821, when its new leader, Iturbide was backed by the creole landowners and clergy, who feared a relatively liberal Spain, though soon Iturbide himself became a victim of this conservative revolution. In 1863, under the supposed protection of Napoleon III, the Archduke Maximilian of Austria accepted the throne of Mexico, but with the end of the War between the States, the Americans insisted on the French troops being withdrawn: by 1867 Maximilian had been shot. A republic was restored under Juarez, who was followed in 1872 by the mestizo, Porfirio Diaz; he presided over the exploitation of the country by American big business until 1911. But his supplanter was soon assassinated, and after dictatorship and civil war, President Obregón established a relatively stable régime in 1920. The democratic experiment thus, to put it mildly, had a chequered history in Mexico.

In South America the prospect appeared at first more promising, the original revolutions being liberal and idealistic. The brilliant Simón Bolívar (1783–1830) was a creole aristocrat – his name is originally Basque – and by 1821 after campaigns of fantastic difficulty he created the republics of Venezuela and Colombia; then Ecuador, Peru and Bolivia were carved out of the Spanish Empire. Further south, San Martin had liberated the Argentine by 1816, then Chile; Paraguay and Uruguay followed, the last not till 1909. Nowhere else had republicanism triumphed over such monstrous geographical obstacles.

In 1821 Brazil, far the largest and potentially the richest colony, had broken away from Portugal; by an amicable connivance, Dom Pedro, son of John VI, becoming emperor of an independent State which became a republic only in 1889. It was Brazil that received the most massive immigration from Europe, by Germans, Italians, Scandinavians and Dutch. Against a background of relative political stability, foreign capital, as in other South American states, began to develop the enormous area – today potentially one of the richest economies in the world.

The independence of South America came about under the auspices of the Americans and British, but these societies were radically different from those in the North. The Europeans were a small minority among the Amerindian population, and in a geographical setting of such far-flung difficulty, the emancipated colonies never formed a federation. Soon government tended to follow the pattern of revolution and dictatorship common in countries ill-suited for self-governing democracy on western lines. The new world, called into existence to redress the balance of the old and developed by western capital, did not take kindly to working western political institutions.

The other vast area of European settlement was on the other side of the world; eastward into Siberia and central Asia. Since 1640 Russian trappers and prospectors had been on the Asian Pacific coast, and by 1820 Russian lumbermen and hunters had got to northern California. With consistent government backing, by 1830 Siberian gold was being mined, and it is estimated that between 1823–81 seven hundred thousand political prisoners and exiles were deported to Siberia. Nor could the government prevent the immigration of land-hungry peasants; by 1914 there were about ten million inhabitants in the huge territory. As in North America, the life of the frontier meant danger and hardship, if sometimes relative freedom; but the settlement had been supervised by government, and no more than in Russia itself, or in the Russian colonial empire in central Asia, had liberal democratic institutions in the western sense been acclimatized, though the subjects of the empire would become 'peoples' democracies' of the Soviet Union.

# III

The overwhelming expansion and political and economic pre-eminence of Europeans and their descendants overseas, most spectacular in the enormous sea-borne British Empire, proved more lasting in areas of European settlement and in science, technology and political ideas than in direct domination over the massive civilizations of Asia and the relatively sparse societies of tropical Africa. But the revolutionary notions of improvement and progress were assimilated, along with the doctrines both of liberal and social-democratic parliamentary democracy and of Marxist–Leninist totalitarian revolution, as government, was interpreted according to history, temperament and setting.

As rulers of India from the Himalayas to Cape Cormorin, of Ceylon since 1802 and Singapore since 1819, as well as of Aden, the British were masters of southern Asia. By the mid-nineteenth century the French were colonizing Indo-China and the Dutch renewed their exploitation of Indonesia, interrupted by the Napoleonic Wars. Malaya, rich in tin and then in rubber, would become, like Sarawak and North Borneo, part of the British Empire and, by 1898, the United States, which had already taken over Hawaii, annexed the Philippines, while the Russians had long been encroaching on Chinese territory in the north-east. The Chinese, whose rulers still considered their civilization conterminous with civilization itself, had been entirely outclassed in armaments and organization, so that their vast empire lay open to exploitation. In 1842, the British imposed the treaty of Canton and obtained Hong Kong and a whole range of treaty ports, including Shanghai; in 1858 they occupied Canton and the Russians founded Vladivostok: in 1860 a Franco–British expedition occupied Peking. The greatest civilization in the Far East had been reduced to colonial status.

The reaction came first in Japan. Their government had long excluded Europeans, but when in 1853 the Americans, determined to obtain a harbour for their shipping from San Francisco to Shanghai, sent Commodore Perry to demand facilities, the Japanese, with characteristic realism, bowed to the inevitable. They then made a revolution: the Tokugawa rulers were removed; in 1864 the emperor was restored to nominal authority and the Meiji régime modernized Japan: Germans trained the army, the British the navy, the Americans devised the constitution. Like the western powers, the new rulers of Japan then tried to exploit the Chinese, whom in 1894 they defeated in a war over Korea, and in 1904 they resoundingly defeated the Russians by land and sea in a war which was decisive in world history, and made Japan the first modern Asian great power. The First World War was their opportunity, and they set about dominating the Far East. While adopting the latest western technology and organization, they had retained the military tradition and intense social solidarity of their past: the army and big business, not the civilian politicians, had the last word.

In China, meanwhile, the corrupt and inefficient Manchu government tottered to collapse. In 1900 following the Boxer Rebellion, the western powers and the Japanese occupied Peking, the Empress Tzu Hsi was compelled to sanction a modernized administration and in 1905 the abolition of the millennially old Chinese examination system. These drastic but belated changes could not avert the collapse of the Manchu dynasty and in 1912 China was proclaimed a republic.

So the democratic experiment in China was made in a more than usually incongruous setting. The western-educated Sun-Yat-Sen now attempted the colossal task of introducing western forms of government and developing the administration and the economy, but though the old imperial order and the ancient predominance of the landed gentry were undermined, the generals who had supported the republic for their own ends now fought one another to control it. External attack then made the new order even less practicable. After Sun-Yat-Sen's death in 1925, China became a prey to the Russians in Mongolia and the Japanese in Manchuria. Despite the formation of the nationalist Kuomintang in 1924 and the emergence of Chiang Kai-shek as its leader, in 1931 the Japanese occupied Manchuria and in the war of 1937–8 subdued the richest areas of China itself. It was out of these catastrophes that the Communist peasant leader Mao Tse-tung emerged. By 1948, following the collapse of Japan, he drove out Chiang Kai-shek and the western-backed nationalists and established his control of China; an event in world history of comparable importance to Lenin's seizure of power in Russia. Thus the brief attempt to import western-style parliamentary government failed in China, and a régime was imposed inspired by a Chinese version of western communist ideas but in Chinese terms, and by the kind of peasant leader who had founded native Chinese dynasties before. He would develop the most populous nation on earth on lines which were at once Marxist-Leninist-revolutionary yet reminiscent of the authoritarian tradition of Chinese history.

While Japan and China reacted to western influence after their own traditions, India, following the abdication of the British and the partition of the subcontinent into the republics of India and Pakistan, attempted with decreasing success to adapt the legacy of British parliamentary institutions and the democratic experiment though the cultural legacy of the British went deep. Iran, once by far the most creative civilization in the Middle East, was slow to adapt to western ways. In 1776 Agha Muhammad Shah had founded the Qajar dynasty: castrated in youth, he was naturally embittered and, in the three years before he was assassinated, had ruthlessly established his power in the new capital Tehran. Then Nasir ed Din Shah (1843–96), after a brief attempt at modernization, executed its chief exponent. His successor, forced in 1906 to convene a Majlis – the nearest thing to a parliament – turned his guns on it. In the First World War Iran fell under spheres of Russian and British influence: then in 1921 Reza Khan, who had risen from the ranks to command a Persian cossack brigade, ousted the Qajars, and by 1925 as Reza Shah Pahlevi, he began to haul his country, now becoming enriched by oil revenues, into the twentieth century; a process that has continued apace under the present Shah. Here, again, the democratic experiment has hardly flourished and western-inspired objectives have necessarily been pursued by traditional and authoritarian means, now backed by immense wealth.

The Turks, of all Asians the nearest neighbours to Europe, have been more strongly influenced by the West. The sultans were still in direct descent from Muhammad the Conqueror of Constantinople, and in 1914 the Turkish Empire, still the greatest Muslim State, sprawled across the Near and Middle East: but already its authority over Egypt had collapsed and in 1876 a palace revolution drove the dethroned Abdul Aziz to suicide. Then in 1877–8 war with Russia led to the independence of Romania, Serbia and Montenegro, while the British took over Cyprus. Abdul Hamid (1876–1909) went back to old-style representative of Muslim orthodoxy, supported by the Turks who resented being levelled with the subject peoples by the western device of a franchise. He countenanced notorious and comprehensive massacres of dissident Armenians. So the modernizing 'young Turks' looked to Germany, whom they wrongly expected would win the coming European war, and, when, after it, the Turkish empire collapsed, in 1922 a revolution led by the dynamic Mustapha Kemal forced the Turks into a modern régime, its capital no longer the cosmopolitan and historic Constantinople, but Ankara, in the original Turkish territories. Since that upheaval, parliamentary government has been acclimatized in Turkey and the policy of deliberate modernization in costume and social customs continued. Fear of Russia, perennial in Turkish history given the Turks' strategic situation, has strengthened their links with the West.

The distintegration of the Turkish Empire exchanged stagnation for conflict. In 1921 the British, having accepted a mandate under the League of Nations for Palestine, sanctioned a 'national home' there for the Jews; a project which after the mandate had been relinquished in 1948, led to the first Arab–Israeli War, and to the establishment of the modern, westernized and militant State of Israel with all the consequences for the Near East.

# IV

The impact of western technology, knowledge and political ideas, both of constitutional democracy and Marxist–Leninist revolutionary dictatorship, on Africa was even more sudden and revolutionary. Only a century ago large areas were still unknown to most of mankind, and it was only in 1884–90 that the colonialist scramble for territory set in. Direct European political control over tropical Africa was much briefer than in Asia. Only North and north-eastern Africa had hitherto been important; Egypt had been civilized when Europe was in prehistoric barbarism and the North African shore and its hinterland had been part of the Roman and Arab empires, while Abyssinia, with her peculiar Christian culture, had contacts with southern Arabia, and the ports on the fringes of East Africa had long traded with India and even China. But by the mid-nineteenth century, with the coming of steamships, the route across the Suez isthmus became more competitive with the long voyage round the Cape to India, and after the Suez canal was opened in 1869, the British soon purchased a predominant interest in it. In 1882 they occupied Egypt, in effect to remain there even after Egypt became independent in 1922, with decisive effect in the Second World War, while from 1899 until 1956 the Sudan became an Anglo-Egyptian *condominium*. All this commitment was strategic: to maintain communication through the Red Sea and Aden with India and the Far East. The main European cultural influence on Egypt was French; but the British administrative legacy remained, particularly in the Sudan, if the British presence also provoked a European-style Egyptian nationalism.

The problems created by the sudden rise of South Africa to be far the richest and best organized area of the continent were more severe. In 1867 the discovery of diamonds along the border of the Orange Free State, and in 1884 of immensely rich gold-fields in the Transvaal, transformed the republics of the pastoral and resolutely provincial Dutch 'Boers' (set up in 1852-4, after their great trek in the 1830s out of Cape Colony into the interior), into a scene of massive cosmopolitan capitalist enterprise.

The freak of fate that located the diamond and gold-fields in the territory of the Boer republics and the clash of their way of life with the worldwide interests of Cecil Rhodes and all he stood for, led in 1899-1902 to the biggest colonial war in British history since the war of American Independence. Eventually the British won, but they lost the peace. The Union of South Africa of 1910 led to an Afrikaner Dutch majority, and though the country fought the Germans in both world wars, it seceded from the Commonwealth and established a régime of *apartheid*, detested by all the states of black Africa. The tension between rich and poor was here complicated by colour, and made more difficult to resolve by democratic constitutional means.

Until the 1890s European commitment in Black Africa had been slow and reluctant: the flag followed trade, not trade the flag. And such was the gap between European and African societies that administration rather than political experiment were bound to have priority. Europeans had traded in slaves, pepper and palm oil off West Africa for centuries, and the West African slave-trade, by the eighteenth century mainly British, had been immensely profitable. But by 1807 the British, and by 1815 most European governments, had made it illegal, and since the British alone could enforce the ban and wished to develop other forms of trade which it had swamped, after 1808 one of their squadrons based on Freetown harassed the diminishing traffic. By 1865, with the collapse of the American Confederate States, the slave-trade with North America came to an end: but not before the British in 1851 had annexed Lagos, ten years later a crown colony, the main slave market on the Bight of Benin.

The full development of the Industrial Revolution now meant a massive demand for oil and soap in Europe, and the palm-oil and ground-nut trade began to flourish. Merchants and missionaries became involved, the responsibilities of government enlarged. In the Gold Coast colony the

Ashanti, who possessed mineral wealth coveted by Europeans, raided the Fanti of the Coast. Hence the Ashanti wars of the 1860s and 1870s, culminating in 1896–1901 in British annexation. In the Oil Rivers colony a chartered company penetrated beyond the rain forest to the Fulani emirates of the north, and by 1914 Lugard had devised a Federated Nigeria, covering a vast area of divergent peoples; some of ancient civilization, others primitive.

By 1862, in central tropical Africa, Europeans had also arrived in the elaborately organized kingdom of Buganda; Livingstone's expeditions, extending from 1852 to 1873, explored the Zambesi, Lake Nyasa, Lake Tanganyika and beyond: Stanley followed the course of the Congo to the sea. In East Africa the British had made Zanzibar a base against the slave-trade with Arabia and the Persian Gulf, and by 1873 had abolished there the largest slave market on the coast. And from Zanzibar they could, if necessary, dominate the interior of East Africa. Already established at Aden and with their political agents on the Trucial coast and in Bahrein, the British in Massawa on the Red Sea had also collided with the Negus Tewodorus of Abyssinia, and in 1868 an army with elephants from India stormed the stronghold at Magdala. The Negus committed suicide, but the British were wise enough not to try to hold the difficult country or impose western institutions on it; and when in 1896 after the scramble for Africa set in, the Italians tried to subdue it, they suffered ignominious defeat. Ethiopia, alone of the African states, save Liberia (founded for liberated slaves), having ancient boundaries and inaccessible territories, preserved its independence.

By 1886 the British, the French, who since 1830 had colonized Algeria and Tunisia, and the Portuguese (the latter with their possessions of Angola and Mozambique, the oldest but least enterprising colonizers) were faced with German ambitions in Africa, set off in part by the private exploitations of the rich Belgian Congo by the king of the Belgians, not by the Belgian State; in part, as an aspect of the new German desire for *Weltmacht*. By 1890 almost the entire continent had been parcelled out by European politicians, often with little knowledge of Africa and with inadequate maps, so that an arbitrary pattern of states was imposed on a variety of tribal societies, in contrasting environments of rain forest and highland, lakeside and desert scrub. These boundaries and an administrative and educational framework, rather than successful democratic experiments, handicapped, in any case, by the absence of an experienced middle class, have been the legacy of Europeans.

The scramble was not occasioned, as some economic theorists have mistakenly argued, by capitalists driven by inexorable economic laws to turn from glutted markets in the developed world to exploit the undeveloped, for the profits of investment in tropical Africa were generally insignificant compared to those made from free trade between the developed states. It was set off by strategic rivalries, and the desire to keep potential enemies out. The Germans, for example, got little good from their colonies in German East and West Africa or the Kameroons, which proved hostages to fortune. Most of these colonies at this stage hardly yielded a profit; only in Algeria, South Africa, Rhodesia and East Africa was there significant European settlement. The Europeans faced a variety of problems: the confrontation with established but often archaic Muslim civilizations, as in Algeria, Tunis and Northern Nigeria, required different policies from those suited to the cultures of the Ashanti or of Benin, while the life style of the warrior Zulu and Matabele, or the pastoral Masai, were just incompatible with the civilization of the West. For the Africans, too, the problem was daunting – not least when, as in Uganda, the Protestant and Catholic missionaries incited their converts to mutual strife. But the Europeans were not, as generally supposed in the nineteenth century, working in a limbo of barbarism: most black African societies, though illiterate, were elaborately organized, with an easy-going habit of endless debate; and the excesses of pagan religions and witchcraft were sustained by a singular resilience of disposition. In general the weakness of African societies was the absence of a trained professional class, so that western-style politics and administration had to be taken over by the army, the nearest alternative. In the West Indies, the Americas and the Middle East the descendants of black Africans had long played their part outside their native continent: now, after this ephemeral but decisive European domination and the emergence of African *évolués*, the whole African continent entered the mainstream of world history and became subject to the competing pulls of western liberal-democratic and Communist ideas both in Russian and Chinese interpretations.

It is therefore not an objective judgement to denounce all aspects of colonialism as mere exploitation, out of which the exploited Africans gained nothing, or write off the democratic experiment among them as a total failure. Given that civilization was bound to impinge on these archaic societies, European administrators and those *évolués* that they trained often diminished the shock; and, the benefits of modern medicine, agricultural methods and technology can not be denied. Well-established populous areas, as in West Africa, or sparsely settled countries in East Africa have both benefited from the brief period of the better kinds of colonial rule. And the wealth of South Africa would not have existed without European initiative. Western concepts of efficient administration and the rule of law are urgently relevant, for problems can better be resolved in a multi-racial society gradually evolved by consent than by dogmatically inspired colour wars and revolutions which would destroy the wealth and civilization attained rather than expand and redistribute it.

# V

Such in very brief outline, against the swift development of technology, appear the main political essentials of two centuries of world politics, briefly and retrospectively considered. They reflect the impact of the civilization of Europeans and their overseas descendants on the rest of mankind. In so compressed a survey much has been omitted, many depths have been unexplored, but one conclusion has emerged with startling clarity. That the great and unprecedented undertaking to create a civilization that includes whole peoples is now common to all governments, whatever their political creeds. This distinguishes our situation from that of any other century before the nineteenth: monstrous and daunting as our problems appear, the objective is sane. The one thing that will prevent its attainment is the insanity of nuclear conflict, and the greatest danger arises from dogmatic nineteenth-century political theories applied in an age of nuclear weapons. Such theories, as were their equivalents in earlier ages in terms of fanatical religions, are a projection of atavistic fear and aggression.

The danger is all the more urgent since, although never in history has political change been so fast, it has lagged behind the technological developments that have dragged mankind after them and created so urgently the need for world order as the alternative to catastrophe.

It is thus essential to buy time so that alternative solutions to the common problem of organizing a mass civilization, whether liberal and social democratic or authoritarian, can be worked out, without nuclear conflict. Perhaps the former, which combines liberty with a pluralistic society operating within a constitutional framework and the rule of law is too exacting: perhaps the liberal experiment hopes too much, and some form of authoritarian rule is the only way to preserve a politically less ambitious civilization. But the price would be heavy. The sacrifice of liberty breeds stupidity and debasement, and the price of a brutal sort of order may be loss of creative power. Only time can work out solutions, now hard to imagine; but the crucial thing is to gain it, and to promote a consciousness of a common interest in survival and an understanding of the achievements of other civilizations instead of intolerance and hatred.

This survey has sketched the cultural and economic as well as the political essentials of the history of the major civilizations up to the Industrial Revolution, with an Epilogue inevitably concentrated, in the space available, on recent technological and political themes.

Can any pattern be observed, or lessons for the present or future be seen, in the vast and kaleidoscopic panorama of world history? The hitherto phenomenal success of the human race, which has now colonized the globe and begun to explore the solar system, is one of the great themes which would surely strike a visitor from a distant planet. The other is the variety of belief, of social organization and ways of life apparent during the relatively brief course of civilized history. Nor is there anything accidental about the coincidence of these two themes. In human biology, as in that of other species, the greater the complexity of an organism, the greater its potential for adaptation and change in the new environments, the greater its chances of survival and success.

Today both the instinct for survival and the flair for innovation and adaptation face new challenges: the threat of total destruction by nuclear weapons; the possibility of overpopulation leading to Malthusian disaster; the danger of exhaustion of the exploitable natural resources of the earth; the polarization of humanity into embittered ideological or racial camps; the spectre of complete totalitarianism based on modern technology of the kind foreseen in Orwell's *1984*. None of these possibilities is mutually exclusive; on the contrary, there is a sinister interrelation between them all: overpopulation and a scramble for diminishing natural resources can readily intensify conflict between the rich (largely white) races of the northern hemisphere, and the poor (largely coloured) races of the tropics; the main danger of nuclear war has arisen, at least hitherto, from the 'bipolar' and intellectually obsolescent ideological rivalry of the United States and Western Europe and the USSR; totalitarianism, national or regional, or even ultimately global, might be seen as the only solution to political or social disorder, or sustained economic crisis; yet surely the greater the suppression of individual freedom, the greater the repression of that inventiveness, initiative and versatility without which the race would not have survived until the present, and without which its future survival might be considered to be of little value even if it could be assumed.

The essential problem in the national and in the international plane can thus be clearly stated. What social and political organization can best reconcile the highest possible degree of individual liberty with the maintenance of political and social order? On the international plane what system will best ensure the independence of national traditions, their chances of continuing freely to develop their own answers, in culture, organization or belief to the perennial problems of human existence, and, at the same time, maintain peace between them? How can the survival, the variety and the creativeness of the human race be assured?

Certain facts point to a way through. First the atomic then the hydrogen bomb have made madness of total warfare between the states capable of producing them, and threatened even the politicians responsible with death or lives of hunted misery. Hence the truce of terror which, at crippling expense, has survived the crisis over Cuba, and which in their own interests, the greatest powers have observed. Though the proliferation of nuclear weapons may make minor wars more of a menace, there remains in the mutual and vital interests of the great nuclear powers a potential source of world order, and the United Nations, its Security Council paralysed by their dissensions and its Assembly by its own irresponsibility, is at least a means of getting them and others off the hook; designed, as Hammarskjöld remarked, 'not in order to bring us to heaven but to save us from hell'.

The economic interdependence of the world has also been greatly enhanced by the latest technology, a fact brought home even to the Europeans and Americans by their present dependence on Middle Eastern oil. Politically, already vast areas of the world have got far beyond the nation state: America is a federal union: Europeans have created their Common Market, a step towards political integration by consent. Examples could be multiplied. There will be pockets of provincial resistance and obtuse insularity, mainly damaging for those concerned, but contemporary technology has so far advanced that communications are almost instantaneous round the whole planet. If civilization survives it seems bound to be cosmopolitan, combining local variety and regional autonomy within a network of world management. Indeed, in the economic sphere such collaboration is already being forced on governments. As Brian Urquhart in his classic biography of Hammarskjöld has put it:

The twentieth century world has dwelt in the shadow of great power rivalries and conflicts which have twice erupted into world wars of an unprecedented horror and destruction. While these disasters have greatly stimulated the natural desire of the majority of nations for peace, the achievement of a representative world order, working in the interests of all states and peoples, is still almost as distant a possibility as ordinary central government must have seemed to the hard-pressed townspeople and peasants of medieval Europe.

But, he continues,

The impetus given by two world wars to the search for an effective international order has been intensified by two effects of the technological revolution: the increasing interdependencies of nations and the active possibility of an instant and comprehensive disaster caused by weapons of mass destruction.[1]

Political *idées reçues* and institutions still lag behind the facts; but in view of them and of the concurrent problems of mass poverty, environmental pollution and the squandering of planetary mineral resources, world management transcending nineteenth century ideologies is a realistic aim; indeed the price of survival. And since statesmanship to be effective needs the support of public opinion, an objective understanding of the rich variety of historic cultures and of their contribution to the civilization of mankind seems necessary and urgent today.

# MAPS

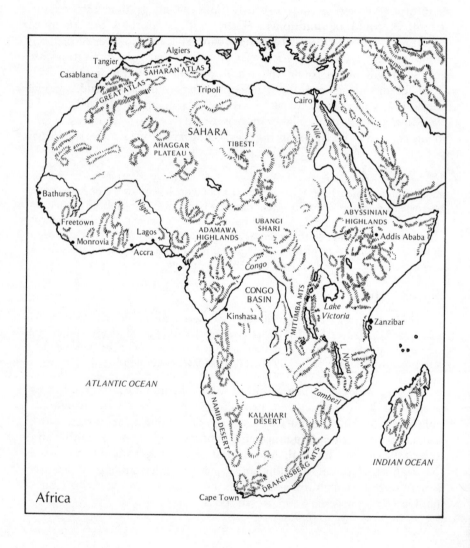

Africa

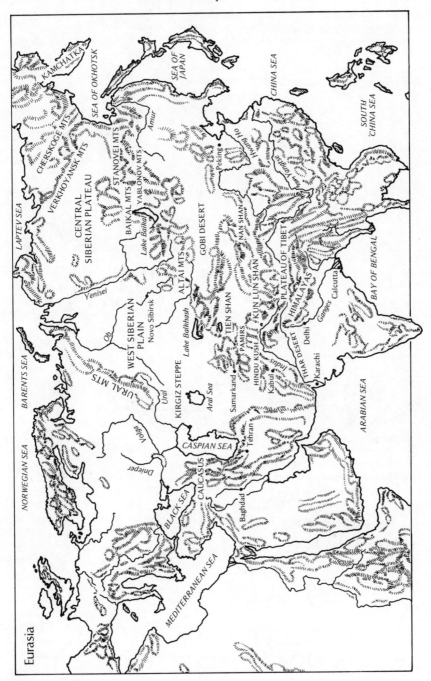

Eurasia

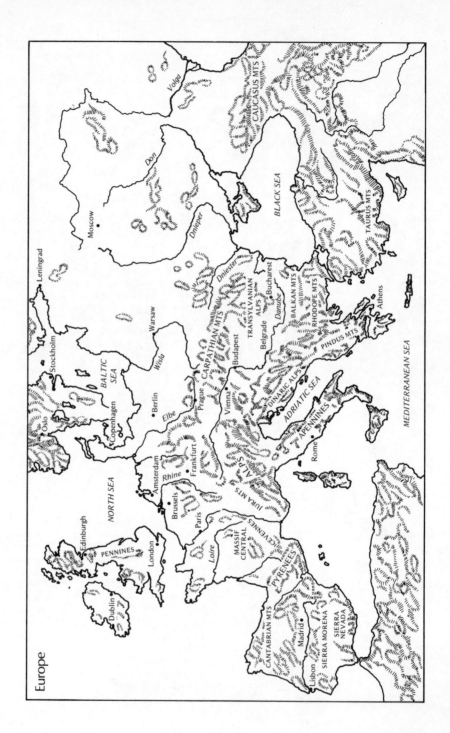

Europe

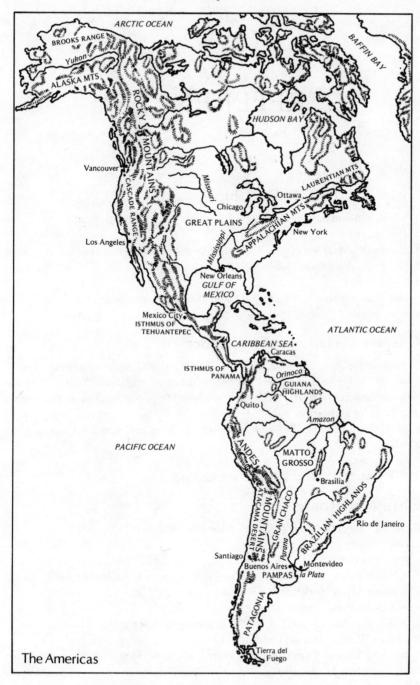

The Americas

# REFERENCES

## Chapter 4  Iran: India: China

1 See R. S. Shamasastry, *Kautilya's Arthasastra* (Mysore 1929), p. 77.
2 *Ibid.*, p. 303.
3 See Radhakamal Mukerjee, *The Culture and Art of India* (London and New York 1959), p. 16. A profound and comprehensive survey.
4 *Ibid.*, preface.
5 Wolfram Eberhard, *A History of China* (London 1960), p. 47.
6 *Ibid.*, p. 50.

## Chapter 5  Hellas and Alexander

1 Thomas Hobbes, *Behemoth*, in *Collected Works* (London 1750), p. 595.
2 See M. I. Finley, *The Greek Historians* (London and New York 1959). An admirable selection, clearly explained, in which Herodotus is taken more seriously than by older authorities.
3 Sir Maurice Bowra, *The Greek Experience* (London and New York 1957), p. 17.
4 *Ibid.*, p. 27.
5 *Ibid.*, p. 29.
6 C. P. Cavafy, *Poems*, trsl. John Mavrogordato.

## Chapter 6  Rome

1 Harold Goad, *Language in History* (Harmondsworth 1958), p. 61.
2 Livy, *History of Rome*, XXI, 35.
3 *Ibid.*, XXVI, 11.
4 See Suetonius, *The History of Twelve Caesars*, trsl. Philemon Holland, ed. J. H. Freece (New York 1930), pp. 260–305.
5 Annals, ch. XVI, p. 16.
6 *Thoughts of Marcus Aurelius*, trsl. T. Jackson (London 1906).
7 Evelyn Waugh, *Helena* (London and New York 1950), p. 139.
8 See *The Satyr of Titus Petronius Arbiter, with its fragments, recovered at Belgrade. Made English by Mr Burnaby of the Middle Temple* (London 1694), reprinted in the Abbey Classics as no. XVIII (no date) with an introduction by C. K. Scott

Moncrieff. He points out the modernity of the characters. For a good modern translation see Petronius, *The Satyricon and the Fragments*, trsl. J. P. Sullivan (Harmondsworth 1965).

9   See Bucol, II, 6–72.

10   *Carmina*, LXXXV.

11   *Ille mi par esse deo videtur*, LX.

12   *Epigrams*, XXVI.

13   *Ibid.*, LXXXVII.

14   Cicero, *De Re Publica*, I, 2.

## Chapter 7   Israel: The Rise of Christianity

1   E. R. Bevan and C. Singer, *The Legacy of Israel* (Oxford 1927), pp. 10–18.

2   'Psalm of Solomon', XVII.

3   *Ibid.*

4   *Cambridge Ancient History* XII, p. 527, for a short and authoritative history of the rise of Christianity and its relation to pagan cults (chs 13 and 14 by Dr F. C. Burkett; ch. 15 by Dr Leitzmann).

5   *I Corinthians* 15:22.

6   *Cambridge Ancient History*, XII, p. 462.

7   See F. Cumont, *Astrology and Religion among the Greeks and Romans* (New York 1912).

## Chapter 8   Sassanians: Guptas: the Far East

1   Mukerjee, *The Culture and Art of India*, p. 24.

2   Eberhard, *A History of China*, p. 78.

3   *Ibid.*

4   *Ibid.*, p. 154.

5   G. B. Sansom, *Japan, A Short Cultural History* (London 1952), p. 136.

6   *Ibid.*, p. 54.

## Chapter 9   The Expansion of Islam

1   See Ibn Battutá, *Travels in Asia and Africa, 1325–1354*, trsl. and selected by H. A. R. Gibb (London and New York 1929).

2   Joseph Schacht and C. E. Bosworth (eds), *The Legacy of Islam* (Oxford 1931), p. 354.

3   Muhsin Mahdi, *Ibn-Khaldun's Philosophy of History* (London 1957), p. 195.

4   *Hafiz of Shiraz; Thirty Poems*, trsl. Peter Avery and John Heath-Stubbs (London 1952), CXXI, p. 40.

## Chapter 10   Byzantium: South and East Slavs

1   Quoted by G. Buckler, *Anna Comnena* (Oxford 1929), p. 60; see also E. Dawes, *The Alexiad of Anna Komnena* (London and New York 1928).

2   *The Chronographia of Michael Psellus (976–1077)*, trsl. E. R. A. Sewter (London 1953), p. 89.

3   *Ibid.*, p. 34.

4  B. H. Sumner, *Survey of Russian History* (London and New York 1944), p. 27.

5  Sir Bernard Pares, *A History of Russia* (New York 1926), p. 28.

6  *Ibid.*, pp. 529 and 531; see also S. H. Cross, *The Russian Primary Chronicle* (Cambridge, Mass. 1930).

## Chapter 11  Western Christendom

1  Sir Mortimer Wheeler, *Rome Beyond the Imperial Frontiers* (London 1954), p. 94.

2  R. H. C. Davis, *A History of Medieval Europe from Constantine to St Louis* (London 1957), p. 162.

3  R. W. Southern, *The Making of the Middle Ages* (London and New Haven 1953), pp. 19–20, for a masterly account.

4  Ingvar Andersson, *A History of Sweden*, trsl. C. Hannay (London 1956), p. 23.

5  *Ibid.*, p. 28.

6  *Ibid.*, p. 33.

7  W. P. Ker, *Epic and Romance* (London 1931), ch. III, section IV.

8  Henry Osborn Taylor, *The Medieval Mind* (London 1911), I, pp. 152–68.

9  'You are locked in my heart.' See *The Penguin Book of German Verse*, ed. Leonard Foster (Harmondsworth 1957), p. 11.

10  'Under the lime tree, by the heath, where we two had our bed. . . . Sweet sang the nightingale.' *Ibid.*, p. 23.

11  J. Masson, *Frederick II of Hohenstaufen* (London 1957), p. 202.

12  *Ibid.*, pp. 209–366.

## Chapter 12  The Heartland of Asia : China : India

1  C. P. Fitzgerald, *China, A Short Cultural History* (London 1954), p. 432.

2  *Ibid.*

3  See *The Travels of Friar John Carpini and Friar William of Rubruquis*, who travelled to the courts of Kuyuk and Mangu Khan.

4  Leonardo Oeshki, *Marco Polo's Asia*, trsl. J. A. Scott (Los Angeles 1960). The author reproduces, in telling contrast, pictures of Kublai at his peak and when suffering from 'gout' in old age.

5  *Ibid.*, p. 225.

6  Fitzroy Maclean, *Back to Bokhara* (London 1959), p. 83.

7  Michael Edwardes, *A History of India* (London 1961), p. 97.

8  Mukerjee, *Culture and Art of India*, p. 295.

9  *Ibid.*, pp. 297 and 304.

10  *Ibid.*, p. 292.

11  *The Travels of Marco Polo*, trsl. R. E. Latham (Harmondsworth 1958), pp. 235.

## Chapter 13  Europe in the Later Middle Ages

1  See his comprehensive *Science in the Middle Ages* (New York 1959), II, to which the following account is indebted.

2 'Vita Karoli Quarti Imperatoris ab Ipso Karolo Conscripta, 1316–46', in *Fontes Rerum Germanicarum*, ed. J. F. Boehmer (Stuttgart 1843), I, pp. 228–70; see also G. S. Walsh, *The Emperor Charles IV* (Oxford 1924).

3 *Ibid.*, p. 36.

4 See his admirable *The English Channel* (London 1959), pp. 153–4.

5 See S. E. Morison, *Admiral of the Ocean Sea. A Life of Christopher Columbus* (Boston 1942), p. 34.

6 *Ibid.*, p. 226. Four hours earlier Columbus thought, and claimed, that he saw a light 'like a little wax candle rising and falling'. At that time he was thirty-five miles off shore, but he got the annuity of ten thousand *maravedos* promised as the reward.

7 *Ibid.*, p. 385.

## Chapter 14 Pre-Columbian America

1 S. G. Morley, *The Inscriptions at Copan* (Washington 1920), p. 397.

2 Aldous Huxley, *Beyond the Mexique Bay* (London and New York 1934), p. 50.

3 *Ibid.*, p. 51.

4 G. C. Vaillant, *The Aztecs of Mexico* (Harmondsworth 1950), p. 76, the authority on which much of this account is based.

5 *Ibid.*, p. 139.

6 *Ibid.*, p. 212.

7 W. H. Prescott, *History of the Conquest of Peru* (London 1908), p. 5.

8 J. Alden Mason, *The Ancient Civilizations of Peru* (London 1957), p. 185.

9 *The First Part of the Royal Commentaries of the Yncas by Garcilasso de la Vega*, 2 vols. (Hakluyt Society), II, p. 171.

10 *Ibid.*

11 *Ibid.*, p. 160.

12 *Ibid.*, p. 210.

13 J. Bartlett Brebner, *Canada, a Modern History* (Ann Arbor, Mich. 1959), p. 11.

## Chapter 15 Medieval Africa

1 Philip Mason, *The Birth of a Dilemma: The Conquest and Settlement of Rhodesia* (London 1958), pp. 64–5, for a good account of the Bantu background.

2 Ibn Battutá, *Travels in Asia and Africa*, op. cit. pp. 319–39.

3 See Richard Hakluyt, *Voyages and Discoveries* (London), pp. 33ff.

4 H. Ling Roth, *Great Benin* (Halifax, England 1903), p. 160.

5 *Ibid.*, p. 40.

6 *Ibid.*, p. 199.

7 Eric Akelson, *South African Explorers* (London 1954), pp. 22–47.

8 Father Francisco Alvarez, *Narrative of the Portuguese Embassy to Abyssinia, 1520–27*, trsl. Lord Stanley of Alderley (1881), in particular pp. 167–9.

9 See *History of Herodotus I*, trsl. E. H. Blakeney (London 1910), pp. 218–22.

10 Mason, *The Birth of a Dilemma*, p. 49.

11 Lord Hailey, *An African Survey* (Oxford 1956), p. 57.

## Chapter 16 The Far East and the Pacific

1 R. L. Hobson, *Catalogue of Chinese Pottery and Porcelain in the collection of Sir Perceval David* (London 1934), p. xxiv, quoted by Fitzgerald, *China*, p. 593.

2 Professor H. R. Trevor-Roper, *The Jesuits in Japan,* Historical Essays (London and New York [as *Men and Events*] 1957), p. 120.5

3 G. B. Sansom, *Japan: A Short Cultural History* (London 1952), p. 465.

4 Trevor-Roper, *The Jesuits in Japan*, p. 119.

5 E. Grilli, *Japanese Picture Scrolls* (New York 1958 and London 1959) for a useful selection. The Japanese also, by way of satire, created brilliant animal caricatures.

6 G. B. Sansom, *Japan: A Short Cultural History*, p. 440.

7 *Ibid.*, p. 483.

8 Andrew Sharp, *Ancient Voyagers in the Pacific* (Harmondsworth 1957), p. 30.

9 Peter H. Buck, *Vikings of the Pacific* (Chicago 1959), p. 35.

10 *The Paddle Song of the Aotea Canoe*, op. cit. p. 283.

11 *Ibid.*, p. 62.

## Chapter 17 The Western Centuries of Genius

1 Jakob Burckhardt, *The Civilization of the Renaissance in Italy* (London 1936), p. 43.

2 *Ibid.*, p. 9.

3 I. A. Richter (ed.), *Selection from the Notebooks of Leonardo da Vinci* (Oxford 1952), p. 341.

4 See Anthony Powell (ed.), *Brief Lives and other Writings by John Aubrey* (London and New York 1949); see also his *John Aubrey and his Friends* (London and New York 1948).

5 A. N. Whitehead, *Science and the Modern World* (Cambridge and New York 1926), p. 58.

6 Lord Russell, *An Outline of Philosophy* (London 1927), p. 170. Most modern philosophers will only admit that 'there is thinking going on', since both 'I' and 'thinking' are highly complicated events.

7 See my *Hobbes and his Critics* (London and New York 1952).

## Chapter 18 Mughal India: Iran: the Ottoman Turks

1 See his *Memoirs*, 2 vols, trsl. J. Leyden and W. Erskine, revised Sir L. King (London 1921).

2 *Ibid.*, I, p. 117.

3 For his appearance see the contemporary paintings reproduced in E. Wellesz, *Akbar's Religious Thought Reflected in Mogul Painting* (London 1952); in particular, plates 18–21, where he is depicted crossing a river on an elephant and holding a battue.

4 *The Commentary of Father Monserrate*, trsl. J. S. Hoyland and S. N. Bannerjee (Delhi 1922), pp. 196–9.

5 Sir George Dunbar, *India and the Passing of Empire* (London 1951), p. 34.

6 *Commentary*, p. 77.

7 Emmy Wellesz, *Akbar's Religous Thought* (London 1952), p. 9.

8 'Finally, it is extraordinary and well-nigh incredible what fierce enmity elephants are apt to entertain towards each other', *Ibid.*, p. 87. 'The camels, when put to it, were 'as nimble and skilful in battle, if I may say so, as horses. Nor are they less fierce. They fight with teeth or feet.'

9 Ed. Sir W. Foster, *The Embassy of Sir Thomas Roe to India. 1615–19, to Jahangir* (Oxford 1926), p. 84.

10 *Ibid.*, p. 86.

11 Thomas Herbert, *Some Years travels into Africa and Asia the Great, especially describing the Famous Empires of Persia and Industan. As also Divers other Kingdoms in the Oriental Indies and Iles Adjacents* (London 1638), p. 206.

12 *Ibid.*, p. 226.

13 *Ibid.*, p. 169.

14 *Ibid.*, p. 156.

15 *Ibid.*, p. 226.

16 A. J. Arberry (ed.), *The Legacy of Persia* (Oxford 1953), p. 255.

17 See his *Arabesques and Honeycomb* (London 1957), pp. 59ff.

18 Arberry, *The Legacy of Persia*, p. 253.

19 G. T. Forster and T. H. Blackburne Daniell (eds), *The Life and Letters of Ogier Ghiselin de Busbecq* (London 1881), I, p. 228. Busbecq, or Busbecqius, was ambassador from 1555 to 1562; his description makes particularly good reading.

20 *Ibid.*, p. 139.

21 See A. H. Lybyer, *The Government of the Ottoman Empire in the time of Suleiman the Magnificent* (New York 1913), p. 15 for the best account.

22 Paul Rycaut (consul of Smyrna from 1623 to 1677), *History of the Turkish Empire* (London 1680), p. 60.

23 *Ibid.*

24 Forster and Blackburne Daniell, *The Life and Letters*, op. cit. II, p. 29.

## Chapter 19 Europe in the Eighteenth Century

1 John Locke, *Two Treatises on Civil Government* (Second Treatise) ed. J. W. Gough (Oxford 1946), chs. 1 and 3.

2 John Aubrey, *Brief Lives*, ed. O. Lawson Dick (London 1950), p. 35.

3 Geoffrey Scott, *The Architecture of Humanism* (London and Boston 1914), p. 245.

4 David Green, *Gardener to Queen Anne* (Oxford 1956), p. 14.

5 Goad, *Language in History*, pp. 154–5.

## Chapter 20 European Expansion Overseas

1 Hakluyt, *Voyages and Documents*, pp. 284–5.

2 *Ibid.*, p. 153.

3 Bartlett Brebner, *Canada*, p. 32.

4 See Silvester Jourdain, *The Discovery of the Bermudas* (1610), with an introduction by Joseph Quincy Adams (reprinted New York 1940), pp. 12 and 15. The adventure, and the consequent sensation, are commemorated by Shakespeare's *The Tempest*.

5 Percival Spear, *Twilight of the Mughals, Studies in Late Mughal* (Delhi 1951), p. 82.

6 *Ibid.*

7 *Ibid.*, p. 83.

8 *A New Voyage Round the World. Describing particularly the Isthmus of America, several coasts and islands of the West Indies, the Isle of Cape Verd, the Passage by Terra del Fuego, the South Coast Seas of Chili, Peru and Mexico, the isle of Tuam, one of the Ladrones, Mindanao, and other Philippine and East India islands near Cambodia, China, Formosa, Luciania, Celebes etc. New Holland, Sumatra Nicobar Isles, the Cape of Good Hope and Santa Helena, their soil, rivers, harbours, plants, fruits, animals and inhabitants. Their customs, religion, government, trade etc., by Captain William Dampier,* 4th edn (1699).

The maps are not inaccurate, save for joining New Guinea to North Australia and for two blank areas for eastern Australia and north-western America, termed 'New North Wales'. On Dampier's later voyage in 1704, the Scotsman, Alexander Selkirk, the original of Defoe's *Robinson Crusoe*, was marooned on Juan Fernandes off the Chile coast, where he lived on crayfish and wild goats, and tamed the cats, relics of some earlier expedition, for company. He was rescued in 1709, pp. 283–4.

9 *Ibid.*, pp. 465–6.

10 J. C. Beaglehole (ed.), *The Journals of Captain James Cook on his Voyages of Discovery. The Voyage of the Endeavour 1768–71* (Cambridge 1955), p. 128.

11 *Ibid.*, p. 171n. Captured, three Maori youths became 'as cheerful and merry as if they had been with their own friends'.

12 *Ibid.*, p. 299.

13 *Ibid.*, p. 378.

## Chapter 22   A Prospect of World Politics

1 Brian Urquhart, *Hammarskjöld* (New York 1972), pp. 3–4.

# INDEX

JOHN BOWLE was educated at Marlborough and Balliol College, Oxford, where he was a Brackenbury scholar. He then taught at Westminster and Eton, and during the war worked in the Air Ministry and the Foreign Office. He was lecturer at Wadham College, Oxford, from 1947–9, and Leverhulme Research Fellow in 1949–50. In 1949 he was Director of the Preparatory Session of the College of Europe at Bruges, where from 1950 to 1967 he was Professor of Political Theory. He has also been visiting professor at Columbia University, New York; Grinnell College, Iowa; the Occidental College, Los Angeles; and the University of Indiana. In 1968 he was visiting lecturer at Smith College, Northampton, Massachusetts. His many books include *Western Political Thought* (1947), *Hobbes and his Critics* (1951), *Politics and Opinion in the Nineteenth Century* (1954), *Henry VIII, a biography* (1964), *The English Experience* (1971), *Napoleon* (1974) and *Charles I* (1975).